# RACISM:
## THE AUSTRALIAN EXPERIENCE
## A STUDY OF RACE PREJUDICE IN AUSTRALIA

### VOLUME 3
### COLONIALISM

VOLUME 1
PREJUDICE AND XENOPHOBIA


VOLUME 2
BLACK VERSUS WHITE

# RACISM:
## The Australian Experience

A STUDY OF RACE PREJUDICE IN AUSTRALIA

Edited by

### F. S. STEVENS

VOLUME 3
## COLONIALISM

TAPLINGER PUBLISHING COMPANY
NEW YORK

First published in the United States in 1972 by
TAPLINGER PUBLISHING CO INC
New York, New York

Library of Congress Catalog Card Number: 70-179992
ISBN 0-8008-6582-0

# PREFACE

With the object of assisting in the celebration of the United Nations International Year for Action to Combat Racism and Racial Discrimination, an *ad hoc* committee of interested individuals was formed in Sydney in October, 1970. Under the chairmanship of Hyam Brezniak, Editor of *The Bridge*, journal of the Australian Jewish Quarterly Foundation, the committee was limited to a small, but balanced representation of university and community leaders. These included:

Sol Encel, Professor of Sociology, University of New South Wales

Frank Engel, Secretary of the Australian Council of Churches

Peter McGregor, Secretary, The Australian Citizens Campaign to Overcome Racial Discrimination (A.C.C.O.R.D.)

Frank Stevens, Senior Lecturer in Industrial Relations, University of New South Wales

After consideration of various ways in which the most direct contribution to discussion of the subject of race prejudice might be made, the committee decided to produce an anthology on the subject, contributed to by people working in the field of race relations.

As a statement of policy, the committee determined that the question of the existence of racism in Australia was to be an open matter and that contributors invited to participate in the series should be selected, not for their opinions on the matter, but on their standing in the field. In all, some ninety invitations to contribute were extended, and approximately one third of the recipients accepted the opportunity. Their contributions are published in full, without any attempt to achieve a strict editorial format tied to the general terms of reference of the main or subsidiary titles of the volumes.

F.S.S.

*Kensington*

*June 71*

The publication of this book has been sponsored by the
United Nations Association of Australia
and the
Australian Committee to Combat Racism
and
Racial Discrimination

# CONTENTS

# AUTHORS

DONALD G. BAKER, B.A. (Denver), M.A., Ph.D. (Syracuse)
Professor of Political Science,
Southampton College of Long Island University,
Southampton, New York, USA.
*(Chapter 1)*

REVEREND R. J. BUCHHORN, B.E. (U.N.S.W.), D.D. (Lateran University, Rome)
Catholic Presbytery,
Quirindi, N.S.W.
*(Chapter 10)*

R. G. CROCOMBE, Ph.D. (A.N.U.)
Professor of Pacific Studies,
University of South Pacific,
Suva, Fiji.
*(Chapter 5)*

S. ENCEL, M.A., Ph.D. (Melb.)
Professor,
Department of Sociology,
University of New South Wales,
Kensington, N.S.W.
*(Conclusion to Series)*

RICHARD V. HALL, B.A. (Syd.)
Private Secretary,
Leader of the Opposition,
Parliament House,
Canberra, A.C.T.
*(Chapter 7)*

LEO J. HANNETT, B.A. (U.P.N.G.)
An East-West Centre Student Grantee, currently studying in Political Science at the University of Hawaii for a Master's Degree in Developmental Public Administration.
A foundation member of the Niugini Black Power Group at the University of Papua & New Guinea.
*(Chapter 2)*

SEKAI HOLLAND
98 Ruthven Street, Bondi Junction, N.S.W.
From Zimbabure, arrived in Australia in 1964, married to an Australian, both temporarily resident in Sydney. Works with any groups fighting racial discrimination in any form in Australia.
*(Chapter 8)*

W. J. HUDSON, B.A. (Qld.), M.A. (Melb.), Ph.D. (A.N.U.)
Senior Lecturer, Department of History,
Faculty of Arts, University of New South Wales,
Kensington, N.S.W.
*(Chapters 3, 6)*

JOHN KASAIPWALOVA

President (1972) of the Students' Representative Council, University of Papua & New Guinea; Editor of *Kovave*, a bi-annual paper devoted to Papuan and New Guinean writings.
(*Postscript*)

A. BARRIE PITTOCK, B.Sc., M.Sc., Ph.D. (Melb.)

Advisory (non-Aboriginal) member of the executive of the National Tribal Council, and Councillor for Land and Legislation;
38 Yackatoon Avenue, Aspendale, Victoria.
(*Chapter 12*)

JOHN J. RAY, B.A. (Qld.), M.A. (Syd.)

Lecturer in Sociology, School of Sociology,
University of New South Wales,
Kensington, N.S.W.
(*Chapter 11*)

JEAN E. SKUSE

1970 Observer at United Nations, N.Y., for World Federation of Methodist Women;
At present, Associate Executive Secretary, Australian Council of Churches (N.S.W. State Council),
Sydney, N.S.W.
(*Chapter 9*)

F. S. STEVENS, B.A. (Syd.), M.A. (Stan.)

Senior Lecturer, Department of Industrial Relations,
University of New South Wales, Kensington, N.S.W.
(Editor, Introduction)

EDWARD P. WOLFERS, B.A. (Syd.)

Fellow, Institute of Current World Affairs, New York;
At present, Lecturer, School of Historical, Philosophical and Political Studies, Macquarie University, North Ryde, N.S.W.
(*Chapter 4*)

# INTRODUCTION

## F. S. Stevens *

This is the last volume in a three part study of race conflict in Australia. In the first two volumes, the major areas of race contact within the country were considered. The present volume deals with Australia's external relations. However, because of the limitations in size necessarily placed on the series, the question of the growth and application of the racially biased Australian immigration policy was considered in the first volume. In some respects the early treatment of that subject must detract from the cohesion of the present study, as the history and practice of racial discrimination, witnessed in the development of the 'White Australia' policy, is the keystone to understanding Australian racial attitudes and the country's foreign relationships. Because of the many years of debate which have gone into its development the 'White Australia' policy stands as one of the few areas which is well documented and widely written about.

As Greenwood has pointed out, 'the task of holding the continent . . . peopled white, an outpost of European civilisation'[1] has been the central objective throughout the short life of the Australian nation.

Without wishing to detract from this analysis in any way, it should be noted that the present series is the first time that a group of scholars has considered the impact of race on the major areas of Australian social, political and economic life. Because of this, the exploration of concepts and fact which these pages contain must be considered as tentative excursions.

Both the editor and the *ad hoc* committee were well aware of the controversial nature of the subject matter which would be covered. We were also conscious of the complexity of the area and of our inability to treat every facet of the problem in the depth and detail it deserves. It is hoped that this initial enquiry will act as the mainspring for further work in the field and, eventually, the elevation of the study of race relations in Australian universities and schools. Indeed, part of the problem with which we had to contend in the presentation of this series relates to the fact that the development of Australians' critical ability concerning their own racial attitudes is greatly restricted by the absence of well developed programmes of racial education and research in schools and universities.

The failure of Australian scholars to give proper consideration to one of the most central concerns in the nation's history is partly due to the dominant role classical anthropology has played in the social science faculties of universities and in the formulation of educational and research policy. For many years, teaching and research in the less formally structured areas of contemporary adjustment of the Aboriginal people has been considered a slightly disreputable area of interest . . . or, at least, not quite as important as classical anthropology. For this reason the nation has no schools of ethnology or race relations, there is no chair in Aboriginal studies and, as might be expected, there are few Aboriginal students in the universities.

This aspect of Australian society is partly the by-product of the matters

*Frank Stevens, University of California, Riverside, California, May, 1972.

*1*

we have had to discuss. Australians, in general do not consider themselves to be racists. Central to this belief, however, is the fact that because of the accomplishment of national racial policies, they are rarely placed in the position in which they are forced to exercise this discretion.

Racist attitudes, however, are not necessarily only those which arise in situations of confrontation between people of different ethnic and biological heritage. For many, it is a way of life, the rules of which not even some of the less prejudiced understand.

The point which should be emphasised, in this regard, is that racism is not merely an interpersonal phenomenon. Over a period of time, it conditions the organisations through which society works. Frequently this is the more damaging aspect of prejudice because of the environment of semi-secrecy in which institutions work. Consequently, it is harder to recognise and more difficult to eradicate. In many ways, people who hold positions of responsibility in the institutions of society have a greater responsibility in ensuring that race prejudice does not condition the decisions they make, as their influence is multiplied many times.

Institutional racism is, of course, the product of human minds. However, once having taken hold of an organisation, it develops its own 'personality' until there is, frequently, an unreal correlation between the racial practices of the institutions and the level of prejudice in the outside community. In the Australian context this irony might be best witnessed in those organisations which have been established, ostensibly, to overcome the problems of race prejudice. One does not need to walk far in that domain to witness the duality of standards which are acceptable to the administrators of the nation's festering Aboriginal settlements and reserves.

The normal defence of administrators, when the depressed conditions of their charges are pointed out to them, is to emphasise the difficulties of overcoming the material gap between the two communities and to demonstrate how much better things are today than they used to be. However, this attitude denies the whole question as to what are the birthrights of the Aboriginal people in their own land.

In over one hundred years of welfare administration in Australia, European administrators have been unable to find one Aborigine who is worthy of appointment to their departments at the same level of opportunity and influence as Europeans. Even within the Commonwealth Office of Aboriginal Affairs, which has shown considerable initiative in many directions, the Aboriginal 'advisers' feel a great sense of frustration and impotency. The refusal of one Aboriginal 'adviser' to participate in these volumes is evidence of the circumscription Aboriginal interests must necessarily suffer whilst being run through European dominated institutions. It is a question of some moment, to judge whether or not this latest contribution to the entangled web of welfare bureaucracy in Australia is not merely another European institution designed for European purposes. At least the structure of its councils and the racial origins of its principles would suggest that this is so.

The administration and continued development of institutional racism in a sophisticated and advanced society such as Australia needs the co-operation and identification of educated people to enable it to function properly. In this respect, the European racists who run the Aboriginal administrations have little difficulty in obtaining 'learned' support for the continuation of their regimes.

One such exercise which has never ceased to amaze me was the co-operation of the Australian National University and the University of Adelaide in an enquiry into the attitudes of Aboriginal women to infant mortality in Central Australian reserves. Whilst the infant mortality rates on the reserves were stabilising at a scandalous rate of over 200 deaths per thousand live births (probably the highest in the world) as a result of a break down in administration and malnutrition, the universities co-operated with the Welfare Branch of the Northern Territory to study the psychological consequences of their neglect and ineptitude. In a small way, the experiments must have taken on the complexion of the 'scientific studies' carried out by the Nazis in German prisoner of war camps.[2]

This is not the only example one can produce of academic 'detachment' from the suffering of the Aboriginal people. It can be duplicated many times. Another example is the refusal of the Commonwealth Department to allow research findings and health statistics on the Aboriginal population to be published. A publication of the Commonwealth Department of Labour and National Service is a further remarkable case. In 1969 they issued the results of a competent looking survey which concluded that Aborigines suffered no particular disadvantage in unemployment. To arrive at this conclusion, they simply excluded figures from the settlements and missions on which most Aborigines reside.[3]

The philosophies of welfare administration rest, of course, on a European base. Apart from the considerations of segregation, on which they were founded, the most recent statements of the objectives of government policy are patently racist. Although the term 'assimilation' might have some emotional appeal, it can only be achieved through the total cultural genocide of the Aboriginal people. Reference to the statement of the policy on assimiliation reproduced in Volume 2 of this series will readily confirm this point. The policy, of course, was created without any reference to the Aboriginal people.

Academic responsibility for this impasse rests with A. P. Elkin the doyen of Australian classical anthropologists and the father of the Australian assimilation programme. Although Elkin rightly claims to have had influence over the change in the nations attitudes to Aborigines, the paternalism of his approach to the question can be clearly documented.[4] In an epoch making article in 1952, he erroneously interpreted the dependent role of Aborigines in Northern industry as 'intelligent parasitism' and consciously denigrated their ability to adjust to and condition the environment within which they live. Following a misinterpretation of their past role and contribution to national development, he wrote off any further opportunities for change in one sentence:

> 'Intelligent appreciation (of their social environment) can only be attained by Aborigines if the white man intends that they should, and helps them to do so.'[5]

It has been this gap which white administrators have been trying to fill for at least five decades. This has been done without consultation with, or the participation of, the Aboriginal people. There should be little wonder that development programmes for settlements languish, and good money after bad is thrown in to fill the breach on missions and reserves—and still Aborigines do not develop sufficient initiative for their elevation. It is obvious that, within the present framework laid down for the administration of policy, there will be no progress, for, as Elkin states, it is a European programme established for European purposes. Based on these terms, the Aborigines can only be excluded from the administration of their own society until 'the white man intends' that they are ready to take over their own affairs. As Goffman has pointed out,[6] the conflict between rationality and the needs of running total institutions effectively prevents them from achieving their stated and intended purpose. In Aboriginal affairs, where the stated objective is dependency, until 'the white man intends' it otherwise, programmes for development and improvement must fail. Indeed, it would seem that this policy can only lay the basis for continuing frustration which, eventually, must be broken by some form of confrontation.

What Australia needs is a new point of departure in relation to the administration of Aboriginal affairs. As a necessary start in this direction, all present administrative organisations must be abandoned and genuinely responsible institutions should take their place. If we can contemplate the possibility of independence for New Guinea in five, ten or twenty years, it is surely a reasonable objective for Aboriginal independence to be established within that period as well. After all, they have had our assistance in the search for independence for over one hundred years. At the present moment, our very enthusiasm for assistance effectively prevents this work accomplishing its stated ends.

Before proceeding with the consideration of the essays contained in this volume, I would like to make two other diversions. The first relates to the future direction of our work and the other is an appeal for greater realism and self criticism in the field.

As mentioned at the outset of this introduction, the essays contained in this series are simply an exploration of the potential of the subject in Australia. If the reviews to date of the series are any real guide, we seem to have adequately accomplished this purpose. However, reviewers have overlooked two important areas of criticism. Had I been amongst their number I would have quickly seized on these two gaps to make a point.

One area of weakness is the fact that, with the exception of the rather general introduction to the first volume by Professor W. E. H. Stanner on the nature of race prejudice in Australia, no other anthropologist is included in the series. This is not because they were omitted from the lists of potential contributors. Their response, in fact, indicated that they had little to contribute. This is partly the product of the concentration on classical anthropology in Australian universities but is equally the product of frustration. Appraising the realities of working within the canvas of the paternalism of Aboriginal welfare agencies, they are turning their minds to areas of interest other than that of the problems of contemporary adjustment. Many refuse to move out of the field of classical studies, as they know that is the only area in which they will be allowed to work by government and semi-governmental agencies. An increasing number of others are turning their attention to problems overseas. This is a tragic loss.

The large mass of writings on classical Aboriginal society is not being matched by similar production and attention to the problems of adjustment. Until this lapse is overcome, policy will continue to work in an intellectual vacuum. It is my feeling that this is exactly where most administrators wish to see it stay. The inconvenience of having to adjust to a forceful and positive enquiry on contemporary affairs is the price that few autocratic administrators want to pay. As a consequence, very little is done. Where something positive looks like being accomplished, the bureaucratic machine has an infinite variety of ways to frustrate it. Until this attitude changes, there can be little hope of real improvement in Australia's most disastrous area of race contact. Whilst Europeans dominate Aboriginal institutions, I doubt whether there will be any significant alteration.

Another area of personal disappointment with the series is the failure of any of the contributors to come to grips with the philosophical foundation of race prejudice in Australia. Although we have been able to travel a short way along the line in this most complex area, we have not been able to penetrate the field sufficiently to delineate the functional from the metaphysical. I am not wishing to detract completely from our contributions as I feel that the efforts in this direction are quite substantial—the work of Hall, McQueen, Brash, Encel, Engel and Hartwig in the first two volumes are significant in this respect. In this volume, Baker's article on the relationships of Australia's racial bias with other Anglo-Saxon communities is also outstanding. However, there is much more work to be done.

A particular responsibility in this direction rests with the Christian Church. Because of the continuing relationships the Church has had with both Aboriginal policy and people, it stands in a unique position of strength. In this respect, I feel that, whilst the Reverend Frank Engel's paper in the first volume dressed up the positive role of the Church, it failed to come to grips with the reasons for failure. That area still remains open. I am hopeful that self-effacement will encourage some students to make enquiries in this area.

Occasionally, whilst working in the field of race relations in Australia, one gets the feeling that one is about to gain valuable insights in this respect, only to be disappointed. There still remains no fundamental analysis of the reason for our racial attitudes along the lines of the work done by Fanon, Hartz, van den Berghe, Kovel or Tucker overseas. Humphrey McQueen's publication, *New Brittania,* is, possibly, a start in the slow process of reappraisal.

It could be, however, that Australian society is not so fundamentally different from the other Anglo-Saxon communities as to make it necessary to mark off the differences. But then, when we try to match up Australian practices with the needs of the community we realise just how basically unsophisticated and prejudiced our attitudes are. My present absence from Australia and my involvement in other peoples' problems have been important in reinforcing my opinions in this direction. Just how insular and provincial our approaches to this whole problem have been might be clearly seen in the *Declaration of Barbados.* This document is the product of an inter-disciplinary conference sponsored by the World Council of Churches in 1971. It provides some interesting proposals opposed to the assimilation/ protectionist philosophies which dominate our thinking. Its contents cannot be thought of as anything other than telling and responsible. As this has not received wide publicity in Australia, it deserves publication in the final volume of the series. It appears as an annexure to this introduction.

Finally to the contents of this volume. As has already been pointed out Professor Baker, of Southampton College, University of Long Island, New York, attempts to set the position of Australia in the framework of prejudice of the Anglo empires. This is a more up to date and sophisticated version of Grenfell Prices' *White Settlers and Native People.* Although Baker visited Australia to gather background for this paper, he was unable to isolate the unique factors of the Australian system. Indeed, he concludes that when viewed from the position of other Anglo colonial outposts the Australian experience seems 'less unique'. This emphasises the need for further work on the fundamental aspects of our predicament.

Unfortunately, I do not think that we are in a position to draw such a wide conclusion as Baker has done. The undeveloped nature of the study of race prejudice in Australia would seem to preclude such a broad judgement. We simply have not paid sufficient attention to the structure of the Australian mentality to determine precisely the complexion of the social and philosophical foundations of the Commonwealth. Indeed, in the introduction to Volume 1, I stated that I did not think our work proved that Australia was a racist country, although I recognised racialism as being of some importance —the difference being practice in the first and ideology in the second. From my appraisal of the material in the second volume, and from conclusions drawn after several years field work in the area, I further concluded that Australia's attitudes and practices towards Aborigines were patently racist. However, the judgement is one of balance. There is also, obviously, a very large reservoir of goodwill towards Aborigines in the broader Australian community. The results of the 1965 Referendum to transfer power over Aboriginal affairs to the Commonwealth government clearly demonstrates this. However, as Mitchell has shown, those people who were most closely exposed to the race contact situation voted less enthusiastically to bring Aborigines into the mainstream of Australian political processes.[7]

This, again, emphasises my appeal for an urgent look at the root sources of prejudice within the country. It could be that my conclusions in relation to conflict between European groups is entirely wrong. Indeed, my conclusions for that purpose were only drawn from the information which was contained within the pages of the study. There is very strong evidence from other sources that race prejudice between European groups rests at a very shallow level in Australian society. The failure to recognise this fact, as Humphrey McQueen has pointed out, has led even responsible and liberal thinkers to draw erroneous conclusions about the nature of the Australian personality and political system.

That a lack of understanding can readily lead to a false impression of the realities of Australian society and produce both complacency and counter-productive policies, in certain circumstances, was brought home to me during a recent reading of Ken Walker's updated study of *The Australian Industrial Relations System*.[8] In his analysis of Australian society and the needs of industrial organisation, he completes his descriptions of the systems without once referring to the issue of race prejudice, the 'White Australia' policy or the multitude of laws which discriminated against Chinese and Southern Europeans in Australian industry. In similar fashion, Aborigines also do not get a mention. On the other hand, the exclusion of Aborigines from the Australian industrial arbitration system for a period of almost seventy years is one of the most obvious examples of racism in Australian Society. The prejudice of the Arbitration Court judges in relation to handling Aboriginal claims before the bench is directly responsible for the continuation of the medieval system for the employment of Aborigines in the North Australian cattle industry and on missions and settlements. It is the supreme example of institutional racism.

With the exception of the Aboriginal problem and Australia's external relationships, and given full employment, the state of mind of European sub-groups towards one another, may be of marginal significance for economic decision making. However, when economic discrimination and unemployment begin to be moulded along ethnic lines, the tinder box for racial conflagration is set. Indeed, this is already the situation with Australian Aborigines. Given the increase in the influence of 'Black Power' groups, it is only a matter of time before certain sections of the more oppressed indigenes rise to the use of the techniques of confrontation adopted overseas. To avert what could be a potentially tragic outcome, we need to determine the roots of overt and covert racism which are so clearly present. There is not better place to start than within the welfare organisations themselves.

Australia's internal relationships are, however, a matter of its own choosing—but the nation does have another role to play. The conditions under which it competes are not all locally determined. Indeed, being one of the leading trading nations of the world, Australia's international image is very much a factor in determining the standard of living its people enjoy. It is here that the nation's attitudes to the question of race come into clearer perspective through being etched in direct economic terms.

The most immediate area of the extension of Australian power and interests was within the traditional framework of international imperialism. Being an outpost of the British empire and facing the geo-strategic problems of isolation, there can be little wonder that Australia readily embraced the European patterns and methods of expansion when its political system and economy were sufficiently strong to support such pretensions. Hudson, in his article on the earliest years of Australia's control of Papua and New Guinea, clearly brings out this point. However, as Hartz has demonstrated,[9] not all European empires have determined the patterns of racial association along the same lines of stratification between indigenous people and imperial associates as those represented in the Anglo-Saxon colonies.

Baker emphasises the points of similarity which bind the Anglo nations together sufficiently for our purposes. But there were, of course, other alternatives for the administration of colonial peoples for Australian representatives in New Guinea to follow. The simple fact is that the Australian territorial government based its techniques of control on those used most widely in the British empire. It was in that direction that they could draw on most experience and examples. Australia's administration of New Guinea, however, has developed its own complexion.

As Wolfers points out 'Colonial policies tend to reflect the domestic preoccupations of the government, or the assumptions implicit in the total national political culture of the colonising power'. If this is so, it is not surprising that the administrative and legal structure of the New Guinea territories came to reflect the prejudice with which Australians of European heritage viewed their relationships with the original inhabitants of the mainland. The fact that both of the dependent peoples were black, naturally assisted in the transfer of attitudes and concepts of organisation. Wolfer's article brings this out in a more than adequate way, and there seems little more to add. However, of greater concern and of more pregnant interest is the current and future pattern of Australia's relationships with the nearest nation to its North.

Professor Crocombe, in his article covering the future pattern of economic development in the Territory, provides ground for concern for even the most conservative student of New Guinea affairs. In clear terms, he demonstrates the rationale for the continuing prejudiced practices of the Australian administration in Papua and New Guinea—that of economic advantage. It is true that certain international pressures are forcing the Australian government to bring forward the time of political independence for the Territory. However, in the meantime, it seems only too obvious that the administration is laying the foundation whereby Australian interests will effectively remain in control of the island's economy regardless of the fate of the national government. As has been shown too often in the past, economic domination is only a short distance from effective political control. With the inevitable confrontation between the forces represented in the position of total independence of the New Guinea Black Power Group and the attempted racial dichotomy suggested in the Australian government's economic five year plan, the foundation for conflict is laid.

As the indigenous student, Leo Hannett, points out:

'It would be naive, simplistic and dangerous for any Nuiginians to think that just the handing over of the outward symbols of political control of (his) country at independence will make (them) *ipso facto* total masters of (themselves) politically, socially, economically and religiously.'

It is obvious from the tone and analysis of Leo Hannett's article that local radical political forces will ensure that the inherent racism of Australian colonial administration will meet its first confrontation with militant nationalism very early during the independence process. It can only be hoped that, by that time, the implications of prejudice will be more clearly understood by the Australian electorate so that local control over indigenous affairs will be granted with dignity, justice and speed—for only in the early equitable settlement of the real questions of power will true friendship and trust be founded. To delay this decision, or even to wrap it up in the paraphenalia of psuedo-sophisticated economic terminology, can only lead to frustration and resolution of the situation by force—a pattern we have witnessed so frequently in the settlement of the affairs of the declining imperial interest in Africa.

The relationship of Australia with the African racial experience is, of course, quite germain to any educated appraisal of the problems or directions of Australian society and policy. Again, Australian isolation and provincialism stands the nation in poor stead. Bill Hudson, in his article on Australian diplomacy and South Africa, delineates what he refers to as the 'sense of rapport with South Africans in the unenviable predicament'. He then goes on to clearly paint the similarities between South Africa's and Australia's problems and the responses to one another they have taken over the years.

Although everyone may not agree with the appraisal of the 'unenviable' situation of white South Africans, which is a self-induced and now forcibly maintained relationship of ultra-racist extremism, it does serve as a well considered introduction to the problems of current relationships and the duplicity of Australia's position on the South African and Rhodesian questions.

In his article, 'South Africa, Rhodesia and Australia: Black Interests and White Lies', Dick Hall clearly outlines the complicity of influential Australian politicians in the machinations of the illegal Smith regime. However, he notes two significant factors—or filters—through which all analysis of Australian racial practices must be viewed. Firstly, that 'world opinion can, and always will, be able to influence Australian policies' and, secondly, that the real interest in Smith's international ambitions was limited to a fairly small number of extreme right-wing Liberal politicians. One might add a further parameter, however, to Hall's analysis. It is obvious from the information provided in his article that the complex patterns of interest produced by race prejudice is barely understood by Australian political leaders. This principle might be applied to internal, as well as international, affairs. This allows the individual to vacillate in relation to this critical area of human association without questioning the moral foundation of his position. Stated alternatively, on the question of race, most Australian politicians are unprincipled.

Jean Skuse's paper on the voting patterns of Australia before the United Nations councils on the question of colonialism and racial discrimination clearly brings this point out. Australia's position on the question of aparthied, for example was appraised by Miss Skuse in the following way:

> 'Couched in general terms, it votes in favour of resolutions (condemning apartheid) but when these require supportive action the response is to abstain or to record a negative vote.'

As we have tried to show in Volume 2 of this series, it is little wonder that the Australian government is unenthusiastic about the positive pursuit of United Nations principles on the question of racial tolerance and minority rights, as her own internal administration continues to violate international conventions on at least ten counts.[10]

The work of Sekai Holland in this volume is a unique contribution to the Australian experience on the question of race prejudice. With the exception of an article which appeared in the American black magazine, *Ebony*, it is the only study I have seen in which a foreign coloured person looks at her experiences in the Australian milieu. As might be expected, we hardly come up to her expectation. No, it is more than this. She quite openly damns us.

I have no defence—but to plead guilty!

The Reverend Dick Buchhorn provides us with a different perspective of Australia's reaction to international racism in the form of prejudice in sport. In balance, I would like to feel that we come out on top in this case. But again, like the questions of our performance before the United Nations councils, there is always the all too frequent possibility that we will side with the forces of darkness. It could be that we are just myopic—or is it opportunistic?

The two concluding articles obviously serve diverse purposes. I cannot help but think that John Ray's piece in defence of the 'White Australia' policy has been purposely written to 'stir things up!' If it does this, it will be well worth attention. However, it does go further through insisting that we clarify our intentions and set out to appraise the costs and benefits of the possibility of change. This principle might well be used in many other of our areas of national policy—especially the consequences of national development through whatever means.

Barry Pittock's article 'Toward a Multi-Racial Society' might now be referred to as a classic statement of racial humanism in the Australian context. Written in 1969, it has long been accepted as the most convincing presentation of the liberal position on the question of race tolerance which has been produced in Australia. Contrasted with Pittock's background in the physical sciences, his writings on the questions of race relations in Australia and overseas are remarkable. It was with some degree of pride that I learnt he had agreed to allow us to run his excellent essay as the final contribution to the series of papers. I feel that it will eventually have greater currency than has been accorded to it at present.[11]

As an epilogue we have included a poem by an indigenous New Guinean student. Apart from the intrinsic beauty of the language and absolutely fresh terminology it carries a hidden warning and a word of hope. In the use of the expletive 'fuck off whitey!' he is providing us with adequate warning to review our moral standards. It is only hoped that we will do it in time.

## REFERENCES

1 GREENWOOD, GORDON. 'National Development and Social Expansion 1901-1914' in Gordon Greenwood (ed.) *Australia: A Social and Political History*, Angus and Robertson, Sydney, 1968 P. 199.

2 *Summary of Aboriginal Research in the Northern Territory Bulletin No. 32 1st October to 31st December, 1971*, P. 3.

3 Commonwealth of Australia, *Labour Market Studies No. 1, Aborigines* Department of Labour and National Service, Canberra, 1969.

4 See ELKINS, A. P., own summary of his influence 'Aboriginal Policy 1930-1950 Some Personal Reflections', *Quadrant* Vol. I No. 4, 1957, Pp. 27-34.

5 ELKIN, A. P., 'Reaction and Interaction: A Food Gathering People and European Settlement in Australia', *American Anthropologist*, P. 174.

6 GOFFMAN, ERVING, *Asylums: Essays on the Social Stratification of Mental Patients and Other Inmates*, Anchor Books, New York, 1961.

7 MITCHELL, IAN S.: 'Epilogue to a Referendum' *Australian Journal of Social Issues*, Vol. 3 No. 4. October, 1968, Pp. 9-12.

8 WALKER, KENNETH F. *Australian Industrial Relations Systems*, Harvard University Press, Cambridge, 1970.

9 HARTZ, LOUIS, *The Founding of New Societies*, Harcourt Brace, New York, 1964.

10 STEVENS, F. S. "Aborigines and the Declaration of Human Rights" *N.S.W. State Conference on Human Rights*, United Nations Association, Sydney, 13/11/68.

11 His contribution to Volume 2 of this series has already been reprinted three times, once in Australia and twice overseas, being translated into both French and German.

## ANNEXURE

### WORLD COUNCIL OF CHURCHES PROGRAMME TO COMBAT RACISM

*The Barbados Symposium was sponsored jointly by the Programme to Combat Racism and the Churches Commission on International Affairs of the World Council of Churches, together with the Ethnology Department of the Univeristy of Berne (Switzerland). A report of the Symposium is in preparation. The views expressed are those of the members of the Symposium, and not necessarily those of the co-sponsors of the Symposium.*

### Declaration of Barbados for the Liberation of the Indians

The anthropologists participating in the *Symposium on Inter-Ethnic Conflict in South America*, meeting in Barbados, January 25-30 1971, after analysing the formal reports of the tribal populations' situation in several countries, drafted and agreed to make public the following statement. In this manner, we hope to define and clarify this critical problem of the American continent and to contribute to the Indian struggle for liberation.

The Indians of America remain dominated by a colonial situation which originated with the conquest and which persists today within many Latin American nations. The result of this colonial structure is that lands inhabited by Indians are judged to be free and unoccupied territory open to conquest and colonisation. Colonial domination of the aboriginal groups, however, is only a reflection of the more generalised system of the Latin American states' external dependence upon the imperialist metropolitan powers. The internal order of our dependent countries leads them to act as colonising powers in their relations with the indigenous peoples. This places the several nations in the dual role of the exploited and the exploiters, and this in turn projects not only a false image of Indian society and its historical development, but also a distorted vision of what constitutes the present national society.

We have seen that this situation manifests itself in repeated acts of aggression directed against the aboriginal groups and cultures. There occur both active interventions to "protect" Indian society as well as massacres and forced migrations from the homelands. These acts and policies are not unknown to the armed forces and other governmental agencies in several countries. Even the official 'Indian policies' of the Latin-American states are explicitly directed towards the destruction of aboriginal culture. These policies are employed to manipulate and control Indian populations in order to consolidate the status of existing social groups and classes, and only diminish the possibility that Indian society may free itself from colonial domination and settle its own future.

As a consequence, we feel the several States, the religious missions and social scientists, primarily anthropologists, must assume the unavoidable responsibilities for immediate action to halt this aggression and contribute significantly to the progress of Indian liberation.

### The Responsibility of the State

Irrelevant are those Indian policy proposals that do not seek a radical break with the existing social situation; namely, the termination of colonial relationships, internal and external; breaking down of the class system of human exploitation and ethnic domination; a displacement of economic and political power from a limited group or an oligarchic minority to the popular majority; the creation of a truly multi-ethnic state in which each ethnic group possesses the right to self-determination and the free selection of available social and cultural alternatives.

Our analysis of the Indian policy of the several Latin American nation states reveals a common failure of this policy by its omissions and by its actions. The several states avoid granting protection to the Indian groups' rights to land and to be left alone, and fail to apply the law strictly with regard to areas of national expansion. Similarly, the states sanction policies which have been and continue to be colonial and class-oriented.

This failure implicates the State in direct responsibility for and connivance with the many crimes of genocide and ethnocide that we have been able to verify. These crimes tend to be repeated and responsibility must rest with the State which remains reluctant to take the following essential measures:—

1 guaranteeing to all the Indian populations by virtue of their ethnic distinction, the right to be and to remain themselves, living according to their own customs and moral order, free to develop their own culture;

2 recognition that Indian groups possess rights prior to those of other national constituencies. The State must recognise and guarantee each Indian society's territory in land, legalising it as perpetual, inalienable collective property, sufficiently extensive to provide for population growth;

3 sanctioning of Indian groups' right to organize and to govern in accordance with their own traditions. Such a policy would not exclude members of Indian society from exercising full citizenship, but would in turn exempt them from compliance with those obligations that jeopardise their cultural integrity.

4 extending to Indian society the same economic, social, educational and health assistance as the rest of the national population receives. Moreover, the State has an obligation to attend to those many deficiencies and needs that stem from Indians' submission of the colonial situation. Above all the State must impede their further exploitation by other sectors of the national society, including the official agents of their protection.

5 establishing contacts with still isolated tribal groups is the States' responsibility, given the dangers—biological, social and ecological—that their first contact with agents of the national society represents.

6 protection from the crimes and outrages, not always the direct responsibility of civil or military personnel, intrinsic to the expansion process of the national frontier.

7 definition of the national public authority responsible for relations with Indians groups inhabiting its territory; this obligation cannot be transferred or delegated at any time or under any circumstances.

## Responsibility of the Religious Missions

Evangelisation, the work of the religious missions in Latin America also reflects and complements the reigning colonial situation with the values of which it is imbued. The missionary presence has always implied the imposition of criteria and patterns of thought and behaviour alien to the colonised Indian societies. A religious pretext has too often justified the economic and human exploitation of the aboriginal population.

The inherent ethnocentric aspect of the evangelisation process is also a component of the colonialist ideology and is based on the following characteristics:—

1 its essentially discriminatory nature implicit in the hostile relationship to Indian culture conceived as pagan and heretical;

2 its vicarial aspect, implying the re-identification of the Indian and his consequent submission in exchange for future supernatural compensations;

3 its spurious quality given the common situation of missionaries seeking only some form of personal salvation, material or spiritual;

4 the fact that the missions have become a great land and labour enterprise, in conjunction with the dominant imperial interests.

As a result of this analysis we conclude that the suspension of all missionary activity is the most appropriate policy on behalf of both Indian society as well as the moral integrity of the churches involved. Until this objective can be realized the missions must support and contribute to Indian liberation in the following manner:—

1   overcome the intrinsic Herodianism of the evangelical process, itself a mechanism of colonialisation, Europeanisation and alienation of Indian society;

2   assume a position of true respect for Indian culture, ending the long and shameful history of despotism and intolerance characteristic of missionary work, which rarely manifests sensitivity to aboriginal religious sentiments and values;

3   halt both the theft of Indian property by religious missionaries who appropriate labour, lands and natural resources as their own, and the indifference in the face of Indian expropriation by third parties;

4   extinguish the sumptuous and lavish spirit of the missions themselves, expressed in various forms but all too often based on exploitation of Indian labour.

5   stop the competition among religious groups and confessions for Indian souls—a common occurrence leading to the buying and selling of believers and internal strife provoked by conflicting religious loyalties;

6   suppress the secular practice of removing Indian children from their families for long periods in boarding schools where they are imbued with values not their own, converting them in this way into marginal individuals, incapable of living either in the larger national society or their native communities;

7   break with the pseudo-moralist isolation which imposes a false puritanical ethic, incapacitating the Indian for coping with the national society—an ethic which the churches have been unable to impose on that same national society;

8   abandon those blackmail procedures implicit in the offering of goods and services to Indian society in return for total submission;

9   suspend immediately all practices of population displacement or concentration in order to envagelise and assimilate more effectively, a process that often provokes an increase in morbidity, mortality and family disorganization among Indian communities;

10   and the criminal practice of serving as intermediaries for the exploitation of Indian labour.

To the degree that the religious missions do not assume these minimal obligations they, too, must be held responsible by default for crimes of ethnocide and connivance with genocide.

Finally, we recognize that, recently, dissident elements within the churches are engaging in a conscious and radical self-evaluation of the evangelical process. The denunciation of the historical failure of the missionary task is now a common conclusion of such critical analyses.

## The Responsibility of Anthropology

Anthropology took form within and became an instrument of colonial domination, openly or surreptitiously; it has often rationalised and justified in scientific language the domination of some people by others. The discipline has continued to supply information and methods of action useful for maintaining, reaffirming and disguising social relations of a colonial nature. Latin America has been and is no exception, and with growing frequency we note nefarious Indian action programmes and the dissemination of stereotypes and myths distorting and masking the Indian situation—all pretending to have their basis in alleged scientific anthropological research.

A false awareness of this situation has led many anthropologists to adopt equivocal positions. These might be classed in the following types:—

1  a *scientism* which negates any relationship between academic research and the future of those peoples who form the object of such investigation, thus eschewing political responsibility which the relation contains and implies;

2  an *hypocrisy* manifest in the rhetorical protestation based on first principles which skilfully avoids any commitment in a concrete situation;

3  an *opportunism* that although it may recognize the present painful situation of the Indian at the same time rejects any possibility of transforming action by proposing the need "to do something" within the established order. This latter position, of course only reaffirms and continues the system.

The anthropology now required in Latin America is not that which relates to Indians as objects of study, but rather that which perceives the colonial situation and commits itself to the struggle for liberation. In this context we see anthropology providing on the one hand, the colonised peoples those data and interpretations both about themselves and their colonisers useful for their own fight for freedom, and on the other hand, a re-definition of the distorted image of Indian communities extant in the national society, thereby unmasking its colonial nature with its supportive ideology.

In order to realise the above objectives, anthropologists have an obligation to take advantage of all junctures within the present order to take action on behalf of the Indian communities. Anthropologists must denounce systematically by any and all means cases of genocide and those practices conducive to ethnocide. At the same time, it is imperative to generate new concepts and explanatory categories from the local and national social reality in order to overcome the subordinate situation of the anthropologist regarded as the mere 'verifier' of alien theories.

### The Indian as an Agent of his own Destiny

That Indians organize and lead their own liberation movement is essential, or it ceases to be liberating. When non-Indians pretend to represent Indians, even on occasion assuming the leadership of the latter's groups, a new colonial situation is established. This is yet another expropriation of the Indian populations' inalienable right to determine their future.

Within this perspective, it is important to emphasise in all its historical significance, the growing ethnic consciousness observable at present among Indian societies throughout the continent. More peoples are assuming direct control over their defence against the ethnocidal and genocidal policies of the national society. In this conflict, by no means novel, we can perceive the beginnings of a pan-Latin-American movement and some cases too, of explicit solidarity with still other oppressed social groups.

We wish to reaffirm here the right of Indian populations to experiment with and adopt their own self-governing development and defence programmes. These policies should not be forced to correspond with national economic and socio-political exigencies of the moment. Rather, the transformation of national society is not possible if there remain groups, such as Indians, who do not feel free to command their own destiny. Then, too, the maintenance of Indian society's cultural and social integrity, regardless of its relative numerical insignificance, offers alternative approaches to the traditional well-trodden paths of the national society.

Barbados, 30 January 1971

Miguel Alberto Bartolome; Guillermo Bonfil Batalla; Victor Daniel Bonilla; Gonzalo Castillo Cardenas; Miguel Chase Sardi; Georg Grünberg; Nelly Arvelo de Jiminez; Esteban Emilio Mosonyi; Darcy Ribeiro; Scott. S. Robinson; Stefano Varese.

# AUSTRALIA AND EMPIRE

# 1

## AUSTRALIAN AND ANGLO RACISM: PRELIMINARY EXPLORATIONS

### Donald G. Baker

### I

Racism is a worldwide phenomenon. It is not an attribute solely of Australians, or of Anglo-Saxons, or of whites. Racism—where a group of one color, or common social or communal heritage, viewing itself as superior, utilizes its power to suppress and/or exploit those of another color or community group—is worldwide. European racism, though, has received the greatest attention in recent years. Joel Kovel, in exploring the foundations of American racism in *White Racism: A Psychohistory* (1970), traces its roots to 'western culture' itself. Elsewhere, in *The Founding of New Societies* (1964), Louis Hartz concludes that racism within the 'fragmented' Anglo settlements (i.e., those societies settled and/or controlled by English: namely, the United States, Canada, Australia and South Africa) derives from their English heritage, a background which, because of its cultural and class basis, rejects the native or nonwhite as equal.[1] Thus Australian racism should be viewed not as an isolated phenomenon, but, rather as part of a broader *Anglo* phenomenon.

As African and Asian societies have shed themselves of European domination, issues of colonialism, neo-colonialism and racism have occupied their attention.[2] Moreover, the Black Power movement in America, having repercussions elsewhere in the world,[3] has also accented the issue of race conflict. Racism, though, is not simply a white phenomenon. Slowly, studies are emerging which recognize the necessity for worldwide comparative research and conceptual appraisal.[4] Most such studies, though, are of a piecemeal nature.[5]

The focus on white racism has evolved, basically, from historical studies of European expansion, settlement and domination over other (normally nonwhite) societies. Under numerous guises (e.g., 'white man's burden', 'civilizing' the native, the 'superiority of white civilization', etc.), European nations earlier settled and/or took control of vast chunks of the world, seeking land, minerals and trade. By conquest or other means, they exploited and dominated native and nonwhite. Whatever form that domination took, a white dominance situation prevailed, racist notions emerged as justification for white privilege and power.[6]

If, as Kovel, Hartz, and others suggest, there are fundamental forces values and attitudes within western culture (or, more specifically, in the Anglo culture) which lead to racism, those factors (and the resulting racism) can be analyzed within societies settled and/or controlled by that western (or Anglo) society. In the Anglo instance, those forces emerge in six countries: the United States, Canada, New Zealand, Australia, South Africa and Rhodesia. They were all either (a) settled essentially by the English or (b) controlled for an extensive period by England. What can be observed, then, is white Anglo society's treatment of the natives, all of whom were, in terms of color, red, brown or black. Similarly, the treatment of other nonwhites (basically, black and/or yellow) can also be observed, for it, too, is suggestive of the parameters of white racist behavior.

There are numerous individual studies of each of these 'Anglo' societies, but comparative analyses of racism in *all* of them are lacking. Given the Anglo cultural-political foundations of each, comparisons do appear feasible. Differences within the countries make contrasts somewhat difficult, but there are numerous similarities, particularly in the treatment of native and non-white. Only a brief comparative sketch is possible here, as the necessary data for a more thorough appraisal is not yet available. These preliminary thoughts might prompt subsequent explorations that will contribute to a broader comparative appraisal of Anglo racism. They might assist, in turn, in putting Australian racism in the broader perspective of Anglo (and white) racism.

## II

The general characteristics of Anglo racism emerge quite distinctly in an appraisal of white settler and native encounters. With the discovery of the New World, there emerged in Europe a Utopian, or Edenic literature in which the Indian was perceived as the idyllic model of man—the 'noble savage'. Henri Baudet, in his study of this literature, suggests that 'the dominant sentiment regarding the Indian—the savage *par excellence*—was one of admiration and esteem.'[7] The European's interest, though, was not the noble savage but the gold, glory, land, minerals, and trade to be gained from newly conquered and settled lands. Whatever the motivation—temporary (or 'sojourner') colonization (for gold, trade, or the extraction of mineral resources) or a more permanent (or 'settler') colonization—the consequence for the native was essentially the same: the loss of his freedom and land.[8] As A. Grenfell Price suggests, European colonization was

> 'in most regions, a brutal age: an age in which swarms of savage invading males slew, raped, plundered, and enslaved the natives or decimated them with exotic diseases, after which they replaced them in some instances by hardier and more complacent slaves.'[9]

In another study, *White Settlers and Native Peoples*, Price compares the Anglo encounters with natives in America, Canada, New Zealand, and Australia. He discerns three fairly distinct stages: first, a period of invasions, when whites decimated natives with gunpowder and white diseases; second, a more humane period, when 19th century philanthropic and religious movements pressured the British government (it still exercised some control over 'native affairs' in Canada, Australia and New Zealand) to curtail settler animosities towards the native; and third, a period commencing in the 1930s, when native programs were reappraised and reform measures were instituted to provide better treatment for the natives.[10]

During the initial period, Anglo settlers used their superior firearms to gain control, possess the land, and subdue the native, often destroying (in the process) the latter's religion, culture and society. The early 19th century philanthropic-humanitarian movement initially pressured for the abolition of slavery in British possessions by the 1830s, then prodded the British Government into protecting native rights in the colonies. The metropolitan Government intervened where settlers mistreated natives, and it encouraged missionary activities. These activities, regarded as humanitarian, nevertheless destroyed native cultures and traditions.[11] After mid-century, the Manchester movement, critical of the high cost of maintaining troops throughout the Empire, pressured for the withdrawal of British forces. The British Government's tempering and restraining influence was thereby removed; and the natives, virtually powerless, were left at the mercy of settlers who coveted and took their lands. Conflicts followed, but white power prevailed. Native populations, increasingly becoming wards of the state and impounded on reserves, generally decreased.

Completing his study shortly after World War II, Price concluded that new, more humane directions initiated in U.S. native policy during the 1930s would ultimately prevail elsewhere. This third stage, Price found, acknowledged the need for more scientific, humane programs aimed at encouraging native cultures and traditions.[12] Price's studies, although dated, represent one of the few comparative appraisals of native treatment in Anglo societies. What are still missing are studies comparing Anglo and non-Anglo white societies in their treatment of native peoples. A few fragmented studies do exist, but their central concern is usually slavery rather than settler-native encounters.[13] Most of the studies focus on the differences in Iberian and Anglo encounters with natives and nonwhites.

Iberian countries and settlers (contrasted with the Anglo) were, apparently, less harsh in their treatment of native and nonwhite. Such factors as religion, class notions, and prior experiences and encounters with nonwhites contributed to this. The religious factor was particularly significant. The Catholic Church, more than Anglican or protestant religious groups, viewed—and accepted—both native and nonwhite as a *person*. It upheld the principle that the slave was, first of all, a *person*, and as such he possessed certain rights.[14] Within the Anglo tradition, however, the slave was generally viewed as a *chattel*, and the Anglican church did not question this. As Hoetink notes, under Catholicism the slave 'was a person—juridically and morally—and not, as in the American and British areas, a chattel.'[15] The Catholic Church also codified, in 1789, the rights of natives and slaves. Settlers sometimes ignored the Church's proscriptions, but the Church did, nevertheless, temper settler treatment of native and slave.[16]

Intersecting economic and religious factors also contributed to Anglo-Iberian variations in native treatment. Hoetink and others have noted the universalistic, hierarchic basis of Catholicism, contrasted with the more atomistic, individualistic basis of religious beliefs of Anglo (and protestant) settlers. The church in Anglo areas had less control over its members. As Tawney, Weber and others have noted, the break from Catholicism had economic consequences, for among protestant groups the individual stood alone, responsible for making his own way in the world, less encumbered by restrictions and controls of a church. This was particularly significant in the economic realm, for the making of money and the accumulation of property were especially significant in Anglo societies. Property, wealth, and power were coveted; and human beings themselves became objects, to be manipulated and controlled where necessary for the acquisition of wealth and power.

These factors converged, bringing forth, in psychosocial terms, other forces at work especially in Anglo societies. As Hartz notes, the Iberian countries were closer to a feudalistic, rigid class structure, whereas in England the class sytem was being modified by capitalist development and the emergence of a comparitively large middle class. This greater degree of 'openness', converging with the more individualistic religious tradition, left the Anglo more isolated, independent, and anxiously struggling to achieve his own 'place' in society. This intensified economic (and social) competition. All individuals were viewed as equal; hence all had to be measured by their achievements rather than their class (or 'non-class'). However, as Hartz suggests, this 'classlessness' left no place for the native or nonwhite *except* as an equal (whereas, in the more feudalistic class structure of Iberian countries, native and nonwhite could conveniently be designated as of the lower class; they were not a threat thereby to the other classes). The Anglo could not accept that situation. Thus native and nonwhite were left *outside* the social system. This resulted, as Hoetink suggests, in the emergence in Anglo settlements of a *segmented* society, i.e., distinct or mutually exclusive social groups, caste-like, with virtually no movement possible from the native or nonwhite segments into the Anglo segment. Color, thereby, became a significant criteria within Anglo settlements.[17]

The major Anglo settlements (the U.S., Canada, New Zealand, Australia, South Africa, Rhodesia) were settler rather than sojourner colonies. The people settled permanently, bringing families with them, becoming, in Hartz's terms, 'fragments' of the larger Anglo society. Many of the Iberian colonies were initially viewed as temporary, the intent being the extraction of resources (gold, silver, and later, sugar, etc.). Interaction with the natives, as a consequence, assumed a role somewhat different from that in Anglo settlements. In the latter, native and white invader fought for scarce resources (land). The struggle often generated racist attitudes. The shortage of labor or other factors often prompted reliance upon slavery within the colonies. Slavery fitted the colonists' needs, and they justified it with racist rationalizations. As Eric Williams has noted: 'slavery was not born of racism: rather, racism was the consequence of slavery.'[18] Although there were differences in Anglo and Iberian traditions, Hoetink, Williams and others also recognized that economic competition often resulted in similar treatment of native and slave. White racism may at times have been different in the Anglo and Iberian settlements, but in both instances it was present.

### III

Hartz classifies most overseas European settlements as 'fragmented' societies i.e., societies which, upon their establishment, retained the major characteristics of the parent country (at that founding point) even though the parent country, in subsequent years, changed.[19] Hartz's thesis provides a shortcut for comparing the six major 'Anglo' settlements: the United States, Canada, New Zealand, Australia, South Africa and Rhodesia. All were, basically, Anglo settled and/or Anglo controlled either in the formative or subsequent developmental period. There are differences among them, but each has a recognizable Anglo culture and institutional foundations, the differences notwithstanding.[20]

Briefly, a few of the similarities can be noted, including the following:—
    1. All were (a) settled initially (and extensively) by English, or

were (b) subsequently controlled by England, power residing initially with the British Government and Anglo settlers, the natives normally powerless.

2. Subsequently, the Anglo settlers themselves, even after the British Government divested itself of control (usually over foreign affairs and 'native' affairs), ended up with political power.

3. All six were settler rather than sojourner colonies, viewed as permanent, and entire families settled. Land was a primary motivational basis for settlement, rapidly bringing settlers into conflict with natives defending their lands.

4. Power, exercised by the Anglo settlers (or through the Imperial Government's potential or actual intervention), was employed to protect and enhance their powers and privileges (over land, resources, trade and opportunities), often at the expense of the non-Anglo settlers (or, later, immigrants) and the natives.

5. All, generally, endured lengthy colonial experiences under British tutelage, and Anglo attitudes (of both settler and the British Government) largely determined behavior (and policies) toward native and nonwhite.

6. In their attitudes toward native and nonwhite, the Anglo settlers and British Government often found themselves in disagreement, thereby exacerbating political tensions between colony and mother country. Where possible, the mother country attempted to retain control over 'native' affairs, thereby protecting the native from settler encroachments on native lands.

7. In all, Anglo cultural and institutional foundations are clearly evident, even though in two of the instances (Canada and South Africa) other European cultural groups retained their own identities alongside the Anglo system.

8. All evolved and have retained (to a great extent) political values and institutions (including the United States) that are essentially English.

9. All encountered native populations, and these often ended in conflict, necessitating the intervention of British military forces. This, in turn, forced the British Government to intervene where possible in protecting natives.

10. An influx of nonwhite immigrant groups in each country subsequently resulted in racial confrontations, prompting discrimination against nonwhite groups, the patterns very similar in all Anglo societies.

Various degrees of racism can be found in Anglo colonies, whether they were settler or sojourner, a factor which, because of its impact on the social structure, contributed to different attitudes toward and interaction with both native and nonwhite.[21] Whatever the motivation for colonization—land, resources, trade, escape and adventure, or opportunity—the settler perceived the native as an obstacle in his quest for power and possessions. Racism, whatever its form, emerged from these early encounters, and it determined the configurations of subsequent settler-native interactions.

The American and Canadian experiences illustrate differences in settler-native encounters. Almost from the beginning the American colonists warred

with the natives, pushing the latter westward as waves of settlers took possession of the land. Settler and native fought bitterly. Viewing the native as
savage and inhumane, the settler thereby rationalized his policy of Indian
extermination.

Power was a significant factor. Whites, when they regarded the native
as powerful (or potentially powerful), were willing to accommodate or
negotiate with the Indian. He was placated. Indeed, at one point whites
proposed that a separate Indian state be established and that Indians send
a delegate to Congress. However, when Indians attempted to confederate
and oust the settlers, U.S. military retaliation was swift. Indian forces were
defeated in 1811; and, with the destruction of Indian power, settler-native
relations assumed a dominant-subordinate status. All ideas of a separate
Indian state with congressional representation were discarded.[22]

Where previously the American Government attempted (though seldom
successfully) to protect Indian territories from settler encroachments, that
changed with Andrew Jackson's presidency (1828-1836). Jackson, who
hated Indians, refused to enforce Supreme Court decisions protecting Indian
rights, and he prompted an 'Indian removal' policy that expelled Indians
from lands east of the Mississippi. Pushed westward and decimated by later
military encounters, the Indian population declined in subsequent decades.
No longer a threat and completely shorn of power, the Indian became a ward
of the state. In recent decades reform efforts have improved somewhat the
condition of the Indian, but the society has continued to discriminate against
him.[23]

Racism has also contributed to the Canadian Indian's deprivation. Historically, he was better treated than the American Indian, but presently the
condition of the two is similar. Significant in accounting for the historical
differences are Canada's original settlement by the French, the role of the
Catholic Church, and the more gradual and less extensive (in contrast to
America) influx of settlers. Early French settlers, trappers and farmers,
intermingled more freely with (and often married) Indians. There resulted a
'mixed breed', or *metis* who, during the 19th century (along with French
Canadians), constituted a substantial percentage of the population. The
smaller number of Canadian settlers resulted in fewer land conflicts between
settler and native. Moreover, Indians were encouraged to pursue farming
and become Christians, and the extended period of French control contributed to a greater acculturation of natives into society.

Political factors determined British policy toward the Indian after it took
control of Canada. Fearful of an American takeover of Canada, the British
curried favor with and relied upon Indians as a buffer in protecting Canada
from the Americans. This view—and policy—continued until mid-19th
century. The British negotiated treaties with the Indians, provided them with
annual gifts and stipends, and protected (to the extent possible) native from
settler encroachments until native affairs were turned over to Canadian
government control in 1860.

With increased settlement in the late 19th century, the Canadian
government, as the American federal government, found itself serving as a
buffer between settler and native. However, there were fewer settlers than in
America, Indian power remained a potential threat, and Canadian settlers,
as a consequence, were less aggressive in their land acquisitions. Moreover,
the *metis* constituted a sizeable percentage of the population, and they,
along with disgruntled Indian tribes, joined in the abortive Riel Rebellions

of 1869 and 1885, which directed attention to the land conflicts. Thereafter, and particularly during the 20th century, the position of the Indian has declined despite government and religious efforts to convert and assimilate him into white Canadian society.[24] As in America, the Indian is discriminated against, and the color factor has contributed to this.

Settler-native encounters in Australia were somewhat similar to those in America. Aborigines were fewer in number than the American Indian, and white weapons quickly dispelled the natives from lands desired by settlers. The British Government, ignoring the existence of the Aborigines, proclaimed as Crown Lands all lands not already claimed by settlers; and, except for Western Australia, it turned over control of native affairs to the state governments during the 1850s. Aborigines were put on reserves, but some (including full and part-Aborigines) moved to cities and towns, where discrimination has perpetuated their continued poverty. Representing less than one per cent of the population, the Aborigine is politically powerless. Power is a significant factor, for the native in America (the red man) has drawn sustenance for his politicization from the developing Black Power movement. However, there is no comparable nonwhite (or white) force in Australia that can support the native in confronting the system.

The relatively comparable power (at least briefly) of settler and native significantly shaped the interactions of those two groups in New Zealand. Early 19th century settler exploitation of the Maori prompted Maori retaliation. Moreover, under the Treaty of Waitangi (1840), directed toward resolving land disputes, the Crown acknowledged Maori possession of the land, guaranteed protection of that land from white encroachment (or purchase), and stipulated that only the British Government could purchase (and subsequently re-sell) Maori lands. Conflict continued, however, resulting in open warfare during the 1860s. The war necessitated the bringing in of British troops, for in New Zealand (as in Canada and South Africa), the Colonial Office had retained control over native affairs.[25]

For a period of time the Maoris were able to withstand the combined settler-British military forces. The defeat of the Maoris resulted in a period of disillusionment and population decline (as has happened with other native groups in comparable situations). Politically, though, the Maoris were somewhat successful, for they gained independent representation in the General Assembly, thereby acquiring a limited degree of political power. Following their defeat Maoris withdrew to their farmlands, shying away from contact with whites, remaining virtually isolated until well into the 20th century. More recently, Maoris have increasingly moved into more urban areas seeking employment. There, they have encountered prejudice and discrimination though in more limited form than found in Australia, America or South Africa.[26]

South Africa and, now, Rhodesia, represent one extreme pole of settler treatment of the native. As elsewhere, early British control over native affairs prevented extremely exploitative settler tactics against the native. The original Dutch settlers utilized their weapon superiority to expel natives from desired lands or to coerce them or imported slaves to work for them. After the British took control in 1806, the Cape Coloreds, the result of white-black liaisons, were accorded limited political rights. The Dutch, who originally accepted British control, increasingly viewed themselves and their white supremacist views as threatened by British support of native rights. The Boer exodus into the hinterlands, where they were far-removed from immediate British control, commenced after the British abolished slavery in 1834. In subsequent decades, despite their hostility to British authority, the Boers called for British military assistance whenever their land aggrandizement policies brought them into conflict with native Africans. Finally, a series of factors (including Boer hostility to and exploitation of the natives; the discovery of gold and diamonds in the Boer territories; and the refusal of the Boers to grant equal rights to Englishmen moving into the Boer areas) prodded the British into reasserting control over the Boer republics of Transvaal and the Orange Free State. This precipitated the Boer War of 1899-1902.

Although victorious, the British desired a rapprochement of Boer and English settlers. They thereby agreed (in negotiations establishing the Union of South Africa in 1910) to ignore native rights, including an earlier promise to support a limited native franchise. Thus, the British put the desire for a rapprochement and potential monetary gains above native rights. Under the Union, the Boers (or, as they came to be called, Afrikaners) ultimately solidified their majority. By 1948, they gained complete control of the political system; and since then the Afrikaner government has utilized its political power to extend the privileges and power enjoyed by the white population. This has been at the expense of the native African, who has been and is exploited under the guise of the nation's 'separate development' (or *apartheid*) policies.[27]

Under the 1965 Constitution, Rhodesia (which unilaterally broke from the Commonwealth), controlled by an Anglo white minority outnumbered nearly 20 to 1 by the native African, has enacted white supremacist policies similar to those of South Africa (where native Africans outnumber whites nearly 5 to 1). Through the uses of political power, the white Rhodesians maintain their privileged position, and native political organizational efforts at achieving political and economic rights are met, as in South Africa, by repression.[28]

In each of the major Anglo countries, then, settler-native encounters ultimately resulted in situations where the Anglo (supported later by other whites) settler used his superior weapons to wrest lands and resources from the native, justifying or rationalizing his hegemony on numerous grounds (e.g., the 'white man's burden', the 'superiority of the white race', 'civilizing the native', etc.). Whatever the justification, the Anglo settler, vying for land, resources, and riches, used his technical skills and weapons to expel or exploit the nonwhite native. And it was the Anglo who emerged with power and wealth.

## IV

Three aspects of power emerge as highly significant in evaluating racist aspects of settler-native encounters, namely: (a) the perception and uses of power in settler-native interactions; (b) the 'external' government's (i.e. the British Government, the American federal government) role in native affairs; and (c) the process of domination and dependency. All have contributed to the development and perpetuation of contemporary racism.

*Power and encounters*

Interpersonal behavior, as Deutsch notes, is determined by forces and by perceptual images which one group holds of another. These factors include: (a) the perceptions (especially of values and power) that each group holds of itself and of others; (b) the forces (the desire for land, etc.), including the intensity of those forces, motivating settler-native confrontations; and (c) the emergent perceptions that result from power encounters and determine subsequent behavioral patterns.

The cultural factor was particularly significant, for the Anglo viewed his culture and heritage as innately superior to that of others. Such ethnocentrism is not uniquely Anglo, for it is a characteristic of most cultures. In his contacts with native cultures, the Anglo concluded that his culture was vastly superior. Color, or the somatic factor, played a major role. As Baudet suggests, the notion of whiteness was highly esteemed, for darker colors, including the skin color of natives, were viewed in less affirmative terms.[28] These factors (the somatic and the cultural), taken in conjunction with his military superiority, the Anglo interpreted as confirmation of his superiority. This superiority, then, was accepted as the justification for Anglo domination and exploitation of the native.

Motivations were also a significant factor, for they determined the settlers' perceptions of and behavior toward the native. The more intense the settler desire for land and the greater the resistance of the native to the expropriation of his possessions, the more prolonged and bitter the settler-native conflict. The intensity of the conflict subsequently influenced the somatic cultural images that the settler held of the native, whose resistance was seen as justifying his extermination. Where the native was momentarily too powerful, the settler negotiated with him (for instance, in his dealings with American Indians prior to 1811, or with the Maoris prior to the 1860s). This did not preclude hostile encounters, but those were resolved normally by negotiations. However, when the settler achieved (or believed he had achieved) a military superiority, he forgot prior agreements and used force to take from the native what he wanted. Where he erred and the native proved more powerful than anticipated, the settler called for outside assistance (e.g., British troops, in the American colonies, New Zealand and South Africa; federal troops on the American frontier). Once having suppressed native resistance, the settler took what he wanted, removing remaining natives to reservations. Where settler-native conflicts were less acrimonious, as in Canada and New Zealand, subsequent native treatment was often less harsh. In some instances it was intervention of the 'external' government that influenced and mitigated settler-native encounters.

*Power of the external government*

Usually, the further removed (in distance and level) the government from the settler, the less intense were pressures to satisfy settler demands at the expense of native rights. Illustrative of this was the British (or metropolitan) Government's dealings with its colonies, where efforts to protect native rights involved it in controversies with settlers.

In the American colonies, for instance, the British tried to separate settlers from Indians by the 1763 Proclamation (prohibiting settlers west of the Appalachians). Covetous of the Indians' rich Ohio valley lands, the settlers resented the Imperial Government's restrictions, and the restrictions precipitated animosities and the war leading to American independence. Subsequently, under both the Articles of Confederation and the Constitution, the American federal government tried (though not always successfully) to protect native rights from settler land aggrandizement. It, like the British

Government, met with limited success as settlers overran Indian lands. This prompted native retaliation, and settlers called upon federal troops for 'protection'—and the expulsion of natives from coveted lands. Under Jackson (and thereafter), the federal government supported settler demands.

In England, early 19th century humanitarian/religious movements prompted the abolition of slavery, then focused on the 'aboriginal question' —the protection of native rights. Parliament, pressured to protect natives from settler encroachments in Canada, New Zealand, South Africa and Australia, retained (in most instances) its control over native affairs. But settler-native conflicts (especially in New Zealand and South Africa) often necessitated the intervention of British troops. Their presence, even if brief, provided British-appointed Governors with momentary leverage for curtailing settler pressures on natives. In other ways, too, the British Government protected native rights, including the negotiation of treaties protecting native lands (in Canada, New Zealand, South Africa), the establishment of buffer zones or native territories to prevent further settler land encroachments (South Africa, Rhodesia), and restricting native land sales to the government, which in turn would sell to the settlers. At least until it surrendered control over native affairs, the British were able to protect native rights.

By the 1860s, numerous forces prompted British retrenchment and withdrawal from the internal affairs of its possessions. The Manchester movement, demanding that colonies be self-supporting, forced the government to curtail its overseas (including military) expenditures. Moreover, mounting settler resentment (and threats of independence movements) prodded the government to loosen its control over native affairs. Finally, British weariness over the constant calling upon British troops to police conflicts both within and without the Empire resulted in a military drawback.

The metropolitan government's role is most clearly revealed in South Africa and Rhodesia. In the 1910 negotiations leading to establishment of the Union, the British, though making symbolic gestures toward native rights, left the native at the mercy of the Union. The Cape Colored's limited right of franchise was protected; constitutional checks were instituted to protect the natives; but the British (as subsequent events confirmed), by not protecting native rights, set the stage for the present apartheid policy.

In Rhodesia, the British retained control over native affairs until the 1920s. Even thereafter they retained some control. Following the demise of the 1950s Federation of the Rhodesias and Nyasaland, white Rhodesia, fearful of native nationalist movements and suspicious of possible British intervention, moved increasingly to solidify its control over the majority native population. To protect their privilege and power, the white Rhodesians declared independence from Britain. Subsequent steps, as in South Africa, have been directed toward the perpetuation of white supremacy.

### Domination and dependency

Racism, resulting from encounters and rationalizations, is reinforced by both the dominant and dependent groups' behavior. As Mannoni and others suggest, dependency behavior (within the dependent group or with the dominant group) elicits specific dominant group responses. For example, parallels are evident in native responses to their apprehensions concerning possible extinction. The American Cherokees and New Zealand Maoris are illustrative of this. Believing there were magical powers in the settlers institutions, they co-opted these for themselves (the Cherokees, a Constitution; the Maoris, the King movement). Such incorporations, it was thought, would assist in repelling settlers. In other instances, both before and after their demise, natives embraced messianic movements (for example, in America, Canada, New Zealand and South Africa) led by self-proclaimed prophets or messiahs who, believing they possessed divine powers, called upon those supernatural powers to assist in expelling the white invaders.[29]

White power prevailed, however. The breaking of native resistance had a traumatic effect upon native populations. Both societal and individual disintegration normally ensued. Characteristic disintegration patterns emerged, including, among others: the breakup and disintegration of family organization and community values; alcoholism; promiscuity; hostility (both intropunitive and toward the community); poverty; cultural disintegration; atomization of the individual; and, often, the decline of traditional authority and leadership.[30] Native groups, powerless, became wards of the state, and individuals were generally characterized by docility, dependency and, often, self-hatred. The internalization of these characteristics, perpetuated by sociological conditions, left native groups dependent upon the dominant white power, which consequently managed to perpetuate its control over and exploitation of native groups.[31]

The native, in many instances, still remains powerless, dispossessed, denied equal opportunity or treatment (whether on reserves or within the white community), and the prey of societies which regard him as racially inferior. Policies pursued continue to discriminate against the native, though the pervasiveness of this discrimination is not as easily visible when natives are hidden on reservations. Thus, racist practices are not always evident where the native is concerned. But it emerges more clearly and distinctly, both historically and at present, in white encounters with nonwhites in these Anglo societies.

## V

Within these Anglo societies, racist practices appear most graphically in the treatment of other nonwhites, especially Asians (more specifically, Chinese, Japanese and Indians) and, in America, nonwhites of African descent. Except for Rhodesia, substantial numbers of Asians settled in the U.S., Canada, New Zealand, Australia and South Africa. Most of the settlements occurred during the latter half of the 19th century, the Asians being brought (normally as indentured workers) or lured by job opportunities. The African, brought as a slave to America, came against his own wishes.

Other nonwhites (Malays, Koreans, etc.) also settled in these countries, but racism is most clearly evident in the treatment of the above groups. At the inception, the host country, because of labor scarcities, encouraged the influx of Asians. In other instances it was the British Government, also seeking cheap labor, which brought Asians into parts of its Empire.[32] Wherever he settled, the Asian encountered opposition, especially from workers who regarded him as an economic threat. This desire for a cheap source of labor also perpetuated slavery in the American South where, land being plentiful, it was virtually impossible for planation owners to find willing workers. After the abolition of slavery, both northern and southern white workers responded with hostility toward black workers. They, like the Asians, were viewed as a threat to the higher wages and job security of white workers.

The initial Asian influx occurred in the 1830s when approximately 3000 Chinese coolies were brought into Australia as contract labor. However, not until the 1850s did large numbers settle in Anglo societies. Australian workers, threatened by that original influx, responded with violence, a reaction that emerged in all Anglo countries.[33] The shortage of farm workers and general laborers, the demand for miners with the gold discoveries of the 1850s onward in California, British Columbia, New Zealand and, later, Queensland, and the scarcity of railroad construction workers commencing in the 1870s, all created acute labor shortages. The Anglo nations—and especially the U.S., Canada, New Zealand and Australia—tried to correct this by bringing in Chinese. Elsewhere, the shortage of sugar cane workers prompted the British to import indentured Indian workers into South Africa, native labor having proven unsuitable. Only later, especially from the 1890s, did Japanese enter, lured by labor scarcities in California, British Columbia and Australia.

Governments initially encouraged Asian immigration. For instance, in 1852, the California governor welcomed Chinese and requested legislative approval of land grants for inducing Asian settlement. But workers felt threatened, and anti-Chinese sentiment prompted racial violence in California, Canada, New Zealand and Australia. Chinese thereafter sought jobs where they were less threatening to white workers; nevertheless, they were accosted as scapegoats during periods of economic distress. Governments, increasingly prodded by angry white citizens, legislated to terminate Chinese immigration.[34]

The Indians, brought in to work the sugar cane fields of Natal, subsequently moved to other colonies of South Africa. Anti-Indian hostily intensified, local governments enacted discriminatory measures, and by 1911, the further importation of Indian indentured workers was prohibited. Efforts to repatriate Indians were largely unsuccessful, and racial violence resulted early in the 20th century. Since the Afrikaners gained control in 1948, the Indians, as the Cape Colored, have been restricted in their freedom and opportunities. Fewer Indians emigrated to the other Anglo societies (i.e. except for the British colonies in the Caribbean and Pacific) of Australia, America or Canada. But, where they did, they too faced discriminatory treatment. More recently, black racism in East Africa has led to the exodus of Indians. Fleeing to England, Indians have increasingly encountered discriminatory treatment there.

During the last decade of the 19th century, Japanese flooded into California and British Columbia, and the fear of a 'yellow peril' prompted new outbreaks of anti-Asian violence. The Japanese government protested. American and Canadian governments, attempting to placate local governments and citizens, negotiated 'gentlemen's agreements' whereby the Japanese government voluntarily restricted the emigration of its citizens. Thereafter, the U.S., Canada, New Zealand and Australia, responding to citizen 'yellow peril' fears, enacted Asian immigration restrictions. With the advent of World War II, anti-Asian racism in America prompted the incarceration of Japanese-Americans. Banished from their homes, their properties confiscated, the Japanese were confined behind barbed-wire concentration camps for over two years.[35]

To a great extent, the blatant racism found earlier in Anglo societies has abated. There have been, and are, exceptions. In South Africa, the Asian is, like the native and Cape Colored, discriminated against. Australia upholds what is, in effect, an immigration policy restricted solely to whites; and immigration laws of other Anglo societies severely limit the number of Asian immigrants.[36] The characteristics of anti-Asian racism are readily evident. In most instances it has been the economic threat of Asian labor competition that has prompted hostilities. Other factors have also exacerbated the animosities. Asians were viewed as untrustworthy, dishonest and corrupt. Indeed, the common stereotype portrayed Asians as evil and immoral; and this generated an image which depicted Asians as sexual perverts who, if given the opportunity, would corrupt the virtue of white women (a comparable view of Afro-Americans is held by white racists).

Finally, white racists claimed that Asians were inferior and could not be assimilated into white culture. To do so would 'pollute' the white race and lead to its 'mongrelization'. Given their lack of power, political or economic, the Asian could not protect himself from white ravages. Only in the instance of the Japanese, where the Japanese government (itself becoming a world power early in the century) protested racist treatment, was any substantive action taken (only palliative, at that) to protect the rights of a minority group in the Anglo societies.

In its 1968 study of racism in America, the President's Commission on Civil Disorders concluded that prejudice and discrimination were widespread in the nation. White racism, it suggested, permeates American life. Indeed, 'white institutions created it, white institutions maintain it, and white society condones it.'[37] The society's treatment of the Afro-American is a graphic example of Anglo (and white) racism. The African, historically, has suffered cruelly at the hands of whites in America, first as a slave, subsequently (after emancipation) as a second-class citizen. Only since World War II, and particularly in the last decade, have changes broadened the Afro-American's opportunities. In some instances those changes are the result of the black American's direct confrontation of the system; in others, they result from the increasing economic and political power he wields, a power which has provided him with the necessary leverage for demanding equal treatment and opportunity.

Viewed historically, the transformation of ethnocentric views into racist notions can be traced during the development of the American colonies.[38] Early in colonial days, the African slave was accorded an ambiguous status, comparable somewhat to that of the indentured worker. But that status changed rapidly. Because of the acute scarcity of labor in the South, the notion of a permanent slavery developed. Society, needing a source of cheap labor and viewing black men as inferior to whites, evolved a series of rationalizations for subjugating and exploiting the Afro-American. Even after emancipation, and extending well into the 20th century, segments of society have developed arguments for maintaining the black American in a subordinate position.[39]

Emancipation brought freedom but not equal opportunity or treatment to the Afro-American. With the withdrawal of Northern troops and the termination of Reconstruction, the white South regained power and utilized it for disfranchising black men. Terror was employed to achieve that end; legislation was enacted to render powerless the former slave; and other discriminatory measures were enacted by state and local governments. The

Afro-American found himself exploited economically, and he was soon caught in a hopeless poverty. Increasingly, the federal government ignored the South's exploitation of black citizens. Indeed, federal courts facilitated repression, for it declared unconstitutional federal civil rights legislation and interpreted other legislative measures in a manner discriminatory to blacks.[40] This process, commencing in the late 19th century, continued, reaching its apex during the presidency (1912-1920) of Woodrow Wilson. Where previously some Afro-Americans had worked their way into comparatively high federal positions, under Wilson blacks were limited to low status jobs. Simultaneously, previously integrated federal public facilities (including cafeterias, restaurants, lavatories, etc.) were segregated, thereby implementing at the federal level the 'separate but equal' facilities which the Supreme Court had declared constitutional in the 1896 Plessy *v.* Ferguson case.

Labor scarcity, along with increasing black protests, prompted the federal and some state governments to enact equal employment measures during World War II. Following the war, civil rights issues were almost totally ignored until the 1960s when society, confronted by an increasingly adamant black minority demanding its rights, moved to prohibit discrimination and unequal treatment. However, even with such legislative and legal efforts, the Presidential Commission's 1968 *Report* admitted that racist practices remain pervasive in society. Racism is equally evident in South and North. In the former, it is more blatant; in the latter, more subtle, though it can be readily detected in education, housing and employment.

There have been improvements. Legislative measures have curtailed discriminatory practices against minority groups. But racism persists. Where, in earlier years, it was essentially Anglo racism, now other non-Anglo white groups (who have gained a niche in society) participate in discriminatory practices, hopeful of protecting powers and privileges they enjoy at the expense of blacks and other minority Americans, including Puerto Ricans and Mexican-Americans.[41]

* * *

Racism, in terms of native and nonwhite, is widespread in Anglo societies. Evident for centuries in America, Canada, New Zealand, Australia, South Africa and Rhodesia, it now manifests itself in England, where once the people were dismayed at the discriminatory practices of their Anglo brethren in settler societies. Racist behavior in England is reflected in the treatment of East Indians and West Indians who have emigrated there, and recently restrictive immigration measures have been enacted to keep out (essentially) nonwhite members of Commonwealth nations.

When viewed from this broader perspective of Anglo racism, the racist practices of Australia (or of any of the Anglo societies) appear less unique. Rather, what is evident is that somewhat comparable forces, based on somatic and cultural predispositions interacting with the desires for power and privilege that have prompted Anglo-native and Anglo-nonwhite encounters, have resulted in racist practices. Racism has, in part, been generated by the bitterness of these encounters. In other instances, the racism has resulted as a rationalization by those with power as a means for justifying the power and privilege they have preempted for themselves. Whatever the forces generating racism, it has assumed an independent existence of its own, accounting for the perpetuation of inequality in Anglo societies. While only a brief sketch has been possible here, the contours of racism in these Anglo societies suggests the possibility of a more thorough appraisal of it on a comparative basis.

## REFERENCES

1 HARTZ, *The Founding of New Societies*. Harcourt, Brace & World, New York: 1964, pp. 16ff. KOVEL in *White Racism: A Psychohistory*. Vintage Books, New York: 1971, esp. ch. 6, traces racism to what he terms the 'obsessive-compulsive, or anal personality' (the 'normal variant' of western man), which is essentially —and obsessively—punctual, orderly, neat, clean, rational, aloof, and dominative. Most of Kovel's illustrations, though, are Anglo rather than European in general.

2 See especially FRANTZ FANON, *The Wretched of the Earth*. Grove, New York: 1968 and *Black Skin, White Masks*. Grove, New York: 1967, and also O. MANNONI, *Prospero and Caliban*. Praeger, New York: 1964. PHILIP MASON, in *Patterns of Dominance*. Oxford University Press, New York: 1970, traces the intersecting of the domination-racism issues.

3 Including the British Caribbean, the Fiji Islands, Papua-New Guinea, and Australia.

4 See, for instance: ANDREW LIND, ed., *Race Relations in World Perspective*. University of Hawaii Press, Honolulu: 1955, WALTER CROCKER, *The Racial Factor in International Relations*. National University, Canberra: 1956; ROBERT BROWNE, *Race in International Affairs*. Public Affairs Press, Washington: 1961; ROBERT GARDINER, Race and Colour in International Relations, *Daedalus*, 96 Spring 1967; RONALD SEGAL, *The Race War*. Penguin Books, Middlesex: 1967; HAROLD ISAACS, 'Color in World Affairs,' *Foreign Affairs*, 47 January 1969; and KOVEL, *White Racism*. Some other studies, particularly of white racism, suffer, unfortunately, from an overemotionalism and self-guilt that leads to a somewhat perverted white self-flagellation. Most illustrative of this is FRANK TUCKER's, *The White Conscience: An Analysis of the White Man's Mind and Conduct*. Ungar, New York: 1969. PETER ROSE is critical of this overemotionalism in 'The Development of Race Studies', in GEORGE SHEPHERD and TILDEN LEMELLE, eds., *Race among Nations: A Conceptional Approach*. D. C. Heath, Lexington, Mass: 1970.

5 The present collection of articles on Australian racism represents, perhaps, the most extensive effort to date. Among the few attempts to study racism (or aspects of it) conceptually and/or comparatively are: TAMOTSU SHIBUTANI and KIAN KWAN, *Ethnic Stratification: A Comparative Approach*. Macmillan, New York: 1965; PIERRE VAN DEN BERGHE, *Race and Racism: A Comparative Perspective*. John Wiley, New York: 1967; R. A. SCHERMERHORN, *Comparative Ethnic Relations: A Framework for Theory and Research*. Random House, New York: 1970; and SHEPHERD and LEMELLE, eds., *Race among Nations: A Conceptual Approach*. Cf., HERBERT BLALOCK, *Toward a Theory of Minority-Group Relations*. John Wiley, New York: 1967 and PHILIP MASON, *Patterns of Dominance*, who also allude to racism in their studies, as does E. FRANKLIN FRAZIER in his earlier (1957) study, *Race and Culture Contacts in the Modern World*. Beacon Press, Boston: 1965.

6 MANNONI, in *Prospero and Caliban*, addresses himself directly to the dominant-subordinate dependency relationship that evolves in colonial settings, and his analysis touches in many instances on the emergence of racist notions. Prior factors, plus the white-native encounters, shape perceptions on which the dominant power members base their behaviour toward the subordinate group. See KARL DEUTSCH, 'Research Problems on Race in Intranational and International Relations', in SHEPHERD and LEMELLE, eds., *Race among Nations: A Conceptual Approach*. CHRISTINE BOLT, in *Victorian Attitudes to Race*. Routledge and Kegan Paul, London: 1971, clearly illustrates the racist under-

pinnings of Victorian English attitudes towards natives in Anglo-dominated societies. MASON, in *Patterns of Dominance* (chaps. 4, 6, 9, 10, 11), touches on the racism issue in selected Anglo societies. VAN DEN BERGHE, in *Race and Racism* (p. 11), defines racism as 'any set of beliefs that organic, genetically transmitted differences (whether real or imagined) between groups are intrinsically associated with the presence or the absence of certain socially relevant abilities or characteristics, hence that such differences are a legitimate basis of invidious distinctions between groups socially defined as races.' Ethnocentrism, where one group views itself as *culturally* superior to other (cultural) groups, is virtually universal, but it should be distinguished from racism, which is based on phenotypical and genotypical traits. It is KOVEL's thesis in *White Racism* that certain attributes of western culture lead, ineluctably, to racism. However, it might be that white ethnocentrism, combined with white dominance and white encounters with native cultures, only later evolved into racist ideology —as a rationalization and justification for white domination. This is implicity suggested in MANNONI, in *Prospero and Caliban*, and explicity stated in ERIC WILLIAMS, *Capitalism and Slavery*, Capricorn Books, New York: 1966. See also BOLT, *Victorian Attitudes to Race*.

7 BAUDET, *Paradise on Earth*: *Some Thoughts on European Images of Non-European Man.* Yale University Press, New Haven: 1965, p. 28. The romantic images of the native Indian in America are also traced in MICHAEL KRAUS, *The Atlantic Civilization*. Cornell University Press, Ithaca: 1949. ROY HERVEY PEARCE, in *The Savages of America*: *A Study of the Indian and the Idea of Civilization.* John Hopkins Press, Baltimore: rev. ed. 1965, traces the transition in white perceptions of the American Indian from the pre-contact period through the Civil War in American literature, illustrating how literature became a subtle means for rationalizing white policies of Indian extermination.

8 The terms 'sojourner' and 'settler' are employed by A. GRENFELL PRICE in his study, *The Western Invasions of the Pacific and Its Continents.* Clarendon Press, Oxford: 1963, pp. 48-52.

9 *Ibid.*, pp. 51-52.

10 A. GRENFELL PRICE, *White Settlers and Native Peoples.* Georgian House, Melbourne: 1949, chap. 1.

11 The United States, no longer under British control, did not feel this influence, and what limited efforts there were to correct abuses generally fell on the deaf ears of a society indifferent toward the Indian's plight. See, for example, HELEN JACKSON's study (first published in 1881), *A Century of Dishonor.* Harper-Row, New York: 1969, documenting the mistreatment of the native population. The British Government, though, did still exercize a degree of power and restraint in Canada, New Zealand, and Australia, as well as South Africa (Rhodesia was not established until later). What is significant is that British power over its Dominions and Colonies often served as a leavening influence against the harsher attitudes of settlers who desired native lands. As long as the British Government retained control over native affairs (which it did within most of these countries for a part of the century), it could influence native policy. This aspect of British power is discussed more fully later.

12 PRICE's study, it should be remembered, carried only through the conclusion of World War II. The new directions he perceived were slowed by World War II, and postwar economic development in these societies diverted attention from the plight and problems of native groups. Recent events do suggest that changes *may* be forthcoming. In general, though, it is quite valid to contend that, except for spotty instances, the condition of the native in the United States, Canada and Australia has improved very little in recent decades, despite efforts of liberal and native groups to bring about changes. The condition of New Zealand's Maoris has, to some extent, improved, though the recent movements of Maoris from rural to urban centres has elicited examples of

previously latent white racism. In both South Africa and Rhodesia, the native, impotent under white hegemony, faces increasingly discriminatory treatment. See, simply as illustrative: HARTZ, *The Founding of New Societies;* D'ARCY MCNICKLE, *The Indian Tribes of the United States.* Oxford University, New York: 1962 and *Indians and Other Americans.* Harper, New York: 1970; VINE DELORIA, *Custer Died for Your Sins.* Avon, New York: 1969, FORREST LAVIOLETTE, *The Struggle for Survival.* University of Toronto Press, Toronto: 1961; JOHN MELLING, *Right to a Future: The Native Peoples.* Anglican Church of Canada, Ontario: 1967; ERIK SCHWIMMER, ed., *The Maori People in the Nineteen-Sixties.* Blackwood and Janet Paul, Auckland: 1968; LORNA LIPP-MANN, *To Achieve Our Country: Australia and the Aborigines.* Cheshire, Melbourne: 1970; PIERRE VAN DEN BERGHE, *South Africa: A Study in Conflict.* University of California Press, Berkeley: 1970; and JAMES BARBER, *Rhodesia: The Road to Rebellion.* Oxford University Press, London, 1967. The articles in this volume on Australian racism represent a major step in appraising the broader ramifications of racism in one society.

13 See especially HARTZ, *The Founding of New Societies,* Part I: H. HOETINK, *The Two Variants in Caribbean Race Relations.* Oxford University Press, London: 1967; VAN DEN BERGHE, *Race and Racism,* chaps. 1, 6; FRANK TANNENBAUM, *Slave and Citizen: The Negro in the Americas.* Vintage Books, New York: 1968; and LEWIS HANKE, *Aristotle and the American Indians: A Study in Race Prejudice in the Modern World.* Indiana University Press, Bloomington: 1970.

14 This notion, upheld in principle by the Church, was not always upheld in practice within the Spanish and Portuguese colonies. See especially TANNEN-BAUM, *Slave and Citizen:* HANKE, *Aristotle and the American Indian:* and HOETINK, *The Two Variants in Caribbean Race Relations.*

15 HOETINK, *The Two Variants in Caribbean Race Relations,* p. 9. This difference is also reflected in the attitude of the French and the Catholic Church in the treatment of the Indian in Canada prior to the British takeover. This French treatment contrasted sharply with Anglo/American treatment in the Colonies and, after independence, in the new American nation. Thus, Eastern Canadian Indians were, over a period of time, more fully assimilated into the French culture. Many Indians became Catholic converts, and French-Indian liaisons and marriages were not uncommon. As a consequence of British control (of Canada) and the American Revolution, the British resorted to the use of Indians as a buffer between the United States and Canada. Canadian Indians, as a result, were momentarily accorded better treatment by the British than the Indians in the United States. See esp. PRICE, *White Settlers and Native Peoples,* pp. 59-69; GEORGE MELLOR, *British Imperial Trusteeship: 1783-1850.* Faber and Faber, London: 1951, chap. 8; and GEORGE STANLEY, *The Birth of Western Canada.* University of Toronto Press, Toronto: 1960, chaps. 10, 11, 13. For a period, British Government control over native affairs in Canada, along with the advent of humanitarian and philanthropic influences, tempered Canadian government and settler treatment of the native. Other aspects of this are discussed below.

16 See HOETINK, *The Two Variants in Caribbean Race Relations,* pp. 9ff.; HARTZ, *The Founding of New Societies,* chap. 1; TANNENBAUM, *Slave and Citizen;* HANKE, *Aristotle and the American Indians;* and DAVID B. DAVIS, *The Problem of Slavery in Western Culture.* Cornell University Press, Ithaca: 1966. Where the Catholic Church played this intervening role (i.e., tempering white encounters with and treatment of the native) in Iberian settlements, the British Imperial Government, until it relinquished its control over native affairs in its colonies, played a somewhat comparable role in the Anglo settled societies.

17 KOVEL, in *White Racism,* explores the underpinnings of these color, or racist, notions. The Anglo tradition, he suggests, compels man to think essentially in

terms of objects or things, over which he has or can exercize control. 'Western man' (though, in reality, KOVEL is describing the Anglo tradition) is essentially an obsessive-compulsive personality, and his training compels him toward punctuality, orderliness, and cleanliness. Likewise, he is, basically, rational, aloof, and thinks in terms of dominating things, including people, Given his obsession with the accumulation of property and power, and lacking a religious tradition that accepted native and non-white as *people*, the Anglo quickly labelled those "others" (i.e., natives and non-whites) as inferior, if not sub-human or nonhuman. Particularly did such notions emerge when the Anglo found the native denying him access to desired land or resources, or when the Anglo found slavery an inexpensive means of labor for growing or extracting the resources of newly acquired colonies. Superior weapons, of course, further led the Anglo to view hostile natives as "objects"—such as nature—to be conquered and brought under control. Given these factors, the development of the notion of slaves being chattel represented a logical progression in Anglo thought.

18 WILLIAMS, *Capitalism and Slavery*. Capricorn Books, New York: 1966, p. 7.

19 HARTZ, *The Founding of New Socities*, chaps. 1-3. He develops this thesis more fully for one society in his earlier study, *The Liberal Tradition in America*. Harcourt, Brace and World, New York: 1967.

20 In Canada and South Africa, the British assumed control over societies earlier established by other groups (the French, in Canada; the Dutch, in South Africa). Each, as a consequence, had from the period it came under Anglo control a substantial non-Anglo white population, and this influenced somewhat Anglo treatment of the native. Despite the surface differences, particularly in terms of political institutions, the American colonists, after Independence, retained what were basically Anglo values, culture and institutions.

21 See, for example, HOETINK's discussion, *The Two Variants in Caribbean Race Relations*, pp. 21-23 and *passim*.

22 See esp. REGINALD HORSMAN, *Expansion and American Indian Policy, 1783-1812*. Michigan State, East Lansing: 1967; and FRANCIS PRUCHA, *American Indian Policy in the Formative Years*. Harvard University Press, Cambridge: 1962.

23 See the McNICKLE and DELORIA books cited in reference 12, as well as STUART LEVINE and NANCY LURIE, eds., *The American Indian Today*. Penguin Books, Baltimore: 1970.

24 See the LA VIOLETTE and MELLING books cited in reference 12, as well as STANLEY, *The Birth of Western Canada*, and J. MELLING, 'Recent Developments in Official Policy towards Canadian Indians and Eskimos,' *Race*, 7 April 1966.

25 KEITH SINCLAIR, *The Maori Wars*. New Zealand University Press, Wellington: 1961; J. D. B. MILLER, *Britain and the Old Dominions*. John Hopkins Press, Baltimore: 1966; JAMES A. WILLIAMSON, *A Short History of British Expansion*. St. Martins Press, New York: 1967; GEORGE MELLOR, *British Imperial Trusteeship: 1783-1850*. Faber and Faber, London: 1951; and ARTHUR KEITH *Responsible Government in the Dominions*. Claredon Press, Oxford: 1928, 2 vol.

26 SCHWIMMER, ed., *The Maori People in the Nineteen-Sixties;* JOAN METGE, *A New Maori Migration*. Athlone Press, London: 1964; HANS MOL, *Religion and Race in New Zealand*. National Council of Churches, Christchurch: 1966; and ALAN WARD, 'Brown Man's Burden: The Maori Today,' *Dissent*, 23 Spring, 1968.

27 See esp. WILLIAM VATCHER, *White Laager: The Rise of Afrikaner Nationalism*. Praeger, New York: 1965; W. M. MACMILLAN, *Bantu, Boer and Briton: The Making of the South African Native Problem*. Claredon, Oxford: 1963; GWENDOLYN CARTER, *The Politics of Inequality: South Africa Since 1948*. Praeger,

New York, 1959; PIERRE VAN DEN BERGHE, *South Africa: A Study in Conflict.* University of California Press, Berkeley: 1970; IAN D. MacCRONE, *Race Attitudes in South Africa.* Witwatersrand University Press, Johannesburg:, 1957; PHILIP MASON, *The Birth of a Dilemma: The Conquest and Settlement of Rhodesia.* Oxford University Press, London, 1958; RICHARD GRAY, *The Two Nations: Aspects of the Development of Race Relations in the Rhodesias and Nyasaland.* Oxford University Press, London, 1960; THOMAS FRANCK, *Race and Nationalism: The Struggle for Power in Rhodesia-Nyasaland.* Fordham University Press, New York, 1960; JAMES BARBER, *Rhodesia: The Road to Rebellion.* Oxford University Press, London, 1967; and CLAIRE PALLEY, 'Law and the Unequal Society: Discriminatory Legislation in Rhodesia,' *Race,* 12 July 1970 and 12 October 1970.

28  HOETINK, in *The Two Variants in Caribbean Race Relations,* proposes the term 'Somatic Norm Image' for 'the complex of physical (somatic) characteristics which are accepted by a group as its norm and ideal,' (p. 120). He prefers this as a somewhat more 'value-free' term for discussing each group's (or culture's) tendency to accept its own physical characteristics and attributes as the more highly esteemed, such characteristics becoming more acutely accented when members of the group encounter individuals (usually of other cultures) who have the opposite, or differing, physical characteristics. This can be a central component of ethnocentric beliefs. The culture itself constitutes another component. One might, in turn, speak of a 'Cultural Norm Image' (the composite of social, political and economic values), which can be viewed as (paraphrasing HOETINK) 'the complex of cultural characteristics which are accepted by a group as its norm and ideal.' Translated into psychosocial terms, these Somatic (SNI) and Cultural (CNI) Norm Images constitute, in part, the underpinnings of the behavioral motivations evident in the Anglo settler-native encounters.

29  VITTORIO LANTERNARI, *The Religious of the Oppressed.* Knopf, New York, 1963.

30  ALEXANDER LEIGHTON, *My Name is Legion.* Basic Books, New York, 1959, chaps. 1, 5, 9. Somewhat similar patterns are observable within slave societies. See, for example, the appraisal in ORLANDO PATTERSON, *The Sociology of Slavery: Negro Slave Society in Jamaica.* MacGibbon and Kee, London, 1967.

31  MANNONI, in *Prospero and Caliban,* describes some of these emergent dependency patterns. FANON, in *White Faces, Black Masks,* takes issue with Mannoni's analysis, but there, as in *The Wretched of the Earth,* he recognizes the psychological impact on the native of the domination/subordination patterns in colonial societies. See, too, MASON's, appraisal in *Patterns of Dominance,* Part II.

32  Elsewhere in the Empire, in desperate need of cheap labor and finding the natives inefficient or unwilling to work, the British imported indentured workers from India for the sugar, copra, rubber and tobacco plantations, particularly in its Caribbean possessions, the Fiji Islands and Malaya.

33  CHARLES PRICE, ' "White" Restrictions on "Coloured" Immigration,' *Race,* 7 January 1966.

34  In appraising the response to Asian immigration (including that of Chinese, Japanese and Indians), see, for example, the following sources: MELLOR, *British Imperial Trusteeship: 1783-1850,* chaps. 3-4; ROBERT HUTTENBACK, *The British Imperial Experience.* Harper and Row, New York, 1966; ARTHUR KEITH, *Responsible Government in the Dominions.* Claredon Press, Oxford, 1928, II, chap. 4; S. W. KUNG, *Chinese in American Life.* University of Washington Press, Seattle, 1962; ROGER DANIELS, *The Politics of Prejudice.* Atheneum, New York, 1970; JACOBUS tenBROEK *et al., Prejudice, War and the Constitution.* University of California Press, Berkeley, 1968; CARL BERGER, *The Sense of Power: Studies in the Ideas of Canadian Imperialism, 1867-1914.*

University of Toronto Press, Toronto, 1970; MABEL TIMLIN, 'Canada's Immigration Policy, 1896-1910,' *Canadian Journal of Economics and Political Science*, 26 November 1960; NG BICKLEEN FONG, *The Chinese in New Zealand*. Hong Kong University Press, Hong Kong, 1959; A. T. YARWOOD, *Asian Migration to Australia: The Background to Exclusion, 1896-1923*. Melbourne University Press, Melbourne, 1964; A. T. YARWOOD, ed., *Attitudes to Non-European Immigration*. Cassell, Melbourne, 1968; VAN DEN BERGHE, *South Africa: A Study in Conflict*. These are simply suggestive, but they provide an initial point for focusing on racism and the Asian immigrant in Anglo societies.

35 See esp. TENBROEK, et. al., *Prejudice, War and the Constitution*.

36 In the American instance, Hawaii has been somewhat of an exception in terms of conflict and exploitation in multiracial encounters. There have been conflicts historically, but in more recent decades that society, composed of Hawaiians, Japanese, Chinese, those of European descent and others, has managed to work toward a high degree of racial harmony in which (generally) equal opportunity and treatment are present. The discriminatory treatment of Japanese during World War II was, of course, an exception to this.

37 *Report of the National Advisory Commission on Civil Disorders* Bantam Books, New York, 1968.

38 The most thorough appraisal of racism in early America is the monumental study of WINTHROP JORDAN, *White over Black: American Attitudes Toward the Negro, 1550-1812*. Penguin Books, Baltimore, 1969. See also KOVEL's discussion of the Anglo underpinnings in his study, *White Racism*.

39 JORDAN, *White over Black*: cf., for later periods, THOMAS GOSSETT, *Race: The History of an Idea in America*. Schocken, New York, 1965; WILLIAM STANTON, *The Leopard's Spots: Scientific Attitudes toward Race in America, 1815-1859*. University of Chicago Press, Chicago, 1960; and I. A. NEWBY, *Jim Crow's Defence: Anti-Negro Thought in America, 1900-1930*. Louisiana State University Press, Baton Rouge, 1965. See also the analysis of slavery and racism in EUGENE GENOVESE, *The World the Slaveholders Made*. Vintage, New York, 1971.

40 Thus, through a series of rulings, the federal courts limited the meaning of constitutional amendments and congressional legislation, thereby limiting the rights of Afro-Americans. It also declared the 1875 Civil Rights Acts unconstitutional; then, in 1896, it accepted the notion of 'separate but equal' facilities in Plessy v. Ferguson, thereby allowing southern states to segregate public facilities that were seldom equal. That doctrine was overturned by the 1954 Brown v. Board of Education decision which held that separate but equal facilities were, by definition unequal, for they placed a stigma of inferiority on the group (Afro-Americans) who were segregated from whites.

41 The literature on American racism is voluminous, and it is difficult to suggest where to begin an appraisal of it. For a brief introduction, see: LOUIS KNOWLES and KENNETH PREWITT, eds., *Institutional Racism in America*. Prentice-Hall, Englewood Cliffs, N. J., 1969; collections of readings such as WILLIAM CHACE and PETER COLLIER, eds., *Justice Denied: The Black Man in White America*. Harcourt, Brace and World, New York, 1970, and SETHARD FISHER, ed., *Power and the Black Community: Racial Subordination in the United States*. Random House, New York, 1970; and the classic study by GUNNAR MYRDAL, *An American Dilemma*. Harper, New York, 1944. For the other American groups noted, see JOHN HOWARD, *Awakening Minorities*. Aldine, Chicago, 1970.

# AUSTRALIA AND NEW GUINEA

# 2

# NIUGINI BLACK POWER

*Leo J. Hannett*

Black Power . . .
Something the white man didn't initiate
Can't propagate
And won't tolerate for Black Consumption.
*David Coleman and Farris Harris*

The Niugini Black Power group was formed at the University of Papua New Guinea on the first of July, 1970. Its inception resulted from one of the many anti-colonialist hate sessions that quite a number of us usually have here at night and which carry on till the small hours of the morning. However, the idea of forming a Black Power group had been bandied around for quite a long time. In August 1969, after the West Irian demonstration for example, when one of us was accused by a noted Port Moresby journalist of being a front man of a white student in organizing the demonstration, serious thoughts were given to forming a similar organisation. However, the idea was given up as it was felt that one would be accused of being swayed too much by the dictates of one's emotions, however deeply felt they may be.

Although the Niugini Black Power group became a reality on that night of the first of July 1970, our first public appearance was at Hohola where we organized a forum to condemn the deplorable Public Order Bill that has since been passed in the House of Assembly. It was significant that at that meeting our members were condemned as emotional and anti-European by some whites and noticeably by some Niuginian members of the Moral Rearmament Movement, considered by our group as opposed to genuine national development.

The reactions that we encountered are fairly representative of the two classes of people that have been resisting us all the time. The first group is that which, from its position of non-committal or non-involvement, sees these issues that we raise as purely academic debatable topics that must be subjected to methodical and clinical examination. Most of these, especially whites, have never been placed in positions of being oppressed or denied their humanity or basic dignity just because they happen to have the wrong colour. To be a coloured person in a white world, defined and controlled by whites, is a unique experience that only coloured people can relate. Too often the so called white liberals, who make out that they understand our cause, in their attempt to help us, invariably end up as being overtly paternalistic and becoming associates of the dispensers of false generosity. The second group, of course, comprises the genuine paternalists, consolidated in their position by fanatical pseudo-religious convictions that human problems can only be solved by following some vague divine providential plan, which places the oppressed in a position of total submission. It is almost beyond hope to convince this type of person, as their naive and simplistic approach to solving human problems is often indubitably based on ignorance and greater personal insecurity than those they oppress. The task of the Black Power group is obvious—to release ourselves from our oppressors first of all, but in so doing, to redeem our oppressors' faith in humanity. For as Paulo Freire puts it—

'This then is the great humanistic and historical task of the oppressed:—to liberate themselves and their oppressors as well. The oppressors, as who oppress, exploit and rape by virtue of their power, cannot find in this power the strength to liberate either the oppressed or themselves. Only power that springs from the weakness of the oppressed will be sufficiently strong to free both. Any attempt to "soften" the power of the oppressor in deference to the weakness of the oppressed almost always manifests itself in the form of false generosity ... which is nourished by death, despair and poverty. That is why the dispensers of false generosity become desperate at the slightest threat to its source'[1].

'True generosity' Paul Freire maintains, 'consists precisely in fighting to destroy the causes which nourish false charity. False charity constrains the fearful and subdued, the "rejects of life" to extend their trembling hands. True generosity lies in striving so that these hands—whether of individuals or entire peoples—need be extended less and less in supplication, so that more and more they become human hands which work and working, transform the world'.[2] It is important to note at the outset, that the Niugini Black Power group does not have a rigid organization that is so tightly structured as to be merely self selving. The binding force that keeps us together is the mutually shared conviction that the philosophy we hold is right and that, by the force of our shared conviction, we must do what we can to bring to reality the desired aims of the group. Our membership is still very small, for it takes quite a while for our people to break themselves off from the dependent mouth-gaping posture they have been used to. The inferiority complex is great. It takes a man of mettle to risk his name and be counted among the 'freaks', the 'ungrateful', the 'communist' and other titles given to those that want to break out from the prescribed virtues or morality of the colonialists. To all appearances, the Black Power group preaches an ideology that is antithesis of all the 'virtues' upheld by the established institutions in the Territory or in other places —such virtues as multi-racialism, law and order, submissiveness to the rightful authorities, Christian brotherhood, Christian charity and forgiveness of those that oppressed you etc. etc.

It may come as a shock to many of our unquestioning critics to know that, basically, we subscribe to most of the fundamental principles mentioned above, except that we do so on one vitally important condition, that the criteria or value judgements which we use to evaluate and bring to reality those ideals are ones in keeping with the black man's dignity, self respect as an individual person equal to anyone in humanity, rights, privileges and duties. To our belief, anyone who preaches anything less than that is an oppressor or an accomplice to the oppression of the blackmen in Niugini. A lot of people who would otherwise agree with most of the aims of the Niugini Black Power group are nevertheless put off by the use of the name 'Black Power'. They argue that to use the name in Niugini is both dangerous and irrelevant. To them black power connotes violence, shooting, looting and hatred of the whites. The name smacks too much of the U.S.A. type of Black Power. They also contend that it is ridiculous to fight for Black Power, where the majority of the people are black anyway and would eventually gain power and control over the country once our political mentors are gone. Our answer to their argument is simply this:— We maintain that the name, 'Black Power' is vitally important for the movement and that it is as relevant to Niugini as the betel nut. It is this name that spells loud and clear the message we want to give. The component parts of the name gives it ginger, pepper and limestuff, the essentials for its vitality. Black Power is precisely what we want, no more, no less. We are adamant in the use of the word 'black' because the crux of our problems here in Niugini is the fact that we are not proud of being black and that, apart from general human values that we share in common with the rest of mankind, we also have been richly endowed with our own cultural, social and religious values which make us distinct as people or as a race. These values alone, give us our corporate personality and identity as a race or as individuals of that race. Black is not used in a narrow sense to mean colour or pigmentation only but, most important of all, it denotes our specifically distinct individuality, racial, cultural, social and religious values. A person with no awareness and no appreciation or urge to develop these characteristics runs the risk of being an empty man filled with straw, an ape or a parrot at that, with no cultural soul which is one of the hallmarks of personal stability. Only when Niuginians know who they are and what ought to be the true and genuine national objectives, will we then seek the means or the real powers to achieve these rightful ends. It would be naive, simplistic and dangerous for any Niuginian to think that just the handing over of the outward symbols of political control of our country at independence will make us *ipso facto* total masters of ourselves politically, socially, economically and religiously. Exchanging the white political actors with black ones and letting them play the same game within unchanged political machinery which works according to a prescribed set of rules, determined and devised under a different governing ideology and set of interests, would only bring about quantitative change but no qualitative change whatsoever. A guillotine is always a guillotine no matter what colour is the person who controls it. Similarly, an oppressive system is always an oppressive system unless there is, first of all, a radical transformation in the whole thinking of the controlling agent, which would necessitate the bringing about of a complete overhaul of the whole political machinery and having it reset to achieve a new set of objectives. It is stating the obvious to say that, when the magic wand of leadership is given to a white-approved Black Leader, nothing will change overnight in favour of the black men. Superficial localization that feeds on personal influence and not governing ideology is colonialism at its worst, for it enslaves the whole country to outside power. A Niuginian who is aware of his national objectives should always be wary and critical of all those talks about 'preparation' and 'development' of the people and the country for independence. The very use of those words, is fraught with preconceived biased and highly paternalistic meanings and attitudes. It is highly questionable whether the dependent people are really being prepared for independence at all. What is most evident in those now independent countries that have been 'prepared' for independence, is that black elites continue to run a colonial type autocracy for the benefit, and on behalf, of the 'mother country'[3]. As B. B. Schaffer once commented, 'the preparatory idea is an extreme instance of the assumption of the possibility and desirability of transferring Western Political concepts, that is, of the political gap approach, not merely in analysis but actually in policy itself'.[4]

Schaffer went on to say that 'in the ideology of preparation there is a fundamental distinction between the preparatory stages which are concerned with the transfer of a system and the process of transfer of power ... Preparation is concerned with the creation and translation of institutions (originally on certain conditions of viability) and transfer of power is concerned with independence'.[5]

One does not have to be an astute analyst to see the present trend of political development in Niugini where our black leaders, working within so-called democratic procedures, have been successful in formulating laws and important policies to consolidate the dominance of the white man in both politics and economics. Take for instance, the Public Order Bill which was passed by the majority of Niugini members in the House of Assembly. This Bill is mainly designed to suppress Niuginians in freely expressing their grievances against the government. The Bougainville Mining Ordinance, which permits only a 20 per cent equity share to our future Niugini Government, with the rest of the shares going to outside shareholders, is another example. The actual owners of the land were grudgingly allowed to receive a 5 per cent royalty, not of the value of the copper, but of the administration's royalty, which is a mere .0625 per cent of the f.o.b. value of the copper concentrate, i.e. an equivalent of 6 cents for every $100 of copper concentrate sold.[6] This is obviously unjust. But such is life; where once we had white exploiters, now we have democratically elected black slave traders in the House of Assembly.

The important point, of course, which the majority of the opponents of Black Power overlook, is that there is, in Niugini, an overwhelmingly dominating White Power in all sectors of life. Like a cancerous growth, it is eating into the very fibre of society. The black person in Niugini is a captive victim of white power. Most of the black men in Niugini have been inveigled into believing that the present order of things, where the white man dominates the black, is the immutable and inevitable instituted order of things.

There is white power in the policies of this country, though discrimination has been officially legislated against. The whole of the political institutions of the Territory reek with discrimination. One finds, for instance, special regulations made to legalize racial salary differentials in the Administration. Here, the obvious qualification a white public servant has over his black counterpart is his white skin and not his skill qualification. Discriminatory differentiation of salaries is quite clear from the definition of an overseas officer (and so an *ipso facto* qualified person) in the Public Service (Papua and New Guinea) Ordinance of 1963, as:

'An Officer who:—
(a) was born outside the Territory; or
(b) was born within the Territory but in respect of whom the Minister certified that it is expedient or desirable in the interest of the Territory that he should be appointed to the Public Service, on overseas conditions'.[7]

So, however much the Administration policies are being articulated in terms of economic rationality, they are still basically racist and discriminatory. The conventional attitudes of expatriates and the imperfect labour market permit the dual system to remain. Because of the racist dual salary structure, there is now an alarming gap in Territory income distribution. For example, between 1950/51 and 1962/63, the share of Niuginian wage and salary earners in national income remained about 25 per cent, whereas the share of non-indigenous wage and salary earners increased from 36 per cent to 45 per cent. Because of substantial wage increases to Australians, the possibility of even further regressive changes in income distribution is imminent.[8]

Another example of this White Power in the Territory is seen in payment of rents in the Public Service. The Treasury rent for a three bedroom high-cost house is $416 per annum. This is what a local officer would have to pay. The overseas officers get a rent allowance of $320 and so only pay $94. All overseas officers live in Treasury houses, and are accordingly at least four times better off than a local officer living in a Housing Commission house. The latter is paying an economic rent. The economic rent comes roughly to 10 per cent per annum of the capital cost. Thus, the precast concrete houses occupied by local officers cost $2,100 and are rented for $210 p.a. The split level type and the two storied flat, occupied by overseas officers, cost $13,000 and should rent for $1,300 p.a. The officer from overseas pays only $94, and is 14 times better off than a local officer living in a Housing Commission house.

Let us take another example. To promote foreign capitalist investment in the Territory, the Niugini Development Bank was formed. Supposedly it was meant to create balanced development and the advancement of the indigenous population, but in practice, as Dr. Curtin observed, most of the bank's loan money has gone to expatriates. After all, the security of a loan is calculated on the whiteman's terms and a Niuginian will always be on the losing side. As he has also correctly pointed out—'Politics is largely about economics, and political power is mainly about economic power. It would be unrealistic to expect good government in Niugini over an essentially foreign economy'.[9]

One could go on recounting more examples to show the predominance of white power in Niugini, *ad absurdum*, but the few already cited are perhaps sufficient to make an Uncle Tomish black think twice about his 'gud fela papa', Australia, and the essential boomerang policy it practices in its so called developmental grants to Niugini. Niugini has, in fact, become an employment camp for unemployed Australians, particularly the dropout of Australian society. So, what used to be a whiteman's grave has now become the whiteman's paradise and the blackman's hell. It will remain so, as long as there are sufficient fools among the blacks to play the role of house boys to them in politics, economics and religion as well as in other fields of life here.

Niugini Black Power is fully aware of the invidious stranglehold white power has on the blacks of this country. Perhaps a summary statement of our views on the problem facing this country is best gathered from the Niugini Black Power Submission to the United Nations Visiting Mission on the 4th of March, 1971.

'In view of the fact that the black man in Niugini today is very much a colonized being, deprived of the real political and economic powers with which to plan and execute a programme of self development, the Niugini Black Power Movement submits the following suggestions to the mission as considerations necessary for a meaningful step towards the creation of a Niugini Nation. The black people of Niugini who constitute the majority within the category of being "backward", will continually be integrated into the political and economic manipulation of whites unless the following rights and powers are handed over the black people or their representatives. We believe that our economic backwardness and political confusion could not be effectively solved unless the black people become aware of and therefore act against the white colonialism. We therefore wish to bring to the attention of this United Nations Mission the following demands:—

1. An all black House of Assembly by 1972.

   Niugini is a blackman's country whose political rights to self determination cannot be realized as long as we maintain a parliament dominated and manipulated by the whites.

   Few non-indigenes may be allowed, subject to special qualifications and stringent conditions dictated by indigenes, elected leaders and the blacks of this country.

2. Foreign investment or enterprise be registered in Niugini.

   This will ensure some checks on the inflow of foreign capital, thereby making foreign investment conscious of the real development of the people of Niugini, instead of merely being concerned with the exploitation of our resources.

3. Niuginian spokesmen in the United Nations be directly responsible to the black people's elected representative rather than to the colonizing power in Canberra.

   This, we believe will counteract Australia's present use of Niugini as a "show piece". With Australia's domination of Niugini affairs at the United Nations removed, Niuginians will then articulate their problems and interests internationally.

4. The borderline between Papua and New Guinea and therefore the legal distinction between Papuans and New Guineans be immediately removed. By so doing, we are putting all black people of this country on a same legal status. This is a positive and necessary step, if we hope to make our people feel and work together as one people.

5. A temporary quasi-citizenship status be created now and should be open to all races in Niugini prior to getting full citizenship after independence. All indigenes are *ipso facto* members. Members of non-indigenous ethnic groups should take a Niuginian quasi-citizenship subject to special conditions if they so wish to reside and enjoy the political rights which now should be only the prerogatives of indigenes. This will ensure racial harmony among the various ethnic groupings now living in Niugini, as well as creating a climate of confidence, co-operation and unity.

6. The next United Nations visiting mission to Niugini should include some members of the Eastern Power bloc. We suspect the past and the present United Nations Missions to Niugini to be biased towards Australia's interest in Niugini rather than to find out the repressed political feelings of the blacks.

7. United Nations should enforce a Black Niugini Policy towards

foreigners in Niugini. Australian Government do not have a multi-racialism society as decreed by their Restrictive Immigration Policy (White Australia Policy) and therefore should not force multi-racialism on the black people of Niugini.

To avoid racial problems we want to have a racial homogeneous black society, perhaps with only a tincture of few non-coloured people.

(This is really a mockery of Arthur Caldwell's insistence on creating a homogeneous society in Australia.)

8. Foreign Aid from other countries be welcomed with such conditions as:—
   (a) aid for non-military purposes.
   (b) aid for the economic development for the rural population be strongly emphasized.
9. Self Government by 1972.
   To ensure an awareness among the black people that real development for us could only be affected when we begin to demand the rights to the control of our political destiny.
10. All minerals in Niugini should be made the property of the people of Niugini. We condemn the Commonwealth of Australia taking the rights over all minerals in Niugini.
11. Universal education be guaranteed to the black people of Niugini and that every possible media be used in the education, i.e. English should not be used as a qualification standard in the formal system of education.
12. A large sector of the Niugini economy be nationalized. We cannot hope to plan for our welfare and development as long as our capital and human resources remain subject to the interests of overseas monopolies.'[10]

The Niugini Black Power philosophy is the only alternative for the black man in Niugini if he is to survive at all as a person worthy of respect and master of his own destiny, for it adheres to the principle that all human beings have these sacred and inalienable right to self respect, self definition or self determination. From such premises are derived the conclusions that we, the black people of Niugini, are not the wards of the white race. We are not the whiteman's burden. We can no longer allow ourselves to be continually defined into the narrow, prejudiced, oppressive and castrating whiteman's image of us.

Niugini Black Power is essentially a philosophy of liberation of the black men who are being oppressed physically or ideologically in matters political, social, economic, religious and cultural. Hence we stand in unity with other movements which seek to liberate the oppressed of any race, sex, colour or creed.

In other words, Black Power advocates the redemption of those oppressed, to the totality of their being as persons, in relation to themselves as individuals or as members of one race, and to members of other groups. It seeks to raise in the minds of the black men first of all, the fundamental questions for which it demands answers about the identity of the black man, his cultural values and the criteria by which he evaluates his acts and those of others. Black power challenges the blackman to define himself, his goals and aspirations as well as his limitations, and the obstacles that hinders him from achieving the full flowering of his personality.

As Stokely Carmichael and Charles V. Hamilton said in their book *Black Power*—'Our basic need is to reclaim our history and our identity from what must be called cultural terrorism, from the depredation of self-justifying white guilt. We shall have to struggle for the right to create our own terms through which to define ourselves and our relationship to the society, and to have these terms recognized. This is the first necessity of a free people, and the first right that any oppressor must suspend.'[11]

It is a pathetic sight to see fellow Niuginians accept without demur such emasculating titles as 'boi', 'manki masta' or 'natives', while the whites are always addressed as 'masta' or 'missis' or 'Taubada' or 'Sinabada' or other titles of respect.

Every time a Niuginian receives western orientated education, he learns the language that is heavily biased against his cultural values. It is ironic that the more education a Niuginian receives, the more he becomes divorced from his own cultural values, at the same time achieving proficiency in a language of self-condemnation. Ask one of the so-called educated Niuginians about traditional values such as 'tribalism', 'animism' and 'polygamy' and you will find they will go to any extent in outdoing white critics in condemning such concepts. The greater the degree of his abhorrence for such customary values the more he manifests and proves the extent of his being 'sophisticated', 'westernized' or 'civilized'. It takes a man of black pride to see positive values in such terms. In fact, in concepts like tribalism, lies the very heart of our identity as people. In all the micro-cultures of Niuginians, there is that latent homogeneity, for in a concept like tribalism, one finds that underlying feeling of brotherhood, that feeling of consolidarity or interdependence that flows within the blood of us all. In nation building, such a concept (if given positive all-embracing width) would certainly form the genuine foundation of nationalism. In animism, again we find our only hope of remaining human and sane. Animism knows no dichotomy between the spiritual and material, and man is one with nature and the total cosmic reality. What has Christianity to offer the blackman? Nothing but self-condemnation, split personality and hypocrisy. As it is today, Christianity, despite its claim to being catholic or supernatural is, in fact, the handmaiden of western civilization. Compare, for instance, the views of an ordinary expatriate planter and that of a Catholic Archbishop towards Niuginians, expressed round about the same period, and one will see very little difference in the attitudes expressed, even though one was supposed to have been motivated by lofty spiritual ideals. An excerpt from *Rabaul Times*, January 25th 1929 shows:—

> 'The local native has a very small intelligence, and in the greater number of cases, what little intelligence he has is used for criminal purposes. Hand in hand with the development of his intelligence goes his advancement in the path of craft and cunning . . .'.[12]

Now consider this view expressed by the saintly Archbishop De Bois-menu of Papua at the second Australian Catholic Congress in 1904:—

> 'The Papuan race is unquestionably of an inferior nature. It has lived too long a prey to original sin. And though it can be christianized, yet the most we can expect is a Christianity of a limited vigor and perfection that must always depend for its existence upon the charity of those nations to whom God has reserved the honour and burden of apostleship.'[13]

The deplorable position of the churches in Niugini where they are deeply engaged in doling charity gifts instead of recognizing Niuginians as men who could be responsible for their own affairs, stems from this typical ethnocentric prejudiced attitude towards us.

But this is the same everywhere, for under the banner of the cross, lands have been conquered and claimed by those who believed themselves to be repositories of the Divine injunction to conquer, civilize and christianize, in obedience to the biblical principle 'to increase and multiply and make the earth yours'. In America, the first settlers from the *Mayflower* were sustained by this ideal for a new ordering of things. 'It was a principle to be expressed in the progress and elevation of civilized men who, striving to imitate their God, would bring order to chaos. America was such a chaos, a new-found chaos. Her natural wealth was there for the taking, because it was there for the ordering. So were her natural men'.[14] Pearce quoted one of the Pilgrim Fathers who wrote saying:—

'All the rich endowments of Virginia, her virgin portion from the creation nothing lessened, are wages for all this work: God in wise-dome having enriched the savage countries, that those riches might be attractive for Christian suters, which these may sowe spirituals and reape temporals.'[15]

There is little wonder, therefore, that people whom we consider exploiters, and who consider themselves expatriates, have no qualms of conscience whatsoever about their divine mission to exploit this country and its people, and deem it their unquestionable natural right to dominate its politics. Might is right; white is right.

Once the blackman in Niugini, through soul searching and self-definition, establishes his goals, he must set about to liberate himself. Freedom is never given—it must be fought for and wrenched from the hands of the oppressors. The blackman must realize that his many and diverse problems rest squarely on his own shoulders, for their solution. We have stressed already that we are not the eternal wards of white civilization, nor are we the whiteman's burden. We are not the 'child' race that must continually be contented to be the beneficiaries of the blessings from the tables of the 'lordly'. The blackman must be the master of himself and of his own destiny. The blackman must realize his own problems and develop a will to solve those problems.

It is shameful to see giant Niuginian tribal leaders who, in a traditional village setting, hold their heads up high in rightful pride, once in front of a white man, however insignificant that person may be, melt before the whiteman's very eye in total submissiveness, filial obedience as it were, and deep obeisance. To many such formerly mighty traditional leaders, younger men and women were wont to say respectfully of their authority: 'When the old men speak let no more words be said'. Now the whole focus of authority is reversed and given unquestionably to any whiteman, old or young. The blackman, both the elders and the young alike, are in a position of an inferior race before a superior race giving undeserved respect and obedience to any whiteman. This total reversal of loyalty from being based on seniority, achievement, and leadership *per se* to being based on just purely racial grounds, is best expressed in this Pidgin English dictum—'Masta tok; tok i dai'. (The master has spoken, all speech must die.) Perhaps Shakespeare has a better equivalent for it in English: 'When Sir Oracle speaks, let no dog bark'.

All that Black Power tries to do is to create a sense of inward-looking self-criticism and self-awareness where one seeks to know who he is, what his values are, and those criteria with which he evaluates his own acts and those of others, instead of continually resorting to those value judgements prescribed for him by others. By so doing, he rises to the level of being a person. After all, the notion of being a person implies the realization of oneself as the subject of one's consciousness, acts and responsibility. This is, however, only the first level of self-consciousness. Above this, there is that level of consciousness which is self-assertive or calls for action and self-realization.

To use the term of Paulo Freire, this form of self-awareness could be called conscientization. This self-assertiveness makes one rise above the complacent mouth-gaping spoon-fed life of the common mob and stand out to face the challenging existential world of here and now. He is no longer just a being subsisting among many beings. He is a proud black person among many blacks whose world is infested and dominated by generally ethnocentric minority groups whose weird practice of the cannibalism of racism has been eating out the very soul of the blackman. From the level of faith in himself the blackman rises to the level of conviction that should lead to action. This propulsive conscientization makes one act black. 'I am black, with my own value, therefore I must act like a black person.'

Only that black Niuginian, governed by his own values and criteria could address himself meaningfully and respectfully to people of other cultures.

Only that black person who respects himself as a person can fittingly respect members of other races without kowtowing to or hero-worshipping them as sacred cows or demigods.

Only those who can speak to each other in a language of respect can have meaningful dialogue. Genuine dialogue is only possible between equals, never between a 'master' and a 'boy', never between a master and a slave. For everytime a 'boi' addresses his 'masta' in a language of obeisance and servitude he demeans himself; he becomes less of a man and more of a thing.

Everytime a Niuginian in a condescending, frog-perspective mentality says 'yesa misis', he allows the whiteman to depersonalize him or castrate his manliness.

Everytime a Niuginian allows himself to be showered with crumbs from the opulent Master's table, he reduces himself to the level of a faithful house dog. This happens when Niuginians do not fight for just wages, better housing, part ownership or shares in companies or firms that employ them.

On a national level, this happens when most members of the House of Assembly pass bills protecting the vested interest of Australians in Niugini, or selling all our mineral rights like that of copper in Bougainville for a pittance.

Everytime a Niuginian melts with gratitude and emotion at the money doled out by racist institutions like the Returned Soldiers League or the Planters' Association he reduces oneself to the inhuman state of beggary.

It has now become quite obvious that the Niugini Black Power Group has no blueprint for nation-building as such. As a small group that acts as a catalyst for creating self-awareness, we do carry out group action education in the form of forums or by involving ourselves in public debates, or by engaging ourselves in writing works of literature to bring about this sense of self-assertion, identity and pride in our heritage and thus create the need for taking steps to have full control of our political, social, economic and religious institutions.

In this educational programme of conscientization, Black Power does not want to convert Niuginians to become Black Power members but to become self-redeemed self-respecting black Niuginian individuals who must play their own role creatively in whatever field of life they have chosen. As redeemed Niuginians they will be certain of building a nation that is ours, founded on our values and our aspirations.

Black man, know thyself and act accordingly.

### REFERENCES

1 Freire Paulo, *The Pedagogy of the Oppressed,* pp. 28-29.

2 *Ibid.,* p. 29.

3 Schaffer, B. B. 'The Concept of Preparation' *World Politics,* xviii (1) October 1965, pp. 42-67.

4 *Ibid.,* p. 45.

5 *Ibid.,* p. 49.

6 Mormis, Fr. John 'Dr. Eugene Ogan; Bougainville' 71 *New Guinea Quarterly.* Vol. 6 No. 2, 1971.

7 *Public Service (Papua and New Guinea) Ordinance,* 1963.

8 Calculated from IBRD *The Economic Development of the Territory of Papua and New Guinea,* 1965, p. 30.

9 Dr. W. P. Curtin 'Niugini's Political Development, Economic Aspect'. *The Politics of Melanesia,* p. 52.

10 Niugini Black Power Submission to UN Mission on 4th March 1971.

11 Stokely Carmichael and Charles V. Hamilton *Black Power,* 1967, p. 49.

12 Valentine, C. 'An Introduction to the History of Changing way of Life on the Island of New Britain' Unpublished Ph.D. thesis, University of Pennsylvania, 1958.

13 Second Australian Catholic Congress 1964.

14 Pearce, Roy Harvey, *Savagism and Civilization,* 1967, p. 3.

15 *Ibid.,* p. 8 'Purchas His Pilgrimes.'

# 3

# AUSTRALIA'S EXPERIENCE AS A
# MANDATORY POWER

## W. J. Hudson

The year 1919 saw the birth of international organisation in the semi-universal form in which we now know it; it also saw the first substantial submission of colonial territories to a system of international accountability. Australia, as a result of her part in World War I, was involved from the first both in the international organisation, the League of Nations, and in this initial shift in colonialism from an essentially domestic to a partly international context. The new colonial phenomenon was, of course, the League's mandates system. It is proposed here briefly to examine Australia's experience as a mandatory power.

The way in which Australia became a mandatory power needs little description. At the request of the British Government and on the clear understanding that Australia was to act merely as an agent, the Australian Government in 1914 secured by force the German colonies to the north of Australia and south of the equator, the major territory being that of German New Guinea adjacent to the Australian possession of Papua.[1] During succeeding war years, a conflict situation developed: within Australia, there developed an assumption of Australian post-war control of the formerly German colonies;[2] overseas, there developed a strong sentiment against territorial aggrandisement and there emerged the notion of international mandates.[3] The resolution of this conflict at the Paris Peace Conference is well known: W. N. Hughes fought for annexation but was at last induced to accept an arrangement whereby Australia would administer New Guinea under the very light trammel of a 'C' class League mandate and would share with Britain and New Zealand the administration of the prize of Nauru.[4]

Considering what Hughes can be assumed to have known about German hostility towards Australia in the Pacific,[5] considering deeply ingrained Australian suspicion of Japan,[6] and considering acute Australian sensitivity on immigration policy,[7] it is fairly clear that Australia's primary motive in seeking control of the island territories to the north was based on security postulates.[8] It is also fairly clear that, having achieved sufficient control over them to neutralise any threat to immigration policy and having achieved, apparently, deliverance from the possibility of nearby fortification by a potentially unfriendly power, Australian governments over the next two decades were inclined to pay a minimum of further attention to them.[9] Financial policy was the then orthodox one of colonial self-sufficiency. As Cook said of New Guinea in his 1921 budget speech:—

'After considerable pruning, the expenditure estimates have been reduced to a sum not exceeding estimated revenue. In accepting the mandate, Australia has entered upon additional responsibility, but no stone will be left unturned to prevent further financial burdens being entailed thereby.[10]

An official report in 1924 noted 'an absence of any constructive policy' in New Guinea and concluded that the territory's administration had so far cost Australia virtually nothing.[11] As McAuley has said of the whole inter-war period, 'there was no thought of promoting development by the deliberate intervention of Commonwealth finance'.[12]

More of this Australian policy will emerge below but, given its basic characteristic of minimum effort, what was the relevant international reaction to it? In general, the reaction was, perhaps predictably, unfavourable. Under Article 22 of the League Covenant and the terms of subsequent mandates agreements, Australia was free to administer New Guinea and (by Anglo-New Zealand agreement) Nauru as integral parts of the Commonwealth. Her only obligations to the territories were to keep them unfortified and observe a number of humanitarian injunctions; her obligation to the League comprised the submission of annual reports on her administration to the League Council on whose behalf the reports would be examined by a Permanent Mandates Commission. This commission consisted of Council-nominated individual experts, and not representatives of states.[13] It might have seemed that a mandatory power would have little to fear from the commission. Certainly, its constitution laid down that a majority of its nine members should be nationals of non-mandatory powers, And, in a statement to the commission at the outset of its work, the first director of the League's Mandates Section, Rappard, spoke of commission members acting as judges and stressed their independence of governments.[14] However, the commission's first chairman, Theodoli, immediately disowned any judicial role: commission members would act as mandatories' collaborators.[15] As for impartiality, all the foundation members came from European powers, except for a Japanese, and all, except two, came from colonial powers. As for independence, the Japanese member for one soon showed a tendency to refer to 'his Government' and to speak in its name.[16] And the commission, initially at least, adopted a tone of extraordinary courtesy, almost of deference, in its dealings with mandatory powers. Yet, despite all this, Australia was not spared by the commission, and least of all by its British members.

The first point to be noted is that the Commission several times tried to elicit a statement of Australia's general policy on New Guinea, but enjoyed negligible success. In 1925, for example, Cook admitted that 'policy has probably never been formally expressed in a comprehensive way within the limits of a single document'. He argued that 'the main heads of policy' could be abstracted from various sources, going on to list items taken mainly from obligations mentioned in the mandate agreement.[17] But the following year, the commission's acting chairman, Van Rees of the Netherlands, complained that 'the members of the Permanent Mandates Commission had not yet obtained any clear idea of the general policy pursued by the mandatory Power in the administration of New Guinea'.[18] Australia's expert witness, Carrodus, again spoke of the 'main items' of policy in a way to suggest that they were to be seen in a mass of statutes, ordinances and regulations. He merely repeated the list supplied the previous year by Cook, with the important but largely imaginary additions of greater participation by natives in the administration and economic development.[19] It would almost seem that the policy statements prepared to help Cook and Carrodus meet commission curiosity themselves became the corpus of otherwise non-existent general policy. Certainly in 1932 when, during debate on the Government's New Guinea Bill establishing an executive and legislative council comprised entirely of nominees, the minister seeing the bill through the House declared that 'the following may be mentioned as constituting the main heads of the Commonwealth Government's policy', he read a list almost identical to the word with the items given years before by Cook and Carrodus.[20]

As late as 1938, Rappard asked if it would not be useful, not so much for the edification of the commission as for the benefit of the administration, to 'formulate a general policy indicating the objects, both material, social and humanitarian, of its policy towards the Territory—in other words, a philosophy of its colonial administration'.[21] The Australian reply to this pleaded inadequacy of finance and personnel and claimed the old objectives, but without any reference to education, political progress or ultimate political goals, or race relations.[22] Rappard did not comment on the reply, but Lord Hailey[23] expressed a reaction when the interrogation moved on to the question of frontier extension. 'Lord Hailey suggested that if the mandatory Power had had a definite philosophy in regard to the territory, as M. Rappard had urged, its attitude might not necessarily be the same. Its criterion now seemed to be whether a given area would prove healthy for missionaries and mining engineers'.[24]

The question of long-term policy also arose in relation to Nauru. As early as 1922, there was commission concern for the fate of the islanders if and when the phosphate deposits should be exhausted.[25] This fundamental question, as Rappard called it, was raised pointedly in 1936, 1937 and 1938 but provoked little evidence of Australian policy or even concern. Australian delegates' replies were variously that the deposits would last for at least fifty years, that estimates of the life of the deposits could only be speculative, that worked out land might support a copra industry, that it was hoped that worked out land might support agriculture, that it was an 'open question' whether worked out land could support agriculture.[26]

Australia's financial policy mentioned above also evoked expressions of commission concern and even, on one occasion, something approaching horror. In 1925, for example, the commission showed considerable interest in the findings of the Ainsworth Report. Cook denied that New Guinea had been 'placed in subjection to, or made dependent upon, the political or economic requirements of the Australian Commonwealth'. He then listed current expenditure down to a sum of £200 on incidental expenses,[27] but the commission was unimpressed and, in its report to the League Council, submitted that Australia had not shown how she planned to meet budget deficits or to provide for the development and more intensive occupation of New Guinea.[28] The following year, 1926, Lugard[29] drew attention to the absence of any regular grant-in-aid by Australia to New Guinea[30] and, in 1930, reminded the Australian representative that, 'in its initial stages, the administration of New Guinea and the surrounding islands must cost a very large sum of money if it were to be effective, more, indeed, than an annual subsidy of £10,000'.[31] However, financial policy remained virtually unaltered. In 1936-7, for instance, when the mandated territory was exporting overseas seven times more copra than Papua, when gold output in the territory was topping £2 million, when the territory had a surplus of almost £ 60,000 compared with a small deficit in Papua, the Australian grant to New Guinea was still only £ 42,000.[32]

Another aspect of financial policy arose in 1930 when one of the Australian representatives, R. G. Casey, sought to answer a query by Lugard as to whether the natives were fairly taxed and a query by Rappard as to whether the territory was being exploited for the benefit of the non-indigenous population. The core of Casey's reply was that 60.3 per cent of revenue raised in the territory was paid in taxes by non-indigenes. Excluding public servants and missionaries, whites were thus paying a per capita tax of £ 70.6 annually. He also pointed out that, in the last years of the old administration, the German population had paid only from £ 20 to £ 49.3 per head, with Germany subsidising the territory at the rate of from £ 46,000 to £ 74,000 a year. (He had admitted that Australia paid a direct subsidy of only £ 10,000 a year.)[33] Lugard thanked Casey, noting, however, that the real issue remained the degree to which expenditure served the native compared with the European.[34] But, in 1931, Casey's statement was attacked scathingly by Rappard, who found it 'hardly . . . convincing', 'hardly . . . accurate' and 'unconvincing'. Indeed, he was astonished that Casey should have 'thought fit to mention the subsidies granted to New Guinea by the former German Government, as the comparison with the very much smaller grants made by the present Mandatory Power was by no means to the advantage of the latter'.[35]

Education was, perhaps, the one field where the commission's views may have had an effect on Australian policy.[36] Throughout the 1920s and 1930s, the commission questioned administration policy which, apparently, was not to encourage school attendance by natives and to leave education, anyway, largely to the missions which, in return for not being subsidised, were let teach how and what they wished.[37] An Australian suggestion in 1934 that education might be handed over entirely to the missions ('perhaps a natural extension of the de facto position', remarked Portuguese member, de Panha Garcia[38]) was opposed by the commission, and especially by Lugard.[39] In 1936, the commission's report wondered if one per cent of the territory's budget was sufficient for education, and, in 1939, the commission's education specialist, Mlle. Dannevig of Norway, observed that 'she knew of no other territory under mandate in which native education progressed so slowly'.[40] However, in 1939, Australia seemed to capitulate with an announcement that in future mission schools would follow an administration syllabus, the administration itself would establish village schools, and the teaching of English would be promoted.[41]

The commission enjoyed less success on another major question, that of native labour. In 1929, 1931 and 1936, for example, the commission expressed concern about the methods and extent of native labour recruitment.[42] In 1936, after Lugard had complained about Australia's failure to answer a request for a statement of policy on the percentage of village manpower which should be indentured, the Australian representative refused to supply a figure.[43] In each succeeding annual report to the Council, the commission expressed concern about the degree of recruitment, asked for information on planned safeguards and registered dissatisfaction with replies received from the Australian delegates or Government.[44]

The commission also failed to have much effect on the pessimistic Australian estimates of the capacity of New Guinea natives to participate in administrative or political institutions. The general Australian view of that capacity was reflected in views expressed by Australian representatives to the commission.[45] The commission was inclined to be sceptical, at times sarcastic (the proportion of indentured labour seemed to be high in a country said to be one step removed from the Stone Age[46]) and occasionally hostile (Lugard and Rappard were openly critical of the failure to allow for any native representation on a suffrage basis on the legislative council which was created in 1933[47]).

The emphasis to this stage has been on the League view of Australian administration.[48] Turning now to the Australian view of the League in its supervisory function, there is an obvious distinction to be drawn between personal and official reactions. At the personal level, Australian delegates on the whole appear to have been urbane and patient during appearances before the commission.[49] At home, relatively little was said in parliament, but the little that was said tended to be somewhat hostile.[50] Outside parliament, interest and, therefore, reaction would seem to have been negligible.[51]

In an area of politics to which party policy scarcely extended, it is sometimes difficult to maintain a distinction between the personal and the official—as, for example, when Cook reflected a degree of 'touchiness' in officially expressing doubts about the admission to the League of slavery-tainted Abyssinia which, as a member, 'would be in a position to criticise those countries, such as New Guinea, where the conditions of life were much more favourable. Abyssinia might examine and criticise countries whose civilisation was more advanced than her own'.[52]

Official reaction took two major forms; fear of losing the mandate and concern for the preservation of domestic jurisdiction. The former led to pressure being brought to bear to minimise even domestic criticism of the Government's handling of the mandate. In 1923, Bruce, for example, appealed to members to say nothing which could be used overseas to reflect on the New Guinea administration.[53] Pearce, in 1926, warned senators that 'everything said in connection with the Mandated Territory is closely scrutinised, including debates in Parliament, and any statements made without backing are used against us at the League of Nations'.[54] Even Beasley was fearful of rumours and misleading information coming from New Guinea to Australia and then being cabled abroad where 'there are those . . . who . . . are eager to place before the League of Nations reports which rebound to the discredit of Australia's administration'.[55]

Two examples of the latter related to petitions and immigration policy. Australia was less than happy with the League Council's decision in 1923 to allow the commission to receive petitions from mandated territories, despite the provision that such petitions might not be considered until the respective mandatory powers had seen them and supplied their comments. Cook felt that 'proper precautions must be taken to prevent such rights of petition being made an instrument in the hands of agitators for the annoyance of the mandatory authorities'.[56] Commission publicity was quite sufficient as a safeguard against abuse of the mandates.[57] When the question of oral petitions was raised (and disallowed by the Council), Australia was utterly hostile. The mandatory power, argued Latham, would have to appear and answer oral petitions and would thus be 'put on trial' on charges which might, after expensive delays, turn out to be frivolous or vexatious.[58]

That control of immigration policy was legally and politically basic to the 'C' mandates was not questioned by the commission as a body, but some members, particularly Lugard, were inclined occasionally to slip in queries aimed at the White Australia policy. There was an example of this pin-pricking in 1923 when Lugard asked Cook whether the thin population spread in New Guinea might not justify a relaxation of the policy in the territory. Cook replied that the policy was in the best interests of the natives. Lugard then suggested that the main purpose of the policy was to keep Australia white and New Guinea, after all, was some distance from Australia. Cook countered this with the argument that one policy could not be applied in one area and another policy applied in an adjacent area under the same authority. Lugard, with some persistence, wondered if the policy might not be relaxed in both areas (Papua and New Guinea). At this point, Cook apparently felt things had gone far enough and cut short this sort of questioning with the observation that it was dealing with the 'well-established and settled policy of his Government'.[59] In 1925, Rappard tried to raise the question but was again stopped by Cook's statement that 'the laws on this matter represented a firm and settled policy'.[60] In 1927, when Lugard returned to the attack, Cook declared pointedly that he was encroaching on 'the settled policy of Australia' and that 'that question would be better left alone'.[61] In 1929, Lugard inquired politely if the White Australia policy still applied to New Guinea and was told, just as politely, that it did.[62] This sort of domestic jurisdiction consciousness on mandate matters reflected the overall Australian attitude to the League as a whole. Through the 1920s, Hughes, Millen, Latham, Pearce and Bruce repeatedly and heavily stressed that the League must not encroach on domestic jurisdiction and that it was in its own best interest not to try to.

Australia, then, received a fair measure of criticism but accepted it without much apparent distress.[63] The structure of the League's accountability system, of course, was such that this criticism came mainly from within the white man's club.[64] A disinclination to accept criticism from lesser breeds like Abyssinians foreshadowed post-1945 developments. Fortunately for Australia, her territories' internal affairs caused her little embarrassment; as one writer put it in 1928, 'the maxim "happy is the nation which has no history" held good for the mandated territories par excellence'.[65] It is clear that Australia was constantly alive to the domestic jurisdiction barrier beyond which she would not tolerate League encroachments.[66] It is equally clear that Australia did not merely accept criticism: she showed some aplomb in ignoring it and going her own way.[67]

## ACKNOWLEDGEMENT

This chapter first appeared in *Australian Outlook*, Volume 19, No. 1, April 1965, while the author was a Research Scholar in International Relations, Research School of Pacific Studies, Australian National University. It is reproduced here with the permission of the Australian Institute of International Affairs.

## REFERENCES

1 That the initiative was Britain's and that Britain reserved the right to negotiate the subsequent disposal of the colonies is clear from documents quoted by Ernest Scott (*Australia During the War*, Vol. XI of *The Official History of Australia in the War of 1914-1919*, Sydney, 1937, p. 763), S. S. Mackenzie (*The Australians at Rabaul*, Vol. X in the same series, pp. 5-6, 149, 159) and C. D. Rowley (*The Australians in German New Guinea, 1914-1921*, Melbourne, 1958, p. 2). After the war, Australian politicians tended to claim that Australia had acted on her own initiative, a view shared

(incorrectly, I believe) by J. P. McAuley (Trusteeship in Practice: New Guinea, Nauru, Western Samoa, in A. H. McDonald, ed., *Trusteeship in the Pacific,* Sydney, 1949, pp. 33-4).

2 As early as 1915, for example, Sir Joseph Cook, then Opposition leader, said that the islands should never have belonged to anyone but Australia and that 'we in Australia expect some little additions to our territorial possessions in the Pacific'. *C.P.D.,* Vol. 76, p. 2367 (April 15, 1915).

3 For a succinct expression of the sentiment and notion in terms of the views of the influential Anglo-American group led by Lionel Curtis, see *Round Table,* Vol. IX, pp. 28-9.

4 For Hughes' use of his cabinet at home to support his New Guinea annexation bid and to excuse his failure to secure sole control of Nauru, see *Scott, op. cit.,* pp. 788, 800.

5 For the text of a German memorandum of July, 1918, see David Lloyd George, *The Truth About the Peace Treaties,* Vol. 1, London, 1938, pp. 126-7.

6 See E. L. Piesse, Japan and Australia, in *Foreign Affairs,* April, 1926, p. 475.

7 'The principle of White Australia is almost a religion in Australia . . . Any surrender of the policy is inconceivable . . .' J. G. (later Sir John Latham, *The Significance of the Peace Conference from an Australian Point of View,* Melbourne, 1920, p. 9.

8 This view is put strongly by Scott, op. cit., p. 773 and by Sir Robert Garran in *Prosper the Commonwealth,* Sydney, 1958, p. 264. There is some evidence to suggest that economic motives probably were not entirely absent.

9 See J. A. Miles, 'The Development of Native Education in Papua and New Guinea', in *South Pacific,* July-August, 1959, pp. 154-161.

10 *C.P.D.,* Vol. 97, p. 1600 (September 29, 1921). See also figures supplied by Page in 1924 (*C.P.D.,* Vol. 107, p. 2735) and Scullin in 1931 (*C.P.D.,* Vol. 130, p. 3529).

11 Parliament of the Commonwealth of Australia, *Report by Colonel John Ainsworth on Administrative Arrangements and Matters Affecting the Interests of Natives in the Territory of New Guinea,* Melbourne, 1924, pp. 7, 13, 39 (in *C.P.P.,* 1923-4, Vol. IV). For corroboration, see K. H. (Later Sir Kenneth) Bailey, in F. W. Eggleston, ed., *The Australian Mandate for New Guinea,* Melbourne, 1928, p. 14.

12 McAuley, *op. cit.,* pp. 35-6.

13 The four places allowed to nationals of mandatory powers were always filled by Britons, Belgians, Frenchmen and Japanese—Australia at no time had a national on the commission.

14 Professor W. E. Rappard, a Swiss, was director of the Mandates Section of the League secretariat until 1924 when he joined the Commission, becoming vice-chairman in 1937. For details of membership, see H. Duncan Hall, *Mandates, Dependencies and Trusteeship,* London, 1948, pp. 181-2.

15 Parliament of the Commonwealth of Australia, *A Selection of Papers Printed by the League of Nations Relating to the Mandatory System,* 1920-1922, Melbourne, 1923, p. 28.

16 *Ibid.,* p. 21. Japanese members rarely contributed much to commission proceedings: see M. Matsushita, *Japan in the League of Nations,* New York, 1929, pp. 134-5.

17 *P.M.C. Minutes,* VI, p. 85.

18 *P.M.C. Minutes,* IX, p. 20.

19 *Ibid.,* p. 21.

20 *C.P.D.,* Vol. 136, p. 1759 (November 2, 1932). The Minister was Charles

(later Sir Charles) Marr, then Minister for Health and Repatriation and formerly for Home and Territories.

21 *P.M.C. Minutes*, XXXIV, p. 163.

22 *Ibid.*

23 Hailey replaced Lugard in 1936 and, with a short break in 1939, served on the commission until its functioning was interrupted by World War II.

24 *P.M.C. Minutes*, XXXIV, p. 165.

25 Austn. Plt., Selection of League Papers, *op. cit.*, p. 53.

26 *P.M.C. Minutes*, XXIX, p. 33; XXXI, p. 51; XXXIV, pp. 19-22.

27 *P.M.C. Minutes*, VI, pp. 85-6.

28 *Ibid.*, p. 180.

29 Sir Frederick (later Lord) Lugard served on the commission from 1923 until his resignation in 1936.

30 *P.M.C. Minutes*, IX, p. 18.

31 *P.M.C. Minutes*, XXVIII, p. 49.

32 See Basil Hall, 'Amalgamation and Mandate', in *Australian Quarterly*, Vol. XI (1939), No. 3, pp. 93-4. Also *Round Table*, Vol. 18, p. 400 and Vol. 27, p. 853; and R. T. Shand, 'Some Obstacles to the Economic Development of Papua-New Guinea', in *Australian Outlook*, Vol. 17 (1963), No. 3, pp. 307-9.

33 *P.M.C. Minutes*, XVIII, pp. 47-8.

34 *Ibid.*, p. 58.

35 *P.M.C. Minutes*, XX, p. 17.

36 It has been suggested to me by an authoritative but necessarily confidential source that the missions' monopoly of native tradesmen may have had more to do with the 1939 switch in Australian policy than the commission's views.

37 According to an Australian statement in 1931, the price of subsidies was the teaching of English. The missions preferred pidgin, a preference they were allowed. See *P.M.C. Minutes*, XX, pp. 24-5.

38 *P.M.C. Minutes*, XXV, p. 48.

39 *Ibid.*, and p. 152.

40 *P.M.C. Minutes*, XXXVI, p. 145.

41 *Ibid.*, p. 161.

42 See *P.M.C. Minutes*, XI, p. 22; XV, pp. 293-4; XX, pp. 23, 232.

43 *P.M.C. Minutes*, XXIX, p. 24.

44 *P.M.C. Minutes*, XXIX, p. 212; XXXI, p. 193; XXXIV, p. 231; XXXVI, p. 280.

45 A perusal of Hansard for members' views on the natives gives an impression of an immensely assured and vaguely benign paternalism, finding ultimate expression in the words of R. James (one of the few, mainly Labor, members to express concern about working conditions of natives) who said of the 'poor unfortunate niggers' in New Guinea that 'even though they are blacks, they are human beings'. *C.P.D.*, Vol. 136, p. 1782 (November 2, 1932). For an extra-parliamentary view, see 'Sydney', 'The White Australia Policy', in *Foreign Affairs*, October, 1925, p. 110.

46 *P.M.C. Minutes*, XX, p. 23.

47 *P.M.C. Minutes*, XXIII, p. 19.

48 Except in 1928, when the commission complained that it was receiving analyses of legislation instead of facts, and in 1929, when it complained of Australian obtuseness in understanding its wants, and on a number of

occasions when it failed to receive adequate answers to specific questions, the commission seemed generally satisfied with Australia's performance of her reporting obligation.

49 Only Cook on several occasions seemed to become exasperated. One such occasion was in 1927 when he was led rashly to ascribe British subject status to New Guinea natives and was somewhat acidly rebuked for not knowing a 1923 Council decision to the contrary.

50 Pearce, for example, could be disparaging about 'philanthropic ladies and gentlemen on the other side of the world'; on the other side of politics, J. A. Beasley objected to 'busybodies in other parts of the world'.

51 P. D. Phillips' view in 1945 that 'it may be doubted whether any but a trifling minority are aware that colonial policies are undergoing re-examination' could undoubtedly be applied to the pre-war period. P. D. Phillips, 'Australia's Attitude to the Pacific Dependencies', in *Pacific Affairs*, March, 1945, p. 76.

52 Parliament of the Commonwealth of Australia, *League of Nations, Fourth Assembly (2nd-29th September, 1923), Report of the Australian Delegation* (Sir Joseph Cook, chief delegate), Melbourne, 1924, p. 32.

53 *C.P.D.*, Vol. 103, p. 929 (July 11, 1923).

54 *C.P.D.*, Vol. 112, p. 315 (January 22, 1926).

55 *C.P.D.*, Vol. 136, p. 1777 (November, 1932).

56 Cook Report, as above, p. 33.

57 *Ibid.*

58 Parliament of the Commonwealth of Australia, *League of Nations, Seventh Assembly (6th-25th September, 1926), Report of the Australian Delegation* (J. G. Latham, chief delegate), Canberra, 1927, p. 6.

59 *P.M.C. Minutes*, III, p. 163.

60 *P.M.C. Minutes*, VI, p. 86.

61 *P.M.C. Minutes*, XI, p. 47.

62 *P.M.C. Minutes*, XV, p. 52.

63 This criticism was not entirely international. Phillips' 'trifling minority' did exist: see the contributions of Stephen Roberts and Sir James Barrett in *The Australian Mandate for New Guinea* mentioned above, and the contribution of J. W. Burton, Snr., in Persia Campbell, R. C. Mills, G. V. Portus, eds., *Studies in Australian Affairs*, Melbourne, 1930.

64 It is, perhaps, a little ironical that Bruce on one occasion complained of the League's European orientation. See Parliament of the Commonwealth of Australia, *League of Nations, Thirteenth Assembly (26th September to 17th October, 1932), Report of the Australian Delegation* (S. M. Bruce, chief delegate), Canberra, 1933, p. 6.

65 Royal Institute of International Affairs, *Survey of International Affairs, 1926*, Oxford, 1928, p. 399.

66 For an expression of fear that a tendency overseas to take tariff and immigration issues out of domestic arenas might ultimately threaten Australia's restrictive immigration policy, 'the heart of our being', see R. G. Casey, *Australia's Place in the World*, Melbourne, 1931, p. 13.

67 There may well have been a feeling that there was no alternative. As Eggleston said in 1927 with reference to Australian policy in New Guinea: 'the main problem facing the Australian people is an internal one: that of the development of our continent'. In J. B. Condliffe, ed., *Problems of the Pacific* (Proceedings of the Second Conference of the Institute of Pacific Relations, Honolulu, July, 1927), Chicago, 1928, p. 5.

# 4

## TRUSTEESHIP WITHOUT TRUST: A SHORT HISTORY OF INTERRACIAL RELATIONS AND THE LAW IN PAPUA AND NEW GUINEA[1]

### Edward P. Wolfers

'Perhaps nothing shows more clearly the progressive development of a young country than a connected account from time
to time of the legislation effected, and of the circumstances
under which new laws are passed or old ones amended.'[2]

Most of the available writing on race relations in Papua and New Guinea
tends to be descriptive of the situation at the time of writing, and essentially
impressionistic. Very little serious attention has been paid either to the
historical background, or to an analysis of the sociological parameters, of
present tensions and problems. The aim of this chapter, then, is to examine
the historical development, and to evaluate the impact, of some of the laws
and governmental institutions through which interracial relations have been
conducted. In carrying out this aim, it will concentrate especially upon those
laws and offices that most directly affected indigenous society at village
level, and when Papuans and New Guineans began to come to town.

### Restraint without Control

'at the outset, the attention of ... [colonial] administrations was
directed primarily to the establishment of law and order, and the provision of those requirements ... which would enable the population
to satisfy its more elementary needs.'[3]

Both Papua and New Guinea remained exceptions to Lord Hailey's
generalisation about Great Britain's African empire for at least the first years
of their administration by outside powers. In both cases, lack of men, money
and interest at home were primarily responsible for their comparative
neglect, although the administration of British New Guinea initially faced a
special set of legal limitations upon its ambitions.

Modern forms of government were imposed upon Papua and New
Guinea. Where the imposition was noticed, it was, at best acquiesced in,
and sometimes even approved of in due course. Given this sequence of
events, the motives of the colonisers were probably of less longterm importance than their actions. Nonetheless, the Reverend Chalmers seemed rather
pleased to report that he had overheard one Papuan confide to another in
the vernacular that the proclamation of a British protectorate over the

southeastern portion of New Guinea should be welcomed. 'Now we are satisfied,' he said, 'now we know that Queen Victoria is our protector.'[3a]

Europeans first came to Papua and New Guinea for the same variety of reasons which took them to Africa and Australia: the desire to make money; to save souls; and to explore. The British government reluctantly declared a protectorate over British New Guinea (later Papua) in November 1884, under pressure from the Australian states, which feared a putative German interest in the area. In turn, the Imperial government sought to control the depredations of the British fortune-, soul- and adventure-seekers there. The protectorate was only a partial success on both counts: the German government annexed the northeastern portion of the mainland and its island outliers in December, and thereby became a power in the area; while the protectorate administration was legally unable to do more than to restrict foreign activity, and to protect the Papuans. It had no legal authority to intervene directly in indigenous affairs, although it was able to control the landing of spirituous liquors, fire-arms, gunpowder, dynamite and diseased persons, as well as the acquisition of land, in the protectorate.[4]

Commodore Erskine's speech at the proclamation of the British Protectorate has become quite famous over the years for its promises 'that evil-disposed men will not be able to occupy your homes . . . . Your lands will be secured to you; your wives and children will be protected.'[5] Indeed, many Papuans know just these portions of the speech off by heart, and are not at all loth to repeat them when arguing the demerits of government policy, especially in relation to land matters.

As soon as the protectorate was declared, however, the Australian states, which had pledged themselves to its financial support, lost interest, and by 1887, South Australia, Western Australia, Tasmania and New Zealand had begun to renege on their payments. Great Britain, New South Wales, Victoria and Queensland alone kept up their payments, until 1898, albeit at a gradually decreasing level.

The protectorate administration was not only in financial difficulties, however, but it was legally hamstrung too. It was empowered by law only to control the entry of foreigners to the area, and to legislate only for its non-indigenous population. If, say, a group of Papuans attacked a European, or a battle between rival Papuan groups threatened European security, there was technically no redress possible. Until such time as it could legally intervene in indigenous society, the administration could only admonish indigenous wrongdoers, as was done when a group of Papuans, who had clearly just arisen from a cannibalistic feast, attended a repeat performance of the protectorate's proclamation near their village. 'Queen Victoria,' they were told, 'doesn't like her children to do that sort of thing.'[6]

Otherwise, the protectorate's administrators had no real alternative to 'shutting up the country', and thereby incurring the wrath of potential investors. As H. H. Romilly observed early in 1885, when he was the protectorate's acting commissioner:—

> '. . . till we get a good working establishment there it would be absurd to allow a rush of white men, and begin our work with a lot of murders and other troubles on our hands . . . .'[7]

Small wonder then, that the protectorate is generally regarded as embracing 'a period of suspended animation'[8] in the actual administration of British New Guinea.

*The Establishment of Government*

British New Guinea was annexed as a colony of Great Britain on, the same day, September 4, 1888, as its first administrator, Dr. (Later Sir) William MacGregor, arrived in Port Moresby. It was MacGregor who laid the basis of the Territory's system of 'native administration', upon lines similar to those set out by Sir Peter Scratchley when he was Special Commissioner of the protectorate (from 1884 until his death at the end of 1885).[9]

Sir William MacGregor has retrospectively acquired a modest reputation as perhaps the harshest head of an administration in Papua's history.[10] Certainly, his methods of establishing government control sounded cruder and more violent than the 'peaceful penetration' policy of his most important Australian successor, Sir Hubert Murray. One suspects, however, that the administration of their policies on the ground may have been more similar than their rhetoric. While MacGregor spoke roughly, he discouraged the mounting of punitive expeditions against groups of offending Papuans. Under Murray, Papuans who resisted the imposition of the *Pax Australiana* too vigorously were sometimes fired upon, or had their houses set alight.[11] MacGregor's claims and actions should probably be read against the background of the extravagant imperial adventurism of his day. In general, he claimed:—

> 'There is only one thing they [the Papuans] respect, that is force. They have the most profound respect for that.... We had first to found our Government stations, and we have been using each station as a centre from which our authority is gradually radiating.... Beyond that there is the old state of things, every tribe fighting its neighbour, so when we go into a new district we almost invariably have to fight the principal fighting tribe of the district. We never fight with them at all if we can possibly avoid it until were are in a position to make it a final and decisive move. We hardly ever have to fight twice in the same district.'[12]

But. in practice, MacGregor seems to have been more reluctant to employ force than appears from the foregoing. In 1889, for example he set out to capture the murderers of two white men at Cloudy Bay (east of Port Moresby), and reported:—

> 'I am very sorry to say that I do not expect to be able to secure any of the actual murders just now. That they will be eventually obtained there can be but little doubt, but this may not be managed until the surrounding tribes are got under Government influence. What has been done already to punish the guilty natives is not to my mind satisfactory, but no alternative presented itself under the circumstances. A fierce and powerful tribe has been defeated in open fight, and been thoroughly humiliated and demoralized; their strongholds have been occupied by us and destroyed, and they are for the time completely expelled from their houses and lands, and we occupy their dwellings and live on their food. They and all their neighbours are aware that, so far, this has been done without any of our party being on the sick list.'[13]

He expected the people of the area soon to come over to the government.

Since MacGregor's day in Papua, and from the beginnings of German rule, the two territories' successive administrations have successfully claimed two rights; to intervene unilaterally in village affairs; and to control the indigenes' rate, and style of entry into the modern world. Intervention can, of course, stimulate change, or repress it; control may be protective (and, therefore, ultimately progressive), or restrictive. The balance is in each case rather fine, and needs to be precisely evaluated in each period, and for each aspect of society in either territory. On both counts, one is tempted to rate MacGregor rather more highly than his German contemporaries, and, given their respective circumstances, even his successors on both sides of the border before World War II.

Very soon after his arrival, MacGregor began to legislate the outlines of his policy of protection. Direct land purchases from the Papuans by anyone other than the administration were forbidden. Arms, ammunition and liquor were not to be supplied to the indigenes, and, in an attempt to bring the recruitment of indigenous labour by expatriates under control, the removal of Papuans from their home districts was declared illegal. At the same time, the general body of Queensland law was brought into force, initially for people of all races.

Only after the passage of the Native Board Ordinance in 1889 was provision made for the establishment of a system of 'native administration', and for the promulgation of a special set of regulations 'bearing upon or affecting the good government and well-being of the natives.'[14] Under Mac-Gregor, however, most conventional criminal offences by Papuans still came under the Queensland code, the only exceptions being those concerned with stealing (1890), injuring another person (also 1890), the careless use of fire (1890) and compelling a Papuan woman to have intercourse, which came under the Native Board Regulations in 1897. Magistrates for Native Matters had the power (from 1890) to summon 'any native' as a witness, in the same manner as a defendant (that is, by arresting and bringing him by force before the court should he fail to appear when duly summoned). Otherwise, the Native Regulations under the British were concerned principally with the protection of the Papuans from exploitation and disease, their paternalistic correction and 'improvement', and the development of the village economy (to provide a potential source of tax-revenue, and to assist in the indigenes entry into a cash economy). The Native Regulation Board Ordinance of 1889 was no more than the legal seed from which Mac-Gregor's Australian successors developed an increasingly bifurcated legal system. Until 1906, the Native Board Regulations dealt mainly with administrative and medical exigencies and requirements outside the normal ambit of British and Australian law.

Under MacGregor, it was legally possible for a Papuan to become an administrative official with the same rights and duties as a European; after 1909, when the Australian administration promulgated a completely new Native Regulation Ordinance, this specific proviso, and official faith in its short term applicability, both disappeared.[15] Under the British, there were also no white policemen in the Armed Constabulary that MacGregor set up in 1890. Unless a magistrate performed the task, all arrests were, therefore, made by Pacific islanders, and they were even used occasionally to guard white prisoners. Despite their good behaviour on these occasions, however, the 1906 Royal Commission into Papua found resentment at the very possibility of being arrested by a member of the Armed Native Constabulary to be so strong among the expatriate population that it seemed advisable to avoid this happening where possible. 'There is always this objection,' the commission felt, 'that, no matter how little a particular white man may deserve the respect of the native, it is still necessary in the interests of all white men that the natives should not be in a position where respect for the ruling race will be jeopardized.'[16] It was not until the 1960s that an Australian administration began to follow MacGregor's precepts again, and appointed some indigenes as commissioned police and patrol officers. At about the same time, the multitude of special, discriminatory, 'Native Regulations', crimes and penalties developed since MacGregor's day were being gradually repealed.

On the administrative side, the pattern established by MacGregor prevailed, almost untouched, until after World War II. As new areas were brought under control, the magistrates, whose duties were initially defined by MacGregor, and their armed indigenous police (who gradually replaced the original force of Fijians and Solomon Islanders), brought government to Papua. It was under MacGregor that the government first began to assert its right to unilateral intervention in village life. Only since 1950, have consultation and an elective local government council system begun to replace the 'native administration' system established during the 1890s.

A 'magistrate' in Papua was more than a judicial officer. He was, and his successor the patrol officer, still is in many areas, the sole local personification of the government: policeman, explorer, roadbuilder, health inspector, social worker, and prison warder; even in court, where he deals with most of the 'lesser offences' against the law, and civil disputes between Papuans, he acts as prosecutor, defence counsel, judge and jury. Only recently have specialized magistrates begun to sit in some rural areas.

Beneath the magistrate, and appointed by him, after an area has come under government control, is the 'village constable'. As Papua was pacified, the number of village constables increased, and the law was enforced in the magistrate's absence. As councils were established after World War II, so elected leaders began to replace appointed officials at village level. By the end of 1970, 86 per cent of the indigenous people of Papua had elected their own councillors, while a few people in the Western District were in process of being 'contacted' for the first time. While the majority was 'relearning' local self-government, a small minority of Papuans was still being, or was about to be, 'ruled' by other Papuans who had been appointed to act on the central government's behalf.

Most of the pre-contact political communities in Papua lacked any centralised authority. There were, in short, no chiefs. MacGregor, therefore, ceased the largely pointless exercise whereby his predecessors had attempted to 'recognise the chiefs', and began to appoint a government official in each village.

The village constable was not a leader, as the regulation (of 1892) creating the position made quite clear:—

> '1. The Administrator may appoint *any* good man to be a Village Constable . . . .
>
> 7. The Village Constable is a *servant* of the Government . . . .
>
> 9. The Village Constable will *listen to and obey the* Magistrate.' (emphasis added).

In MacGregor's day, each village constable was given a medallion to wear around his neck, or a special staff. Later on, he was given a uniform, and paid a modest annual allowance.

The altogether alien nature of the village constable's position became clear as the system developed. He had no specific legitimate role in indigenous society. His sole legal power of arrest had no precedent, and therefore probably no substantive meaning, even where it was known. A special regulation had, therefore, to be promulgated (in 1895) to restrain appointed constables from ill-using their people 'and, at the same time, ... [telling] the people that the Government approves of their bad behaviour which is a lie ...'; and to protect the indigenous public from those who falsely claimed to have been appointed by the government. Under Australian rule, the increasing number of penalties and demands placed upon these constables only emphasised their role as servants of the government, and probably undermined the autonomy of those officials who had become leaders in their own right. As time passed, their duties were ever more specifically set out and their authority circumscribed by government decree.

The dividing-lines between protection, correction and development are vague. Here, they will be used very broadly to help organise the data rather than to make an important analytical point. To take an example: in 1893, the following regulation was promulgated by the Native Regulation Board:—

> 'White men know that sorcery is only deceit, but the lies of the sorcerer frighten many people. The deceit of the sorcerer should be stopped.'

Was this paternalistic injunction intended to protect the people from the vengeance of the bewitched? to correct an erroneously held set of beliefs, or evil practices? or to prepare the people of Papua for the secular world of development? Anyway, as Sir Hubert Murray once remarked, 'Sorcery is an offence which is of course imaginary . . .'[16a], with no possible evidence, other than the belief of the ensorcered, or the boasts or protestations of the practitioner, either way. How, then, could and did European Native Magistrates sentence the guilty to up to three months goal, and (native) Native Magistrates dispense sentences of up to three days? If anything, their actions only showed, as Sir William MacGregor realised[16b], that the Administration took sorcery very seriously, and thereby became in one anthropologist's eyes, 'a powerful ally of the native sorcerer against all would-be educative agencies . . . [in that the convicted sorcerer] and all others inevitably take the view that the white man shares in his conception of sorcery as actually and directly powerful'![17]

In 1911, the anti-sorcery regulation gained a more precise and readily enforceable definition. It then became illegal to practise or to pretend to practise sorcery; to threaten its use either by oneself or through another; to procure or to attempt to procure a sorceror; to be found in possession of 'implements or charms [both left undefined] used in sorcery'; or to accept payment, or presents in the shape of food or otherwise 'when the obvious intention of making such payments or presents is to propitiate a sorcerer.' An accused can at least be found guilty or not guilty, according to fairly objective criteria, if he is charged with pretending to a certain skill, threatening or procuring its use, possession of certain classes of goods, or extortion. Unfortunately, most sorcerers are only discovered after someone has suffered, and the suffering or death is retrospectively attributed (often through the use of magic too) to the apparently malevolent character of someone's secret (and therefore effective) actions.

Otherwise, on the purely protective side of their longterm economic interests—Papuans were forbidden altogether from disposing of their land, by will or through any other means, to any person at all, other than by custom.

In the medical field, to protect the indigenes from disease, to correct previous unhealthy practices, and to develop better standards of hygiene it became illegal (in 1890) to bury the dead within an occupied village, and especially to keep them near one's house, as many Papuans had previously done. In 1902, magistrates had been empowered to order the removal, abandonment or destruction of any village which they found 'objectionable' on any, but particularly health, grounds. In 1904, it became compulsory to report all cases of venereal disease to the magistrate, for the sick to wash with water every day, and to avoid all physical contact with their neighbours. By 1905, it had become legally compulsory to improve, and keep one's village clean, on pain of seven days in gaol, or the enforced destruction of one's house. At the same time, magistrates could order all diseased dogs and pigs to be destroyed, and village water-supplies to be kept clean, and fenced. Medical development required what was best, not what was wanted or persuasive.[18]

More generally, it became illegal in 1891 to spread lying reports, and to use threatening language. Although the first regulation was originally introduced to deal with the large number of seemingly definite and circumstantial accounts of massacres of white men in the early days which the administration had felt bound to investigate,[19] it came to be increasingly employed over the years to deal with those who disturbed the administratively-imposed quiescence of an area by preaching or expecting that the millenium of European-style affluence for Papuans was close at hand. The latter charge dealt with those who challenged the government's authority or whose verbal assaults seemed likely to lead to a breach of the peace.

Colonial governments have tended to define 'development' in two broad ways: as an economic phenomenon, or in terms of their own administrative convenience. Protection and correction, too were often defined in terms of the interpreted 'real' interests of the governed, not their immediate desires. Thus, magistrates were empowered, (in 1891) to prosecute anyone who destroyed (even his own) coconut palms, (from 1895) took sap at the wrong time from a rubber or guttapercha plant, or blocked a water-channel; to order the men of any village to plant a given number of coconut palms each, and to tend them properly (in 1894); and, in 1903, to order other trees to be planted for food and trade where the ground was unsuitable for coconuts. From 1894, magistrates could order the people they administered to build, and maintain, local 'roads', more accurately broad and shady tracks, to make patrolling and more general movement between villages easier. Administrative convenience or development?

The wide and shaded lanes along the Papuan coast, flanked by neatly planted and carefully tended coconut palms on either side bear mute testimony still to the immediate efficacy of the government's injunctions. The failure to replant many of these palms after sixty years, of now rapidly decreasing production, are witness to the longterm inefficiency of economic development through compulsion (at least without continued compulsion). Consultation was regarded as impossible.

A number of other 'Forbidden Acts', as offences against the Native Board Regulations were called, were defined over the years to assist the government in its self-appointed task of administering, and therefore developing the country. As a regulation of 1897 rather unctuously put it, 'The work which the Government do [sic] is for the good of all the people of the land . . . .' As its officers could not patrol without carriers to convey their goods from place to place, each illiterate 'chief' was compelled to keep a list of potential carriers in his village, who could then be compelled, in return for rations and nominal pay, to help to magistrate on his way.

Only administrative convenience, for law-enforcement and, later, census-taking purposes, could really explain the need for a regulation (of 1902) forbidding people to abandon their old homes in settled villages and scattering themselves in small groups over the country. This practice was, however, outlawed, technically because it increased superstitious fears, bred animosities, and 'debase[d] those that follow[ed] it'. Like adultery and wife-stealing (in 1891), the practice was made an offence really because of the threat that enmity, perhaps caused by a spouse's sexual infidelity, and expressed, then exacerbated, in the division of small communities, posed to the peace. Even traditionally isolated small groups containing no more than three dwellings could be compelled to remove themselves to a regular village within a specified period.

Government control had brought peace and the ability to live and move more freely. It had also placed quite new demands for labour, 'improvement', and administratively more efficient living, upon the village.

Perhaps the most optimistically-based requirement that 'development' placed upon the Papuan people, however, was a regulation of 1897, which was introduced with the same sort of patiently paternal explanation that prefaced many of the regulations of the day:—

> children learn these things or not. It is therefore for the good of the now growing up will by the time they become men and women need to know more about reading, writing, and arithmetic, than their parents do. But some foolish parents do not care whether their children learn these things or not. It is therefore for the good of the children that this law is made.'

Thereupon, a clause followed making it compulsory for all children between five and thirteen years to go to the nearest school on at least three days per week, on pain of a fine of five shillings or three days gaol for the parents of defaulters. In a territory that supported not a single government school, nor more than a handful of mission-sponsored educational institutions, the regulation was a little difficult to implement justly or effectively.

One final regulation from the interregnum period[20] of continued joint British and Australian rule (1901-1905), while the assumption of full and formal responsibility for Papua's administration in 1906 by Australia was still pending, deserves special mention. In 1902, Papua set a rather gruesome legal precedent. In that year it became a Forbidden Act, on pain of one month's gaol, 'to barter, give, sell, offer or procure, whether for any consideration or otherwise, any human skull or other human remains'. Thus, cannibalism, headhunting as a *rite de passage* in many communities, and certain classes of museum-collecting, were technically outlawed in a single sentence.

*Papua under Australian Rule*

Australia became legally responsible for the administration of British New Guinea with the proclamation of the Papua Act in 1906. The story of the colony's administration from then, until World War II was the familiar one of a continued Australian lack of interest, and neglect. Policy was made, and its implementation supervised, by a single man, J. H. P. (later Sir Hubert) Murray, from his appointment as Acting Administrator in 1907, and then Lieutenant-Governor in 1908, until his death in 1940. Throughout the period, 'the Murray System', as it became known, was Australian policy.[21]

Murray's reputation is presently uncertain. On the one hand, many Papuans remember his aloof paternalism and frequent personal tours of the territory with affection, while, on the other hand, at least one writer has claimed that there never was a 'system' at all, 'except in so far as the claims of Europeans who had been induced to invest money in Papua, were balanced against the well-being of the original inhabitants'.[22] Lord Hailey, the eminent author of *An African Survey* and other famous works on colonial administration, was however probably his most pointed critic. By 1948, when he wrote, 'the Murray System' had become a legend, a potent legitimating symbol in the arguments between the pre-war European settlers who saw it in its continuation the best that they could still hope for, and the proponents of 'a new deal for the natives', who spoke of the logical next step from Murray's policies. Rather to the discomfort of both sides, Lord Hailey described Murray's 'system of administration [as amounting] . . . to no more than a well-regulated and benevolent type of police rule'. This judgment was not intended as 'any disparagement of Murray's reputation . . . . Little more was perhaps possible within the slender financial resources available.'[23]

In a curious way, Murray had been well aware of the differing standards by which he would one day be judged. Perhaps he alone had been consistent as his territory, and colonial policies elsewhere, developed—ahead of his time at the beginning, quaintly old-fashioned at the end, and always hampered by lack of funds and the Australian government's monumental indifference to Papuan affairs:—

> 'The outstanding criticism of the Papuan Government used to be that it was "pampering" and "coddling" the natives and encouraging them in habits of idleness. The tide seems now to be turning, and it is likely that in the future we shall be accused, rather, of overworking the Papuan and driving him too hard. This is not evidence of inconsistency, it is due to the fact that different people are talking . . . .'

His capitalist critics, who wanted to develop Papua in their own interests were, in time, replaced by 'the enthusiast for native races who takes an entirely opposite view'. 'Eventually', Murray thought, 'the enthusiast also will satisfy himself that we know exactly what we are doing, and that our administration is not so bad after all'.[24]

However, despite Murray's claim to consistency, his policy 'was not as clearly formulated and as static as both critics and admirers tend to assume. . . . [His] practice changed and developed . . .,'[25] as the society around him changed. Nonetheless, he seems to have remained quite consistent, in his gradual implementation of his policy-responses, to certain general notions about the place of the Papuan in society, and the sort of 'improvements' he should undergo. And, although he tried to leave indigenous custom untouched, Murray felt that his legislative and regulatory enactments 'set a high standard for the Papuan (far higher than we would ever dream of setting for ourselves) and ... that the Papuan responds on the whole extremely well'.[26]

In order to provide some organisation for the data that are available, we shall consider the pre-war Papuan administrative system, and its policies, under three heads: (1) the development of the MacGregor tradition of unilateral intervention in village affairs; (2) the protection of the Papuans; and (3) the preservation of European interests, standards, and society.[27]

## 1   *The Development of the MacGregor System*

One cannot obtain a proper understanding of the true long-term historical importance of the 'native administration' system in Papua from a study of the Native Regulations by themselves. They were essentially but a continuation, and an intensification of certain elements, of the regulations promulgated by MacGregor. Their historical significance derives, rather, from the length of time—nearly sixty years in some areas—during which they remained the principal, if not the sole, point of contact between the villager and the central government, and the ways in which they moulded village life. The manner of their administration was, in the end, as important as their purpose.

As the geographical area under government control expanded after 1906, so too did the areas of village life in which the government asserted its right of unilateral intervention. The style of that intervention was as oppressively paternalistic as its interference seemed ubiquitous. By World War II, the government had effectively established the right to intervene when and where it chose, and had effectively stifled or demoralised almost every source of independent initative and leadership outside its own institutions and appointees.

At the most general level, resident magistrates had been empowered (since 1890) to initiate prosecutions upon their own complaint and to summon 'any native' as a witness. In 1911, they were told, for the first time, that they might use their 'discretion as to taking notice of matters that are civil claims'. They were permitted now to intervene in anything at all 'to appease quarrels and disputes about the property and rights, real or imaginary [of the people], and to prevent as much as possible the strong taking advantage of the weak'. Although not allowed to decide the ownership of land or water, magistrates were to do all they could to prevent trouble or 'immoral' conduct (which was often a direct cause of trouble) in the village.

Magistrates were, of course, allowed to do more than just avert trouble. They were to assist in the development of the village, and the improvement of the people, in their charge. In 1913, disobedience of any 'lawful order' of a magistrate became punishable by a fine of ten shillings or one month's gaol. In 1920, the range of these 'lawful orders' was expanded to embrace 'any act which ... [any native had to do if the magistrate considered it to be] for the good government and well-being of the natives'. After 1931, magistrates were empowered to summon anyone they suspected of committing a 'forbidden act', whether or not a complaint had been laid. In short, Papua's resident magistrates not only had quite wide powers to enforce the law, but were gradually invited to legislate almost as they chose.

Out in the bush, the precise wording of the regulations probably did not matter much anyway. The magistrate was prosecutor, judge and jury in his own court. In an extremity, he alone was armed. Murray presumably handpicked his officers for just these reasons: out on patrol, a man's character was a more likely determinant of his conduct than the law. From that realisation, it was but a short step to give the virtual power of legislation to his field staff.

At a narrower level, the range and number of regulations kept on increasing too. A few regulations, such as that (in 1909) forbidding the wearing of a shirt, long-sleeved singlet or hand-protection other than gloves while 'feeding machinery' were an obvious response to the need to provide legally for an increasingly complex, developing society. Others, such as the regulation (of 1930) enjoining village constables to find someone to feed a motherless child who was still at breast, were probably no more than expressions of a neurotic paternalist's unnecessary fussing.

In the medical field, parents who lived within ten miles of Port Moresby were legally compelled to seek medical attention for their children if so ordered (in 1909); the isolation of sick people could be ordered, and communication within a village restricted (also in 1909) to prevent the spread of sickness; Papuans with dysentery were forbidden to enter the town (in 1912), and communication between any village where an infectious disease was rife, and outsiders, could be outlawed (in 1916). In 1919, inoculations became compulsory on the orders of a resident magistrate or the Lieutenant-Governor,[28] while in 1930, a fine of one pound, or two months gaol, was provided for any offender who left a canoe with water in it (and which was, therefore, a likely breeding-ground for mosquitoes) near a village. In 1913, abortion had been outlawed, although the effectiveness of this measure may be gauged from the large number of references to Papua and New Guinea to be found in a bibliography on abortion in primitive society which was published more than forty years later.

As regards the general health and welfare of the village as a whole, the house and village cleaning regulations were tightened up (in 1911), as were the road-cleaning and maintenance provisions. Additions to villages built partly over the sea, for defence reasons before contact, had now to be made over the sea too but this time for health reasons (in 1911), while magistrates were empowered (in 1905) to issue orders to repair, and later (in 1921) to extend, or to rebuild, overcrowded, insanitary or badly neglected houses. In 1921, magistrates were given the quite arbitrary power 'from time to time [to] select a native house as a standard and type to be followed in the erection of new houses in a village'—and not infrequently the model so selected has been aesthetically quite pleasing; if considerably more dangerous to health than the still and stuffy warmth of a house that had proved more satisfactory over the previous few thousand years of existence in an area. In some areas, however, the magistrates had to employ the same regulation to achieve the opposite end: to discourage villagers from abandoning their traditional style of housing for a more 'modern', if rather less healthy, style.[29]

In 1905, resident magistrates were empowered to order that diseased pigs and dogs be destroyed without compensation for their owners; in 1914, coconut trees with root disease had to be carefully cut down, dug out, and burnt; in 1915 and 1917, respectively, war was declared on the rhinoceros and red palm beetles, and in 1922, upon noxious weeds and plants; and in

1916 a biannual inspection of all ships, boats and gear was ordered. After 1907, children who failed to attend school regularly could be whipped (in addition to the punishments still meted out to their parents), although, in 1929, recognition was finally given to indigenous custom. A teacher or magistrate was then allowed to excuse a child from school 'for so long as in his opinion such attendance would interfere with the proper observance of a recognized native ceremony'. On the other hand, once a missionary had possession of a man's body and/or soul, it was quite a serious offence (from 1931 on) for a Papuan to interfere with the performance of a burial ceremony according to the usages of the deceased's religious denomination.

Perhaps the most charming regulation contained in the 1911 revision and consolidation of the old Native Board Regulations was one allowing the owner of a garden to kill any pig or goat that trespassed upon it for a second time, after its owner had been warned, and provided the latter was informed afterwards. If, however, the gardener then ate the animal or gave its carcase away rather than buried it, he could be charged with theft.

In sum, then, the preceding regulations were but an increasingly paternalistic and interfering continuation of the old MacGregor regulations. Murray's real regulatory innovations tended to centre on the towns, on some new forms of protection for the indigenes, and in controlling the Australianisation of the Papuans. Yet, it was at village-level, through the extension of the system of village administration established by MacGregor, that the increasing dependence of many Papuan leaders upon European advice and guidance was built up.

In 1933, for example, the Lieutenant-Governor was empowered to declare any cult illegal. Thus, some quite irrational revivalist movements were driven underground, together with other movements that were the products of a tough and innovating, if sometimes misguided, indigenous leadership. In short, leadership as a relationship between a capable Papuan of ambition and his followers was abolished. Leaders were now men appointed to obey the central government, rather than selected to initiate, or organise local group action.[30] When Murray finally saw the need for, or the desirability of, negotiation or consultation between the government and the governed, an aggressive and articulate indigenous leadership was no longer available for training in the operation of Western-style institutions. Instead, the people of the Port Moresby area were, as Murray himself reported, reluctant to have village councils set up for them to run:—

> ' "Why should we have Councillors?", they would ask. "It is the white man's business to carry on the Government; we do not know anything about it, and do not want to. We are quite satisfied with things as they are." '[31]

Even today, a number of the longest-governed and best-educated groups of Papuans feel the same way, at least about the national government. The ubiquitous interference of the administration in indigenous affairs, and the oppressive paternalism of the Murray years, have made many Papuans extremely dependent upon European advice and guidance, and too unsure to take the plunge (say, towards self-government) alone. For them, government and leadership do not require participation but obedience; independence often means desertion. Many of those who are most nearly 'ready' for self-government may be numbered among those who are least willing to shoulder its responsibilities.

## 2 *Protecting the Papuans*

A colonial policy designed for the protection of indigenous interests may operate both so as to prevent abuse and exploitation, as well as to avoid what Sir Hubert Murray called 'the effects of . . . "the material disturbance" caused by the white man's arrival'. In the latter case, Murray claimed to prefer 'to encourage [the] population in habits of industry',[32] although, inevitably, he had also to restrict, or at least control, its contacts with the modern world. Once the Papuans had been protected from abuse, Murray thought it most important to encourage those forms of (especially agricultural) development which would help 'to conserve and stabilize the native race, and to prevent the native from losing his individuality, and from sinking down into the position of a tenth-rate white man, aping the lower and more contemptible aspects of the white man's culture, but unable to recognize or appreciate the higher'.[33]

Under the first head—that is, the prevention of exploitation—Murray was more willing than his predecessors to alienate indigenous-owned land for development, but just as careful to keep control of the whole process in official hands. Thus, the administration alone was allowed to buy land from the Papuans, and then only after a full investigation into the likely future needs of its owners. Australian and other overseas investors could only lease land from the government, while their labour-lines were rather more stringently controlled than in MacGregor's day.

As Murray believed in the longterm compatibility of overseas investment and the indigenes' welfare, the protection afforded by the Native Labour Ordinance embraced both the employer and the labourer. Both 'signing on' and 'paying off' were supervised by the local magistrates. The use of undue influence or inducements to sign a contract was illegal, as was desertion by a labourer. The duration of the indenture,[34] and the food, pay, housing and hours of work for indigenous labourers were set down by law, as were the penalties for misusing an employer's property or ill-treating his animals. These penal sanctions upon the labourer and his master remained in force until after World War II, when some of the restrictions upon the labourer became enforceable only as civil suits, for breach of contract.

Even where recruits were willing, the administration tried to protect them from themselves—and, for fear of a labour-, and then a food-,shortage, it would sometimes close a village, or an entire area, for recruitment. On the other hand, the administration quietly circulated lists of men who should not for some reason be re-employed to government offices, and plantations. Appended to some of the names was a note to the effect, 'not to be employed where he is likely to come into contact with European women and children'.

In 1930, a special Order-in-Council under the Native Labour Ordinance was issued. No Papuan from the Gulf or Delta Divisions (in Western Papua) was henceforth to be employed as a domestic servant outside his own district. Employers with such men working for them were invited to have their contracts cancelled and to send them home. Employers were 'further earnestly advised not to employ such natives casually'.

Just why this special order was issued remains unclear. Present-day officials are embarrassed that it ever existed, for it was clearly not intended to prevent over-recruitment in the area—the tone was too urgent for that. On the other hand, despite their rather unsavoury—if ill-founded—reputation (among Europeans) for sexual violence and excess,[35] there were no more Gulf and Delta Division men on the lists of men not to be employed again, nor among those convicted of sexual offences, than there were men from other areas. It seems clear from the sketchy evidence that is available, however, that the European population of Port Moresby was considerably more fearful of Gulf and Delta men than any others, perhaps only because of their reputation for general lawlessness and for interfering with, and robbing, other Papuans as they travelled between their place of work in Port Moresby and their compounds in the Badili area, about one and a half miles away.[36] By 1931, they had been forbidden (also under the Native Labour Ordinance) to enter or remain in Port Moresby between 7 p.m. and 6 a.m. without the written permission of a resident magistrate. In case of doubt as to a man's origins, the normal procedures of British justice were reversed, for 'under this Regulation the averment that the native concerned is a native of the Gulf Division or the Delta Division shall be deemed sufficient evidence of the fact until the contrary is shown'.

Protection under the Native Labour Ordinance, therefore, worked both ways. Generally, however, it probably worked to the advantage of the literate, and those who knew the law. Most Papuans had to wait until they found, or were noticed by, a European who recognized their plight, before they could assert their rights. Nonetheless, people of both races were charged, and convicted, for breaches of the ordinance.

Sir Hubert Murray's attitude towards unwholesome kinds of change lay somewhere between his desire to protect Papuans from abuse, and his continued assertion of the government's right to unilateral intervention in the village. As Murray himself put it, in a characteristically paternalistic vein:—

> 'The principle on which we have generally acted, and which I think is the right one, is to tolerate all customs, of course within reasonable limits, which were in existence among the natives before the Europeans came here; but to prohibit others which are new to them, and which we think may have a bad effect, even though we may continue to practise such habits ourselves . . . .'[37]

Thus, in 1906, it became illegal to play cards or to gamble after 9 p.m. while all gambling was outlawed in 1907, and the fine (one pound for a first offence) could be deducted from a labourer's wages. The supply of alcohol to, and its possession by, Papuans had been illegal since the declaration of the protectorate, and the drinking of *gamada* became so in 1911. In the case of *gamada*, however, Murray personally was perfectly consistent. *Gamada* is an intoxicating drink like *kava*, made from the roots of a plant in many parts of Western Papua.[38] Murray opposed its proscription on the ground that it was a traditional vice of the people concerned, although he was not prepared to repeal the regulation banning its consumption, which was brought into force while he was absent overseas.[39]

Paternalism had many faces. In 1913, Papuans were even protected from influence by their fellows, when it was made illegal for one Papuan to try to persuade another to spend his wages with another person, if the first Papuan hoped to gain from the attempt. Ten years later, in 1923, it became illegal under the Native Labour Regulations for a European to attempt such persuasion, or to charge a Papuan customer more than a reasonable price for his purchases. Bribery and corruption of village officials were, of course, illegal, but so too (after 1911) were 'All noise shouting beating of drums and dancing . . . in . . . [gazetted] towns and villages [after] 9 o'clock each night unless the Magistrate gives permission . . .'. Clearly, pacification and steel tools had provided the time, and money some of the wherewithal, for new forms of crime. A patient government had now not only to protect the Papuans from their own desires and crimes, but to do what it could to ensure a good night's sleep for all who had to work on the morrow.[40]

Murray was, however, well aware that his policy of encouraging the Papuans to follow the preachments, rather than the actions, of their mentors may have appeared less noble to them than it did to him. Forbidding the Papuans access to alcohol was both prudent and wise by his lights. 'Still, to the native it must', he concluded, 'appear rather strange':

> 'Perhaps, if he thinks about it at all, he concludes that the supply of liquor is limited, and that the white man selfishly wants to keep it all to himself, and has no mind, as an old miner put it many years ago, to "waste good stuff on a b——y nigger".'[41]

### 3  Preserving European Standards

'The colonial world', as Frantz Fanon insisted in *The Wretched of the Earth*, 'is a world divided into compartments'. It is 'a world cut in two'. As a matter of sociological analysis, and official explanation, its boundaries can be seen to be demarcated by differences in power, wealth and status. But when their actual operation is experienced, these boundaries soon fade or coalesce. For the colonized, 'it is evidence that what parcels out the world is . . . the fact of belonging to or not belonging to a given race, a given species'.[42]

Australians have never really thought of Papua as a 'colony'; it is a 'territory'. Yet, until very recently indeed, the actual conduct of its administration, its actual forms of contact with the Papuans, were colonial in the extreme. At the time of their repeal in 1959, Papua and New Guinea's curfew laws had few contemporaries left, outside southern Africa, and no parallels at all in most other areas of law-making for 'native administration' and control.

The world of Papua's expatriate settlers before the war was a dusty, lower middle class, Australian version of the British Raj. It lacked the grace and the magnificance of the Empire at its zenith. Its security derived less from a sense of pride in its technological superiority and splendour than from a mean and pedantic insistence on the importance of innate racial differences. Nonetheless, its sexual fantasies about its subjects rivalled those of the French in Malagasy as described in O. Mannoni's *Prospero and Caliban*,[43] while its image of 'the natives' was pure Fanon, albeit without the starvation, or the excitement of 'the native town'. In fact, Papua, as we shall see, was never allowed to have a 'native town'.

Otherwise, many a European settler in pre-war Papua would—rather incongruously—have found himself agreeing with much of Fanon's description of 'the native's' lustful look upon the settler's world—his 'look of envy; . . . his dreams of possession—all manner of possession: to sit at the settler's table, to sleep in the settler's bed, with his wife if possible. The colonized man is an envious man . . . for there is no native who does not dream at least once a day of setting himself up in the settler's place.'[44]

The British administrators of Papua before 1906 displayed little legislative interest in the sexual and other insecurities of the territory's European settlers. They may have been less conscious than their successors of the need to place restrictions upon the nature and extent of interracial contacts, although it seems more likely that such problems did not yet require legislation. In other words, the precision of the Australians' legislative discrimination between the races may have owed more to their penchant for exploration and pacification, and the consequent establishment of 'contact' with rapidly increasing thousands of people, than to any real difference between the racial sensitivities of the two administering nations.

### (i)   Clothing

Australian policy in both Papua and New Guinea has always traversed a narrow path between devotion to the civilising mission, and contempt for those who need it. Papuans and New Guineans have, therefore, always been expected to dress and act like Europeans if they want to be taken seriously, but are often treated with contempt and dislike for most of their attempts to play the part. The shock of recognition at the improperly clothed semisophisticate, perhaps the fear of unconscious parody of themselves, have led many Australians to subscribe to a sort of 'big bang' theory of the civilisation process. Papuans and New Guineans are welcome to be like Australians (although most of those who try are failed by their examiners); their attempts at becoming so are repressed, or dismissed with disgust. The history of the Papuan clothing regulations, and the changing basis of their justification, demonstrate this theory well.

The very first legislative reference to the desirability of clothing any Papuans at all appeared in the provisions concerning the uniforms of the armed constabulary and village constables. In 1906, the very first Native Regulation issued by the territory's blushing Australian administration required all male Papuans in the Port Moresby area, except small children, to wear a loin-cloth when in public. In 1909, all indentured labourers had, by law, to be provided with a new loin-cloth every three months.

By 1917, it had, however, become clear that many Papuans were incapable of wearing modern clothing properly. In that year it became an offence for a Papuan even to possess an article which was used, or which was capable of being used, for clothing or bedding if a magistrate considered it to be in such a condition that it constituted a potential source of danger to the owner, or to any other Papuans. Magistrates were empowered to order the destruction of such articles by fire, and without compensation to the owner.

In 1919, a patient legislative lecture was preached to the clothed and erring:—

> 'Clothes are good to wear if they are kept clean, and if they are taken off when they are wet and dried before they are put on again. Otherwise they are bad, for they cause sickness and death. Some natives know how to keep their clothes clean and do not wear them when they are wet, but many others are foolish, and wear them when they are very dirty, and keep them on, and even sleep in them, when they are wet. To protect these foolish men and women it is necessary to make a law about the wearing of clothes.'

From 1920, all Papuans, both male and female, were forbidden to wear clothes on the upper part of the body, on pain of a fine of between ten shillings and one pound, or imprisonment for between one and two months, plus the destruction of their clothes. Crown servants, policemen, village constables and other government employees, contract labourers and mission teachers, students and other residents of mission stations were exempt from the provision, as were any other Papuans who had been given a special exemption by their local magistrate. From 1921, contract labourers required the written permission of their employer or of a resident magistrate to wear a singlet, shirt or pullover, and from 1924 so too did crown servants, members of the constabulary and other government employees. Clothes made of traditionally used materials were always quite legal.

The clothing regulations outlined above remained in force until 1941. Only then were most Papuans and New Guineans legally permitted to clothe themselves as modestly as many missionaries had preached they should.[45] In addition, those mountain-men who had taken to the regular use of soap and water were, for the first time, presented with a viable alternative to feeling cold: in place of the pig-grease with which they had traditionally smeared their bodies for warmth, shirts, pullovers and cardigans could now be worn.

The clothing regulations have had another unintended consequence. In the days when all indigenous employees were paid in cash and kind, the latter category had included the provision of a length of cloth—called a *rami* in Motu, and a *laplap* in Pidgin—to be worn around the waist, by males and females alike, in the manner of a skirt. Few Papuan and New Guinean men could afford a pair of shorts, and some Europeans discouraged their purchase by indigenes as presumptuous (and claimed them to be contrary to the regulations compelling adult males to wear a loincloth—which they insisted be worn over an indigene's pair of shorts). The old waist-cloths were, in consequence, resented as reflecting the inferior social status and rights of the indigenes.

By 1964, however, even the police had succeeded in impressing upon their superiors the need for a new uniform with shorts instead of a waist-cloth. Now, only some hotel bar-men and waiters, village constables, administration interpreters and aid post orderlies wear a *laplap*, and resentment in some sophisticated circles has been replaced by pride. A *laplap* is regarded by some comparatively well-educated graduates of the old regulations as a special sort of badge—a symbol of one's colour, and a mark of affinity with the traditional waist-cloth-wearers of the other Pacific islands. Indeed, a former student of mine, used to employ his *laplap* as a sort of weather-gauge: when he was happy with the world, eager for progress, or just plain conformist, he would wear shorts, long socks, and black shoes to lectures. However, when he was angry, specifically with the Australian government, or white men generally, he would arrive for work clothed in a Fijian *sulu* or waist-cloth and sandals. A handful of the more radical members of the first House of Assembly seemed to wear their *sulus* too, as a form of sartorial protest against the conservative, suit-wearing majority.

(*ii*) Urbanisation

Port Moresby in 1938, seemed to one of Murray's most famous magistrates, Jack Hides, to be to Papua

'. . . what Rome was to that ancient civilization. There all roads meet. Port Moresby is the seat of Government; the constabulary headquarters is there; and the principal jail, where new "students" constantly arrive to take their course in breaking stones. From Port Moresby all news and learning are spread wherever police and labourers go.'[46]

Urban development has only recently become a problem in Papua and New Guinea. Until the 1960s, and then only by default, it was simply not allowed to become one. Papuans and New Guineans were allowed to work in town, and to go to gaol there. They were not allowed to live there. The towns of Papua and New Guinea were white men's towns, places where many Papuans and New Guineans are still made to feel quite alien.

Port Moresby and the other towns of Papua and New Guinea have never served as the political and social melting-pots which towns have been in other colonies and new states. Papuans and New Guineans have been restricted, and later discouraged, from coming there to meet people from distant areas, to exchange ideas and undergo new experiences; in short, to suffer the difficulties and excitements of detribalisation. Instead, the indigenous people of both territories have been encouraged to maintain, and protected from the disruption of, the integrity of village life. They were actively discouraged from seeking more than temporary urban employment, even when they were able to obtain the sort of education that made such a proposition viable.

The officially gazetted towns of Papua by 1950 were: the administrative centre for the territory, Port Moresby, and Rouna in the mountains nearby; Daru, in the west; Buna in the north; and Samarai, Kulumadau (on Woodlark Island) and Bwagaoia (on Misima Island) in the east. They were all administrative centres and/or close to areas of comparatively intense European commercial and mining activity. Their location and the manner of their administration bore little relation to the needs, and potential requirements for development, of the indigenous population.

Indeed, no attempt was made even to cater for the problems of the Papuans when they did come to town. Labourers were usually recruited without their wives; they were housed in barracks; and their movements around town were restricted.

Unlike those colonial governments that have recognised the problems of urban drift, and have, therefore, attempted to control or organise lowcost housing areas by supplying them with roads, police and garbage disposal facilities, the Australian government has always ignored the problem. It has, in effect, attempted to discourage indigenous desires to come to town by making no provision for the indigenes when they do come, and by vigorously insisting on the maintenance of Australian standards of living, housing construction and maintenance. The unintended consequence has been a proliferation of substandard fringe settlements just outside the legal boundaries of the towns, and a widespread feeling among Papuans and New Guineans that they are aliens in town.

Before World War II, Port Moresby was, as Jack Hides pointed out, the centre of a particular kind of acculturation process—a place where European insecurities were allowed full play, and Papuans were allowed only for employment, and to bear witness to the overriding power of the government. Papuans were not wanted there unless brought; and, once there, their activities were strictly controlled. The texture of their urban existence must surely be one of the most important reasons for the slow development of nationalism among a people who were never allowed to mix freely together away from home, and to meet people from far-distant places. The only experience common to most Papuans has been a distant awareness that they all came under the same paternalistic 'native administration' system; in New Guinea, the plantations tended to be limited, if relatively uncongenial, meeting-grounds instead of the towns.

The villager who comes to town for the first time is generally also free for the first time in his life from the sources of restraint and security that contain and organise his life in the village. The administration's response has been to restrict his activities rather than channel or organise them. Papua's wouldbe urban dwellers were excluded from the towns rather than educated there.

In 1906, all Papuan labourers were required to be indoors, and in their assigned quarters, after 9 p.m. unless they were absent with the written permission of their employer, or had some other sufficient excuse. In 1925, the curfew was altered to last from 9 p.m. until daylight, although even a letter from one's employer could not allow an absence after 11 p.m.

The towns were the administrative and cultural centres of an employee culture for the Papuans. The wouldbe sightseer was a nuisance. In 1925, for example, Papuans were forbidden—naturally enough—wilfully to obstruct or impede the passage of other people along a road or path, and they were also subject to a fine for loitering upon any footway to the inconvenience of passers-by. In 1926, it was declared to be illegal for any Papuan other than a contract labourer, or a mission or government employee, to come within five miles of Port Moresby, or to Samarai, or to any other gazetted area, unless he were able to give a good account to a magistrate of his means of support. If the account were deficient in any respect, the magistrate could order an offender to return home, and if he did not do so within a reasonable time, then he could be forcibly removed to the prison nearest his home area for up to three months. From 1930, a Papuan who repeated this offence within six months was liable to six months imprisonment with hard labour. A Papuan who had been convicted of an offence against a white woman or girl was forbidden—under the Native Offenders' Exclusion Ordinance of 1930—ever to return to any town.

In 1922, it became illegal to be found on any town premises other than those of one's employer (if any) between 9 p.m. and 6 a.m. unless one had a lawful or a reasonable—both of which terms were left undefined—excuse. An invitation to be present upon such premises that was issued by a Papuan of either sex was, however, explicitly stated not to be a sufficiently lawful or reasonable excuse.

In 1931, the places to which the curfew provisions applied were more precisely defined. The forbidden areas of Port Moresby during curfew were laid down as embracing any 'lands, wharves, jetties, houses and buildings of any description, roads, streets and buildings' other than the quarters supplied by a man's employer. Further, the onus of proof lay upon the accused to furnish written evidence that he had his employer's permission to be absent from his assigned quarters, and it was specifically laid down that it was not a lawful or reasonable excuse to plead that one was present upon any premises at the invitation of another Papuan.

Gradually, then, Port Moresby, and other gazetted towns were sealed off from their surrounds. There was even a fence between the main peninsula on which Port Moresby was built, and the area where indigenous labourers were quartered.[47] If one were unemployed, Port Moresby was completely out of bounds during most of the night, and even those Papuans who were able to show that they had reasonable means of support would have had difficulty in walking to town, and back beyond the five mile limit, within the legal time. Only the surrounding bushland, and the small size of the local police force, effectively safeguarded them from arrest. In 1933, even those Papuans who were employed were excluded from the town area altogether unless required to wash their masters' dishes, or to sweep their floors. In that year, it became compulsory under the Native Labour Regulations for all Papuan employees other than domestic servants to be quartered outside the town area, and to have the written permission of a magistrate or a labour inspector to be in town after 7 p.m. In 1930, the administration had shown itself to be unhappy with the presence of Papuans from the Gulf and Delta Divisions in town. By 1933, it had evidently decided that it was best to keep all unemployed Papuans out of town, and all employees except domestic servants after seven o'clock at night.

One group of Papuans, the Hula from east of Port Moresby, was able to circumvent the regulations quite easily: they moored their boats between the high and low water marks upon the beach (which area was outside the town boundary), and could not be legally removed.[48] Their canoes, which also served as houses, provided evidence that they had an adequate means of support to be within five miles of the town, even after dark.

A number of other laws and regulations had primarily urban applications. In 1915, for example, Papuans were forbidden by regulations made under the Land Ordinance to trespass in the Port Moresby swimming baths or their adjacent premises, and in 1928, the same provision was extended to the Samarai baths. Even without these specific regulations, however, it would have been illegal for most—and certainly the least sophisticated—Papuans to bathe there: neck to knee clothing was compulsory in the baths, and most Papuans were forbidden to wear clothes above the waist. At Ela Beach, where Port Moresby's European population swam after World War II, the relevant authorities carefully 'avoided the trap which had closed on their counterparts in other colonial countries with a colour bar, by erecting two notices. One read *European Swimming Beach* and the other *No Dogs Allowed*'.[49]

The Places of Public Entertainment Ordinance of 1915 also had primarily urban application. Its subordinate regulations seemed to ensure that almost all urban entertainment was illegal, and, where legal, racially discriminatory in the manner of its presentation.

Under these regulations,

> 'Places of public entertainment to which Europeans and natives are admitted shall be provided with separate means of ingress, accommodation, and egress for Europeans and natives, placed and constructed to the satisfaction of the Director of Public Works.'

In addition, the Government Secretary or his appointees could prohibit the attendance of any Papuans at any place of public entertainment altogether, or at any given performance therein, and all films which Papuans were to be allowed to see were censored first. After 1926, films could no longer be shown at all if Europeans and Papuans were present at the same time, and this provision embraced even the theatre-owner's indigenous assistants. At other forms of public entertainment, separate seating for both races had still to be provided. In 1931, the regulations were liberalised somewhat, and recognised educational institutions were not only allowed to show films without a permit (though a magistrate could order that he be shown them first), but European members of staff were permitted to be present at a showing at the same time as their Papuan students.

Town was not a very exciting place to be, then, for most Papuans—at least when compared with what Australians could do there. Drinking, dancing and singing after 9 p.m., movement at night, and bathing in a swimming pool were all illegal. Films were censored—generally for the weaknesses they revealed about the ruling whites, or the socially upsetting ideas they might contain. From 1918, it was even illegal for a Papuan to allow himself to be filmed by any means capable eventually of being reproduced in moving pictures without a resident magistrate's permission.[50] But still the Papuans came to town . . . primarily to watch . . . . And, in 1930, a cautious government empowered European Officers of the Armed Constabulary (under the Police Offences Ordinance) to enter private premises and to search both that portion of them where Papuan employees were housed as well as canoes without a warrant. Papuan policemen could do the same only if an assault or trespass had been reported, and, in the case of canoes, only if they went in pairs, and if one of the pair were a sergeant.

Gradually, the outlines of a society that was almost completely cut in two began to emerge. Whatever the administrative reasons for the duality, many Papuans clearly resented being cut off even from the possibility of gaining access to what they wanted. The extent of their resentment and the degree of their dislike for Europeans are unclear—memories, rather than written records, constitute the bulk of the available evidence. That there was considerable interracial tension, rather than humble gratitude among the Papuans for the assistance rendered them by their benevolent white rulers, we do know. Why else was it necessary (in 1922) to introduce a regulation to control the behaviour of Papuans in their villages towards Europeans?— in the only place and situation where the balance of power was biased towards the Papuans. Even in their villages, Papuans were legally obliged to recognise their inferior social station:—

'If any native in or in the vicinity of any village—
  (a) uses any threatening, abusive, insulting, jeering or discrespectful language to any European; or
  (b) behaves in a threatening, abusive, insulting, jeering or disrespectful manner towards any European; or
  (c) begs for money, tobacco or other property from any European;
  (d) wilfully or wantonly throws any stone or other missile to the damage or danger of any person;
  (e) wilfully obstructs the passage of any vehicle [which was almost always European-owned], or holds on to any vehicle whether in motion or not;
he shall be guilty of an offence . . . .'

Papuans who were guilty of an offence against this regulation were liable to up to three months in gaol if they were fourteen years of age or over, and to up to ten strokes with a strap if they were younger.[51] Although they were legally forbidden to strike them, Europeans who abused, insulted, jeered or cast hurtful or racially biased slurs upon Papuans were not liable to being charged with committing any special offence at all. They could only be sued for slander, or libel. Where discrimination among people of different racial background was not legally enforced, it was illegal for Papuans.

(*iii*)    Protecting the Fair of the Fair Sex

A number of writers have devoted quite a deal of attention in recent years to exploring the role of sexual fears, fantasies, and rivalries, in generating interracial tensions in colonial society. O. Mannoni, in his book, *Prospero and Caliban,* for example, has carefully analysed how the casual sexual liaisons of the explorer and adventurer on the frontier are gradually replaced as settlement comes, by the permanence of marriage,[52] and the desire to protect one's family from the depredations of, and contamination by, the surrounding society.

In Madagascar, Monsieur Mannoni observed, 'the European women are far more racialist than the men'.[53] They are not itinerant exploiters of casual interpersonal relationships, but are accustomed to 'protection' by their men at home, and anxious to preserve the wholeness and traditional character of family life abroad.

With settlement, and the development of familial life, and a vigorous society-away-from-home, among the colonisers, direct interaction with the colonised becomes both more infrequent, and less personal. 'Native administration' is both systematic and detached. Directly gained knowledge, and the understanding born of shared experience, are supplanted by rumour and myth, second-hand knowledge gained from the files, and insecurity towards the colonised. In time, the colonisers begin to project upon a people who have not themselves changed, an unconscious 'mental derangement' as Jung called it. Gradually, the coloniser's image of the colonised becomes, as Mannoni points out, 'simply a reflection of . . . [the coloniser's] inner difficulties'.[54]

Many of the ordinances and regulations described above may be interpreted as the legal reactions of a colonial society afraid of the unknown; anxious as to the actions and reactions of a people it did not really know; fearful to avoid problems through an attempt at asserting its control, even over the private lives of its subjects. Whereas the protectorate administration had attempted to protect the Papuans from the sexual depredations of its own British subjects, the Australian administration of Papua sought to protect expatriate colonial society from either attack, or corruption, induced from without.

In pre-war Papua, the fears and fantasies of the colonisers were heightened by the inability of most Papuans and Europeans even to speak the same language. Police Motu, the official *lingua franca,* was spoken and understood by a minority of either race, and there was generally no alternative common language of communication available. Thus, with even the possibility of interracial communication rendered so remote, projection tended to serve instead of knowledge.

Many Papuans developed elaborate theories, founded on traditional beliefs, about where the white man came from, and how he gained his knowledge and material wealth. European society, for its part, generated as fanciful a set of beliefs about the customs and behaviour of the 'natives' as it was possible to have. In the end, fear of the unknown, and legend, replaced the mutual education derived from interaction.

According to this sort of analysis, the clothing regulations can be interpreted as an ambivalent attempt to make the Papuans more modest in their dress, while also preventing the primitive from aping the more civilised. 'If they look like us', so the argument runs, 'we may mistakenly expect them to act like us, and be hurt when the attempt fails; or they may even begin, again quite mistakenly, to aspire to supplant us.'

The regulations restricting the entry of Papuans to town, and especially their movement at night, may well be, on the lines of the foregoing analysis, the results of fear, of anxiety aroused at the prospect of dark-skinned prowlers and peeping eyes, lurking unseen in the night. At night, the very Europeans who so brashly and wantonly asserted their racial superiority, their right to be served first and to proceed unhindered on their way by day, kept fearfully to their houses, grateful to be legally safe from prowling Papuans. A special amendment to the Criminal Code (in 1920) made it an offence to loiter upon the curtilage of a dwelling house with intent indecently to insult or annoy a female within. This provision, which carried a penalty of up to a year's imprisonment for the guilty, was widely regarded as being especially designed to deal with 'peeping toms'.

Perhaps the most dramatic and important piece of evidence for any theory about the sexual antagonisms and projective fantasies of colonial society in pre-war Papua is the White Women's Protection Ordinance of 1926 (as amended in 1934, when the possession of knuckledusters was also separately outlawed).

Shortly before its passage, Sir Hubert Murray observed that Papua had hitherto been mercifully free of assaults by Papuans upon white women. Nearly every reported attack had proved upon investigation to be without foundation, and there had been only two or three serious cases to date.[55] However, during 1926, 'an epidemic of assaults by natives on white women' was reported, a phenomenon which Murray was inclined to attribute to 'the carelessness of the white women themselves, who do not seem to realise that a native is a man with a man's passions, and commonly very little self control'.[56] In 1929, there were a further two serious offences (one of indecent assault and one of attempted rape) upon white women,[57] and in his *Annual Report for the Year* 1933-34 Murray announced that a mission-educated Sergeant of the Armed Constabulary had been sentenced to death for an offence against a child.[58] When first enacted, then, the White Women's Protection Ordinance was the legislative product of anxiety, of doubts projected from the insecurities of Europeans upon the Papuans, rather than of social need. By 1929, it may, however, be said to have received a measure of subsequent justification, although injuring a person had been illegal under the Native Board Regulations since 1890, and so were rape and other forms of sexual assault under the Queensland Criminal Code.

Offences under the White Women's Protection Ordinance, then, were in a category of their own. To begin with, the penalty for rape or attempted rape against a European female was death, whereas the maximum penalties for the same offences under the Queensland Code were life imprisonment for rape, and fourteen years with hard labour for attempted rape. In 1934, the White Women's Protection Ordinance was amended so that a person who could be charged under the Criminal Code or the newer ordinance had to be charged under the latter. Indecent assault of a Papuan by another Papuan had carried a penalty of only six months imprisonment under the

Native Regulations since 1913. Under the new ordinance, unlawful or indecent assault and carnal knowledge could lead to imprisonment for life, with or without hard labour, and with or without a whipping. The number, and kind, of whippings to be administered to an offender were laid down with precision. Indigenous offenders under the ordinance were also excluded, under the Native Regulations (in 1926) from ever again entering the boundaries of any town in Papua, on pain of six months gaol for each such offence. Until then, the Commissioner for Native Affairs, had had the power (under the Native Labour Ordinance) to refuse to allow labourers who had committed an offence to re-engage, but not to send them home or to order that they stay there.

In essence, the White Women's Protection Ordinance was a product, *nonpareil*, of the anxieties and fantasies of colonial rule, and special measures were taken to ensure that Papuans throughout the territory were told of it. Indeed, a warning that the death penalty had been agreed to and would be enforced was translated, with the assistance of the missions, and widely circulated in the principal indigenous vernaculars. The ordinance stated quite explicitly that where a Papuan and a European woman suffered for the same offence (against them), the attacker of the second should be more severely punished. White women required, and got, greater protection under the law.[59]

Thus, Murray was not just reassuring a nervous white community, but was stating a simple fact about the effectiveness of his protective policies, when he wrote in 1925:—

> 'On the whole I should think that there are few civilized countries, if any, where life is so safe and serious crime so rare as in the settled parts of Papua to-day.'[60]

By the end of the 1930s, the towns were safe from crime; the Europeans from any meaningful contact with the Papuans; and the Papuans in the pacified areas were protected from the more violent and 'uncivilized' elements of their previous way of life, as well as from many of the disturbances of development. And then, in 1938, Father (now Bishop) Louis Vangeke returned from his studies for the priesthood in Madagascar to show up (deliberately or not) by his mere presence some of the absurdities and contradictions which had hitherto remained concealed within the general developmental policies and the particular administrative practices of the Murray administration. Not only did some Europeans resent the very existence of a Papuan who was better educated than themselves but, as Sir Hubert wrote to his niece:—

> '. . . a difficulty has arisen. Being a native . . . [Father Vangeke] is not allowed to drink any intoxicating liquor; but he is used to wine in Madagascar, all the other priests drink wine, and it seems hard that he should have to stand out of it. And we can not help him for it is an Australian statute [the Papua Act] that forbids him, and we can not alter an Australian statute. Then again, being a native, he can not be out after nine o'clock in any township, and he can not wear clothes on the upper part of his body—so, strictly speaking, he should say Mass stripped to the waist. But these are local regulations and we can remit them.'[61]

*The Style of German Administration*

Throughout British New Guinea, the administrative official was generally the effective colonial pioneer; in German New Guinea, it was usually the trader. This difference in the personnel who pioneered the frontier was an important element in the differences in both style and impact between the two territories' administrations.

Great Britain, it will be remembered, declared its protectorate in New Guinea with considerable reluctance. It acceded to the expansionist demands, and strategic fears of a foreign presence there, of the Australian states only after German interest in the area had become quite clear, albeit some weeks before the German protectorate was finally declared.

The German government, too, was not eager to become officially involved in New Guinea. Bismarck was not anxious to expand Germany's imperial responsibilities there except insofar as it seemed necessary to provide legal protection for pre-existing German settlements and investments. In August, 1884, therefore, he had reluctantly promised the immediate progenitors of the German New Guinea Company (*Deutsch Neuguinea-Kompagnie*)

'...protection...*after* the company had negotiated and taken possession...of harbours and stretches of coast for the purposes of cultivation and for the installation of trading settlements...' (emphasis added).[62]

Under Bismarck, the flag followed trade, provided that it did not cost too much to keep the flag flying afterwards.[63]

The Imperial German government was, as might be expected from the foregoing, even less interested in administering and developing its new possessions for their own sakes than the British. Indeed, within six months of the protectorate's declaration in December 1884, the German government proceeded to withdraw itself as much as possible from direct involvement in the area, and granted an Imperial Charter to the New Guinea Company. As 'against the obligation to meet the cost of and to maintain the government institutions, also the cost of an adequate legal system', the company was given 'the corresponding right of sovereignty together with the exclusive right to take into possession unclaimed land and to dispose over it and to conclude treaties with the natives over land and land rights,...under the supreme surveillance of...[the] government which will promulgate the necessary decrees for the preservation of vested rights of property and for the protection of the natives'. The Imperial German government retained direct responsibility only for the 'order and administration of justice as well as the regulation and direction of relations between the protectorate and foreign governments....'[64]

Except for a brief period—from 1889 to 1892—the German New Guinea Company was responsible for the protectorate's administration from 1884 until, in financial difficulties, it handed over to the German government in 1899. Naturally enough, the chartered company was rather less interested in administration and the expansion of control for their own sakes than the administrators of British New Guinea. Its policies and administrative activities were directed by the search for profit.

The New Guinea Company was, therefore, concerned with the safety of its own investments rather than pacification as such, and the development of village life. It intervened as little as was necessary for its own security in indigenous society. Under the company, the administration of German

New Guinea protected New Guineans from certain vices (for example, alcohol), and potential sources (excessive land alienation, adultery) and means (firearms and ammunition) of conflict with Europeans. In 1887, it also began to control the recruitment of New Guineans for labour overseas.[65] The German notion as to how much land could reasonably be alienated, however, was far more liberal (towards European economic interests) than the British, as were the conditions on which expatriate investors held their land—as direct owners rather than lessees from the colonial government. On the other hand, Asians and New Guineans who were not literate in a European language were not allowed to buy or lease alienated land at all. A few Asians eventually leased some land, but none ever owned any freehold.[66] When the Australian government took over in New Guinea, it returned a considerable amount of alienated land to the indigenes, and continued the land alienation procedures which had been introduced by the German government in 1902, and under which (as in Papua) the government alone was empowered to alienate land, which could then be leased to prospective planters and developers.

As mentioned above, pacification was not an end in itself under the company. Rather, pacification and settlement or labour recruitment went hand in hand. The administration was not concerned to intervene of its own accord in village life. Rather, it tended to intervene only when forced to, and, even then, as little as was necessary, in retaliation for attacks and raids, or a lack of co-operation by indigenous communities. The punitive raid was a more prevalent feature of the German administrative style than of the British.[67] S. W. Reed was not unique among historians of German rule in New Guinea when he wrote in *The Making of Modern New Guinea*:

> '. . . one inevitably receives the impression that native life was cheap in German times as compared with white life.'[68]

If the German administration of New Guinea was brutal—and it was so, especially under the company—it was at least quite definite as to the rights and status of New Guineans. In Papua, the desire to develop and protect the indigenes led to an uneasy balance between paternalistic intervention, and a racially-orientated lack of faith in indigenous abilities and potential. Many Papuans were never quite certain where they stood in European eyes, while the MacGregor tradition of unilateral administrative intervention into almost every aspect of village life gradually demoralised, and sapped the potential for initative, of what indigenous leadership there was.

In New Guinea, the Germans let New Guineans know more exactly where they stood: they had almost no status at all in expatriate society, except as labourers, although the structure and texture of their village lives were largely left alone. Where the two segments of society came into conflict, the Germans made sure that they prevailed. They were generally less interested, and also lacked the means, to intervene in village life unless forced to do so. But when they punished, they did so very thoroughly and definitely—through punitive expeditions against their attackers, hangings, imprisonment, floggings, and enforced hard labour (with or without a gaol sentence in addition), all of which punishments were authorised in 1888.[69]

Well might Sir Hubert Murray later criticise his German counterparts as being comparatively more brutal than his own administration, and more concerned with the development and improvement of towns than with his beloved 'outside work',[70] although he did have a high regard for Dr. Albert Hahl, who was the Imperial Judge from 1896 to 1899, and then Governor (including a brief spell as Acting Governor) of German New Guinea from 1901 until 1914.[71] When, after 1896, the German administration began to establish a 'native administration' system, however, it did say so by 'recognising' indigenous leaders and giving them new, defined responsibilities rather than 'creating' them from scratch. Not a few older New Guineans even today speak fondly of the German period. Time has given what was once brutality a new appearance of precise and thorough justice; racial prejudice at least made them certain as to their status. Yet, what these old men often call the *gudpela taim bipo* (Pidgin for 'the good old days'), before the Australians came, was different from what followed in at least one vital respect: men were men, and generally left alone, rather than dependents.

The earliest German criminal regulations for the New Guineans were but unadorned extensions of domestic German law. The means whereby they were enforced—for example, through a punitive raid—rather than their substance, were adapted to local circumstance. Even the law forbidding adultery was probably an application of domestic law, rather than the elaborate adaptation to peculiar overseas conditions it was supposed to be in Papua.

Under the 1888 criminal law for New Guineans, the German New Guinea Company was specifically empowered to arrest and penalise New Guineans for transgressions of the law. In general, however, prosecutions could only be launched for what were crimes or misdemeanours under German domestic law, and judgments and penalties too were supposed to follow current practice in the metropolitan country.

The death penalty was provided for murder, arson or killing in the execution of another criminal offence. Riot, rebellion, serious assaults, indecent assaults, rape and robbery were all offences for which imprisonment, with not less than six months hard labour, was prescribed, and two years if someone were killed in the process. Persons accused of these offences were legally entitled to the protection of qualified counsel.

If the judgments meted out to indigenous offenders were often harsh, they were arrived at with the assistance of two indigenous assessors who could be appointed to assist each judge. In addition, some concession was made to local custom in the law, specifically to the principle of reciprocity in indigenous society: where a sufferer from some form of attack was customarily entitled to compensation from his attacker, the judge could—if the local chiefs confirmed the existence of the practice—order such compensation to be recognised as part of his judgment.[72]

Very little serious attention at all was paid to the problems of 'native administration' in New Guinea, either by the German New Guinea Company or the Imperial government itself, until 1896. In that year, Dr. Albert Hahl, who initiated and developed what administrative system there was before 1914, arrived in New Guinea as a judge. His actual duties were more than those of a normal judge however, as he later wrote:

> 'I was the judge of first instance, was responsible for general administration, was endowed with consular powers, looked after tariff, harbour and quarantine matters, and was registrar of births, deaths and marriages.'[73]

Within a year of his arrival in New Guinea, he had also established the territory's first indigenous police force, and begun to lay the outlines of a full-scale system of village administration. He was—as deputy governor from 1901, and governor from 1902 until 1914—the architect of New Guinea's administrative system.

Although most of the standard histories, like this chapter, treat the pre-war histories of Papua and New Guinea as two separate entities, there were, in fact, more similarities and cross-influences[74] between the two than are generally supposed. Both Hahl and MacGregor, for example, believed in the use of force when establishing the government's authority. Unlike Mac-Gregor, however, Hahl survived into a period when such a belief was no longer fashionable—for long enough to give the German administration a reputation for brutality, especially in the unctuous eyes of Papua's Australian administrators. Hahl's police force was also largely set up (in 1896) on the same lines as MacGregor's. Generally, however, Hahl's administrative system was less inclined towards unilateral intervention in village life than Mac-Gregor's, and ultimately, therefore, less demoralising in its effects on indigenous leaders and initiative. The Papuan head-tax, which was introduced in 1918, on the other hand, was probably derived, at least in part, from Hahl's model, which was instituted in 1907—to force more indigenes into the cash economy (and, therefore, to increase the available labour supply), and to ensure that the development of indigenous society was paid for primarily from within. The *kiap's* (Pidgin for 'patrol officer's') plantations that were compulsorily developed in many New Guinean villages were a product of this policy.

The first village officials in German New Guinea were appointed by Hahl in 1896. They were not so much appointed servants of the government as leaders, who were 'recognised' and granted certain specific powers, which they exercised on the governments behalf, in addition to the powers that derived from their traditional authority.

There is some doubt among anthropologists as to who the *luluai* was, and what he did, in pre-contact Tolai society.[75] He was definitely powerful in war and also in land matters, however, and may have been—quite exceptionally for Melanesia—the holder of a position and a title, rather than an individual who had acquired his authority purely by virtue of his personal achievements. To the extent that the *luluai* was an office-holder rather than an influential leader, so was his position inappropriate as a model for most New Guinean societies.

As an appointed official of the colonial administration, however, the *luluai* nonetheless remained a recognised local leader rather than an appointed servant of the government. He received a uniform, but not a salary. He had the authority to arbitrate in local disputes, to settle local level court cases, and to represent his people to the government. His executive tasks—for example, supervising his village's compulsory roadwork, or collecting the head-tax (for which he retained a ten per cent commission)—were really only added as an afterthought.[76] In Papua, on the other hand, village councillors were only appointed after 1921, to advise the resident magistrate of the people's wishes, while the village constable enforced the law. In New Guinea, leadership only gradually gave way to administration, specifically when the Australian government undertook responsibility for the area's government, and redefined the *luluai's* role in 1921-2, as follows:—

> 'He acts as representative of the Administration in the village, and sees that all orders and regulations are observed. He is responsible

for maintaining good order, and he reports promptly to the Administration any breach of the peace or irregularity that may occur. He adjudicates in quarrels on minor matters of difference among the people.'[77]

The Australians, in short, emasculated the *luluai's* position.[78] The wise leader and arbitrator of his people became a servant of the government, a mere law-enforcer (albeit still with considerably greater judicial powers than the Papuan village constable).

Under the Germans, the *luluai's* role as local leader was accentuated by the lack of a requirement that he even speak the *lingua franca,* Pidgin. Communication between the *kiap* and the *luluai* was through a Pidgin-speaking *tultul,* who also carried out the latter's administrative functions. A medical *tultul* was often appointed in many villages, to carry out the administration's health policies. By the middle of 1970, the *luluai* and the *tultul* were still the only medium of contact between the village and the government—other than the quadrennial House of Assembly elections—for 9.9% of the population of New Guinea.

The German administration in New Guinea never developed as complex a legal system for village administration as the British and Australians did in Papua. Lack of money for the task was, however, less important as a determinant of this policy, than lack of interest. The German government was simply not interested in the administrative aspects of development, nor overly concerned with the indigenes' longterm welfare. It was both harsher in approach, and less concerned with changing New Guinean society. Rather than train New Guineans for certain labouring tasks, or offer them additional inducements to work, or even pacify to increase the area from which recurits were drawn, the German administration was content to import Asian labour for the plantations. Unlike its counterpart in Papua, it was not concerned to maintain the 'White Australia' policy in immigration, even into the territories, although it did warn its sea-captains in 1894 not to allow those Chinese coolies who did not wish to return home to enter British ports in Australia, and British New Guinea.[79]

In 1907, Bernhard Dernburg, the first Secretary of State for (German) Colonies, gave a speech in which he outlined the principal elements in the Imperial government's colonial policy, as being the 'improvement of the soil, its resources, the flora and fauna but above all of the inhabitants for the benefit of the economy of the colonising nation which is obliged to give in return its higher culture, its moral concepts and its better methods'.[80] In return for much of their lands, and a great deal of labour, indigenous New Guineans received a regular system of centrally controlled village administration, a somewhat toughened version of contemporary German law, and the conventional colonial preachment to the colonised, to work harder for their own improvement. It would, however, be unfair to criticise the German record on its own, for the essential features of the German administrative system were carried on by its Australian successor, while the revised labour law that the Germans had proposed to introduce in 1915 was implemented (with a few changes) by the Australian military administration in the same year.

The regulations governing the New Guineans' lives under German rule were less restrictively protective and interventionist in character than their Papuan counterparts. In general, German law applied, with a few additions.

There was, perhaps, no time for the development of a separate system of special laws and regulations for 'the natives'.[81] Just as the British had done, however, the governor of German New Guinea ordered, in 1897, that (with some exceptions) firearms and ammunition be not supplied to ships manned only by New Guineans, although, after 1909, they were allowed to apply for permits to possess them. New Guineans were also forbidden to have explosives in their possession (in 1904), and spirituous liquor, although 'natives belonging to other coloured peoples' as well as New Guineans could, after 1909, apply for permits to drink.

In 1900, the German governor of New Guinea issued a special set of orders covering the employment and treatment of New Guinean labourers. The penalties were tougher than in Papua. A New Guinean who neglected his duty, for example, or was lazy, refractory, absent without cause or otherwise neglected his work, could be flogged or birched, confined in a separate room with or without chains, or fined. Once again, the conditions for a flogging were laid down with precision—although, as government officers could appoint other Europeans to act on their behalf in such cases, much of the detail as to who would be beaten how remained unchecked in practice. The pay, working hours, duties, days off, and provisions regarding the labourer's safe return home at the expiration of his contract were also laid down in the familiar way. Significantly, the German government was more concerned to regulate the working conditions and duties of New Guinean labourers than with other aspects of indigenous society. It did not attempt to regulate many other areas of indigenous life, except to require official approval for all transactions between 'natives and non-natives' in which a New Guinean was liable to pay money or other movable property, on pain of a penalty for the non-New Guineans involved (in 1909).

As regards the developmental aspect of its work, the German administration did not allow New Guineans to sell coconuts to Europeans except as copra. This had the effect of increasing the amount of work they had to do, as well as the money they received. After 1903, the goverment empowered its officials to require labour without payment from New Guineans for up to four weeks *per annum*, on works required as a result of natural calamities, as a form of war-service, or for the improvement of roads and government plantations. Although its provisions were more sweeping than those of its Papuan counterpart, the German regulation was not different in effect. It required New Guineans to work for 'development' as the government defined it, when and where it said, within limits set down, and enforced, by government officials.

If, however, the German administration of New Guinea was appreciably tougher in its demands and more ruthless in their execution, than its Papuan contemporary, the difference was one of style rather than legal substance. Its officers were hard and racially discriminatory, but, at the same time, quite certain of the indigenes' status, and less inclined to interfere in the domestic affairs of the village. The German administration was, in sum, less paternalistic and protective, more brutal and direct where it did intervene in indigenous society, than the MacGregor-Murray tradition had allowed its officers to be. German interests and activities in New Guinea, then, were of the classically imperialist kind—primarily directed towards economic gain. Administrative theory, and even practice, concern with the development and welfare of the indigenes, were all of quite secondary importance in the German Imperial tradition.

*The Australian Army in German New Guinea*

On September 12, 1914, those New Guineans who happened to be in Rabaul at the time were informed—in what officialdom mistook for Pidgin—that they now came under a 'new feller flag . . . belonga British (English); he more better than other feller . . . .' The Australian Naval and Military Expeditionary Force (the A.N.M.E.F.) had arrived, and captured what was now officially referred to as 'The Late German New Guinea'. As the proclamation of the Australian takeover said:

> ' . . . now you give three good feller cheers belongina new feller master.
>
> NO MORE 'UM KAISER.
> 'GOD SAVE 'UM KING.'

—primarily because 'he no fighting black boy alonga nothing'.[82] And so, again, the New Guineans who had attended the proclamation ceremony did as they were told, and New Guinea welcomed its latest group of uninvited rulers.

The Australian force's arrival in New Guinea changed little but the nationality of their rulers as far as most New Guineans could see. Existing labour contracts remained in force; and the territory's laws remained largely unchanged (but for their translation into English), as militiary law required. As the Australian government reported to the League of Nations in 1922:

> 'It was the object of the [military] Administration to follow the German law and to retain the German arrangements for government, so far as was possible in the circumstances of a military occupation, and to maintain the economic condition of the Territory in the state in which it was found at the commencement of the occupation . . . .'[83]

Uncertainty as to the territory's future, and inexperience in colonial administration on the part of its temporary rulers, ensured continuity in both the style of execution and the substance, of the law. The Australian government favoured outright annexation; President Wilson advocated a mandate with Australia as trustee; while Sir Hubert Murray hoped to become the chief administrator of a combined territory of Papua and New Guinea. Until the territory's constitutional status was resolved, with the granting of a League of Nations C class mandate in 1921, it was better, then, to do nothing to compromise the future. In the interim, an ignorant and inexperienced administration found the advice of the pre-war settlers not unhelpful. There were, after all, few alternative counsellors available. Indeed, until the translation of the German laws into English began in April 1915, the pre-war German settlers had virtual control over even the administration's access to the past.

Rabaul, which remained the administrative centre of New Guinea after 1914, was divided into three quarters: 'Rabaul proper', where more than 1,600 Europeans (of whom more than 1,100 were Germans) lived; Chinatown where about 1,450 'non-indigenous natives', including Malays, dwelt; and the Native Compound, with a population of nearly 200 'police boys', and 300 contract labourers, including thirty women. The territory's 236 Japanese were treated, by both the German and Australian administrations as honorary whites, and lived and were buried with their 'fellow Europeans'. The Chinese (who were generally treated as New Guineans with certain special privileges), and the New Guineans themselves had their own separate cemeteries and living quarters.[84] The New Guineans who lived and worked in town lived in big barracks, 'only the "boss boys" and their Marys having small wooden huts, one room being allotted to each couple. In the native compound ... [was] also situated the police-masters' residence, the jails [one each for Europeans, Asians, and New Guineans], magazine and the Government stables.'[85] The Chinese and the New Guineans represented, in effect, two successive generations of indentured labour; the Chinese having been brought in by the Germans until New Guinean labour became more efficient and readily available, and until the 'White Australia' policy was applied.

The first Administration Order issued by the new military government was of a kind similar to those that have characterised the early days of a military occupation elsewhere. All inhabitants were required to submit to the directions of the officers of the occupying force; there was a curfew between 10 p.m. and 6 a.m.; meetings, the printing, publication and issuing of newspapers, circulars or printed matter, and the sale or manufacture of alcohol were all outlawed. If telegraph or telephone lines were injured and those responsible could not be discovered, the inhabitants of the neighbourhood where the damage was inflicted were to be fined.[86] Among the more charming precautions taken for the war were the requirement that the owners of homing or carrier pigeons should have a permit, and a provision (also under the War Precautions Order) forbidding non-British subjects from changing their names, except in the case of women who married after the commencement of the war. Under Garrison Standing Orders, New Guineans were forbidden entry to the barracks, and all visitors to Company quarters. No one other than officers of the garrison and the military police when wearing their badges, was allowed to visit Chinatown without permission. Early in 1915, in an attempt to prevent the spread of dysentry and to tighten up on discipline generally, the military posted a New Guinean policeman at the roads entering the town, and two on the foreshore, 'to prevent back-country natives from entering Rabaul'; soldiers were forbidden to visit villages; holiday trips were declared to be illegal for local New Guineans; fruit and vegetables were ordered to be dipped in boiling water if they were to be eaten uncooked; dysentery was to be treated immediately; and a detailed set of sanitation measures, dealing mainly with stagnant, unclean, drinking and aerated water, were introduced. In addition, those soldiers who had managed to befriend New Guineans across the legal barriers set down by the military administration were advised that 'under no circumstances will natives be permitted to accompany the Troops returning to Australia'. A few months later, the soldiers were forbidden to allow New Guineans to loiter about the barracks, and the curfew was amended so that it applied only to persons other than British subjects. While most German laws, and especially the labour law, remained in force, the German gun law was found to be inadequate. Henceforth, gun-licences were only to be issued to residents of 'localities where danger may be apprehended from the Natives', and the only to 'white men, who ... [were] held responsible for the conduct of such Natives in their employ, as may be named in the license as having permission to shoot birds or animals for food'.

In July 1915, the first translated 'Regulations Governing the Recruiting and Employment of Native Labourers' were published. For the time being, employers of New Guinean labourers were enabled to seek a licence to punish their employees for breaches of their duties (but not of the criminal law)—by flogging or birching them, if the employer had a licence, and paid due attention to the age (over sixteen), sex (male), and health (which had to be good) of the victim, as well as to the maximum number of strokes (ten per fortnight) which could be inflicted. If corporal chastisement were not enough, or an inappropriate form of punishment for a particular offence, a labourer's employer could fine him up to twenty marks (four months pay), to be deducted from his wages; or he could be confined in a single room for up to three days—with or without a light and with or without chains, for serious offences.

By August, 1915, someone in authority had evidently read the translated regulation, for corporal punishment was then restricted so that it could henceforth be administered only by government officials appointed to carry out a judge's order or the sentence of a court, although employers could still punish (through confinement, with or without chains and/or light) or fine their labourers for serious offences in relation to the duties imposed by their contract of service. However, if an employer flogged or chastised corporally in any other way, he could be fined (2,000 marks) or gaoled (for six months). In October of the same year, the application of corporal punishment was further curtailed—to serious crimes (such as murder, attempted murder, rape, sodomy, attempted sodomy and defilement of girls under twelve), the circumstances surrounding which presented features of cruelty, deliberation, violence, torture, or immorality. Early in 1916, District Officers were empowered to authorise floggings, and the range of crimes for which a flogging could be ordered was extended to include cases of (attempted) assault, robbery, theft, arson, gross insubordination and desertion from employment in which the aforementioned circumstances or 'defiance of authority' were special features. The length of a labourer's term of imprisonment could also be added to the length of his contract.

However, despite the restriction of flogging to officials, it seems quite likely that the practice did not disappear among the planters overnight.[87] Early in 1918, it became illegal for an employer to deprive a detained or confined labourer of daylight, although chains could still be used, a situation which Sir Hubert Murray thought would be impossible in a British colony.[88] At the same time, adultery and the making of false statements at an enquiry conducted by a District Officer were added to the list of offences for which a flogging could be ordered, as was housebreaking in 1919. In May of 1919, flogging was completely outlawed, although the prevalent opinion among expatriates in New Guinea, even the officials, was that its abolition, at the behest of the Australian government, was a mistake.[89] Thus, it is not perhaps surprising to find that the legislation of the Australian Army's Field Punishment No. 1, in 1920, for use as a punishment for offences of a serious nature, represented no more than the granting of legal power to do what was already being done illegally.[90] The punishment, which remained in force until 1922, could only be carried out with the approval of the Administrator, or where his consent could not be obtained without delay, that of a commissioned officer. The official description of the offender's position during its execution was as follows:—

'(A) He may be kept in irons, that is, in fetters or handcuffs, or both fetters and handcuffs, and may be secured so as to prevent his escape.

(B)  When in irons, he may be attached for a period or periods not
exceeding two hours in any one day to a fixed object, but he
must not be so attached during more than three out of any four
consecutive days, nor during Twenty-one days in all. (D) [*sic*]
Straps or ropes may be used for the purpose of these rules in lieu
of irons.

(C)  He may be subjected to the like labour, employment and
restraint, and dealt with in like manner as if he were under a
sentence of imprisonment with hard labour.'

The punishment had to be inflicted 'in such a manner as is calculated not
to cause injury or to leave any permanent mark on the offender', and it
had to be discontinued if a responsible medical officer felt that the continu-
ance of any portion of it 'would be prejudicial to the offender's health'.

Apart from the reforms wrought to the system of punishing offenders
against the law, the military administration changed very little of the legislation that was in force at the time of the Australian takeover. In 1915,
it declared the killing of deer and pheasants, the felling of trees upon the
foothills and slopes between Rabaul and nearby Namanula, and the making
and eating of 'Pipe na loun' from certain roots illegal, the last because of 'the
effect it induces of exciting a propensity to unrest and violence . . . .' New
Guineans found guilty of this offence could be fined up to two hundred
marks (the equivalent of more than three years pay). In 1916, labourers who
lost or damaged their employers' property could have its monetary value
deducted from their pay; labour recruiting was forbidden for varying periods
in New Ireland, New Hanover and parts of New Britain (in 1915), in
the Markham Valley, west of Aitape, Manam Island (in 1916), and later in
other areas (presumably, to prevent over-recruitment); and mission teachers
and students were exempted from paying head-tax (to encourage education). In 1918, a German ordinance forbidding the use of shell-money as
barter was rescinded, although in 1920 the use by Europeans of saucepans
from Siassi Island in barter was outlawed. In 1919, it became necessary for
a recruiter to inform a District Officer beforehand where he intended to seek
labour. In the same year, one minor form of legal differentiation between
men of different race was eliminated: henceforth, New Guineans had to pay
six (instead of two) shillings, from a monthly wage with a cash component
of five shillings for unskilled males and four shillings for females, to register
their dogs, although they still paid less than people of other races to attend
the cinema and the hospital.

In 1918, detailed regulations were issued concerning the use by the
public of the Rabaul Botanic Reserve, and in 1919 for the Kaewieng (now
spelt, 'Kavieng') Botanic Reserve. In both cases, New Guineans were forbidden to use garden seats and other conveniences provided for the public,
or—a superfluous provisions perhaps—to soil or disfigure them. They were
also forbidden to use seats and other conveniences in the avenues and streets
of either town. If a New Guinean transgressed the law in either reserve,
he could be charged in addition or instead under other laws, and, until 1919,
could, therefore, be corporally chastised for his offence. Perhaps the most
important symbol of the New Guinean's social and legal status—as labourer
or almost nothing—was the extremely wide range of his life which came
under the Native Labour Ordinance of 1917. This ordinance did more than
just set out the terms and conditions of employment; it extended even

into a precise delineation of who (not New Guineans without a permit) could go abroad, and why (to learn a trade or a profession), and as to the various classes of crime for which a flogging could be ordered (until 1919). Of the seventeen flogging offences (as of early 1918), only two—gross insubordination and desertion from employment—bore the remotest relationship to the New Guinean as labourer.

In the labour and employment field, the ordinance offered several forms of protection to New Guineans: their pay, conditions and hours of work, the requirement of a passage home at the expiration of a contract and that wages be paid in current coinage rather than counters or tokens, and some protection from ill use by an employer, were all laid down. They were even protected from themselves by a provision rendering it illegal for a labourer to sell or barter his approved rations (although, in practice, the compulsory tobacco ration was excluded from this provision), or to receive the rations of another man. In return for the legal requirement that each labourer be supplied with a loincloth, a blanket, bowl and spoon, the law ensured that their recipients would not be 'spoiled': the cost of the last three items and of any loss or damage caused to another person could be compulsorily deducted from each labourer's meagre salary by his employer.

In order to see that someone 'ran' the village, *luluais, tultuls* and traditional chiefs were forbidden to 'sign on'. In addition, the order issued by the Administrator, Colonel S. A. Pethebridge, in 1916, that 'Interference with native women is strictly prohibited' remained unmodified: from 1917 on, unmarried females (who had to be at least nine years of age) could be employed as domestic servants only by married European women who possessed a special permit; and if a married woman were recruited with her husband, and the marriage then broke up, the woman had (as from 1918) to be returned to her place of recruitment.

A person's racial origins, occupation and social and legal status tended to correspond quite closely in New Guinea. New Guineans, for example, were not even regarded as potential employers. Labour-recruiting was legally restricted to Europeans, people with 'the same rights as Europeans' (that is, Japanese), and, only later, to some Chinese. In 1917, it even became illegal for a recruiter or a ship's master to send a New Guinean ashore, armed or not, to recruit for him, unless the New Guinean were 'in the personal company of and under the personal charge or control of a . . . person having the status of a European.' New Guinean labourers who deserted their employers could be flogged and gaoled. If they held a naked light and endangered property, or did not help to put out a fire, they could be gaoled or fined. If, however, a New Guinean labourer were convicted for a crime, or created or fostered 'a bad influence among his fellow labourers', or endangered his employer's interests through disobedience or neglect of his duties, he could be dismissed. If he were very ill or insane or proved, through no fault of his own, 'unfitted for the work for which he . . . [was] recruited', he could again be sacked. If, however, a New Guinean wished to terminate his employment for his own reasons, he could do so only through mutual agreement with his employer. At least his employer was no longer legally empowered to flog him, or to punish him for criminal offences.

As the regulations concerning the granting of labour recruiting licences implied, the racial heterogeneity of New Guinea allowed the Australian administration to discriminate quite finely between the rights and duties of people of different racial backgrounds. In Papua, such finesse was virtually impossible until it was no longer relevant, for, until the late 1950s, only a single Chinese tailor, and his associates, were allowed into Papua (during the 1930s). Until the late 1950s, the 'White Australia' policy in immigration was applied quite firmly to Papua, and only a few mission-workers from other parts of the Pacific (the Solomons, Fiji, Samoa and Tonga, especially) and the handful of men mentioned above, slipped through the net.

New Guinea's curiously labelled 'non-indigenous natives', who were mainly Chinese or Malay in origin, were subject to a special set of regulations and restrictions. Only in October, 1915, was the section of the Native Labour Regulations authorising 'persons having the same rights as Europeans' to apply for recruiting licences amended 'to include Chinese of approved character who are engaged in a substantial business or who are planters on land leased or purchased by them',[91] while Chinese, Malays and persons of 'other non-European races' had to apply for special licences to purchase intoxicating liquor (without being allowed to take it from the saloon, hotel or tea-house where it was bought). Even after they had been brought into the same general legal system as Europeans and Japanese, in December 1915, the Chinese and Malays still lacked certain rights and privileges, especially in commerce. That they were, however, suspected by officialdom of having been able to circumvent some of their legal disabilities was implied by the coupling of the redefinition of their legal status with a prohibition on the acceptance by A.N.M.E.F. and administration officers of 'any gift present fee gratuity reward payment commission or consideration' from non-Europeans in a single ordinance.

In 1917, the Control of Chinese Trade Order came into force. It was, however, more important for what it tried to do than for what it actually achieved, for an embarrassed government withdrew the order after it had been in operation for only twenty-three days.

Under the order, Chinese persons, firms and companies were forbidden directly to import goods wholesale, or to export on their own or a client's behalf. The detailed provisions of the order revealed that it was designed at least as much to protect European, especially Australian, profit-margins (and, therefore, living standards), as to prevent exploitation of the New Guineans.

During the order's short-lived period of application, all Chinese exports were placed in the hands of the Controller of Customs, who could charge a commission of five percent. All imports for Chinese businessmen or planters required the controller's permission, and all such transactions could only be carried out by European firms, for a commission of twenty per cent of the value of the imports (half of which commission went to the controller as government revenue). In addition, all sales and wholesale deliveries whatsoever to or for Chinese required the controller's written consent, and this would only be forthcoming if the vendor's or deliverer's profit was at least twenty per cent of the value of the goods concerned. All defaulters under the order were liable to six months imprisonment or a fine of one hundred pounds, and confiscation of the goods involved in an illegal deal. And the controller was empowered to inspect a business's books to assist him in administering the law. Finally, to prevent exploitation, the controller could reduce both profits and charges (which were additional to normal import and export duties) where he saw fit. In 1920, all non-indigenes of non-European origin who were over fifteen years of age were required to register at the nearest district office and to produce a personal registration card upon demand. In addition, the lucrative trade in beer, wine and spirits for the troops was reserved for persons of European origin (and their employees) by an ordinance (of 1920) restricting liquor licences to sell to the A.N.M.E.F. to them alone.

After an order to regulate both the price and the barter-rate for coconuts and copra had been issued early in 1917, an additional Ordinance Relating to Trading in Copra and Coconuts, was applied on the Gazelle Peninsula from April 1917 until February 1918, to regulate trading between people of different races (generally, to the advantage of Europeans), and to apply pressure upon New Guineans to enter into the cash (and, therefore, tax-paying sector of the) economy. The ordinance contained a number of provisions of the familiar interventionist type, that have already been outlined in the section above on Papua.

To begin with, New Guineans were forbidden to pick (even their own) green coconuts except for food. Otherwise, they were to restrict themselves to making use—generally as copra—of coconuts that had already fallen to the ground. They were, however, not allowed to leave their coconuts on the ground for more than two months, or after they had begun to germinate, unless they had the Administrator's written permission. They were required to sell their coconuts, or to cut out their copra, and dispose of it to the nearest (European) trader with the least possible delay.

European businessmen, especially long-established companies, were also given some protection from certain kinds of competition (mainly by Chinese) under this ordinance. In the first place, New Guineans were forbidden to buy coconuts or copra on behalf of a trader or sub-trader except in those areas where trading stations did not already exist. In addition, all traders were ordered to stay near their own trading-stations. In other words, existing businesses were protected from competition by the indigenous agents of newcomers, and were also discouraged from entering one another's areas. Neither provision worked to the advantage of the New Guinean grower. Indeed, it was the trader who saved on every count: competition as such was restricted; 'free natives' (that is, New Guineans who had not signed an indentured labour contract) were ordered to deliver all of their coconuts and copra to the nearest trading-station; and, finally, an official rate of exchange, which had to be adhered to, prevented the indigenous seller from bargaining for more, or being forced to take less, than his copra's official value in tobacco, salmon, *lavalavas* (or waistcloths), etc. Europeans who breached the ordinance were liable to lose their licences, to be fined up to one hundred pounds, or to be gaoled for six month for each offence. New Guineans who did not want to sell their produce, who tried to get a better price in another area, or who traded for a European trader where this was illegal, were liable to imprisonment, as well as to 'be put to work upon the roads for any term not exceeding twelve months'. The onus of proof of compliance with the order was placed upon the person charged, although the officer conducting an enquiry or proceeding under the order was instructed 'to take all necessary steps to ensure that the various Chiefs of villages are adequately represented so that the interests of the Natives may be safeguarded in a fit and proper manner'. So important was the order that the Officer-in-charge of Native Affairs in Rabaul, and the District

Officer at Kokopo were instructed each to provide a constant patrol of 'Native Police in charge of a White Non-Commissioned Officer' to enforce it on the part of the Gazelle Peninsula which was his responsibility.

Upon the repealing of the Trading in Copra Ordinance early in 1918, a German regulation of 1903 came back into force. A licence to buy copra from a New Guinean was still compulsory, whatever the purchaser's race, while it remained illegal for New Guineans not to cut out the copra before selling to traders, unless the coconuts were being bought for planting or food, or the Administrator had expressly permitted the export of whole coconuts. In 1920, the purchasing of copra was confined to trading stations or to freehold or lease-hold land of which one of the parties to the transaction was the proprietor. A few months later, a potentially lucrative source of income for the dishonest labourer was closed off by a provision outlawing the purchase of copra from an indentured labourer.

Over all, the Australian military's administration of New Guinea from 1914 until 1921 tended to cleave fairly closely to the pre-war German legal pattern, and to follow the advice of the German settlers who remained in the less formalised areas of interracial relations. Most of the New Guinean policemen whom the Germans had recruited and trained were kept on,[92] and a number of German ordinances remained in force. After all, the Germans had known 'how to handle natives', and the military did not. An aloof Papuan administration preferred to wait until it could take over altogether, rather than render advice to the inexperienced military. Thus, as C. D. Rowley has written, 'the civil administration of the Mandated Territory of New Guinea commenced operation on 9 May 1921 without a native policy . . .',[93] other than a skeletal administrative structure and a loose set of racial attitudes inherited from the Germans. The period of New Guinea's military administration had seen few major changes: the nationality of the territory's rulers had been changed, as had the legal basis of their authority; trade with German firms had been outlawed, and German property expropriated,[94] without fundamentally altering the favourable attitude adopted by the incumbent administration towards expatriate commercial and planting activities; and then continuity was preserved through the permanent appointment of a substantial number of army men to positions within the new civilian administration. By 1921:

> 'The only signs of a new order were the doffing of uniforms by those holding civilian appointments, and the dispossession and shipping away of the Germans.'[95]

## Australian New Guinea

The Australian officials of the two pre-war administrations, as well as the expatriate planting and commercial communities, in Papua and New Guinea had scant regard for one another's attitudes and methods. Historians have tended to accept the apparent pattern of these antipathies very much at face value, and to treat the pre-war histories of Papua and New Guinea quite separately. It is the contention of this section of the chapter that, from the legal and administrative perspective adopted here, the differences were not as great as is generally supposed—more a matter of style than substance (hence the lack of detail in this section compared to the analysis of Papua, above). After all, the head of the New Guinea Department of Native Affairs in 1921 had been trained in Papua,[96] and two resident magistrates from the same territory were sent to New Guinea to assist in the establishment of the mandated territory's administration;[97] the Queensland Criminal Code and some nineteen Papuan ordinances (few of which, admittedly, impinged at all seriously upon indigenous society) were taken over and applied in New Guinea;[98] and both territorial administrations had to deal with similar kinds of people, and terrain, against a common Australian background of their own, under a single Commonwealth department.[99] In March, 1934, the department even organised a meeting, chaired by the Minister in charge of territories, of all of Australia's leading colonial administrators, from Papua, New Guinea, Nauru and Norfolk Island. In the circumstances, it would have been peculiar if there had been no cross-fertilisation of ideas. Nonetheless, the tensions and differences between the territories respective expatriate populations were quite real.

Throughout the inter-war period, the 'Papuans'—as many of the Australian settlers in Papua called themselves—were envious of the comparative affluence of the New Guinea administration. The New Guinea administration was economically self-supporting, at a higher level of affluence than the Papuan which had to rely on a small annual subvention—never more than fifty thousand pounds—from Australia. While official Papua unctuously despised the comparative harshness and alleged brutality (especially in obtaining, and maintaining, indigenous labour) in New Guinea, not a few Papuan settlers were enthusiastic about the 'realism' of the New Guinea administration's handling of the indigenes. New Guinea's settlers and officials, for their part, were contemptuous of Sir Hubert Murray's 'pampering' and 'mollycoddling' of his indigenous charges. Gradually, these mutual envies and contempts became part of the stock of political and social attitudes that developed among the Australians in either territory.

In 1920, Sir Hubert Murray was in a minority of one (to two) on the 'Royal Commission on Late German New Guinea' in favouring the two territories' administrative amalgamation (under himself, as their joint head). However, all of the members of the commission felt that the old German system of administration should be superseded. What was needed was the British system's tendency towards 'the fatherly supervision of the interests of the natives'.[100] In Murray's minority report, he claimed that considerations of economy and efficiency in administration, and the similarities between the geography, the racial characteristics of the indigenes, the natural productions, and the economic development, of the two territories, all showed the value of amalgamation in furthering this aim.

However, in 1939, H. L. Murray, Sir Hubert's nephew and Official Secretary, and the 'Papuan' representative on the three-man Committee to Survey the Possibility of Establishing a Combined Administration of Papua and New Guinea, was carefully briefed to oppose amalgamation. By then, Sir Hubert was fearful that his own lifework would be undermined once the Papuan and New Guinean planters and investors gained access to one another's labour, and economic resources, respectively.[101] Now, H. L. Murray agreed with his two fellow-commissioners that the amalgamation of the two territories was both undesirable, and impracticable. The existence of two separate legal systems, and sets of administrative methods and conditions, as well as differences in the financial position of the two territories (plus the mandate), were all cited to lend credence to this view.[102]

The two territories' early official antipathies were often echoed in the private relations of their expatriate inhabitants. Officials, and planters, from the two territories rarely spoke to one another, except in a spirit of derogatory jocularity, on the ships from Sydney to 'the islands',[103] although there were occasional exchanges of sporting teams between Port Moresby and Wau.[104] During World War II, when most of the pre-war settlers from both territories had been evacuated to Australia, and shared a common interest in protecting the former *status quo* from its wouldbe reformers, their roof organisation, the Pacific Territories Association in Sydney, had an equal number of Papuan and New Guinean 'old hands' on its executive.[105] Within A.N.G.A.U. (the Australian New Guinea Administrative Unit), too, the army experienced difficulties caused through the rivalries of the two pre-war administrative services, which were now combined in uniform.

Generally, then, the two administrative services, and the territories' expatriate populations, thought of themselves as following two separate traditions. In fact, however, the Papuan Native Regulations and the Native Administrative Regulations which were promulgated in New Guinea in 1923, were very much alike and tended to change in much the same ways at the same times as one another. By the time that World War II reached the area in 1941-42, they differed only in detail, and especially in their style of execution. The paternalism and interventionist protectionism of the pre-war Papuan system had gradually come to New Guinea.

The immediate aims of the Australian administration in New Guinea in 1921 were, in effect, to tidy up and humanise the old German system, along lines not unlike those that then prevailed in Papua:

'(a) to stop evils which in the past have been connected with recruiting and in particular to encourage recruited native men to bring their wives with them.

(b) To improve the health of the natives.

(c) By the introduction of model villages, with cleaner and more moral surroundings, to create in the native a desire for better conditions.

(d) To encourage the natives to make plantations of useful trees and crops.

(e) To educate the natives.

(f) To introduce healthy forms of amusement.

(g) To extend the influence of the Administration through the parts of the Territory not yet under Government control.'[106]

Even the structure of the village administration system was altered along Papuan lines (as mentioned above), as the *luluais* lost their judicial powers, and became increasingly but law-enforcers.[107] During the 1920s, however, the Papuan administration, began to experiment with new forms of consultation—village councillors—and during the late 1930s, the New Guinea administration began to follow suit, and *kivungs* (or village committees)—with primarily dispute-settling functions—were set up near Rabaul.[108]

In general, New Guinea's Native Administration Regulations imposed harsher penalties than their Papuan counterparts—and, from 1923, all prison sentences for offences against the Native Administration Regulations, were deemed to 'be with hard labour unless it . . . [was] expressly enacted' that the reverse was to be the case. They were geared to the requirements of a plantation society, and only secondly to the protection of the village. In New

Guinea, the indigenes were always at least potential employees; in Papua, villagers, to be protected from the effects of uncontrolled social change, and economic exploitation. Many of the Native Administration Regulations were, however, directly derived from the MacGregor-Murray tradition of asserting the administration's right of unilateral intervention in the village, rather than the German tendency to concentrate its legislation upon the urban and commercial points of contact between the New Guinean and 'his' administrators.

In 1924, Colonel John Ainsworth, former Chief Native Commissioner in Kenya, was sent to New Guinea by the Australian government to report on the 'administrative arrangements and matters affecting the interests of the natives'. Although they dealt specifically with New Guinea alone, his comments provide a fascinating insight into the contemporary status of both the Papuan and—it could be argued, increasingly Papuan-influenced—New Guinean systems of 'native administration'. At that time, few of the field officers in New Guinea had had any experience of 'native affairs' or of judicial procedure, he observed, and the consequences of their inexperience, and the nature of the regulations, seemed quite clear:

> 'It seems to me that the provisions of the Native Administration Ordinance and the Regulations thereunder are—as they stand— so framed as to aim at a form of direct administration of native affairs by white officials, that cannot be helpful to the development of native society in the Territory; besides which, if the services of the native authorities are not developed and taken advantage of as fully as possible, more white officials will be necessary.'[109]

Neither Murray in Papua, nor his contemporaries as Administrator of New Guinea, Brigadier-Generals E. A. Wisdom (1921-32) and Thomas Griffiths (1932-4), and Sir Walter Ramsay McNicholl (1934-42), ever seriously heeded Ainsworth's prescient advice.

Like its Papuan counterpart, New Guinea's Native Administration Ordinance (of 1921) empowered the Administrator-in-Council to 'make regulations ... with regard to all matters relating to, or affecting, the good government and well-being of the natives'. And, despite Colonel Ainsworth's recommendation that both the Native Administration Ordinance and the regulations thereunder should generally be reconsidered,[110] the regulations that followed from 1923 continued in the Papuan tradition, both in their provisions for the village, as well as for the towns.

At the most general level, administration officers were given legal sanctions (in 1923) to ensure that all of their orders, and those of their village officials were obeyed.[111] In addition, *tultuls* were required to obey their *luluais* and both had to see to their people's adherence to the law, and could be removed for misbehaviour, or on grounds of their incapacity, by a district officer.[112] It was also compulsory for New Guineans to assist in the apprehension of an offender, if so requested.

As in Papua, *kiaps* were empowered to summon and try indigenes against whom no complaints had been laid. Indigenous witnesses could be summoned by a court, while 'non-natives' could only be requested to give evidence, to a Court for Native Affairs, a distinction between the official treatment accorded men of different race for which Colonel Ainsworth could see no clear reason, and which seemed to him 'to be open to adverse comment'.[113] And if mediation failed in civil cases, the *kiap's* decision could be legally enforced, through the threatened imposition of a fine, or imprisonment, for recalcitrants. Administration field officers were, however, legally supposed to 'take judicial notice of all native customs and give effect to them', unless they were inhumane, or contrary to law. They were required to do all they could to make themselves acquainted with such customs, and to record them.

In general, then, custom was to be allowed subject to the rest of the law, and certain discretionary powers. Thus, some traditional burial practices, or preservation of the dead in the village, as a mummy, were made illegal, as unhealthy, while the Administrator was, for example, empowered to forbid the customary marriage of an indigenous woman if she objected, and had been educated in European surroundings, or had acquired European habits. In the case of divorce, custom was regulated, in that a divorce was only valid, if it accorded with the customs of the woman's group. Wills, too, had to accord with custom (and the law), and, as in Papua, could not legally dispose of land (or things growing on, or attached to, it).

In the health field, customary guardians could be punished (as from 1940) for failing to ensure that children under fourteen years of age received medical assistance when it was required, and accessible. From 1923 on, *luluais* were required to report unusual amounts of sickness in their areas, and district officers could order a villager to be medically examined or treated, and a *luluai* or *tultul* to ensure that the villager was seen by a medical officer or assistant. Either a district officer or a *luluai* (or from 1924, a medical officer or assistant) could order a sick villager to be isolated, and *luluais* had to take those who were suffering from a venereal disease to hospital, and then report to the local *kiap*. In addition, New Guinean villagers could be ordered to present themselves for inoculation against disease (1923), to keep their houses well-built and their villages in a sanitary condition (1934), and to clean out drains and ditches in which mosquitoes were liable to breed (1940). Village water-supplies had also to be kept clean (1940), water-channels were not to be obstructed (1923), refuse had to be disposed of daily (1940), and latrines provided (also 1940).

More generally, but still at village level, able-bodied men could be ordered to plant, tend, harvest, and store crops for themselves and their families (1924), both to ensure that they had enough to eat themselves, as well as enable their more ready entrance into the cash economy.[114] Diseased or trespassing animals (on the second occasion) could be destroyed, but not consumed (1923). Attendance at an official census was compulsory, and it was illegal either to be absent oneself, or to assist another to avoid having his name recorded (1923). Under both these regulations (from 1933), and the Roads Maintenance Ordinance (1922), every owner, lessee or occupier of land was obliged to maintain the adjacent half-width of any road or track, on pain of a fine of two pounds. imprisonment for two months, or an order to recover the costs of such maintenance as was necessary from defaulters.

The range of offences covered by the Native Administration Regulations was similar to the Papuan model: sorcery, adultery, threats, assault, abuse, insults, obscene language, the spreading of false reports (all in 1923), homosexuality among males (in 1936), and riots (in 1940), were all illegal, and generally carried penalties of a fine of up to three pounds, or six months imprisonment, or both. The possession of alcohol (1923) and knuckledusters (1933); or razor-blades without lawful excuse (1933), the onus of proving which lay upon the offender, were all illegal. Bribery of village officials; the careless use of fire, or the use of fire by an individual where he had no traditional rights to its use, or did not warn his neighbours, and gambling, were also offences under the 1923 regulations, as was the misuse of authority (as in Papua). One minor provision which was unique to New Guinea was that requiring that animals and birds be carried only in baskets or crates capable of carrying the creature's entire weight. Breaches of this regulation carried a fine of one pound, or two months gaol, or both.

New Guineans who wished to travel were subject to much the same restrictions as Papuans. Potential emigrants required a permit to leave the territory altogether, while within the territory, it was illegal to remain in Rabaul (from 1932 to 1940), and then in any town, for more than four days without employment, or for a non-resident to enter there during the curfew hours. Otherwise, movement was relatively free, subject only to the Administrator's right to order the removal of a New Guinean whose continued residence in a district in 1924, and later (from 1930) a town or place, was detrimental to the peace and good order of that district, town or place, or was likely to be so. After 1927 (except during a brief lapse in 1929-30), the person being removed could be kept in custody while in process of removal. As from 1936, a New Guinean's freedom of movement could be restricted not only through forbidding him to remain somewhere, but through the issuance of an order by the Administrator preventing him or her from leaving a specified district, area or place without permission.

In 1923, District Officers were empowered to prevent New Guineans from proceeding into Districts which were in the *kiaps'* opinion hostile or dangerous to the lives of the indigenous visitors. Under the Uncontrolled Areas Ordinance of 1925—on which the Papuan ordinance of the same name was apparently modelled in 1936, until the 'uncontrolled areas' of Papua were thrown open in 1939[115]—the entry of non-indigenous non-officials into the unpacified areas of the territory was forbidden, unless the entrants had a permit. In this way, the administration hoped to prevent the exploitation of the unsophisticated and unpacified by outsiders, as well as to prevent bloodshed through the meeting of the two. In 1936, a provision was added to the Native Administration Regulations under which New Guineans could be forbidden to enter any area or place in which they were not under the immediate control of a European. The new measure had a threefold purpose: to protect the primitive—mainly Highlanders—from the sophisticated coastal New Guineans; to avoid conflict between the two groups; and to allow the administration to control the movement of particular groups of New Guineans into areas where they might come into conflict with the locals and/or would not be under direct government control.

New Guinea during the inter-war period was more highly urbanised (and less thoroughly explored and pacified) than Papua. It had, in short, more, and more isolated, islands of white security than Papua. During the period, more than a dozen towns were officially proclaimed: Rabaul and Kokopo (New Britain), Kavieng and Namatanai (New Ireland), Lorengau (in the Manus area), Kieta (in Bougainville), Madang, Morobe and Aitape (on the coast of the New Guinea mainland) during 1924; and Salamaua (in 1926), Wau (1930), Lae (1931) and Wewak (1937), which were all on the mainland too.

New Guineans who came to town were insecure: they could not for example, carry a weapon there after 1929, except to sell it, to remove it after buying it, or to carry it to or from work. The towns became a sort of (legally-enforced) neutral meeting-ground for hostile groups.

Life in town was not exciting either: the same curfew (9 p.m. to 6 a.m. after 1924, altered from 6.30 a.m. in 1923) applied as in Papua, and was enforced in Rabaul from 1923, Kavieng, Madang, Kokopo and Lorengau from 1924, and in every town from 1937, with the same maximum permitted extension as from 1932 (to 11 p.m.), unless the New Guinean, was out of town, or working.[116] Singsings could not be held (after 1929) without a district officer's permission, and, after 1940, they could be (but never were) outlawed in any given area altogether. Anyway, from 1923, all noise, shouting, beating of drums, singing and dancing had to cease at 9 p.m., while street games were illegal. Under the Native Labour Ordinance of 1922, New Guinean workers were legally cut off from the hustle and bustle of urban living as well as expatriate society by a provision requiring their huts to be built so that they neither adjoined nor faced any main street. Not only could New Guineans not be housed in or under houses in which Europeans usually resided unless they had a special permit, but their huts had to be at least one hundred yards from any road or street, and fifty feet from any European dwelling. From 1924, New Guineans had, under the Native Administration Regulations, to live on their employers' premises, or 'in a reserve set apart for the use of natives'. They were allowed to play sport only in specially proclaimed areas (1923), and needed a district officer's permission even to play football on their employers' land (1933). Under a series of regulations that were issued (under the Administrator's Powers Ordinance) in 1929, New Guineans were forbidden the use of 'any garden seat, arbour, summerhouse, or other convenience provided for the public' in the Rabaul Botanic Reserve, and of any seat or other convenience that was provided for public use in the public streets, roads, parks and gardens of Rabaul, Kavieng, Morobe, Madang, Namatanai, Aitape, Lorengau, Kokopo, and Kieta townships. Finally, New Guinean labourers and servants everywhere required special permission to attend (even an otherwise authorised) singsing after 11 p.m.—in case they might not be fresh for work on the morrow.

As in Papua, it was illegal (from 1923) for New Guineans to be photographed for moving or living pictures of a dramatic character without an official's permission,[117] while the films that they, in turn, could see were censored too. New Guinea's Cinematograph Films Regulations (which were made under the Administrator's Powers Ordinance in 1927), however, did not just require that all films be seen, and then perhaps cut, by an official before being shown to indigenes. They simply could not be shown at all unless they came under one or more of seven categories. Films which New Guineans were permitted to view at all had (a) to deal with educational matters; (b) to portray descriptions of scenery, or (c) travels or voyages, or (d) events of public importance or general interest; (e) to deal with industrial matters; (f) to portray cartoons, or (g) to be 'pictures in which all the actors taking part in the exhibition or the film are natives'. Films in which people of all races appeared had, in other words, to be of a relatively serious, uplifting kind, unless they were cartoons. And, under the Places of Entertainment Regulations (issued under the Licences Ordinance), the Government Secretary was empowered (in 1927) to prohibit the attendance of New Guineans at specific places of entertainment or performances, while in 1929 it was laid down that separate seating accommodation for indigenes and non-indigenes should be provided at such places.

The clothing regulations in New Guinea were much the same as Papua's, although, in one respect, they were carried to a further logical extreme. All New Guineans other than small children had to wear a loincloth (from 1923), and it was illegal for men to wear a non-traditional covering on the upper part of the body.[118] Under the Native Labour (Supplies and Rations) Regulations of 1927, female labourers could be issued with 'a sarong or other garment which adequately and decently covers the body of the native' in place of the usual monthly blouse and *lavalava*. Then, in 1934, New Guineans were forbidden to ride bicycles in Rabaul, unless they actually carried a government officer's written permission with them—reputedly, because they tended to get their waist-clothes caught up in the bicycle chain. They were, however, allowed to purchase cars and trucks.[119]

In general, the New Guinean administration's legislation during the mandate differed from that of its Papuan neighbour only in detail (especially in the precise punishment to be meted out for each offence), and in the timing of the introduction of some of its new measures and amendments. Where the differences were substantial, the New Guinean legislation tended to be harsher and to separate the races more firmly than its southern counterpart. In 1927, when the sexual anxieties of Papua's European population were at their height, the New Guinea Criminal Code was amended to inhibit the activities of 'peeping toms', through making it a misdemeanour to be upon the curtilage of a building with the intent indecently to insult or annoy its female inmates. At the same time, in cases involving carnal knowledge of a 'native girl', the averment that she was of under any one of a series of specified ages (each with its own penalties for the offender) did not have to be proved as it did in the case of European girls. Proof that the girl 'had developed a state of puberty' was acceptable as an absolute rebuttal and avoidance of any averment as to her age. In cases where there was some doubt as to whether the girl was legally a 'native' or not, the relevant Court was empowered to determine her status once it had seen the girl. And then, in 1934, in the same year that Papua's White Women's Protection Ordinance was amended, the New Guinean administration amended its Criminal Code so as to make white women almost completely inaccessible to New Guineans. Through two provisions that were the reciprocals of one another, the government declared:

> 'Any European woman who voluntarily permits any native (other than a native to whom she is married)[120] to have carnal knowledge of her shall be guilty of an indictable offence.'

*    *    *

> 'Any native having or attempting to have carnal knowledge of a European woman (other than a European woman to whom he is married) with her consent shall be guilty of an indictable offence.'

The penalty for an infringement against either provision was one year's imprisonment. Here indeed, it could be argued that sexual anxiety had induced officialdom to move beyond a situation in which social taboo and stern, informal prescription had maintained 'white prestige' and separation, to the employment of judicial sanctions to enforce them.[121]

Under the Police Offences Ordinance of 1925, a police officer (and from 1926, any member of the New Guinea Police Force) could, without a warrant, take into custody any person for whom he suspected a warrant had been issued, any person whom he believed to have been correctly charged with a felonious assault, and 'any native found committing, or suspected of having committed any crime, misdemeanour, or simple offence'. In 1941, the hand of white authority was strengthened yet again *vis-à-vis* that of the New Guinean population by an amendment to the Police Offences Ordinance which allowed any police officer—by definition a 'European Officer of Police or Warrant Officer'—who had been authorised by the Superintendent of Police or an Inspector to enter into and to search, without a warrant any house or land (and anything that they contained) which was ordinarily occupied exclusively by New Guineans, and to use force, if necessary, to do so. In addition, the same ordinance also contained what can only be described as one of the most absurd (and unintentionally discriminatory) provisions ever promulgated by a legislature in modern times —a dramatic demonstration of the truth in the proposition that the laws of one society (in this case, Queensland) are not always appropriate in another.

Throughout most of the inter-war period, it was an offence to be found anywhere in New Guinea 'with an unlawful intent... [and one's] face blackened or wearing felt or other slippers, or dressed or otherwise disguised ...'. In Papua, the slippers were not forbidden under the Queensland Criminal Code, although a blackened face earned a longer sentence than in New Guinea (three years with hard labour and seven years if the defendant had been previously convicted of a crime relating to property, instead of two years of simple imprisonment). Depending upon the definition of 'blackened', then—as an inherited cutaneous complexion, or as the product of applying colouring to the skin to hide at night—not only those Highlanders who traditionally wore charcoal on their faces, but, over all, nigh on two million persons were quite possibly guilty of an offence under this provision, according to a recent Crown Solicitor of Papua and New Guinea.[122]

Thus, New Guineans were legally prevented from dressing like, and effectively discouraged from consorting with, Australians, while, on the other side, the internal caste-rules of 'white prestige' were gradually reinforced too. In 1938, the Police Offences Ordinance was amended so that it became an offence, carrying a penalty of up to twelve months imprisonment, for 'Any person, not being a native or the child of a native, ... [to be] found lodging or wandering in company with any of the natives of the Territory ...', unless he or she could give a good account to a court that he or she had a lawful, fixed place of residence and adequate means of support, and that he or she was wandering or lodging with the indigenes for some temporary and legal occasion. An Australian who spent too much time with, rather than over, New Guineans, was thought to imperil the entire structure of territorial society, although, in fairness, one should also point out that this provision prevented the exploitation of New Guineans by beachcombers and loafers who tried to live off, through living with, them. By 1963, when this provision was finally repealed, the normal vagrancy provisions of the criminal law were deemed sufficient to protect New Guineans from exploitation by those few 'poor whites' who slipped past the scrutiny of the enforcers of the immigration laws.

## World War II

World War II is widely regarded 'as a kind of watershed in the development of race relations in [Papua and] New Guinea'.[123] It is, however, arguable that, although the Australian government's attitude towards, and actual involvement in, the social, political and economic development of Papua and New Guinea changed quite considerably, if not dramatically, during the war and early post-war years, the newly combined territories' problems and administrative systems retained considerable continuity with the pre-war past.[124] Indeed, very few of the new policies that were put forward, and accepted, in Canberra between 1942 and 1950 produced visible results at village-level until the 'reconstruction' process and been completed and 'development' could begin during the early 1950s. Nonetheless, the changes that did occur, such as the removal of penal sanctions from indentured labour contracts in 1947, and the improvement of indentured labourers' working conditions were of sufficient symbolic importance for many old-time residents of the two territories to see history as consisting of two periods, 'time now' and 'time before': the post- and pre-war periods.[125]

The expatriate populations of both Papua and New Guinea entered the war with greater self-assurance than they emerged with from it, for, during the war it became increasingly clear that whatever the nature of the past, and however great the territories' previous isolation from world affairs, the future would be different. The old colonial order was being questioned, even in Australia.

During the war, Australians heard a great deal about the 'Fuzzy Wuzzy Angels'.[126] Afterwards, many of the Australians who had served in 'the islands' and not a few of their indigenous assistants, began to romanticise what they had heard, or experienced for themselves, and even to believe their myths.[127] Only the pre-war settlers were caught: where once they had proudly claimed responsibility for the loyal hard work of the indigenes, they had now to denigrate it in order to secure their own positions, and, if possible, return to the pre-war *status quo*. Thus, the Murray years in Papua became a sort of golden age in the eyes of many pre-war settlers from both territories,[128] while many New Guineans began to perceive that not all white men were the same. Before the war, some of the indigenous inhabitants of the Markham Valley said, New Guinea had been ruled mainly by men whom they called 'the English' whose 'chief concern had been to "keep them in their place".' While many administrative officers obviously were still 'English', the war had brought a large number of 'Australians' to New Guinea, men who were 'better disposed towards . . . [New Guineans] and . . . more concerned for their welfare and their progress than their pre-war rulers'.[129]

During the war, a small body of academic and professional men who were then in uniform (in the Army's Directorate of Research and Civil Affairs), and missionaries who came mainly from the missions that were least heavily involved in the planation industry, began to press—with some success—for greater attention to be paid at the policy-making level in Canberra to the longterm prospects of improving the indigenes' welfare, and of including them too in the 'development' process. Their main short-term achievements were in the field of labour regulation, but it was from their plans and advocacy that the development of co-operatives and local government councils especially later proceeded.

For many Papuans and New Guineans, the most dramatic and immediate change brought by the war was the sudden departure of the two territories' expatriate communities in late 1941 and early 1942, which was followed by a short period of lawlessness and confusion as men who had been employed were left to loot and then to find their own way home. In mid-February 1942, civil administration was suspended in Papua, and from then on, until October 1945,[130] the Australian Army, through the Australian New Guinea Administrative Unit (A.N.G.A.U.), was the effective administration in those areas of Papua and New Guinea which were not under Japanese control. It combined the functions of a fighting unit, a government with almost total power under the Australian National Security (Emergency Control and External Territories) Regulations,[131] and the pre-war plantation industry, which A.N.G.A.U. effectively took over and continued to operate even after the pre-war settlers began to return in 1943.

Some Papuans and New Guineans supported the Japanese, and even sent their children to Japanese schools (in the Sepik).[132] Many fought heroically behind the Japanese lines for the Australians, or the seemingly wealthy Americans. Generally, however, they tended to acquiesce to whomever seemed to hold local sway, and did what they were told—as coastwatchers, soldiers, carriers and roadbuilders, for the Allies, or the Japanese. In the words of a man from Yasa, Manam Island:

> 'You see, we do not understand. We are just in the middle [of nowhere]. First the Germans came—and the Australians pushed them out. Then the Japanese pushed out the Australians. Later, the Australians and the Americans forced the Japanese to go. It is beyond us. We can do nothing, When a *kiap* . . . tells us to carry his baggage we have to do it. When a German told us to carry his baggage we had to obey. When a Japanese told us to carry his baggage we had to do it. If we did not we might be killed. All right, there it is. Take it or leave it. *Nogat tok.* I didn't say anything, that's just how it is, that's life.'[133]

The normal processes of civil administration simply ceased in some areas 'for the duration', or were restricted (and changed somewhat) to the compulsory recruitment of indigenous labourers and carriers. By the end of 1944, when perhaps 55,000 Papuans and New Guineans were serving the Allied cause in a variety of capacities, it seems true to say that 'the burden of war was weighing . . . more heavily, man for man [upon the indigenous people of the territory] than on the general run of Australian citizens.'[134]

In some areas, health services were increased and improved considerably by A.N.G.A.U. In others, the insensitivity of men with no previous experience of Papua and New Guinea, and the demands of war, created difficulties in the government's relations with the village people which were to persist well after the war was over.[135] However, despite the feeling of many officers of the pre-war Papuan field service that the Murray tradition of sympathetically despotic[136] rule was being 'swamped' by the larger number of pre-war *kiaps* and planters who now patrolled for A.N.G.A.U., one outside observer seemed to feel that many of the changes that occurred owed more to the subordination of peacetime practice to the exigencies of war than to the dominance of pre-war New Guinean administrative values over those that had pertained in Papua. As Mr. J. V. Barry, K.C., the royal commissioner who investigated the suspension of civil administration in Papua, observed:

> 'No administration possessing a military character could satisfactorily discharge the obligations of trusteeship in respect of the natives that have arisen from our acceptance of the Territory of Papua and of the obligations under the Mandate in respect of the Territory of New Guinea. The Australian New Guinea Administrative Unit . . . was an essential and invaluable body to meet the urgencies to which the Japanese assault on the island of New Guinea gave rise, and it has, from the military viewpoint, been successful in its handling of native affairs, but the fact that it is a military unit has meant that when the supposed needs of the Army have conflicted with the welfare of the natives, Army requirements have triumphed.'[137]

In addition, experienced field staff were in short supply, and there was a shortage of accurate guidance for the newcomers on the A.N.G.A.U. field-staff as to the nature of their responsibilities and the limits of their power.[138]

In principle, the Army was unable (legally) to commit any future Commonwealth government politically.[139] Nonetheless, two important precedents were set during the war: large sums of money were spent in Papua and New Guinea by an Australian government that later felt it owed a debt to those who had helped it to fight; and, as the war progressed, the two territories' administrations were effectively combined under a single military unit, A.N.G.A.U., with its headquarters in Port Moresby, the only major centre in either territory never to fall into Japanese hands. By the middle of 1943, the Army was not only the effective government of Papua and New Guinea, as well as its sole employer of often compulsorily recruited labour, but the plantation industry had been taken over and was being run by the Australian New Guinea Production Control Board.

During the war, Australians promised a great deal, both collectively and individually, directly and by implication, to their indigenous helpers.[140] Some Papuans and New Guineans can still recite the promises made to them at the end of the war by the commandant of A.N.G.A.U., Major-General B. M. Morris, word for word.

An interesting vignette concerning these promises of a 'new deal' after the war has been re-told by a New Guinean resident who was present when three thousand indigenous troops were assembled together at Vunakanau, on New Britain, for a final parade before being demobbed. Australia, they were told in Pidgin, was grateful to them; their future was assured; progress and development would be theirs. The Motu translation was, however, left to an officer of the pre-war Papuan administration, who translated: 'the war is over; go home quickly; don't steal anything; and don't be "bigheads" '.[141] On their way home, not a few soldiers and carriers had their war-time issues, and presents given them by grateful foreign troops, confiscated by administration field officers suspicious that they had been stolen.[142]

In Australia, however, what was, in fact, quite often but the enforced assistance of a conscripted labour-line, in a strange, half-comprehended war, was remembered afterwards as heroic co-operation. Sometimes it was; but very often it could not have been, simply because news of the war had deliberately been kept from many Papuans and New Guineans until the Japanese attacked. Considerations relevant to the preservation of white prestige had prevented a public admission of the likelihood of attack from the north.

Among the troops in Papua and New Guinea, there was a widespread and mindless self-confidence about the role of the Allies in the war. There was no real need to convince the indigenes of the justice of the Allied cause, for the whites were loved. As a booklet, entitled *You and the Native,* which was prepared on behalf of the General Headquarters in the South-west Pacific Area in 1943, for distribution to the troops, put it:

'The natives are used to us, as white men; they feel we belong, whereas the Japanese are in every respect strangers. Natives don't like strangers. Therefore, their natural inclination is to side with us.'[143]

In addition:

'The native has always looked up to the white man. He admires him because of the marvellous things that white men at large can do—make electric torches, fly in aeroplanes, etc. You may not be marvellous yourself, but he will think you are, merely because you are one of the white race.'

And nearby was a picture of a European soldier with a puffed-out chest, and the caption: 'Worth Acting Up To.'[144]

At the policy-making level in Canberra, new plans for the future were being developed. In Papua and New Guinea, however, the men who knew from experience—not theory—'how to handle natives' set the pace. Experts in 'native affairs' advised the army, and the latter's officers learnt quickly. In time, even such 'new chums' to the Territory as Lieutenant-Colonel W. J. Reinhold—the officer-in-charge of the road-construction project across the roof of Papua and New Guinea from Bulldog to Wau—were prone to theorise, and give advice about race relations, as well as the indigenes' habits:

'Fraternisation between whites and natives must be deprecated.[148] The native reverences dignity and control in his superiors. Whoever neglects these and becomes familiar with him is at once no longer his superior. All natives have a deep-rooted regard for signs of authority, whether they be material or by character. Among his own people, the hats of the Tultul and Luluai, the stick of office that the boss boy carries, the belt of the police boy, are no vain trappings but are real and important to the native mind. No white man may shed his dignity and retain his status in the eye of the native . . . .

'Concentration of native work is necessary. Natives are gregarious. They move in masses, they sleep in masses, they live in close communities. Working them in a line that is as close as the work reasonably allows has three advantages—it makes supervision easier; it brings a mass effect to the task, and it allows competitive effort that the natives enjoy. The native does not like work. Work is a menial office that in the village is relegated to the women folk. But when he signs on to work he does it best with his fellows.'

There were, however, not just special ways in which to treat Papuans and New Guineans in order to get the best from them, but highly developed, and fanciful, speculations as to what they really liked:

'The native labour was supervised by ANGAU personnel, and amongst them were some of the most experienced men in New Guinea in the handling of natives and in the control of work. They were a tower of strength in inspiring others. As the result of experiment, a high efficiency of work and support was attained. It was found impossible to regard the natives as being generally more intelligent than white children of about the age of eight or nine years. They had much the same pleasures and outlook. To treat them as of more companionable age neither impressed them nor added to their pleasure or the task in hand. They lived in the immediate present. Like many children, they craftily sought all material advantages, but they were not concerned if unreasonable demands were not met. A boy, justly punished, never bore a grudge. But he did if punished unjustly.

'A guiding feature of control was there there be no humbug from either side. What is promised to them they expect, whether it be food, tobacco, rest days, or punishment for offences. Leniency that is based on weakness they appreciated at its true and only worth. But although (like white men) they may try to loaf and to take advantage of weak control, they will give full effort, without nonsense and amicably, however firm the control, if there is no humbug given to them.'

'Realists' such as Reinhold had no time for sentimental myths about 'Fuzzy Wuzzy Angels'. Such myths were not, he believed, borne out in practice:

'Feed him well, treat him justly, look to his health, and work him intelligently and firmly. The native works magnificently when handled correctly but, like ourselves, he is no angel.'[146]

However, despite the official booklets and the advice of those with pre-war experience in either territory, the average soldier probably tended to treat the Papuan and New Guinean labourers with whom he came into contact with quite cheerful familiarity. The A.N.G.A.U. officers, who were in charge of the labourers, were, in fact, so concerned with the conduct of the troops in the Sepik that a special set of instructions was issued in the middle of 1945 to bring them back into line:—

'(a) Natives will, under no circumstances, be picked up or carried in jeeps. This in no way affects the carrying of natives in the back of large vehicles on duty.[147]

(b) No native will enter camp areas except on duty and then only under the supervision of Angau overseer or boss boy.

(c) Troops will not enter native compounds except on duty.

(d) Natives will not be allowed to visit picture shows or other forms of entertainment.

(e) Troops will have no dealings with natives outside the course of duty.

(f) Natives will not be given grenades or explosives for fishing.'[148]

Before leaving the real world of 'proper' techniques, and separate drinking taps, transport, messing and sleeping facilities,[149] and compulsory recruitment—a mere continuation, in extremity, of the pre-war *status quo*—one ought perhaps to turn again to *You and the Native*. After all, it had its touching, rather human side too, as in this quotation from an old New Guinea prospector:—

> 'Generally speaking, . . . natives civilised and uncivilised are friendly and therefore should be treated as friends, not as black bastards who intend to murder you at the slightest chance . . .,'[150]

as well as its more typically settler touches:—

> 'Joke with him [the native] by all means; even lark with him. He likes it as much as you do. But while you play the fool don't forget that you have to maintain that pose of superiority. Don't go too far.
>
> 'Don't deliberately descend to his level. He has not been used to that from the white man; he will consider it unfitting and think less of you.'[151]

It is only recently, now that Papuans and New Guineans are beginning to be allowed to make—and can also write—history, that the myths about the wartime combatants sharing a common cause, and common perils, have begun to be edged out by the bitterness and hostility of the conscripted who were then spurned, forgotten or mistreated.[152] Somewhere between the two sets of beliefs lies the truth. But it is a truth that arose out of the realities of interaction in emergency, rather than the narrow constraints of precisely laid down (and discriminatory) law.

### The Early Post-War Years

Colonial policies generally tend to reflect the domestic preoccupations of the government, or the assumptions implicit in the total national political culture, of the colonising power.[153] Before World War II, no Australian government took much interest in, nor had a systematic policy towards, Papua or New Guinea, apart from the generalised assumption that it was better, for defence reasons, for the territories to be in Australian than in foreign hands. Both administrations were, therefore, left relatively free to work out their own political and administrative balance, between the indigenes' putative interests (as conceived by expatriates), and the European settlers' fears, and economic interests. Before the war, Australians were as little interested in the problems of 'native administration' and development in their external territories as they were at home in the Aborigines.

The much-vaunted 'New Deal for the Natives' promised by the Australian Labor government during the war, for implementation once hostilities had ceased, was the first genuine policy-initiative (other than the various attempts at annexation) taken by an Australian government in 'the islands'. A number of its most important provisions, however, were but a continuation of A.N.G.A.U's *ad hoc* decisions during the war (the amalgamation of the two administrations, and the provision of government money for development), long-overdue reforms left over from the pre-war period, or measures designed to restore the territories to at least their pre-war level of affluence and amenity. Such measures as the decision to compensate many Papuans and New Guineans for damage or injury suffered during the war, and to rebuild the towns (and some villages), fell into the last category. Lae, for example, was deliberately set out into separate European, Chinese, Papuan, mixed race and general indigenous labour, housing areas,[154] while local European settlers were extremely critical of the administration's plan to rebuild Hanuabada village, near Port Moresby, at government expense. On the other hand, a number of the reforms that were promised or implemented, bore all the marks of being no more than extensions of traditional Labor foci of domestic political interest into Australia's dependencies.

In general, Labour promised to improve the standards, and quantity of indigenous welfare, health and education facilities, to foster economic development (through co-operatives, especially), and to provide for indigenous representation both in the combined territories' Legislative Council, and at village level (through native village councils). Labor's most detailed and precise reforms were concentrated in the field of labour and employment, the party's main traditional area of interest. In the labour field, reform was relatively easy to implement.

In the developmental categories for governmental action (health, education, political and economic development), however, the Labor government could do little. Throughout its period of office, reconstruction and repair absorbed most of the available funds and personnel, and development had to be left to the Australian Liberal-Country Party government, which came to power at the end of 1949. In these fields, only tokens of future change—some co-operatives, a few more schools, the beginnings of a public health policy, and the invitation of some Papuans to government house—were possible. But, as the first post-war Administrator (from 1945 to 1952) of Papua and New Guinea, Colonel J. K. Murray noted in 1946, a 'new spirit, new ideas, new demands and standards' seemed to have spread through the indigenous community during the war, and, he vowed:

> 'I do not propose to attempt, even if I could hope to succeed, to stifle that spirit so that European employers can return to the standards of a vanished world.'[155]

In the labour field, the government allowed all wartime labourers to return home to their villages when civil administration was restored—and as a symbol of its commitment to change, the first announcement that all existing labour contracts had been cancelled was made directly to the general public, over the radio, and in Motu.[156] Most of them had been impressed, rather than recruited of their own free will, and had worked harder and for longer than was usual. Against the protests of the planters, who were short of money after the war, and labour, because of the foregoing release, the government then scrapped the penal provisions in the Native Labour Ordinance,[157] in favour of allowing civil actions for desertion, neglect of duty, etc., and promised to abolish indentures altogether within five years. The pay for indigenous labourers was made uniform and raised to fifteen shillings per month, five shillings more than the pre-war Papuan minimum, and ten shillings more than the old New Guinea base, all plus keep; the minimum age for employment was raised to sixteen (a rise from fourteen, and twelve for domestics), the working week was shortened to 44 hours (from 55 in New Guinea and 50 in Papua), and the period of indenture was limited to one year (as opposed to a maximum of four years in pre-war Papua, and seven 'on the other side'). All of these changes, of course, probably made the business of 'native administration' easier, and less tense, and interracial relations, therefore, all the easier. In the interests of uniformity, it also became illegal in Papua, as it had been in New Guinea before the war, for an outsider to create disaffection towards their employer among indigenous employees. Clearly, the Australian Labor movement's philosophy had its limits in the territory. On the other hand, few changes at all were made in the pre-war Papuan Native Regulations or New Guinea's Native Administration Regulations, or in related areas of 'native administration' and interracial relations not specifically covered by them.

During the late 1940s, the Labor government quite unselfconsciously reported to the United Nations Trusteeship Council that, in New Guinea:—

> 'All elements of the population are secure in the enjoyment of human rights and fundamental freedoms without discrimination as to race, sex, language and religion.'[158]

Protection was not yet regarded as discrimination, and paternalism was the only safeguard against exploitation.

There were certainly some dramatic, if symbolic, gestures towards the building of a multiracial society. In 1944, the Minister for External Territories (Mr. E. J. Ward) refused to allow himself to be carried ashore from a boat by some Papuans. He preferred to take off his shoes and wade— a gesture that was widely derided by expatriates at the time, and not repeated by one of his successors as Minister for External Territories (Mr. C. E. Barnes), who allowed himself to be carried ashore by some Papuans in 1969.[159] In 1946, some Papuans visited government house for tea,[160] and earned the then Administrator of the territory (Colonel J. K. Murray) the title of which he is now reputedly most proud—'Kanaka Jack'. For some time, the old-time settlers—or 'B4s'—boycotted government house at a protest against even such token integration.

Although few of the pre-war regulations were changed, where there were differences between the two territories' previous practices, uniformity was aimed at.[161] Among the few, minor changes that were implemented were a reform of the New Guinea clothing regulations (in 1946), to bring them into line with the Papuan regulations of 1941, so that all dirty, wet or insanitary clothes were henceforth illegal to wear (unless the suspect had a reasonable excuse)—but not Western-style clothes in general. In 1947, the Cinematograph Censorship Regulations of both territories were simplified somewhat so that any District Officer was empowered to view a film that had been imported into the territory, and to censor it if in his view it were 'prejudicial to the public welfare or the morality of the community'. Express permission was, however, required for all films, even those that had been cleared for 'public exhibition', to be shown to an indigenous audience, and the Director of Education, any designated 'Censor', and (only) European Police Officers were given the authority to enter without charge and to view any film that was being shown. In 1948, attendance at a government census was made legally compulsory in Papua, and riotous behaviour was outlawed there too, as it had been in New Guinea in 1940. All but slight changes in the interest of uniformity, albeit still under two separate sets of territorial laws.

In 1946, Papuans and New Guineans were protected, for the first time, from one small type of discrimination. Under the Trading with Natives Ordinance of that year, all wouldbe salesmen to, or buyers from, Papuans and New Guineans required a licence, and were supposed to display both a price-list, and the weight on every package, as well as to issue receipts. Although Papuans and New Guineans were usually not allowed into most stores unless purchasing for a European, and had to be content to be served from a shutter at the side,[162] shopkeepers and other traders were henceforth compelled to charge indigenes and non-indigenes the same prices, and were further told that they

'... shall not, without reasonable cause, refuse to sell to a native any goods held ... for sale if the native tenders in cash, the price of the goods as shown in the price list ... .'

Papuans and New Guineans were now not only to be protected, from themselves, and others, but were given some small rights. The effectiveness with which an illiterate and submissive indigene could assert his rights against a wealthy European, who naturally knew everyone else who mattered in a small town, was not properly thought through at this stage; but a breakthrough had been made. As the Administrator saw it, the role of the administration in a plural society was a delicate one:—

'Where the European group interacts with the native group, institutions of culture contact arise, e.g. the native labour system or the forms of native Christianity, and the Europeans tend to insist that their notions and needs shall be the paramount factor in the shaping of these institutions. The native community is not able to exert an equal pressure for the protection of its desires and interests; hence the duty thrust upon the Administration to disentangle itself from its European associations and prejudices and hold the balance as fairly as it can between the groups ... .'[163]

### The Ending of Legally Enforced Discrimination

'The idea ... [of trusteeship] is a simple one. When we, a civilised people, accept the tasks of government in a country largely populated by a primitive and dependent people, we recognise that we are not governing them to serve our own advantage or to place our own gain above their welfare, but we consciously accept an obligation towards them and we regard ourselves as having a trust to discharge towards them. We have had seventy years of trusteeship in Papua and nearly forty years of trusteeship in the former mandated territory of New Guinea.'[164]

Thus spoke an increasingly self-conscious Minister for Territories in 1956. By then, trusteeship and paternalistic protection were no longer altogether fashionable ideas outside Australia. Elsewhere in the colonial world, the former stress on the need to protect the indigenous inhabitants of the colonies from being exploited and (mis-)led by the non-official members of their expatriate communities was being discarded in favour of an increasing official recognition and advocacy of the inevitability and imminence of self-determination, after which the interests of the new nations' citizens would have autonomously expressed primacy.

During the early 1950s, the process of building a multiracial society in Papua and New Guinea tended to be conceptualised as one in which the indigenes required protection, from themselves and others, in their own separate segment of society—and under white control. As time passed, however, and the pace of decolonisation elsewhere quickened, so the Australian government became ever more self-conscious—that is, self-aware as well as awkward and uneasy—about the content of its policy.

In its report to the United Nations Trusteeship Council on the administration of New Guinea during 1952-53, for example, the Australian government still denied that there was any racial discrimination there, although, for the first time it added a rider:—

> '... except to the extent that it is still considered necessary to pre-
> serve certain provisions relating to the indigenous inhabitants in order
> to protect their interests, particularly in such matters as land acqui-
> sition, trading and industrial matters.'[165]

It is debatable whether criticism of Australia's territorial policies at the United Nations constituted a form of pressure at the time, or simply served to make Australian policy-makers aware of the contemporary incongruity of their attitudes. Either way, the Minister for Territories, Mr. P. M. C. Hasluck—the first fulltime, and longest-serving incumbent (1951 to 1963) of that portfolio—seemed to become ever more aware of the need to justify his policies, as in the following section of the address already quoted:—

> 'It will probably be objected by those who love to deal with colonial
> problems by the use of cant phrases that ... [his policy as stated]
> is mere paternalism. We should remember that paternalism in its true
> nature is good. Paternalism should not be accepted as a term of
> abuse or criticism. At the same time, we need to be aware, as all
> fathers need to remind themselves, that the paternal attitude is only
> good for small children so long as they need the protection and the
> guidance of their parents. Paternalism becomes oppressive if it is
> carried too far and for too long, and if it is exercised not for the
> good of the children but for the comfort and well-being of the
> father. If it checks the growth of the child, after the child has grown
> up, then it can become a tyranny. A colonial power that recognises
> its paternal responsibilities must also be great enough and under-
> standing enough to be able to give up the duties and the privileges
> of fatherhood, no matter how emotionally satisfying they may be.'[166]

Less than two year later, the process of revising the laws of Papua and New Guinea to remove some of the more glaring examples of legislatively sanctioned and administratively enforced discrimination got under way. However, the cumulative effect of more than sixty years of 'native admini-stration' in Papua, and over forty years in New Guinea, required much more effort to undo than the simple repeal and revision of legislation. Indeed, some ten years after the foregoing ministerial defence of paternalism, when the more crudely discriminatory aspects of the concept had been largely stripped away from the protective, the prevailing attitude of the Administra-tion still seemed to a cautious Indian observer to be one of 'separateness':—

> 'For the people of New Guinea the good Australian Administrator
> has sympathy, even affection, but no sense of affinity. The "paternal-
> ism" strikes one as fairly genuine and there is pride and satisfaction
> at the achievements of the "native". But there is no concept, dream
> even, of a multiracial society.'[167]

The first two-thirds of the decade of the 1950s, were spent in tightening some regulations, liberalising others, and in evening out the application of a few more. In short, what legislative changes there were, were no more than variations upon a well-worn theme.

In 1950, for example, the curfew regulations were given greater flexi-bility, in that the Director of District Services and Native Affairs was empowered to vary the duration of the curfew for any public place or street; and liberalised, in that an employer's written permission—called a 'pass'—was deemed to provide sufficient authority for the normal hours to be disregarded. Under United Nations pressure, the curfew hours were reduced so that after 1955, they applied from 11 p.m. until 5 a.m. A United Nations Visiting Mission, in 1956, then used the lack of any evident rise in the urban crime rate in consequence of the reduction, as ammunition in its plea for total abolition of the curfew, while the Australian government sternly warned:—

> 'These people [the indigenes] cannot be expected to conform to a European code of ethics until they know what it is, and in the meantime in the interests of law and order and of safety, some restriction must be placed on free movement . . . .'[168]

The expatriate population was not alone in its fears and resentments at the sexual activities of people of another race at this time. Since the very beginnings of European contact in the area, one loophole had consistently been allowed in the regulations governing marriage and sexual relations between people of different races: white men had been free to seduce, or marry, indigenous women.

Finally, however, in 1951, this last avenue for miscegenation was partially sealed. Twenty-five years after the passage of the White Women's Protection Ordinance, and for four years after its repeal (that is, until 1962), Papuan and New Guinean women were legally shielded from some of the attentions of European men. Henceforth, white prestige was protected through the restrictions placed upon the comfortable pursuit of unmarried indigenous women, who were, in turn, protected from their white suitors —at the insistence of their own indigenous male leaders.[169] It was now illegal under the Native Women's Protection Ordinance for—

> '. . . a female native . . . to reside or be in or upon any premises or the curtilage of any premises occupied by any person other than a native between the hours of six o'clock in the evening and six o'clock in the morning, unless the occupier of the premises has obtained the prior written consent of the [local] District Commissioner . . . ,"

or the woman's husband was with her, or habitually lived upon the premises. The penalty for causing or permitting breaches of this law was a fine of one hundred pounds or six months imprisonment.

In 1954, the Native Women's Protection Ordinance was amended so that the Administrator could prohibit all non-indigenes from entering or being in a village or an area occupied solely by Papuans and New Guineans between 9 p.m. and 6 a.m. without a district officer's permission. Individuals and certain classes of persons (for example, doctors) could be exempted from any notice issued under this provision. In 1957, a female Papuan or New Guinean was allowed to live upon premises occupied by non-indigenes if she were accompanied by her husband, father, mother or guardian 'by native custom'—a slight liberalisation of the husband'only provision of 1951.

Other regulations with a primarily urban application were promulgated or amended during the period under review here. In 1950, the pre-war regulations forbidding the making of noise, shouting, beating of drums and dancing after 9 p.m. were repealed, although the provision that forbade the holding of a singsing in a New Guinean town without permission remained in force. In 1952, however, it became unlawful in both territories of the administrative union to make a noise by shouting, beating a drum or dancing during the curfew hours set down by the Department of District Administration if the noise were a nuisance to a resident of the town, although permission could still be given for a singsing to be held during these hours in New Guinea. In 1955, the hours of legally enforced silence were set down to last from 9 p.m. to 6 a.m., and remained so until both the noise and singsing regulations were repealed in 1959. In 1952, it became illegal in New Guinea (through a regulation that closely resembled a Papuan provision that came into force in 1922) for an indigene to be in another indigenous employee's quarters without the employer's permission. In the same year, it also became possible for a Papuan or New Guinean to seek permission to possess methylated spirits, for heating, and lighting purposes only, while administration medical assistants were permitted to employ alcoholic liquor for medicinal purposes. In 1953, an anxious administration forbade all indigenous employees to possess any weapons at all (including wooden swords), other than tomahawks, axes or knives required for their work, and Papuans and New Guineans were generally forbidden to carry weapons in town unless they were on their way to sell, or work with them, or *en route* to a hospital, a court, or to their village upon expiration of a 'native labour contract'. The Cinematograph Censorship Regulations were also amended—to allow for the movement of a film from Papua to New Guinea, and vice-versa, without being censored for a second time. However, a special permit to show a film to an indigenous audience remained necessary until 1962, when censorship of films, slides, and advertisements for the showing of both, became uniform for people of all races. Henceforth, films had to be blasphemous, indecent, obscene, injurious to morality, likely to incite to crime, offensive to people of a friendly country, or undesirable 'in the public interest' to be banned.[170] It is, however, of some interest to note that even after 1962, films were generally censored on racial, rather than moral, grounds—most recently, and notoriously, *The Comedians*, allegedly because it showed black Haitians mistreating whites.[171]

In 1951, the Samarai Swimming Baths By-Laws were relaxed so that swimmers need no longer wear neck-to-knee costumes. In 1952, the use of the facilities of the Rabaul Recreation Reserve was opened to all races, and the Port Moresby Recreation Reserve followed suit in 1954.

As early as 1946, Colonel J. K. Murray warned that it was impossible to 'continue to use the word *native* as if it meant less than *man*'[172] and in 1954, following United Nations practice, a circular from the Department of Territories forbade the official use of 'native' as a noun (the use of *boi* or 'boy' to describe adults had been outlawed some years earlier). Henceforth, Papuans and New Guineans were called 'indigenes' when they were officially referred to as the subjects or objects of a sentence, and as having 'native' attributes only when referred to adjectivally. However, in June 1956, Simogun, a fairly conservative nominated member of the Legislative Council, and one of its minority of three indigenous members, reported:—

> '... recently I have had meetings with many Papuan and New Guinea people and they ask me "Why does the Administration and the Europeans in this country refer to us as natives? All the time it is Native, Native, Native". We are Natives of this country, but the European is not called a Native he is called after the name of his

country, and we ask . . . that this custom of calling us Native now cease and we be known as Papuan men, New Guinea men, or Papuan women, New Guinea women. Natives ask me why we are called Natives and I assure you they are asking that the Administration ceases to use this word and to call them by the country in which they live.'[173]

In 1962, the United Nations Visiting Mission led by Sir Hugh Foot found the use of 'native' as a noun to be widespread still, albeit 'not . . . in a derogatory sense'.[174] In 1969, the Administrator of Papua and New Guinea issued a further circular to his officers banning the use of *boi* (or 'boy') again, *kanaka*, and *meri*, even in Pidgin, when speaking or writing of or to indigenes, and—a concession to multiracialism—the use of *masta* (or 'master') in return,[175] although all of these terms are still in frequent use, by people of all races.

In 1953, the Papuan Native Regulations were amended to bring them into line with their New Guinean counterparts, by making it illegal for a Papuan to remain within a town for more than four days without employment unless he or she were there to attend a hospital or court, were awaiting a passage home after the ending of a labour agreement, or had the permission of a Magistrate for Native Matters or that of a police officer. In 1957, the regulation restricting the entry of Papuans and New Guineans into the town was amended so as to give wider discretionary power to the *kiaps*. A new regulation was promulgated, which allowed a patrol officer to order any Papuan or New Guinean who left his area to return home. It was, however, formulated as a general vagrancy measure, to remove the simple sting of appearing just as an urban exclusion law:—

'A foreign Native [that is, one absent from his tribal area] who does not give a good account of his means of support to the satisfaction of a Court, when called upon to do so, may be ordered by the Court to return to his tribal area within such time as to the court may seem reasonable.'

In the same year, the Papuan Public Entertainment Regulations and the Places of Public Entertainment Regulations that applied in New Guinea were amended to allow the Administrator to permit the separate seating provisions for Europeans and indigenes to be dispensed with for a particular meeting, assembly, entertainment or exhibition. In 1958, the separate seating provision was dispensed with altogether. It was not until 1962, however, that the Administrator finally lost the power to prohibit the attendance of Papuans and New Guineans at particular places of public entertainment or performances therein.

The early 1950s were a period of relative legislative quiescence at village level. The administration still interfered when and where it chose, and became, if anything, even more protective. An increasing number of villages were placed off bounds to labour-recruiters, and, although the Liberal-Country Party government—unlike Labor—allowed Highlanders to be recruited to work on coastal plantations, recruitment there was kept firmly and exclusively in government hands.

In 1950, the Administrator was empowered to declare any area of the territory to be liable to famine, and to order the men there to plant as much food as he saw fit. After 1951, it became necessary to seek official permission to light a fire even on a man's own land, and, from 1953, the owner of an animal could be ordered to forbid its trespass upon 'non-native' land, if it were adequately fenced.

In 1952, the New Guinean Police Offences Ordinance was amended to restrict the power to arrest indigenous witnesses to people who were not residents of a town—that is, 'to cases in which it . . . [was] really essential.'[176] In 1953, the police were empowered in both territories to apprehend Papuan and New Guinean witnesses and to take them to a District Court in New Guinea or a Court of Petty Sessions in Papua as soon as 'reasonably practicable' for an order to segregate or detain them. From 1963 on, the courts alone could order a person of any race who was required as a witness to be detained.

In 1955, a number of Papuan regulations were amended in order to make them uniform with their New Guinean counterparts. The Administrator was empowered to declare any area of Papua to be one in which an indigene could not reside unless he were under the immediate control of a 'non'-Native'[177] (here the word reappeared as a noun, one year after Mr. Hasluck's aforementioned instruction).[178] Two areas of the New Britain District, and parts of the Namatanai and Kavieng subdistricts (of New Ireland) were proclaimed during the same year to be off-limits under the New Guinea regulation. The Papuan adultery regulation was amended to make it an offence for a married indigene to commit adultery and for an unmarried Papuan knowingly to have sexual intercourse with one who was married, and a complaint against an offender could henceforth be laid (as in New Guinea since the 1920s) by either spouse or by 'his or her nearest available relative'. It also became illegal in Papua to behave indecently or offensively as well as to speak or act in a threatening manner towards 'any person', and the penalty for a breach of this regulation was raised to a fine of three pounds or a sentence of six months imprisonment.

After 1956, all of the territory's discriminatory laws and 'native administration' regulations were progressively liberalised. The United Nations Visiting Mission of 1956 had been critical of the curfew laws, and other forms of discrimination, while the Australian government had become quite self-conscious as to how incongruous the authoritarian paternalism of the *kiap* and the preservation of a racially divided society must have appeared at the height of the anti-colonial world's push to independence. Change was, however, more probably the result of the Australian government's sense of being out of step, than of international pressure. While most of the rest of the colonial world prepared to leave, Australia began to liberalise the structure, and the legislation, of its rule. As yet, the indigenous population was too little educated, unorganised in modern forms, and too peripherally involved in extra-local affairs, for international anticolonialism to find any sizeable group of Papuans and New Guineans with whom it could make common cause.

During 1957, a few minor changes to the Native Administration Regulations, and the Native Regulations were introduced. *Kiaps*' courts were allowed to decide on the spot as to the rights to use and occupy, but not to own, land. The regulation compelling the supply of carriers for government patrols in Papua was amended to make such assistance purely voluntary (as it had always been, at least legally, in New Guinea), and that allowing for the removal of 'foreign natives' from an area repealed.

In 1958, Papuans and New Guineans were also allowed to buy tickets in approved lotteries, and to wager at certain sporting events.

Towards the end of the same year, Asians residing in the territory—less than a handful of whom had been allowed to enter Papua so far—were allowed to apply for naturalization as full Australian citizens. In 1957, however, the Minister for Territories had still to reassure a nervous expatriate population that this measure did not signify the end of the colonial order:—

> 'Those who will be affected by the decision are people living wholly in the European manner alongside, or integrated with the European community. They have no home except the Territory, and in all the implications of the term they can be regarded as good citizens.'[179]

After all, he added, those who wished to be naturalized had a good education in English, were Christian, and well fitted to be equal with other Australian citizens.

Gradually, the plurality of racially-determined social, political and economic statutes that had hitherto been a feature of Papua and New Guinea's colonial society was being reduced to two. Thus in 1962, people of mixed racial origins were allowed to apply for Australian citizenship too, although the government seemed reluctant to accede to their requests (at least until 1964).[180] At time of writing, most of Papua and New Guinea's mixed race and Chinese population have applied for Australian citizenship, primarily to take advantage of the higher salaries and better conditions enjoyed by those who are technically 'overseas officers' of the Public Service, and to secure a foreign refuge for themselves should an independent Papua and New Guinea prove to be uncongenial. Those people of mixed racial origins who have not been naturalized are treated as indigenes, or given an intermediate status for salary-purposes by private enterprise—hence the persistent proliferation of advertisements for indigenous, mixed race or expatriate workers, according to what prospective employers think they can afford to pay.

Nowadays, then, the Australian government's provision of the possibility of naturalization is part-cause and part-effect of the differentials that pertain between the salaries, housing and other conditions that workers of different racial origins receive. Technically, of course, Papuans are Australian citizens, although they cannot exercise their 'right' to live in Australia (unless they are married to a white or mixed race Australian); Chinese and mixed race people who have been granted citizenship can. New Guineans are Australian protected persons. And, to press home the point as to the difference between the white Australian and the non-white almost-Australian, till 1968 Papuans and New Guineans had to apply to a District Officer for a 'Permit for a Native to Leave, or to be Removed from, the Territory', before they went abroad. In 1967, the Migration Regulations were amended so that a female Papuan or New Guinean with an expatriate spouse was spared the embarrassment of having to apply for permission to be 'removed' by her husband, and, from 1968 on, all indigenes had only to apply to any authorised officer for a 'Permit to Leave the Territory'. The Administrator can, however, prevent the emigration of any person or class of persons by declaring them to be 'protected'—a safeguard against exploitation of the unsophisticated, and against the departure overseas of the wealthy but relatively un-Westernised.

During 1958, the administration set up a special committee to review all existing legislation in order to remove all racially discriminatory provisions therefrom. Then followed a flood of amendments and repealing ordinances. Among the first reforms was the repeal (in 1958) of the White Women's Protection Ordinance and of the provisions of the New Guinean Criminal Code that had outlawed intercourse between a New Guinean male and a consenting white woman. New Guinea girls were also given protection from certain forms of sexual abuse until the age of seventeen, in line with the protection afforded expatriate girls by the Criminal Code—a modest advance from the former notion that indigenous girls could be seduced from puberty on. However, the process of officially-sponsored law reform alone could not eradicate prejudice nor bring about that willingness to interact from which a truly multiracial society may grow.

In 1959, for example, the spirit and sexual neuroses of the pre-reform world were still shared even by the kind and thoughtfully paternalistic:—

> '[Expatriate] Missionaries must beware of becoming too friendly with the opposite sex. The native has very strong sexual drives which he often is unable to control. Because of this natives have set up rules for themselves, chief among them being that boys and girls must not mix freely. . . . To be so friendly as to ask a little souvenir or gift from the other sex can only mean one thing. The natives apply this to Europeans also. European men and women should remember this and not mix too freely.

> 'Respect for the European has declined considerably. The main reason for this is the laxity of morals the European has showed in recent years. . . . Immodest dressing is a temptation to our natives and has frequently led to the abuse of white women in the Territory'[181]

—and the same message, in rather more restrained and oblique form, still appears in many tourist brochures[182] and handbooks for newcomers to the territory.[183] For the more scientifically inclined missionary of a separatist bent, there was the medical advice contained in a booklet published by an Anglican mission doctor and still widely sold in Papua and New Guinea during the 1960s:—

> 'Prevention of Malaria.

> . . . [*Inter alia*] keep natives away from your house at night. They are infectious just as a case of scarlet fever, except that the "germ" needs a mosquito to carry it from the native to you.'[184]

In answer to the second request by a United Nations Visiting Mission, the curfew and absence-from-quarters regulations were repealed in 1959. In a separate series of amendments, the powers of *luluais*, *tultuls* and village constables were passed on to Native Local Government Councils as they were slowly established, and those of medical *tultuls* to Council Aid Post Orderlies. Where possible, a field officer's powers under the Native Regulations and the Native Administration Regulations in relation to a number of matters passed to the councils too: in relation to playing football in Rabaul, the giving of gifts to prisoners, the burial of the dead, streams and watercourses, census-taking, proceeding into a hostile district, and assisting in the apprehension of offenders, all in New Guinea; in relation to court appearances, escape from custody, absence from a village and the presence in town of the unemployed, deserted wives and childern, films, the recruiting of minors, clothing and bedding and isolated dwellings in Papua; and in relation to the carrying of weapons in a town and a large number of medical matters in both territories. Thus, many of the powers that enabled the patrol officer to intervene unilaterally in the village passed from the central government to the councils, although they were still exercised on the councils' behalf by the *kiaps*.[185] Most of the restrictions on freedom of movement, except into 'restricted area' (that is, those not yet under administrative control), were repealed, although it remained unlawful until 1968 for a Papuan or New Guinean to be in a town without employment for more than four days.

From the very beginnings of British and German rule over Papua and New Guinea, it will be recalled, 'the demon drink' was placed beyond the reach of indigenes. Under Australian rule, the provisions outlawing the possession or consumption of alcohol by Papuans and New Guineans were entrenched in the two territories' very constitutions, the Papua Act and the New Guinea Act respectively. It was not until the Papua and New Guinea Act of 1949 came into force that it was legally possible for a local body, the Legislative Council, to make exceptions to, or to change, the rule. And, as a result of this change in the law, the Arms, Opium and Prohibition Ordinances of both territories were amended in 1950 to allow Papuans and New Guineans to use sacramental wine in a recognized religious service.

In 1953, a new Liquor Ordinance was passed to allow Papuans and New Guineans to possess methylated spirits provided that it was not for human consumption, to drink alcohol for medicinal purposes, and to transport it (if it were securely packed) for an expatriate. Most importantly, it allowed the Administrator in Council to exempt 'a Native or class of Natives from the whole or a part of the provisions' of the Ordinance. A 'Native' was legally defined as an aboriginal inhabitant of Papua and New Guinea, an island or archipelago adjacent to the territory, Australia, the British Solomon Islands, Netherlands New Guinea, any Pacific Island, the East Indies and Malaysia, or anyone, including people of mixed racial origins, who followed, adhered to, or adopted the customs of, an indigenous Papuan or New Guinean. The exemption provision was not intended to allow Papua and New Guinea's resident 'Natives' to drink—although from 1948 to 1956, selected mixed race people were able to apply for a permit to do so[186]—but to enable the Administrator to avoid painful incidents with 'distinguished [if technically 'Native'] visitors'[187] by allowing them to drink.

Of all the discriminatory legislation in force during the 1950s, the legal prohibition of alcoholic beverages seems to have been the most bitterly resented by Papuans and New Guineans, especially during the second half of the decade.[188] In turn, the territorys' hard-drinking expatriate population —with a *per capita* consumption (including, men, women, children and missionaries) double the Australian rate[189]—seemed quite self-conscious about this measure.[190] Finally, however, during the visit of a United Nations Visiting Mission in 1962, a special committee of inquiry was set up to investigate the desirability of allowing Papuans and New Guineans to drink alcohol.[191] 'The time has come', the Visiting Mission felt, 'to sweep way all survivals of racial discrimination'.[192] By the end of 1962, it was legal for Papuans and New Guineans to purchase any alcoholic beverage to consume in a licensed hotel, and to take beer alone away. One year later, in November 1963, they were allowed to purchase spirituous liquors at retail stores for consumption somewhere else.[193] The specific prohibition of *gamada*-drinking was also repealed in 1962.

After a further special investigation (which commenced in 1960) into the territory's legal system, legislation was passed (also in 1963, although it came into effect only in 1966) to replace the old *kiaps'* courts (New Guinea's 'Courts for Native Affairs' and Papua's 'Courts for Native Matters') with a uniform system of 'Local Courts', which deal with lesser offences committed by people of all races. Today, fulltime indigenous magistrates are increasingly—although still only in relatively few areas—being used to administer a uniform code of low-level criminal and civil justice to people of all races. Higher up, the courts had always been fully integrated, in terms of whom they called before them. In 1965, local government councils were enabled to become multiracial: at long last, people of different racial origins were given a stake in one another's affairs. And quite often, Papua and New Guinea's indigenous council rule-makers are harder on their own people than the central government's law, or the *kiap*, ever were in fostering 'development'.

In 1961, a Companies Ordinance that had been in force in New Guinea since the 1930s was repealed to remove certain clauses which had effectively prevented New Guineans from forming companies for a great number of purposes.[194] In 1963, some of the more restrictive provisions of the Transactions With Natives Ordinance were amended (on the initiative of a non-official member of the Legislative Council) so that Papuans and New Guineans could henceforth be sued for the recovery of debts in excess of fifty pounds, and so that their creditors could no longer be fined for lending them money or selling them goods worth more than fifty pounds without official permission. What had once been a form of protection against exploitation had by then become a restriction on normal business activity and development, although the Administrator could still require certain contracts to be approved by an authorized officer. In the same year, a new Native Employment Ordinance abolished the old protective restrictions on the employment of casual workers, who were henceforth free to work for a cash wage alone and were no longer bound to take their wages partly in food and clothing.[195]

In some fields, however, the emerging indigenous leaders of Papua and New Guinea were not as eager for change as their expatriate mentors. In 1962 (the same year as that in which Papua's Native Offenders Exclusion Ordinance was repealed), the government moved to repeal the Native Women's Protection Ordinance. Several of the twelve indigenous members of the thirty-seven member Legislative Council were opposed to the repeal of the ordinance, as they wished their women still to be protected from the attentions of expatriates, and for the small number of educated Papuan and New Guinean women to be reserved to become wives for the rising generation of educated men. However, John Guise, the member for Eastern Papua, saw quite clearly that the elimination of discrimination and the lifting of certain forms of protection went together—although true progress in the constitution of a multiracial society could only be achieved if the rights of Papuans and New Guineans were properly recognised. As he said during the debate on the ordinance's repeal:—

'I think . . . that if the Government repeals this law, it should make a clear statement in this Council for every councillor to hear that

Papuans and New Guineans should enjoy all the liberties and rights in everyday practice which European people enjoy; that if our young Papuan and New Guinean men make friends or become engaged to white girls or white girls make love to Papuans they will not be arrested by the authorities and get into trouble; that there will be no more blacklisting of Papuans; and that if Europeans are found molesting Papuan women they should also go to gaol just like any other person under common law.'[196]

Legally enforced discrimination and certain forms of paternalism (outside the fields of land and labour law) were almost at an end, although such pieces of indirect discrimination as differential conditions for persons recruited for the public service overseas still remain in force, as does the Australian barrier on the free entry of indigenes into the Commonwealth. Now, gradually, Papuans and New Guineans are being increasingly well protected, at least legally, from discrimination in their own country, although the old Papuan Native Regulation that made threatening, abusive, insulting, jeering and disrespectful language and behaviour towards a European a special offence remained in force until 1968.

*Laws Against Discrimination*

It needs to be remembered when reading the foregoing account that many Papuans and New Guineans—including probably most of the territory's 800,000 Highlanders[197]—were never aware of the exact layout of the law. Very few of them could legally, or had the means to, go to town, or earnt enough money to buy clothes. Even fewer could read the law, or write in protest. At most, they saw the *kiap* two or three times each year—and often less. While he was on his way to see them, they cleaned the village, moved back to their census point from the surrounding bush, and took off their (dirty) clothes. Then, as they prepared to help him on his way, they sent word ahead to the next village to do the same. In short, most of the laws and regulations cited above were symbols of the government's intentions, rather than expressions of administrative reality. But, when the law was applied, justice was meted out quite firmly.

Just as the country's natural terrain and the administration's lack of financial manpower resources meant that the law could be administered only intermittently, and then quite arbitrarily, so the removal of discrimination as such involves more than legal rights. Those who are discriminated against must have the means to resist, or to seek redress. A hotel that kept out indigenes through requiring its patrons to wear shoes could only be integrated by those who knew the law, or, in this case, how to circumvent it. Here, some enterprising Papuans and New Guineans bought multiple sets of shoes, to hire to would be drinkers. But sometimes—as in those hotels that are designed simply to discomfort any man not wearing a tie and long trousers—a man's own pride or personal resources alone can force integration.

Nonetheless, discrimination of certain sorts was made illegal—if not always enforceably so—under the Discriminatory Practices Ordinance of 1963. Henceforth, if the Secretary for Law (an expatriate government official) consented, the holder of a liquor, restaurant, traveller's, pedlar's, entertainment, trading ('with natives'), meat-selling, copra- or cocoa-buying, or any other official buying, selling, dealing or trading licence could be prosecuted (and fined one hundred pounds) for discriminating between people 'for reasons only of race or colour'. A person who acts in an insulting, provocative, or offensive manner, or endeavours to incite another person so to act, on licensed premises, can be gaoled for two months. And the definition of 'discrimination' is broad:—

'... "Discriminatory practice" means discrimination either of an adverse or of a preferential kind practised by a person or group of persons against or in favour of another person or group of persons for reasons only of race or colour, and in particular includes—

(a) the setting aside of portion of any premises, vessel, aircraft or vehicle the subject of a license for the exclusive use of persons or a class of persons of a certain race or colour;

(b) the failure to attend to persons in the order that those persons enter or approach any premises, vessel, aircraft or vehicle the subject of a licence;

(c) the selling or buying of goods at different prices or on different terms to different persons or classes of persons; and

(d) a course of conduct which distinguishes between persons or classes of persons of differing races or colours and which may reasonably be expected to result in mental distress or suffering by a person or a member of that class of persons; .... '

Under a revised version of the ordinance which was approved by the House of Assembly during 1969, the definition of 'discrimination' was broadened to cover differences not only of colour and race, but of an ethnic, tribal or national kind. Now, Papuans and New Guineans cannot discriminate against each other, nor can expatriates differ in their treatment of people of different indigenous or expatriate sub-groups. Abuse and threats were also added to insults as possible causes for legal action. Finally, as in Great Britain, it was declared to be illegal—

'... with intent to stir up hatred, ridicule or contempt against any section of the public in the Territory distinguished by colour, race or ethnic, tribal or national origin—[to]—

(a) publish or distribute written matter which is threatening, abusive, insulting, provocative or offensive; or

(b) use in any public place or at any public meeting words or behaviour which are or is threatening, abusive, insulting, provocative or offensive,

being matter, words or behaviour likely to stir up hatred, ridicule or contempt against that section on grounds of colour, race or ethnic, tribal or national origin.
'Penalty—

(a) on summary conviction, Four hundred dollars or imprisonment for six months, or both; or

(b) on conviction on indictment, Two thousand dollars or imprisonment for two years, or both.'

Evidence of the need for the 1969 ordinance was provided almost as soon as it had been passed by the House of Assembly, when a monthly journal (with a circulation reputed to be about 4,000) which was published in Port Moresby went out of business, with an editorial that proclaimed:—

> 'In June this year, the dignified House of Assembly of this fleabag collection of semi-humanity describing itself as a rising nation approved legislation to prevent the publication of written matter which could be construed as "threatening, provocative or offensive to people of other races or tribes".
>
> 'This particular piece of legislation . . . has now in official circles become popularly known as the "Anti-BLACK and WHITE Magazine Law".'[198]

The magazine, which had been described by an Australian writer as 'a promoter of racial hatred'[199] claimed at its demise to have 'reflected the ideas and opinions of the majority of expatriate people of this Territory'.[200]

*Conclusion*

Racial discrimination and selective segregation are no longer legislatively sanctioned and administratively enforced in Papua and New Guinea, at least not explicitly. However, just as the laws outlined above did not tell the full story of their times, in that they could not account for individual acts of care, kindness and assistance in development[201] across the castebarriers of colonial society, so the passage of the Discriminatory Practices Ordinance did not presage the sudden arrival of a society in which race is of no account.

What the 1968 United Nations Visiting Mission to New Guinea referred to as 'Social incidents of a minor but irritating nature'[202] still persist: adult male Papuans and New Guineans are still called '*boi*'; expatriates tend to receive priority from salesmen of all races in many stores; and Papuans and New Guineans are made to feel uncertain and unwelcome in a number of licensed premises. However, as deliberate and systematic discrimination by expatriates against Papuans and New Guineans declines, so there is arising an increasing tendency for indigenes to resent the presence of expatriates in their bars and taverns[203]—perhaps a logical extension of the unduly exuberant and appreciative welcome given to expatriate visitors to a 'native bar' during the late 1960s.

'Social separateness' still seemed quite pervasive, then, to the 1971 United Nations Visiting Mission, and was to 'some extent . . . the result of disparities in living standards which are very marked'.[204] It may be realistic, if not just, to pay and house overseas public servants better than their local counterparts, but the separateness that results retains many important links with the past. The public rationale for inequality has changed, but to the disadvantaged it must surely often seem that 'The cause is the consequence':[205] informal racial segregation. The lines of economic cleavage remain largely continuous with their racist predecessors.

Except when it deals with immigration, wages, working conditions and certain kinds of land dealings, the law is generally indifferent to a man's race—indifferent, not impartial, for it is often still as blind to the indigenous people's needs and aspirations as was its more partial, racially-orientated antecedent. Objectively, then, Papuans and New Guineans are as free as expatriates, and are even protected from certain forms of injustice at the latter's hands. But, objectivity is still all too often directed against those who have legal rights but lack the resources to enforce them.[206]

If the wouldbe applicant for a house or land can overcome his discomfiture sufficiently to seek access to the appropriate officials, who are usually expatriates with no relevant linguistic skills, and is not humiliated or intimidated by them, he must then fill in complicated forms in English, to compete economically against much better-paid expatriates to lease land for a house which must conform to regulations that were laid down with Australian living standards, and, therefore, economic conditions, in mind. There simply is no provision for the poor and ill-educated to live securely in town, and so semi-legal squatter settlements abound on the fringes of most territory towns. However, the racial element in this form of discrimination is now only incidental. Here, thoughtlessness and the application of inappropriate standards have replaced racism to achieve much the same effect, albeit one to which the rising indigenous inheritance elite is largely blind. Seated in their cars, the absence of footpaths in Port Moresby now seems to them to be an economic problem rather than an example of racist indifference to local circumstances (in which, until recently, almost all privately owned cars belonged to expatriates). And they are becoming increasingly right . . . .

Until 1960, the majority of the members of the legislatures of either territory were government officials. They, and through them the Australian government (and its British and German predecessors) were responsible for the legislation that was enacted, and later repealed. Even since then, the official members in the House of Assembly have had the resources and support to get their way. The successive colonial administrations of Papua and New Guinea cannot shirk their responsibility for the past, both for the construction and the dismantling of the 'native administration' systems. To date, there have been very few anguished liberals or reforming activists among Papuans and New Guineans. A handful of young educated men and women see a need to discriminate in favour of Papuans and New Guineans (particularly in the economic sphere), but the majority of contemporary indigenous leaders are so fearful of the nearness of the pre-contact past, and so uncertain as to the range of possible alternatives before them, that they cling dependently to an authoritarian emulation of the Australian administration's values (even to multiracialism when it is to their followers' disadvantage).

The foregoing account has, therefore, concentrated upon official actions and values, because it was appropriate so to do. It would be foolish, however, to pretend that they tell the full story. But, to the extent that economic histories of Papua and New Guinea have been written without taking account of the legal restrictions upon indigenous financial and commercial activity and access to the towns; histories of race relations without mention of the various restrictions on interracial sexual and social liaisons; and political histories without an analysis of the legal media through which government and people came into most regular and systematic contact; the legalistic emphases of this chapter would seem to have been justified by the oversights of other scholars. Eventually, it is hoped, others will investigate the impact of the law, but when they do, will they discover that each charge and conviction is evidence that the law was vigorously enforced or more widely disobeyed? and will negative evidence be any firmer? In the interim, this chapter is intended to stand as a history of successive colonial governments' intentions and reservations in the contact situation in Papua and New Guinea, and as a *memento mori* to those who preach multiracialism as a doctrine of expatriate-dominated stability when change is necessary.

## REFERENCES

1 This chapter is a revised version of 'Race Relations I: Two Systems of Law', Newsletter, EPW-20 of October 23, 1969, published by the Institute of Current World Affairs, New York, to which body grateful acknowledgement is made for permission to republish.
The Newsletter was originally intended to provide only a preliminary account of the development of the 'native administration' systems in Papua and New Guinea, for a wider project on the impact of European law and the history of interracial relations there. It is best read in conjunction with one of the wider-ranging general histories of Papua and New Guinea.

2 MACGREGOR, SIR WILLIAM, in Victoria, *Annual Report on British New Guinea from* 1st July, 1891, to 30th June, 1892; *with Appendices.* Brisbane, n.d., p.v.

3 *Native Administration and Political Development in British Tropical Africa: Report by Lord Hailey,* . . . 1940-42, London [1944?], p. 3.

3a D. C. Gordon, *The Australian Frontier in New Guinea* 1870-1885, New York, 1951, p. 251.

4 There was, in fact, some doubt as to the powers that could be exercised by the Special Commissioner. For a discussion of the issues at stake, see MAYO, J. 'The Protectorate of British New Guinea 1884-1888: An Oddity of Empire') in *The History of Melanesia*, Port Moresby, 1969, pp. 17-31; and Queensland, *Report on British New Guinea, from Data and Notes by the Late Sir Peter Scratchley, Her Majesty's Special Commissioner by G. Seymour Fort* . . ., Brisbane, 1886, pp. 26-27.

5 LEGGE, J. D. *Australian Colonial Policy: A Survey of Native Administration and European Development in Papua*, Sydney, 1956, p. 46.

6 GORDON, D. C. *op. cit.*, p. 252.

7 ROMILLY, H. H. *Letters from The Western Pacific and Mashonaland* 1878-1891, London, 1893, pp. 219-210.

8 LEGGE, J. D., *op. cit.*, p. 32.

9 A careful reading of Queensland, *Report on British New Guinea . . . by G. Seymour Fort* (*op. cit.*, especially pp. 3-20) reveals the justice of M. Groves.' assessment that 'It was in the experience of those four years that the outlines of Papua's subsequent constitution and administrative system were formulated' (GROVES, M., 'The History of Papua: Some Notes on Research Resources, Achievements and Problems', *Historical Studies: Australia and New Zealand,* 5 (20), May 1953, p. 393). If the practical achievements of the protectorate administration and the policies set down by Sir Peter Scratchley are carefully distinguished, then the seemingly divergent views of the protectorate held by Legge (above) and Groves seem (*pace*, HASTINGS, P., *New Guinea: Problems and Prospects,* Melbourne, 1969, p. 46) to be quite compatible with one another.

10 Lewis Lett, for example, has accused MacGregor of acquiring from the Colonial Office the notion 'that the humiliation of rebellious tribes was an essential to the inculcation of respect for the governing power, and that dignity must be upheld by force' (LETT, L., *The Papuan Achievement,* Melbourne, 1942, p. 59). 'And nothing could be plainer than his persuasion that force, subjugation, assertiveness, were the roots of governmental power, and a humble attitude an essential to docility' (LETT, L., *ibid.*, p. 60). See also LETT, L., *Sir Hubert Murray of Papua,* Sydney, 1949, p. 125 for a similar view. In a rather fairer analysis, J. D. Legge still felt that MacGregor

'tended to maintain prestige by the use of force' (LEGGE, J. D., *op. cit.*, p. 69) on occasions when it may not have been necessary to do so. For another attempt to judge MacGregor by the standards of his time, see JOYCE, R. B., 'William MacGregor: The Role of the Individual,' in *The History of Melanesia*, *op. cit.*, pp. 33-44.

11 As MacGregor himself remarked:

'The best work of an administrator is seldom heard of, because it is not spectacular. I have often received thanks and congratulations for the accomplishment of tasks that required force; but only once have I been thanked by a Secretary of State for peacefully composing trouble that threatened into civil war' (SIR WILLIAM MACGREGOR, 'Introduction', in MURRAY, J.H.P., *Papua or British New Guinea*, London, 1912, p. 26).

Despite the subsequent attempt of his admiring biographer, Lewis Lett, to compare their two administrations to MacGregor's disadvantage, Sir Hubert Murray seems have sympathised with MacGregor's complaint that the successful use of force received greater public recognition than the more routine tasks of administration (MURRAY, SIR HUBERT, *Papua of To-Day or An Australian Colony in the Making* (hereinafter cited as *Papua of To-Day . . .*), London, 1925, pp. 12-16).

12 Conference with Australian Premiers, January 1888; Accession CP 1/1 (New Guinea Correspondence, 1885-98, in the Archives Division, Australian National Library, Canberra), Bundle 6, quoted in LEGGE, J. D., *op. cit.*, p. 70.

13 Victoria, *British New Guinea. Annual Report by Her Majesty's Administrator of the Government, from 1st July, 1889, to 30th June, 1890 . . .* Brisbane, n.d., p. 31.

14 Unless otherwise indicated, the source of the ordinances and regulations cited or quoted in this section is the relevant year (often indicated in brackets) of the *British New Guinea Government Gazette*, which was indexed every year from 1888.

15 When an attempt was made, after 1929, to employ Papuan assessors (in groups of four) in the trial of cases involving Papuans, the Lieutenant-Governor, Sir Hubert Murray, did not expect them to be

'. . . of assistance to Magistrates in the present generation, but the idea is to train them up to some idea of Court procedure so that eventually— not I think in the lifetime of any of us now living—they may be able to dispose of cases themselves, without the intervention of Europeans. . . . There are of course innumerable obstacles in training Papuans to a true conception of judicial impartiality; personal likes and dislikes, the fear of sorcery, and other disturbing elements must be banished. I know many intelligent natives, . . . but I do not know any that I could trust with the trial of a case however simple. Still, in the next generation, the prospect may be more promising . . . .'

MacGregor had attempted to involve Papuans in the judicial process, Murray said, but he had failed (The Parliament of the Commonwealth of Australia, *Territory of Papua, Report for Year 1930-1931* [hereinafter cited in the form *Territory of Papua, Report for . . .*], p. 20).

16 The Parliament of the Commonwealth of Australia, *British New Guinea. Report of the Royal Commission of Inquiry into the Present Conditions, including the Method of Government, of the Territory of Papua, and the Best Means for their Improvement . . .*, Melbourne, 1907, p. xlii.

16a Sir Hubert Murray, *Papua of To-Day . . .*, p. 65.

16b R. B. Joyce, *op. cit.*, p. 44.

17 FORTUNE, R. F., *Sorcerers of Dobu: The Social Anthropology of the Dobu Islanders of the Western Pacific*, London, 1932, p. 290.

Cf. Hogbin, H. I., 'Sorcery and Administration', *Oceania*, VI (1), September 1935, pp. 31-32; and the comments of the Secretary for Law (L. J. Curtis) on the Sorcery Bill 1970, in Territory of Papua and New Guinea, *House of Assembly Debates*, II (13), p. 4138.

18 In his autobiography, Albert Maori Kiki describes most revealingly how even a seemingly quite generous administrative act such as the giving of a cash bonus to Papuan mothers or a thorough medical inspection could affront indigenous *mores* (Kiki, A. M. *Kiki: Ten Thousand Years in a Lifetime: A New Guinea Autobiography*, Melbourne, 1968, pp. 83-84).

19 Murray, Sir Hubert, *Papua of To-Day . . .*, p. 65.

20 Gibbney, H. J., 'The Interregnum in the Government of Papua, 1901-1906', *The Australian Journal of Politics and History*, XXI (3), December 1966, pp. 341-359. During this period, both Queensland and Great Britain sought to pass the financial buck to a reluctant federal government in Australia, and 'nobody was prepared to take responsibility for major decisions. Le Hunte [the Lieutenant-Governor from 1898 to 1903] could do no more than keep routine matters functioning and postpone all questions of higher policy' (Legge, J. D., *op. cit.*, p. 104).

21 Recent Studies, such as Nelson, H. N., 'Hubert Murray: Private Letters and Public Reputation', *Historical Studies*, 14 (56), April 1971, pp. 612-621, should, however, prompt the student to be cautious in identifying Murray personally with every aspect of the system he administered. Several of the least attractive items in his administration's legislative record were enacted during his periodic absences from Papua, while the Australian government, some of his subordinate officers, and the territory's expatriate population managed to block—politically, administratively, and/or economically—some of his most forward-looking proposals, for example, that Papuans be seated in the Legislative Council.

22 Hall, B., 'The Murray System and the War', *The Australian Quarterly*, XVIII (2), June 1946, p. 66.

23 Lord Hailey, 'Introduction', in Mair, L. P., *Australia in New Guinea*, London, 1948, p. xvi.

24 Murray, Sir Hubert, *Papua of To-Day . . .*, pp. 282-283.

25 West, F., *Hubert Murray: The Australian Pro-Counsul*, Melbourne, 1968, p. 205.

26 Murray, Sir Hubert, *Native Administration in Papua*, Port Moresby, 1929, pp. 17-18.

27 Unless otherwise indicated, the source of the ordinances and regulations cited or quoted in this section is the relevant year (often indicated in brackets) of the Territory of Papua, *Government Gazette*, which was indexed every year until 1940.

28 The tensions that such a seemingly straightforward (and perhaps necessary) health measure could create, for other reasons, have been well described in novel-form, in Eri, V., *The Crocodile*, Milton (Queensland), 1970, p. 22. The women of Moveave walked away from their inoculators 'ashamed and crying. The doctor had seen and felt their husbands' property' when their bottoms were injected.

29 Maher, R. F., *New Men of Papua: A Study in Culture Change*, Madison (Wisconsin), 1961, pp. 53-54.

30 Indeed, even the village constables' private lives were subject to administrative interference through an Executve Order forbidding them from taking an additional wife after their accession to office. This position, Murray said, had been

'distorted into evidence of a persecution of polygamy. It is, of course, nothing of the kind for we are careful never to interfere with native customs. The most obvious reason for the order is one of police; if the Constable has a crowd of relations-in-law he is likely to favour them in his administration and to overlook their misdemeanours. And there is the further consideration that the Constable, being only human, is likely to misuse his power ... by "cornering" the most eligible girls in the village' (MURRAY, SIR HUBERT, *Native Administration in Papua, op. cit.*, pp. 7-8).

31 MURRAY, SIR HUBERT, *The Machinery of Indirect Rule in Papua*, Port Moresby, 1935, p. 5.

32 MURRAY, SIR HUBERT, *Papua of To-Day . . .*, p. 253.

33 'I would sooner see a native a good agriculturalist than a good scholar or even than a good carpenter' (J. H. P. Murray, 'Native Administration in Papua', paper read before the Royal Anthropological Institute, London, May 1923, quoted in the same author's *Notes on Colonel Ainsworth's Report on the Mandated Territory of New Guinea*, Port Moresby, 1924, pp. 3-4).
Some years later, Murray commented that, although it was scientifically quite impossible to compare the innate capacities of different races:

'My own opinion, . . . which probably coincides with that of most of the European residents of Papua, is that Papuan and European overlap; that is I think that the best Papuans are superior to the worst Europeans, but that Europeans as a whole have an innate superiority over Papuans. . . . Personally, I have no doubt that Papuans could be found who could be educated to the standard of an ordinary professional career; but ... I am quite opposed to the creation of a Papuan intelligentsia, and would rather aim at the diffusion of an elementary education, with a knowledge of English, over as wide an area as possible' (*Territory of Papua, Report for . . . 1937-1938*, Canberra, 1939, p. 20).

34 By limiting the term of labour contracts to three years, and the time that a Papuan could remain from away from his home village to four years, Murray both prevented the excessive exploitation of the labourer and hoped to prevent 'detribalization' (*Territory of Papua. Annual Report for . . . 1928-1929*, p. 6).

35 According to one of Murray's resident magistrates, secret societies only existed to the west of Yule Island, where 'bestiality, human sacrifice, incest, and other abominable crimes' were practised. He assumed that there was, therefore, some connection between them (MONCKTON, C. A. W., *Experiences of a New Guinea Resident Magistrate*, London, n.d., p. 212). Some years later, when the Papuan Government Anthropologist visited the Orokolo area, he investigated rumors, that circulated among Europeans, of 'sexual abominations' in connection with the *Hevehe* ceremonial cycle. 'In the course, however, of a most wholehearted endeavour to learn everything possible about the cult', he reported 'I have discovered nothing to verify them; nor can I imagine when, where, or how they are supposed to take place in the cycle' (WILLIAMS, F. E., *Drama of Orokolo: The Social and Ceremonial Life of the Elema*, Oxford, 1940, p. 248).
A decade later, however, the Kerema area still seemed to be associated in some expatriates' minds with sexual excess. Indeed, to one writer, 'rape appear[ed] to be a national pastime, and an accepted method of retaliation for personal affronts' there (GROVES, M., 'The Criminal Jurisdiction of the Supreme Court of Papua-New Guinea: Part II', *The Australian Law Journal*, 25 (10), February 21, 1952, p. 640).

36 Indeed, one of the headlands between the town and Badili became popularly known as *Tau Erema Iduka* (Police Motu for 'the headland of the Kerema men'), because it was there that the Gulf and Delta men waited in the bush to waylay and rob other Papuans as they walked along the path to town to hawk their fish (Albert Maori Kiki, personal communication).

37 MURRAY, SIR HUBERT, *Papua of To-Day* . . ., p. 71.

38 LANDTMAN, G., *The Kiwai Papuans of British New Guinea: A Native-Born Instance of Rousseau's Ideal Community*, London, 1927, p. 106.
According to Landtman, copious consumption of the drink was 'likely in a short time to impair the nervous system' (p. 107). The only time that Landtman noticed a mutinous spirit among the usually submissive Kiwai was when discussing *gamada*, for to them it was more than an intoxicating drink. It was their principal means of invoking the spirit-world, and, therefore, 'one of the most essential instruments of the people's welfare. It was associated from the beginning with man, for according to a folktale both have sprung from the same origin . . .' (p. 108).

39 MURRAY, SIR HUBERT, *Papua of To-Day* . . ., pp. 64-65.

40 Murray himself was opposed to the argument that feasts and dances should be forbidden because they gave occasion and opportunity for sexual immorality. While he agreed that immorality should, if possible, be checked, 'to suppress the dances would be merely to treat the symptons and would leave the cause untouched.' Rather than discourage feats, he hoped to utilise them in furtherance of good government—to celebrate the giving of prizes for the best village and the best Papuan-owned plantation in a district, and the distribution of the baby-bonus (MURRAY, SIR HUBERT, *Native Custom and the Government of Primitive Races with Especial Reference to Papua: A paper read . . . at the third Pan-Pacific Science Congress, Tokyo, 1926*, Port Moresby, 1926, pp. 14-15).

41 MURRAY, SIR HUBERT, *Papua of To-Day* . . ., p. 72.

42 FANON, F., *The Wretched of the Earth* (translated by Constance Farrington), Harmondsworth, England (Penguin edition), 1967, pp. 30-31.

43 MANNONI, O. *Prospero and Caliban: The Psychology of Colonization* (translated by Pamela Powesland), New York (Praeger, second edition), 1964.

44 FANON, F., *op. cit.*, p. 30.

45 Some missionaries had, self-consciously, advocated the course that was finally enforced by the regulations after 1920. The Reverend J. Chalmers, for example, wrote in 1884:
'I fear I shall shock many of my friends and a large number of Christians in what I am now going to propose. The natives of New Guinea now under British rule do not wear much clothing, and it is desirable that they should be encouraged to use only a very little. The women in many parts are clothed enough, and in others, where their clothing is scant, they should be encouraged to take to the petticoats and nothing more. Nowhere do the men want more than a loincloth, and every effort should be used to discourage anything more. . . . [C]lothed natives are, I believe, only hurrying along an easy and respectable road to the grave. To swathe their limbs in European clothing spoils them, deteriorates them, and, I fear, hurries them to premature death' (James Chalmers, in LOVETT, R., *James Chalmers: His Autobiography and Letters*, Oxford, 1902, p. 257).
Some years later, the discouragement of clothes-wearing had become widely accepted as an important way in which to prevent a further decline in the indigenous population of Melanesia (see, for example, RIVERS, W. H. R., (ed.), *Essays on the Depopulation of Melanesia*, Cambridge, 1922, *passim*). According to the Reverend W. J. Durrad, for example, many Melanesians washed and dried themselves in their clothes, and became ill with influenza, colds and coughs in consequence. In his view, a skirt without a bodice was sufficient for the women, in that it provided 'the maximum of decency and the minimum of risk' (DURRAD, W. J., 'The Depopulation of Melanesia', in RIVERS, W. H. R. (ed.), *ibid.*, p. 9).

46 HIDES, J. G., *Savages in Serge*, Sydney, 1938, p. 138.

47 Stuart, I., *Port Moresby—yesterday and today*, Sydney, 1970, p. 252.

48 Stuart, I., *ibid.*, pp. 117-118.
Oram, N. D., 'The Hula in Port Moresby', *Oceania*, XXXIX (1), September 1968, p. 6 says that the Hula did not use their canoes as dwellings while they worked in Port Moresby until 1943. Until then, they seemingly came to town only on brief annual visits.

49 Stuart, I., *op. cit.*, p. 157.
The Ela Beach sign was about as subtle as the present signs on the toilets between the District Office in Port Moresby and the Supreme Court: 'Ladies'; 'Gentlemen'; '*Hahine*'; '*Tatau*' (the last two being the Motu terms for 'Women' and 'men' respectively). For some comments on how skilfully the administration has avoided the appearance of discrimination through the obliquely meaningful juxtaposition of such signs, see Kiki, A. M., *op. cit.*, p. 92.
According to another writer, the sign at Ela Beach, post-war, simply said: 'No Dogs or Natives Allowed' (D. M. Hogg, in Anderson, J. L. and Hogg, D. M., *New Guinea*, Sydney, 1969, p. 163).

50 Sir Hubert Murray was, it seems, as anxious to prevent inexact reporting of conditions in Papua as to assuage the fears of those Papuans who believed that a camera could somehow capture their spirit. In Murray's view, irresponsible travellers and writers were bad enough, but
'Photographers' are perhaps the worst offenders. They certainly turn out some wonderful pictures, but when one hears that a respectable resident of the Port Moresby village, who has been working for years as a hospital orderly, is represented as a head-hunter stalking his prey through the long grass, and one's own washerwoman as queen of an unknown tribe in the interior, one begins to wonder whether uncontrolled publicity is much of an advantage after all (Murray, Sir Hubert, *Papua of To-Day* . . ., p. 291).

51 At the same time, the older regulation forbidding the spreading of lying reports that tended 'to give rise to trouble or ill-feeling amongst the people as a whole, or between individuals'; the use of threatening language and similar behaviour; and the utterance of obscenities 'within the hearing of any other person', carried a penalty of a fine of up to two pounds or imprisonment for four months. It remained in force during the life of the regulation quoted in the body of the text, and even after the repeal of the latter.

52 Cf. Lind, A., 'Inter-Ethnic Marriage in New Guinea', *New Guinea Research Bulletin*, 31, August 1969, Chapter 2, *passim*.

53 Mannoni, O., *op. cit.*, pp. 114-115.

54 Mannoni, O., *op. cit.*, p. 197.

55 Murray, Sir Hubert, *Papua of To-Day* . . ., p. 94.
However, in speaking to the bill in the Legislative Council, the Government Secretary (H. W. Champion) said that there had been no convictions recorded for offences by Papuan men against white women between 1904 and 1913; only two during the following five years; three between 1919 and 1921; while 'for the following four years ending 1925 not only were the cases more serious but there were no less than eight convictions, with two more cases pending' (Territory of Papua, *Legislative Council Debates*, Meeting No. 1, January, 1926, p. 2).

56 West, F. (ed.), *Selected Letters of Hubert Murray*, Melbourne, 1970, p. 119.
For a description of the 'carelessness' of some white women, see Eri, V., *op. cit.*, p. 41.

57 *Territory of Papua. Annual Report for* . . . *1929-1930*, p. 3.

58 *Territory of Papua. Annual Report for* . . . *1933-1934*, p. 6.

59 *Territory of Papua. Annual Report for . . . 1925-1926*, p. 9.
Murray, however, felt that the ordinance had been 'very generally misunderstood outside Papua'. Contrary to a widespread misconception, the white man and the Papuan were liable to the same penalty (death):

> 'The distinction is the victim of the outrage. Thus the rape or attempted rape of a white woman is a capital offence; the rape or attempted rape of a native woman is punished, as before, with imprisonment. So an indecent assault of a white woman may be punished with imprisonment for life; an indecent assault of a native woman carries a punishment of two years' imprisonment.' (*ditto*, p. 9).

According to Murray, there had by mid-1927 been only two cases of attempted rape of a Papuan woman by a European man, and both had been acquitted. The sentences for a rape of a Papuan woman by a Papuan man were generally between one and three years imprisonment (*ditto*, p. 10).

60 MURRAY, SIR HUBERT, *Papua of To-Day . . .*, p. 96.

61 WEST, F. (ed.), *op. cit.*, p. 208.
A group of Papuans who went to Sydney in 1933 to train as medical assistants were allowed to dress in European clothes for the trip. However, the resultant controversy among Port Moresby's expatriate community meant that their successors were sent South in 1934 dressed in Boy Scouts' uniforms (NELSON, H. 'Brown Doctors: White Prejudice. Oh to be a medical assistant in the 1930's!', *New Guinea and Australia, The Pacific and South-East Asia* [hereinafter cited as *New Guinea*], 5 (2), June-July 1970, p. 24).

62 'The Imperial Charter Granted to the New Guinea Company', Appendix I to MOSES, J. A., 'The German Empire in Melanesia 1884-1914; a German self-analysis', in *The History of Melanesia, op. cit.*, p. 59 (translated from MELNECEKE, G. (ed.), *Koloniales Jahrbuch*, Vol. 1, 1888, pp. 245-247).

63 MOSES, J. A., *op. cit.*, p. 46.

64 'The Imperial Charter Granted to the New Guinea Company', *op. cit.*, pp. 59-60.

65 'Strafverordnung, betreffend das Verbot der Verabfolgung von Waffen, Munition, Sprengstoffen und Spirituosen an Eingeborene, sowie der Wegführung von Eingeborenen aus dem Schutzgebiet als Arbeiter', in Riebow (publisher), *Die deutsche kolonial—Gesetzgebung. Erster Theil. Bis zum Jahre 1892*, Berlin, 1893, pp. 532-533.

66 The Parliament of the Commonwealth of Australia, *Report to the League of Nations on the Administration of the Territory of New Guinea, from September, 1914, to 30th June 1921* (hereinafter cited in the form *Report... on the Administration of . . . New Guinea, from . . ., to . . .*), p. 15.

> 'Japanese had the status of, and in most matters received the treatment accorded to, persons of European race; whereas persons of other non-indigenous races—the most numerous of whom were the Chinese and the Malays—had the status of, and in most matters received the treatment accorded to, indigenous natives' (*ditto*, p. 15).

67 The *Deutsches Kolonialblatt* lists forty main punitive expeditions that were mounted by the administration of German New Guinea between 1898 and 1912 (MOSES, J. A., *op. cit.*, p. 54). On the other side, it has been pointed out that 'almost every German factory is said to have experienced bloody incidents' and attacks during the first twenty-five years of German rule (REED, S. W., *The Making of Modern New Guinea, with special reference to Culture Contact in the Mandated Territory*, Philadelphia, 1943, p. 134).

68 REED, S. W., *ibid.*, p. 137.

69 'Verordnung, betreffend die Erhaltung der Disziplin unter den farbigen

Arbeitern', in Riebow (publisher), *op. cit.*, p. 552. I am indebted to P. Biskup for drawing my attention to this source.

70 The Parliament of the Commonwealth of Australia, *Report by His Excellency the Lieutenant-Governor of Papua to the Honourable the Minister for Home and Territories, on an Article on 'Three Power Rule in New Guinea', by Mr. Rinzo Gond,* Melbourne, 1919, *passim.*

Although he thought that reports of atrocities in German New Guinea were 'almost certainly exaggerated', Murray felt that 'the British method [of colonial administration] is the only one which is worthy of a civilized nation...' (*ditto*, p. 9). The German colonies were, he felt, 'looked upon simply as so many German commercial establishments, to be conducted solely in the interests of those who have invested money in them, while in the British colonies the interests and the general well-being of the native inhabitants are recognized as being certainly of not less, and probably even of greater, importance than of any other consideration whatever' (*ditto*, p. 7). See also 'Report by Chairman, His Excellency, J. H. P. Murray, C.M.G., Lieutenant Governor of Papua, in The Parliament of the Commonwealth of Australia, *Interim and Final Reports of Royal Commission on Late German New Guinea,* Melbourne, 1920, pp. 54-56.

71 MURRAY. SIR HUBERT, *Papua of To-Day*..., p. 212.

72 'Strafverordnung für die Eingeborenen', in Riebow (publisher), *op. cit.*, pp. 557-558.

73 HAHL, A., *Gouverneursjahre in Neuguinea,* Berlin, 1937, p. 23, cited in BISKUP, P., 'Dr. Albert Hahl—Sketch of a German Colonial Official', *The Australian Journal of Politics and History,* XIV (3), December 1968, p. 345.

74 Murray, for example, corresponded and exchanged new ordinances with Hahl (BISKUP, P., *ibid.*, p. 347, n. 19, where a personal communication from Peter Sack is cited as the source).

75 SALISBURY, R. F., 'Depotism and Australian Administration in the New Guinea Highlands', in WATSON, J. B. (ed.), 'New Guinea: The Central Highlands", *American Anthropologist Special Publication,* 66 (4), Part 2, August 1964, pp. 225-226; ROWLEY, C. D., 'Native Officials and Magistrates of German New Guinea—1897-1921, *South Pacific,* 7 (7), January-February 1954, p. 773; and BISKUP, P., *op. cit.*, p. 350.

76 BISKUP, P., *op. cit.*, p. 349.

77 *Report*... *on the Administration of*... *New Guinea from 1st July, 1921, to 30 June, 1922,* p. 40.

78 'There is no evidence that any of the Australian Military Administrators [between 1914 and 1921] understood what the Germans were trying to do for the creation of viable local government units. They were not colonial theorists. Therefore they kept the luluai and continued to use him more or less as they saw him, as part of the structure of order, and the contact man for the Administration in the village' (ROWLEY, C. D., *op. cit.*, p. 775).

79 'Bekanntmachung, betreffend die Auswanderung chinesischer Kulis aus dem Schutzgebiete der Neu—Guinea—Kompagnie nach Australien', in ZIMMER-MANN, A., *Die deutsche kolonial—Gesetzgebung; Zweiter Theil 1893 bis 1897,* Berlin, 1898, pp. 67-68.

80 DERNBURG, B., 'Zielpunkte des Deutschen Kolonialwesens', *Deutsches Kolonialblatt* 1907, Part I, cited, in MOSES, J. A., *op. cit.*, p. 54.

81 Unless otherwise indicated, the source of the ordinances and regulations cited or quoted in the rest of this section is *Report*... *on the Administration of*... *New Guinea, from September, 1914 to 30th June, 1921,* pp. 40-43.

82 'Proclamation. Read to Natives on the Annexation of the late German Possessions in the Pacific. Rabaul, September 12th, 1914', *British Admini-*

*stration—German New Guinea, Government Gazette,* I (2), 1 November 1914, p. 7.

83 *Report . . . on the Administration of . . . New Guinea, from September 1914, to 30th June, 1921,* p. 6.

84 In 1918, there were several different cemeteries in Rabaul: number one for Europeans and Japanese; number two for Chinese; number three for Malays and other persons of European status except for those previously mentioned. By 1921, cemetery number three was reserved for the exclusive use of Malays, while a number four cemetery had been established for other persons of European status. It was illegal to bury a body in Rabaul in a place other than the cemetery reserved for people of the same race as the deceased.

85 LYNG, J. G., "Rabaul and Neighbouhood", *British Administration—late German New Guinea, Government Gazette,* II (2), 15 February 1915, p. 1.

86 Unless otherwise indicated, the source of the ordinances and regulations cited or quoted in this section is the relevant year (often indicated in brackets) of the *British Administration—German New Guinea, Government Gazette,* I (1), 15 October 1914 to 8 (11), 7 May 1921. An index to the Gazette appears in *Report . . . on the Administration of . . . New Guinea, from September, 1914, to 30th June, 1921,* pp. 31-39.

87 OVERELL, LILIAN, *A Woman's Impressions of German New Guinea,* London, 1923, pp. 171-180.
Allegations that floggings still persisted, together with reports alleging the use of forced labour, were widely publicised in Australia in 1923, although an official enquiry tended to the conclusion that 'if there were any assaults, and . . . [the investigator had] no evidence to this effect, they would be blows struck on the spur of the moment and . . . not of a serious nature, and certainly do not justify the use of the word "whipping" let alone "flogging" ', ('In the Matter of the Mandated Territory of New Guinea and the Investigation of Certain Charges Ordered in Reference Thereto by the Commonwealth Government: Report of A. S. Canning, the Person Appointed to Make the Investigation', in *Report . . . on the Administration of . . . New Guinea from 1st July, 1922, to 30th June, 1923,* p. 123).

88 'Report by Chairman, His Excellency J. H. P. Murray, C.M.G., Lieutenant-Governor of Papua', *op. cit.,* p. 55.
The Germans, Murray believed, regarded the 'native . . . merely as a means to an end—as an instrument of the employer; he is to be well treated, because if he is not well treated he will not work, but he may be flogged, because by that means he can be made to work better.' The Australian military administration in New Guinea had, he thought, been 'necessarily . . . influenced by and imbued with German principles'. The 'disciplinary punishments' which were in force still late in 1919 (that is, before Field Punishment No. 1 came into force), were, he felt, 'impossible in a British colony'.

89 'Report by Chairman, His Excellency J. H. P. Murray, C.M.G., Lieutenant-Governor of Papua', *op. cit.,* p. 55.

90 ROWLEY, C. D., *The Australians in German New Guinea 1914-1921,* Melbourne, 1958, p. 149.

91 According to the *Report . . . on the Administration of . . . New Guinea, from September, 1914, to 30th June, 1921,* p. 22, most of the holders of recruiting-licences were Chinese, and 'many of them have been quite unscrupulous in their methods'. Renewal of licences was, therefore, refused by the administration to 'persons not of known good character'.

92 TOWNSEND, G. W. L., *District Officer: From Untamed New Guinea to Lake Success, 1921-46,* Sydney, 1968, p. 41.

93 ROWLEY, C. D., *The Australians in German New Guinea 1914-1921, op. cit.,* p. 333.

The nearest thing to a 'native policy' enunciated by the military was a General Order to the troops which was issued by the Administrator, Colonel S. A. Pethebridge, and then gazetted, in January 1916:

'You are cautioned as to your relations with the natives; they are entitled to your consideration, and you are expected to treat them with firmness but absolute fairness. Upon you depends their conception of British justice and honesty of purpose. Interference with native women is strictly prohibited.

※ ※ ※ ※ ※ ※

'By your example and conduct your are relied upon to do nothing to lower the reputation of the British soldier, or impair in any way the prestige of the British Empire.'

94 Including houses, plantations, furniture, and household goods, among which was the linen (TOWNSEND, G. W. L., *op. cit.*, p. 27). Many Germans, including all officials, were repatriated to their homeland.

95 ROWLEY, C. D., *The Australians in German New Guinea 1914-1921*, *op. cit.*, p. 334.

96 *Report . . . on the Administration of . . . New Guinea from 1st July, 1921, to 30th June, 1922*, p. 51.

97 TOWNSEND, G. W. L., *op. cit.*, p. 108.

98 Under the Second and Third Schedules of the Laws Repeal and Adopting Ordinance 1921.
Unless otherwise indicated, the source of the ordinances and regulations cited or quoted in this section is the relevant year (often indicated in brackets) of Prime Minister's Department (compiler), *Laws of the Territory of New Guinea*, Melbourne, I (1921-1922)—XV (1939, 1940 and 1941).

99 Essentially, the foregoing argument is intended to do no more than to urge that the two territories' pre-war administrations should be compared (for their similarities as well as their differences) rather than treated quite discretely. It is not an attempt to counter the careful and close, if impressionistic, account of the differences between the two territories' judicial systems contained in GROVES, M., 'The Criminal Jurisdiction of the Supreme Court of Papua-New Guinea', *The Australian Law Review*, 25 (9), 25 January 1952, pp. 582-588, and 25 (10), 21 February 1952, pp. 636-641.

100 'Report by Majority of Commission (Messrs. Atlee Hunt and Walter H. Lucas)', in The Parliament of the Commonwealth of Australia, *Interim and Final Reports of Royal Commission on Late German New Guinea*, Melbourne, 1920, p. 29. Hunt was Murray's former departmental head in Australia, and Lucas a director of Burns Philp. According to WEST, F., *op. cit.*, p. 198, Murray 'particularly disliked' his two fellow-Royal Commissioners.
Among the reasons that Murray's two opponents advanced for opposing the amalgamation of the two territories was 'the very different composition of the non-native populations. In Papua there are practically none but British subjects; in the Mandated Territory there are at present, apart from the Military Forces, only a few British, but many Germans,[and shades of "White Australia"!] Chinese and Japanese' (*ditto*, p. 23).

101 By 1939, Sir Hubert Murray was even prepared to concede that familiarity with German methods had not imbued the New Guinea administration with German rather than British ideas of 'native administration'—in order to ensure the separate survival of his 'home . . . [and] own creation', Papua (Sir Hubert Murray, *Notes on the Suggested Combination of the Administrations of Papua and New Guinea*, Port Moresby, 1939, pp. 2, 18-19).

102 The Parliament of the Commonwealth of Australia, *Report of Committee Appointed to Survey the Possibility of Establishing a Combined Administration of the Territories of Papua and New Guinea, and to Make a Recommendation as to a Capital Site—(1) For the Combined Admini-*

*stration if that is Favoured, or* (2) *for the Territory of New Guinea if the Retention of Separate Administrations is Recommended,* Canberra, 1939.

103 McCARTHY, J. K., *Patrol into Yesterday: My New Guinea Years,* Melbourne, 1963, p. 9; and BASSETT, MARNIE, *Letters From New Guinea,* 1921, Melbourne, 1969, p. 11.

104 WOLFERS, E. P., 'Games People Flay: Whose Ethnohistory?', *New Guinea,* 6 (1), March-April 1971, p. 51.

105 WOLFERS, E. P., 'The Unsettled Settlers: New Guinea in Australia, 1942-6', *The Journal of the Papua &New Guinea Society,* 1 (2), 1967, p. 10.

106 *Report . . . on the Administration of . . . New Guinea, from* September, 1914, to 30th June, 1921, p. 22. Cf. *Report . . . on the Administration of . . . New Guinea from 1st July, 1921, to 30th June, 1922,* p. 51.

107 *Luluais* who had held office under the Germans were replaced by the Australian administration (SALISBURY, R. F., *Vunamami: Economic Transformation in a Traditional Society,* Melbourne, 1970, p. 44).

Despite their loss of the legal power to take part in judicial matters, *luluais* in the Rabaul District were reported to be hearing cases and exacting fines in 1924 (The Parliament of the Commonwealth of Australia, *Report by Colonel John Ainsworth, C.M.G., C.B.E., D.S.O. (Late Chief Native Commissioner, Kenya Colony) on Administrative Arrangements and Matters Affecting the Interests of Natives in the Territory of New Guinea* (hereinafter cited as *Report by Colonel John Ainsworth . . .*), Melbourne, 1924, p. 17.

108 McCARTHY, J. K., *op. cit.,* pp. 231-232.

109 *Report by Colonel John Ainsworth . . .,* p. 23.

110 *Report by Colonel John Ainsworth . . .,* p. 24.

Although Ainsworth specifically condemned a number of Native Administration Regulations that were very similar to provisions contained in the Papua Native Regulations (see, for example, footnotes 111, 112, 113, 114, 117 and 118 below), Sir Hubert Murray's sixteen-page booklet in reply did not even mention them. However, in answer to Ainsworth's suggestion that Asians should (continue to) be imported to assist in the development of New Guinea (*ditto,* 12-13), Murray replied that the exclusion of such labour was 'a heavy handicap, but . . . we . . . [have] shouldered the load deliberately and would carry it to the end.' Speaking particularly of Papua, he feared 'a race problem in the future' as well as 'the danger of Asiatic immigrants crossing the comparatively few miles of intervening ocean' from the territory to Australia. He expected the latter consideration would weigh more with an Australian than with an officer of the Imperial Service (MURRAY, J. H. P., *Notes on Colonel Ainsworth's Report on the Mandated Territory of New Guinea, op. cit.,* pp. 5-6).

111 Dealing as it did with illiterate villagers, this provision gave Colonel Ainsworth the (quite accurate) impression 'that the intention . . . [was] to catch any and sundry who may have escaped the many other offences contained in the Regulations' (*Report by Colonel John Ainsworth . . .,* p. 24).

112 Colonel Ainsworth was quite firmly of the opinion that the power to appoint and dismiss *luluais* should be vested in the Administrator of New Guinea, or the Native Commissioner. As things stood, *luluais* were 'liable to be dismissed because of some momentary and possibly trivial disagreement with the district officer and, at that, possibly a newly-arrived or acting man who may have ideas different to those of his predecessor.' A *luluai* who had been dismissed without serious reason was very likely to become 'an undesirable element in a district' (*Report by Colonel John Ainsworth . . .,* p. 18). According to SALISBURY, R. F., *Vunamami: Economic Transformation in a Traditional Society, op. cit.,* pp. 44-45 the Australians not only dismissed the *luluais* who had been appointed by the Germans, but each new European official

on the Gazelle Peninsula between 1922 and 1930 (and in the Highlands during the closing years of World War II) 'felt dissatisfied with the appointments of his predecessor and made new and additional appointments.'

In 1927, the power to dismiss *luluais* was legally vested in the Administrator, although District Officers were able to suspend them from office for up to six months, and to dismiss *tultuls* and medical *tultuls.*

For some accounts of how *luluais* (like village constables) managed to employ their official positions for personal aggrandisement, see BROWN, PAULA, 'From Anarchy to Satrapy', *American Anthropologist,* 65 (1), February 1963, pp. 1-15; EPSTEIN, A. L., *Matupit: Land, Politics, and Change among the Tolai of New Britain,* Canberra, 1969, p. 252; HOGBIN, H. I., 'Government Chiefs in New Guinea', in FORTES, M. (ed.), *Social Structure: Studies presented to A. R. Radcliffe-Brown,* Oxford, 1949, pp. 189-206; SALISBURY, R. F., 'Despotism and Australian Administration in the New Guinea Highlands, *op. cit.,* p. 228; SALISBURY, R. F., *Vunamami: Economic Transformation in a Traditional Society, op. cit.,* p. 45.

As in Papua, many village officials in New Guinea were former prisoners who had first come into regular contact with the government and learnt the territorial *lingua franca* in gaol (REED, S. W., *op. cit.,* p. 171, n. 35). One can only speculate as to how the behaviour of the ex-convicts compared with that of the men described by Brown and Hogbin above.

113 *Report by Colonel John Ainsworth . . .,* p. 24.
    Under the Police Offences Ordinance 1925, a New Guinean witness in a District Court case could be apprehended and detained in the same manner as a defendant.

114 *Report by Colonel John Ainsworth . . .,* p. 8.

115 *Territory of Papua. Annual Report for . . . 1938-1939,* p. 5.
    Practically all of Papua had been explored, although much of the territory was 'not yet under control, just as the slum areas of great cities can hardly be said to be under control . . .' (*ditto,* p. 6).

116 Curiously, the report of the commission of inquiry into the 1929 Rabaul strike recommended that 'the Native Labour Regulations be amended to provide that no native labourer be permitted to be abroad in Rabaul township after, say, nine or ten at night, unless he is in possession of a pass issued by the police officer' (*Report . . . on the Administration of . . . New Guinea from 1st July, 1928, to 30th June, 1929,* p. 109, and WORSLEY, P., *The Trumpet Shall Sound: A Study of 'Cargo' Cults in Melanesia,* London, 1957, p. 47)—some six years after a nine o'clock curfew had been introduced, and three years before it became permissible to extend the curfew-hour in certain cases to eleven o'clock.

117 Again, Colonel Ainsworth's comments provided a useful gauge of the standing of the New Guinea legal system by British colonial standards:
    'How is an illiterate native to know when he is being photographed (natives in the vicinity of Rabaul and at some of the out-stations where steamers call, are constantly being photographed) whether the photograph is capable of being reproduced in moving or living pictures. If the intention of the Administration is to prevent the appearance of exaggerated pictures or, indeed, whatever the idea is, the only reasonable course is to apply the clause in question to the photographer. It seems both unjust and absurd to place the offence on the native' (*Report by Colonel John Ainsworth . . .,* p. 24).

In 1925, it became illegal under the Police Offences Ordinance to take, buy or sell a negative, photograph or film of a New Guinean that could be used in moving or living pictures of a dramatic character. The penalty for this offence was a fine of one hundred pounds or a gaol sentence of six months (as against a three pound fine and/or six months imprisonment for any New Guinean who was photographed).

118 To Ainsworth, it seemed 'quite wrong to put a person in prison for wearing a shirt or a hat' (*Report by Colonel John Ainsworth . . .*, p. 24).

119 EPSTEIN, A. L., *op. cit.*, p. 31; and EPSTEIN, T. S., *Capitalism, Primitive and Modern: Some Aspects of Tolai Economic Growth*, Canberra, 1968, p. 47.

120 The first marriage between a male New Guinean and a female European did not take place until the early 1960s.

121 REED, S. W., *op. cit.*, p. 245.

122 JOHNSON, S. H., 'Criminal Law and Punishment', in BROWN, B. J., (ed.), *Fashion of Law in New Guinea: Being an account of the past, present and developing system of laws in Papua and New Guinea*, Sydney, 1969, p. 83.

123 REED, S. W., 'New Guinea', in THOMPSON, E. T., and HUGHES, E. C.(eds.), *Race: Individual and Collective Behaviour*, Glencoe (Illinois), 1958, p. 287.

124 STANNER, W. E. H., *The South Seas in Transition: A Study of Post-War Rehabilitation and Reconstruction in Three British Pacific Dependencies*, Sydney, 1953, p. 2.

125 WHITE, O., *Time Now, Time Before*, Melbourne, 1967, p. 15.

126 The name came from a poem entitled 'Fuzzy Wuzzy Angels' by Sapper H. 'Bert' Beros. Prior to its publication in a booklet entitled *The Fuzzy Wuzzy Angels and other Verses* (Sydney, n.d., pp. 11-12), it was published in the Brisbane *Courier-Mail* and then the *Australian Women's Weekly*. After being printed in *The Marist Messenger*, it was reprinted in *The Annals of Our Lady of the Sacred Heart* (LIV (4), April 1943, p. 69). It also appeared in BODGER, J. D., *Fuzzy-Wuzzy Angels of Papua: The native background to the Papuan Campaign and its influence on the future of the Territory* (*Toronto*, n.d., p. 2), and COCKETT, C. B., *The Australians, Americans and Fuzzy-Wuzzies of New Guinea: Christian Missions Help to Save the Pacific*, Sydney, n.d., p. 10-11.

127 WOLFERS, E., 'Return to Kokoda', Newsletter EPW-9 of the Institute of Current World Affairs, New York, 15 November 1967.

128 MAIR, L. P., *Australia in New Guinea*, London, 1948, p. 13.

129 READ, K. E., 'Effects of the Pacific War in the Markham Valley, New Guinea', *Oceania*, XVIII (2), December 1947, p. 108.

130 A.N.G.A.U. was formally set up in March 1942. On 30 October 1945, the administration of that portion of Papua and New Guinea to the south of the Markham River was handed back to a provisional civil administration. By 24 June 1946, the whole of Papua and New Guinea had finally been restored to civilian control.

131 Government of the Commonwealth of Australia, *Statutory Rules made under Commonwealth Acts during the Year 1941 also Prerogative Orders, etc., with Tables and Index*, Canberra. See also 'Defence—National Security' in the 1943, 1944, 1945-1946, and 1947-1948 volumes. The National Security Regulations were made under the Australian National Security Act.

132 SOMARE, M., 'In a Japanese School', *Journal of the Papua and New Guinea Society*, 4 (1), 1970, pp. 29-32.

133 BURRIDGE, K., *Mambu: A Melanesian Millenium*, London, 1960, p. 12. Cf. HASTINGS, P., 'Race Relations—I: Prospero's Other Island', *New Guinea* 2 (1), March—April 1967, p. 56.

134 LONG, G., *The Final Campaigns*, Canberra, 1963, p. 83.

135 In 1950, the people of Wabag in the Western Highlands were still 'felt to be non-co-operative with the Administration', at least partly because the

Army had resumed 'a piece of more or less level garden land, a Wabag rarity', in 1943, as well as a ridge site for a house without discussion with the owners, and without payment (ELKIN, A. P., 'Delayed Exchange in Wabag Sub-District, Central Highlands of New Guinea, with Notes on the Social Organization', *Oceania*, XXIII (3), March 1953, p. 162.

136 MURRAY, J. H. P., *Review of the Australian Administration in Papua from 1907 to 1920*, Port Moresby, n.d., p. 42.

137 *Commission of Inquiry under the National Security (Inquiries) Regulations and National Security (General) Regulations into the circumstances relating to the suspension of the Civil Administration of the Territory of Papua in* February, 1942: *Report By J. V. Barry, K.C., (Commissioner)*, 1944-1945, p.57.

138 According to MAIR, L. P., *op. cit.*, p. 194, only 58 members of the 178-man A.N.G.A.U. field staff in April 1944 had had pre-war experience in the field of 'native administration'; 28 had been government officers in other departments; 35 had been unofficial residents of Papua and New Guinea before the war, and 57 were new to the territory. Copies of the Native Regulations and Native Administration Regulations were extremely hard for the newcomers to obtain. As a result, 'Patrol officers with no clear idea of the extent or limits of their powers sometimes adopted methods more high-handed than the most convinced exponents of "bashing" would have condoned in normal times . . . .'

139 A.N.G.A.U., 'Conference of Officers of Headquarters and Officers of District Staff', *Papers and Discussion*, Port Moresby, 7-12 February 1944, Vol. 1, p. 1.

140 Cf. LAWRENCE, P., *Road Belong Cargo: A Study of the Cargo Movement in the Southern Madang District New Guinea*, Melbourne, 1964, p. 124.

141 Major D. Barrett, when delivering a paper entitled 'The Pacific Islands Regiment' to the Second Waigani Seminar, in 1968.

142 BEIER, U., 'The White Man's Burden: As a group of carriers saw the war', *New Guinea*, 4 (3) September—October 1969, p. 35; KIKI, A. M., *op. cit.*, p. 60; and READ, K. E., *op. cit.*, p. 110.

143 Allied Geographical Section, South West Pacific Area, *You and the Native: Notes for the Guidance of Members of the Forces in their Relations with New Guinea Natives*, 1943, p. 1.

144 Allied Geographical Section, South West Pacific Area, *ibid.*, p. 2.

145 Cf. HELTON, E. C. N., *Booklet on Pidgin English as used in The Mandated Territory of New Guinea. With Dictionary of Nouns and Phrases*, Brisbane, n.d., p. 10.

146 REINHOLD, W. J., *The Bulldog-Wau Road*, Brisbane, 1946, pp. 37-38.

147 Cf. HOGBIN, H. I., *Transformation Scene: The Changing Culture of a New Guinea Village*, London, 1951, p. 278. Hogbin was criticised for allowing a New Guinean servant to accompany him in a staff car to an airfield, instead of ordering a special truck for him. It was better, so some members of A.N.G.A.U. seemed to think, 'to use up petrol than to endanger the status of European'.

148 LONG, G., *op. cit.*, p. 380.

149 HOGBIN, H. I., *Transformation Scene: The Changing Culture of a New Guinea Village*, *op. cit.*, p. 278.

150 Allied Geographical Section, South West Pacific Area, *op. cit.*, p. 12.

151 Allied Geographical Section, South West Pacific Area, *op. cit.*, p. 3.

152 BEIER, U., *op. cit.*, *passim*, and ERI, V., *op. cit.*, p. 128, *et seq.* Although

not history in the formal sense, Eri's novel gives eloquent expression to the attitudes of the disenchanted.

153 LORD HAILEY, 'Introduction', *op. cit.*, p. xii.

154 ROFE, R. B., 'Urbanization—Lae, Territory of Papua and New Guinea', in *Urban Problems in the South Pacific: South Pacific Commission Technical Paper*, No. 152, Noumea, April 1967, p. 42.

155 MURRAY, J. K., *The Provisional Administration of the Territory of Papua—New Guinea: Its Policy and Its Problems*, Brisbane, 1949, pp. 25-26.

156 MAIR, L. P., *op. cit.*, p. 210.
The expatriate community resented the tone of the broadcast as well as the failure to forewarn them of the measure so that they might attempt to persuade their employees to re-engage.

157 Unless otherwise indicated, the source of the ordinances and regulations cited or quoted in the remainder of this chapter is the relevant year (often indicated in brackets) of *The Laws of the Territory of New Guinea 1921-1945 (Annotated) in force on 29th October, 1945, together with Tables and Indexes*, Vols. I-V, Sydney, 1947; *The Laws of the Territory of Papua 1888-1945 (Annotated) in force on 29th October, 1945, together with Tables and Indexes*, Vols. I-V, Sydney, 1948; *Laws of the Territory of Papua-New Guinea, 1945-1949 (Annotated) made between 30th October, 1945 and 30th June, 1949 . . .*, Sydney, 1952; and *Laws of the Territory of Papua and New Guinea 1949-1951 (Annotated) . . ., et seq.* The latest available index to the post-war ordinances and regulations of Papua and New Guinea is Territory of Papua and New Guinea, *Alphabetical Tables of Ordinances and Instruments with References and Appendices from 1945 to 3rd April, 1970: Supplement to Volumes V of The Laws of the Territory of Papua 1888-1945 (Annotated) and of The Laws of the Territory of New Guinea 1921-1945 (Annotated)*, Port Moresby, 1970.

158 The Parliament of the Commonwealth of Australia, *Report to the General Assembly of the United Nations on the Administration of the Territory of New Guinea from 1st July, 1948, to 30th June, 1949* (hereinafter cited in the form '*Report . . . on the administration . . . of New Guinea from . . . to . . .*), p. 37. The same words appeared in the *Report . . . on the Administration . . . of New Guinea from 1st July, 1949, to 30th June, 1950*, p. 57.

159 Compare the much-celebrated picture of the Honourable E. J. Ward wading ashore in the west of Papua in 1944 (*Pacific Islands Monthly* [hereinafter cited as *P.I.M.*] XIV (10), 17 May 1944, p. 7), with that of the Honourable C. E. Barnes being carried from boat to shore in the Milne Bay District some twenty-five years later (*P.I.M .*,40 (5), May 1969, p. 35).

160 *P.I.M.*, XVI (9), 16 April 1946, p. 11.

161 According to GROVES, M., 'The Criminal Jurisdiction of the Supreme Court of Papua-New Guinea: Part I', *op. cit.*, p. 583, the post-war Supreme Court for the Territory of Papua and New Guinea was still functioning during the early 1950s as if there were two separate territories each with its own legal system. One judge heard the New Guinea cases, another those from Papua.

162 BELSHAW, C. S., *The Great Village: The Economic and Social Welfare of Hanuabada, an Urban Community in Papua*, London, 1957, p. 241.
According to Belshaw, one large store in Port Moresby did not take out a native trading licence so that it could refuse Papuans permission to buy, except with a 'chit' from their expatriate employer.

163 MURRAY, J. K., *op. cit.*, p. 39.

164 HASLUCK, P., *Australia's Task in Papua and New Guinea*, Perth, 1956, p. 14.

165 *Report . . . on the Administration . . . of New Guinea from 1st July, 1952, to*

*30th June, 1953,* p. 61. The same words were used in successive Annual Reports up to and including that for 1959-1960.

The same formula was employed in Commonwealth of Australia, *Report to the General Assembly of the United Nations on the Administration of the Territory of New Guinea from 1st July, 1960, to 30th June, 1961,* (which version of the *Annual Reports* is hereinafter cited), Canberra, 1962, with the information that all of the territory's legislation was being revised to remove all discriminatory provisions other than those that were 'needed to guard the well-being of the people, in defined circumstances, or to respect their own customs' (p. 103). In the 1961-1962 *Report,* the foregoing wording was repeated together with the advice that the process of revision was 'almost complete' (p. 102); and the same was said in 1962-1963 (p. 92). The 1963-1964 *Report* announced that discrimination had now come to an end except 'to protect the interests of the indigenous people in such matters as land acquisition and employment' (p. 94), and the same formula was repeated in succeeding annual *Reports* up to and including that for 1969-1970. In the 1968-1969 and 1969-1970 *Annual Reports* the reference to employment was explained in terms of employment 'being subject to the *Native Employment Ordinance* 1958-1968' (pp. 112 and 127 respectively).

166 HASLUCK, P., *op. cit.,* pp. 27-28.

167 SARKAR, C., *Window on Asia,* New Delhi, 1967, p. 58.

168 United Nations, *United Nations Visiting Mission to Trust Territories in the Pacific 1956: Report on New Guinea together with the Relevant Resolution of the Trusteeship Council* (hereinafter cited in the form *United Nations Visiting Mission to . . .*), Trusteeship Council Official Records, Eighteenth Session, Supplement No. 5, New York, 1956, p. 36.

169 Leaders from Hanuabada Village near Port Moresby were among the most vocal advocates for the passage of the Native Women's Protection Ordinance. For a description of the relations that pertained between village women and European men from Port Moresby, see BELSHAW, C. S., *op. cit.,* pp. 237-241.

170 'Customs (Cinematograph Films) Proclamation 1962', in Territory of Papua and New Guinea, *Government Gazette,* 28, 19 June 1962, pp. 323-327.

171 Book censorship has generally been rather less strict in Papua and New Guinea than in Australia. *Lady Chatterley's Lover, Lolita,* and *In Praise of Older Women* were all sold freely in the territory before they became available in Australia. During the mid-1960s, it was, however, widely believed by expatriates and indigenes alike that a large number of communist books were (or, in the view of some expatriates, should be) banned. They were, in fact, not illegal imports at all, but very hard to obtain in Papua and New Guinea. Edward's Lindall's novel, *A Time Too Soon* (London, 1967) was seized from one bookshop soon after publication lest it offend young Papuans and New Guineans, though it was subsequently sold elsewhere in the territory. *Playboy* is less frequently seized by customs in the territory than in Australia, although the Army, for example, has warned its European officers not to give it to their domestic servants lest they become agitated by the notion that all white ladies look like those in *Playboy* without their clothes.

172 MURRAY, J. K., *op. cit.,* p. 55.

173 Territory of Papua and New Guinea, *Legislative Council Debates* (hereinafter cited as *L.C.D.*), Second Council: Fifth Meeting of the First Session, 28th May to 1st June, 1956, p. 86.

174 *United Nations Visiting Mission to the Trust Territories of Nauru and New Guinea, 1962,* Trusteeship Council Official Records: Twenty-Ninth Session, Supplement No. 3, New York, 1962, p. 30.

175 *Papua-New Guinea Post Courier,* 17 September 1969, p. 3.

176 The Secretary for Law (W. W. Watkins), in *L. C. D.*, First Council: Second Meeting of the Second Session, 6th October to 18th October, 1952, p. 46.

177 The New Guinea regulation was amended, too, to replace 'European' with the slightly broader 'non-Native'.

178 'Native' still appears as a noun in both the Papuan Native Regulations and the New Guinea Native Administration Regulations.

179 Commonwealth of Australia, *Parliamentary Debates*, 6 Eliz. II, Vol. H. of R. 16, p. 174.

180 TUDOR, JUDY (ed.), *Pacific Islands Year Book and Who's Who*, Sydney, (9th edition), 1963, p. 309.

181 *Handbook on New Guinea Living for Lutheran Missionaries*, Madang, 1959, pp. 48-49.

182 A Rabaul tourist brochure advised still in 1969 that 'it is customary for women to avoid wearing excessively brief garments which are considered unsuitable for a multi-racial community.'

183 WYATT, JESSIE, *A Guide to Newcomers to Papua—New Guinea*, Port Moresby, n.d. (196?), p. 16:
'In the home, on the streets, and even in the field of sport and swimming, bear in mind the phrase "revealing clothing leads to provocation".'

184 JAMES, C. S., *Tropical and other Diseases commonly met with in Melanesia and Polynesia (Pacific): Their Diagnosis, Prevention and Treatment*, Auckland, (Revised fifth edition; first edition, 1937), 1963, pp. 9-10.

185 For a fascinating, critical account of the modifications wrought to the old 'direct rule' tradition by the introduction of local government councils, see CROCOMBE, R. G., 'Local Government in New Guinea: An Example of Conflict Between Policy and Practice', *The Journal of Pacific History*, 3, 1968, pp. 131-134.

186 BURTON-BRADLEY, B. G., 'Mixed-Race Society in Port Moresby', *New Guinea Research Bulletin*, 23, March 1968, p. 5.

187 The Director of District Services and Native Affairs (A. A. Roberts), in *L.C.D.*, First Council: Fifth Meeting of the Second Session, 16th November to 23rd November, 1953, p. 41.

188 According to CLELAND, SIR DONALD, 'An Administrator Reflects', in *The History of Melanesia, op. cit.*, p. 219, 'Every time the Minister for Territories came up on a visit the urban natives always raised the question when they were going to be allowed to drink.' Cf. KIKI, A. M., *op. cit.*, p. 91; SIMOGUN, PETA, in *L.C.D.*, Second Council: Second Meeting of the First Session, 21st March to 5th October 1955, p. 24, and *L.C.D.*, IV (3), p. 365; *United Nations Visiting Mission to Trust Territories in the Pacific, 1956*, Trusteeship Council Official Records: Eighteenth Session, Supplement No. 5, New York, 1956, pp. 43-44; and *United Nations Visiting Mission to the Trust Territories of Nauru and New Guinea, 1962*, Trusteeship Council Official Records: Twenty-Ninth Session, Supplement No. 3, New York, 1962, p. 30.

189 WOLFERS, E. P., 'Alcohol and Social Structure', Newsletter EPW-11 of the Institute of Current World Affairs, New York, 14 January 1968, p. 2.

190 In 1955, the administration introduced a bill into the Legislative Council to enable Papuans and New Guineans to apply for a permit to drink alcohol. It was, however, withdrawn in the face of opposition by the non-official members (including two of the three indigenes), and an all-expatriate select committee of five was set up to investigate the question (*L.C.D.*, Second Council: Second Meeting of the First Session, 21st March to 25th March, 1955, pp. 21-25, 26-29, 62-71; and Second Council: Third Meeting of the First Session, 27th June to 30th June, 1955, pp. 2-4). The select committee recommended against the immediate introduction of a permit

system, (*L.C.D.*, Second Council: Fourth Meeting of the First Session, 24th October to 28th October, 1955, pp. 5-10), and the permit provisions of the ordinance were withdrawn (*ditto,* pp. 52-60, and 110-111).

In 1958, the amount of methylated spirits that an indigene was permitted to possess was restricted, and two official members of the Legislative Council reported that there was widespread illegal drinking taking place, especially among the Tolai of New Britain. One of these official members, Mr. J. K. McCarthy (the chairman of the 1955 select committee) was openly in favour of a permit system (*L.C.D.*, IV (3), pp. 360-361, and 363-364).

191 For a discussion of the relative importance of the various pressures for change, see NELSON, H. N., 'New Guinea Nationalism and the Writing of History', *Journal of the Papua and New Guinea Society*, 4 (2), 1970, pp. 23-25.

192 *United Nations Visiting Mission to the Trust Territories of Nauru and New Guinea*, 1962, Trusteeship Council Official Records: Twenty-Ninth Session, Supplement No. 3, New York, 1962, p. 30.

193 OGAN, E., 'Drinking Behavior and Race Relations', *American Anthropologist*, 68 (1), February 1966, p. 182.

194 Under the New Guinea Companies Ordinance of 1933, no company having for its object or one of its objects, the engaging in agricultural, pastoral or forestry pursuits or aerial navigation could be formed or registered unless at least two-thirds of its shares were held by or on behalf of British subjects. Holding companies were required to apply for a declaration that they adhered to this provision, or they could be ordered to be wound up.
A little later in 1933, mining companies could be exempted from the two-thirds provision by the Administrator, although, in 1936, companies engaged in mining for oil, coal or iron ore were brought back under it. In 1938, oil companies were again exempted, although the exploitation of their discoveries was controlled anyway under an Ordinance relating to the Mining for Petroleum (Territory of New Guinea, *Legislative Council Debates*, Eighth Session: 24th to 25th August, 1938, p. 26).
The original aim of this particular Companies Ordinance was to conserve the territory's wealth for local use, and to prevent foreign exploitation (*ditto*, p. 26; Territory of New Guinea, *Legislative Council Debates*, Meeting No. 1, 1936: 25th to 28th February, 1936, p. 44; and *L.C.D.*, VI (1), p. 22). However, by 1961, it had become clear that the ordinance also effectively prevented the formation of companies with a more than one-third New Guinean shareholding, as indigenous New Guineans were not British subjects. The ordinance was, therefore, repealed.

195 Under the Native Labour Ordinance of 1946, casual workers could be paid in money alone instead of a small amount of cash, plus keep. From 1952, restrictions were placed upon the granting of permits to casual workers to buy their own food, and from 1960 an 'Advanced Workers Certificate' had to be obtained from a district officer to do so. Since 1963, casual workers have not required a permit to be paid in cash alone, although many agreement workers on plantations are still paid in cash and kind (Territory of Papua and New Guinea, *Report of Board of Inquiry Investigating Rural Minimum Wages under the Native Employment Ordinance 1958-1968, Minimum Wage-Fixing Machinery and Related Matters*, Port Moresby, 1970, pp.7-14.

196 *L.C.D.*, VI (5), p. 444.

197 Until 1947, when the Supreme Court finally gained jurisdiction in New Guinea's Central Highlands District, homicide cases were tried as cases for assault by the District Officer. In areas of recent contact, it was thought to be better to treat murders 'as problems of immediate local administration, which have to be in the hands of the pioneer administrative officer' than to introduce the full panoply of western judicial procedure all at once (GROVES,

M., 'The Criminal Jurisdiction of the Supreme Court of Papua-New Guinea: Part II', *op. cit.*, pp. 638-639).

198 'The Last Editorial', *Black and White,* July-August, 1969, p. 3.

199 HARRIS, M., 'Browsing: A Few Blacks and Whites on New Guinea,' *The Australian,* 26 October 1968.

200 'The Last Editorial', *op. cit.*, p. 3.

201 See, for example, FINNEY, B. R., ' "Partnership" in developing the New Guinea Highlands, 1948-1968', *The Journal of Pacific History,* 5, 1970, pp. 117-134.

202 United Nations Trusteeship Council, *Report of the United Nations Visiting Mission to the Trust Territory of New Guinea, 1968,* Thirty-fifth session: Item 6 of the provisional agenda (T/1678, roneoed), 22 May 1968, p. 100.

203 Territory of Papua and New Guinea, Liquor Licensing Commission, *3rd Annual Report by R. G. Ormsby, Chairman on Operation of Liquor (Licensing) Ordinance 1963-1968 and Generally on the Operation of the Licensing System in the Territory* (roneoed), n.d., p. 29.

204 United Nations Trusteeship Council, *Report of the United Nations Visiting Mission to the Trust Territory of New Guinea, 1971,* Thirty-Eighth session: Item 6 of the provisional agenda (T/1717, roneoed), 6 May 1971, p. 99.

205 FANON, F., *op. cit.*, p. 31.

206 Cf. FANON, F., *op. cit.*, p. 61.

# 5

## AUSTRALIAN PLANNING IN THE
## NEW GUINEA ECONOMY[1]

### Ron Crocombe

One cannot blame Australia for planning New Guinea's economy. Given the trusteeship status, the indigenous demand for higher incomes and the very few New Guineans with specialist skills in this field, it was necessary. The first big step came with the publication, in 1968, of the *Programmes & Policies for the Economic Development of Papua & New Guinea* (known as the Five Year Plan 1968-73).

The plan is a notable achievement, but this article aims to highlight its most serious defect, i.e. the fact that it claims to provide for maximum indigenous participation, but neither it nor government action made the necessary provisions to put this into practice. Moreover, the plan takes too little cognisance of the social and political consequences of the way in which the economic changes are to be brought about. The danger is that the economic goals will not be achieved (not that economic goals should be paramount) and that a major reason for their non-achievement will be the social and political effects of the plan itself, and particularly of inadequate New Guinea participation.

Even if applied economics was an exact science (which it is not) it could only be applied if the policy objectives were complementary. But, in New Guinea, four of the main policy objectives are in conflict in important respects. These objectives are:—

(a) to maximise economic growth in terms of Gross National Product;

(b) to minimise dependence on external aid;

(c) to increase welfare in terms of goods and services, personal freedom, racial harmony, etc.; and

(d) to institute representative government.

As the government has not defined precise priorities, any economist advocating any particular policy can only do so by making personal value judgments about priorities. Moreover, when economists move from theory to practice, they can only deal with a very limited number of variables on the basis of very limited, incomplete, and often inaccurate data. Some of the variables they cannot process are more important than some they can. Absentee economists, like the rest of us, can only make informed guesses from assumed facts. The matter in dispute is the validity of the assumptions.

### The Myth of Maximum Development

Let us, for discussion purposes, take the 'maximum development' argument to its fullest extent, and assume that all persons involved in the

148

New Guinea economy have only 'economic qualities', such as particular skills, economic motivation and amounts of capital. We then draw up a plan for 'maximum development' and move people into the positions where they would contribute most to economic growth. It would proceed at a fantastic rate, with many Japanese, Americans, Chinese, Australians, Indians and others in a variety of roles. But, alas, we are dealing with humans, so we must take note of the 'social qualities'—race, nationality, feelings, etc.—of the people who have been positioned on economic criteria alone. The existence of so many foreigners in those roles would be likely to cause such a political and even physical reaction from New Guineans that the economy would be more likely to be disrupted than to grow, i.e. the social and political consequences of such a plan would negate its economic goals.

One of the paradoxes of the plan is that during the period in which Papua-New Guinea will probably cease to be a colony of the Australian government, it could well become a colony of Australian business interests. It may be true that total growth of 'the economy' will be most rapid if any form of outside capital is attracted into New Guinea for any purpose. It is most unlikely, however, that this would be in New Guinea's best interests. Some forms of capital should be encouraged, others should be accepted under certain circumstances, and others should not be accepted under any circumstances.

At the end of the five-year plan, 52 per cent of all commercial agriculture is to be in expatriate hands and, even in the 1980s, nearly half the value of rural production, and hence of rural income, is still to be controlled by foreigners. No proportionate details were given for commerce and industry, yet it seems that by the 1980s, if the plan is followed, at least 90 per cent of all business and industry, and probably over 95 per cent of all business profits, will be in the hands of foreigners. If this is so, the verbal reiteration of the paramountcy of indigenous interest hides, perhaps unconsciously, the real consequences of the plan.

There is an implicit tendency to regard it as in some way equitable for the 98½ per cent of the population which is New Guinean to get an eventual 50 per cent of gross rural income while the other 50 per cent goes to the 1½ per cent of foreigners. The inequity is even greater in relation to industry and commerce.

The plan claims that local people will slowly catch up with foreigners in entrepreneurial activity, but by the time they are in a position to do so, most of the highly profitable enterprises will be held by foreign interests. It is difficult to see the processes by which the indigenous people will catch up, for the plan made no adequate provision to enable them to achieve this objective.

Although it suggests that the maximum indigenous participation is being provided for, this is not so. Perhaps it is partly because those who drafted the details of the plan are not aware of alternative ways to increase the proportionate participation of New Guinean people, but partly it is a question of inevitably divided loyalties when the interest of Australia and New Guinea are neither complementary nor parallel. In some ways, the interests of Australian capital and New Guinean people are at one, but in many ways they are not. In the latter situations, the planners have come down on the side of foreign capital. The assumption throughout that the interests of expatriate and indigenous people are common is simply not true.

Great emphasis is given to the part to be played by the 'private sector' which will, in practice, be largely a foreign, and predominantly an Australian sector. The plan seems to imply that there should be equal opportunity for all participants in private business in New Guinea. Given the very unequal backgrounds, this would be most unfair.

It is questionable to encourage Australians into New Guinea to compete with New Guineans in those enterprises which the latter could run, when New Guineans are not permitted into Australia to work in tasks where they could effectively compete with Australians to the considerable advantage of the New Guinea economy. About half of the 4,500 trade stores are operated by expatriates. Such persons should not be granted licences to trade or run trucks or other enterprises which New Guineans could operate. It is hypocritical to suggest that New Guineans should compete on equal terms with Australians when Australia will not allow Indian, Japanese or Filipino traders of the same kinds to compete with Australians in Australia, nor to compete with Australians in New Guinea.[2]

The example of the acceptance of Torres Strait Islanders in industrial occupations on the Australian mainland makes an interesting comparison. With many cultural similarities the Torres Strait Islanders are in demand in Australia for many tasks for which their output averages higher than that of white Australians.[3] Figures quoted for the laying of railway tracks, for example, show that the Islanders are up to 30 per cent more efficient than European Australians. Remittances from this employment are one of the mainstays of the Torres Strait Islands economy. For American Samoa, Niue and the Cook Islands, one of the important sources of income and capital accumulation (and skills which are in many cases used back home) is from the islanders working in the USA and New Zealand. As Papuans are legally Australian citizens, denying them access to appropriate work opportunities in Australia is unjust in an economic as well as a legal and moral sense. Indeed, in many ways, this policy effectively denies New Guineans gaining access to one of the main sources of elevation of both their skills and capital accumulation. A reversal of the policy could be one of the most effective practical solutions to the problem of social and economic development in the northern Islands.

If New Guineans could see that they had ample openings in fields within their present and developing skills, they would be much happier about foreign involvement in areas where they do not have either the capital or the skill.

Over $20,000,000 worth of primary produce in New Guinea is marketed by non-indigenous organisations. In many parts of the Pacific, produce marketing is reserved exclusively for local individuals, co-operatives or governments. It could also be so in New Guinea.

Tolais ran taxis in the 1930s. There were 141 licensed taxis in New Guinea in January 1969. Every one was foreign owned. Every one could have been New Guinean owned, but the new licences continued to be awarded to better financed, established foreign companies. In the Northern District, various indigenous people, including a particularly experienced indigenous entrepreneur with the necessary cash, applied for the first local bus licence. It was issued to an Australian planter who was undoubtedly more experienced, but who had already been granted a $50,000 government loan to develop a plantation. In Rabaul, the franchise for a small new bus service, well within the competence of a New Guinean, was, in 1970, granted to an expatriate company.

There were 28 licensed hairdressing salons in New Guinea in 1970, almost all of them owned and run by expatriates. Does New Guinea really need to import barbers?

The Purdy Islands, which were unused for decades as the lessee lived in Australia, recently became available for leasing. Indigenous people who claimed traditional rights were among various indigenes who wanted to acquire the group, but it was granted to the highest bidder, an expatriate trader. Pak Island Plantation, a very large copra enterprise, is also owned by absentees who recently decided to sell it. The former landowners wanted to buy and the vendors wanted to sell to them, but the Development Bank at that time declined to lend the necessary money, though this is now understood to be under re-examination. If they emphasise development of indigenous enterprise, they will almost certainly lend, but even if they emphasise Gross National Product this may be a good investment. Indigenous entrepreneurship may be one of the most valuable factors in increasing Gross National Product.

Action was required to reserve certain categories of enterprise, such as taxis, rural trade stores, hair-dressing, most trucking, etc., for indigenous people. The Minister for Territories said on 9 April 1969, that the government would like to see indigenous participation in ownership and management of large foreign enterprises. Presumably only slow progress will be made in this field until he requires (as in the U.S. Trust Territory in Micronesia) indigenous participation in most major foreign industries (including airlines, shipping and produce marketing) as a prerequisite to their being granted entry and the land, tax and other concessions that are justifiably given to many industries.

Guy Hunter, an authority on African development, believes that accelerated economic growth and social balance can only be attained 'by creation of opportunity at the low level rather than an attempt to maximise national income through the efforts of a small entrepreneurial group'.[4] A noted development economist, Clifton R. Wharton, notes the dangers of improved growth if it is achieved by increasing the gap between rich and poor, and cites the recent death of 43 persons in a riot in India as a product of this.[5] The continuing Rabaul riots show similar influences at work in New Guinea.

*Social and Political Consequences*

The plan assumes, in its budgeting, two categories of income and privilege based on race, i.e. expatriates are to be paid much higher rates of pay and be given more favourable conditions of employment than indigenous people. The extent to which indigenous people will tolerate such a state of affairs is yet to be seen, but reaction against it already has been considerable.

An unintended consequence of the plan is that foreign firms become involved in political processes, both through contributions to campaign funds and through more widespread and pervasive influences. They will thus have a disproportionate influence on who gets elected and on what policies get adopted.

The plan will result in making the rich richer and the poor poorer, for poverty is a relative concept. The increasing total income of Cuba during the 1950s did provide spill-over benefits to Cubans, but as so many of the basic resources and institutions were controlled by foreigners, the latter got most of the increase. This led to total rejection of American interests. Whether this was disadvantageous or otherwise does not alter its having happened. Similar situations have occurred in Indonesia and many other parts of the world. Plans to avoid such a situation in New Guinea must be built now, for when the crisis arrives it is too late.

The Territory Production Account should, but does not, show the relative incomes accruing to expatriate as against indigenous people. Likewise, references to increases in average incomes would be more meaningful if the actual average incomes of indigenous and expatriate people were shown. To avoid revealing such figures is to hide one's head in the sand, for this is a crucial economic and political factor for the future.

### External Subsidy

The Australian grants are large, given with benevolent intent, and are appreciated in New Guinea. They are urgently needed for creating infrastructure such as harbours, schools, etc., for acquiring local interests in commercial enterprises, and even more important for developing the skills and capabilities of New Guineans. These grants have great advantages because they have no long-term strings, i.e., the infrastructure is put in and, so long as it is effectively maintained, continuing benefit is derived. Excessive foreign investment, on the other hand, could leave New Guinea as a permanent colony paying a large part of its income to Australia and Australians.

### Credit Structure

There are co-operative societies, savings and loan societies and some forms of government credit. Some banks have loaned small sums to New Guineans. But, looking at the total picture, the proportion made available to indigenous people has been 'dismal', to quote the New Guinean economist, Henry To Robert. Only a tiny fraction of indigenous savings was lent back to New Guinean individuals, organisations or institutions. Most is loaned to Australians who are a better financial risk. Indigenous participation at present is not acquiring for them a significantly increased proportion of ownership in New Guinea's enterprises, though in 1970 and 1971 the Development Bank made strenous efforts to improve this situation.

A strong case can be made for a policy of active private enterprise in the development of many of New Guinea's resources, but it is much more difficult to support when the backing is predominantly for enterprise which is almost exclusively foreign. It can lead to average per capita income appearing high, only because the incomes of the foreign component are high.

The great need is to provide local people with positive plans, and with detailed guides to their implementation, so that they can get into ownership as well as specialised training. This will not just happen, and it is pleasing to note that more positive steps in this direction were taken in 1971.

### Agriculture and Livestock

Apart from peasant farming, the major indigenous participation in this area is to be labouring at lower pay than some other places pay for workers doing the same work, producing the same crops for the same international markets. Much labour in New Guinea is indeed inefficient, but the most effective way to persuade planters to make it more efficient is probably to force the payment of higher wages. It had this effect in the New Hebrides and the British Solomon Islands. There is no advantage in commercial development if it makes the people unskilled workers for whom the quality of life is not improved.

The philosophy of nucleus estates needs much closer examination. The tea estates in the highlands are highly capitalised, prosperous foreign cells surrounded by peasant farmers who will see themselves by comparison as poor and deprived, and whose livelihood is dependent on the factory they surround. Price for the product is determined by the factory which has an effective monopoly. It would be difficult to devise a system which could so quickly affect race relations adversely. The number of indigenous workers on tea estates is expected to rise to 14,000. But, if they are to be paid $4.00 per month plus keep, or 60 cents a day without keep, it is a moot point whether the prospective figure of 14,000 is an encouraging or a frightening one.

The Administration's decision to take a substantial equity in the first oil palm estate and processing factory is to be commended. A great deal more of this and other kinds of local involvement are urgently needed and are, at last, being encouraged.

As in many other aspects of the plan, one must applaud the sentiments expressed, but having heard them before without significant action, and seeing little detailed provisions in this plan for how they will be implemented, one must remain a little cautious. There is an urgent need to restrict certain imports, or perhaps better, to tax particular categories of imports which could be locally produced (of which there are many), and to use the tax revenue for the development of urban markets, for the extension of market gardening, and for assistance with marketing arrangements.

Even in 1973, at the end of the five-year period, New Guinea people are expected (in the plan) to own less than one-quarter of the beef cattle, and expatriates more than three-quarters. If indigenous beef production cannot possibly be increased at any faster rate, there may be a good case for not developing expatriate beef production as rapidly as now proposed.

Land is said to be alienated for foreign planters only after 'prior and adequate investigation' to ensure that it is surplus. But surplus by what criteria? The 'white highlands' of Kenya were so regarded, and after investigation and consideration of indigenous need that was thought fully adequate at that time, as were the German estates in Samoa (and near Rabaul and Madang also!), and in Nauru, the Gilbert Islands, Fiji, the Solomons, New Zealand, Indonesia and the Caroline Islands. In all of the above cases, however, and in most others, the colonial administrations have been found in the long term, to have been working from economic, demographic and political assumptions which were in fact false. The post-war New Guinea alienations for foreign settlers, including some quite recent ones, will probably come to look even less appropriate than some of the early colonial examples referred to above.

The statement that Administration promotion of foreign planters has not used resources which could have helped increase indigenous output is true where the capital has come from private sources, and some co-existence of foreign plantations and indigenous smallholders can be mutually advantageous. But the government, through the former ex-servicemen's credit scheme, allocated to foreign settlers twelve times the acreage and fifteen times the loan funds allocated to indigenous settlers, and the indigenes probably planted as many trees per unit of capital as the expatriates.

*Forestry*

The main objectives of the forestry programme reflect those of the plan as a whole, i.e., to increase export earnings and local employment, to foster a measure of Territory (whether expatriate, indigenous or governmental is not, but should be, clarified) participation, and to 'increase the levels of training and employment of indigenes in the industry'. No major effort to increase indigenous ownership of the industry is provided for, though forestry lends itself to indigenous participation at that level. Indigenous people own much of the forest land and are paid royalties in cash which are largely dissipated. Where it is saved, it is usually in savings banks where the rate of interest barely keeps up with the depreciation in the value of money. If, however, instead of taking cash, a considerable proportion of that money was invested in the industry, then the proportionate value of their resource would probably increase all the time and they would participate in the industry in a very real sense. No significant consideration was given to these possibilities in the plan,[6] though some steps in this direction are now being taken.

*Capital Formation*

This is one of the crucial issues in the whole plan. There is a wide range of ways in which capital formation by the indigenous people could and should be speeded up.

When land is purchased in New Guinea, the indigenous people are paid in cash even though they are not familiar (and cannot be made immediately familiar) with its full potential worth. There is a tremendous incentive to spend it quickly and unwisely, despite the fact that officials usually advise them to bank it. In New Zealand, similar monies used to be paid to the Maori Land Trust Boards or to the Maori Trustee on behalf of the land-owners. The principle is clear and applies in New Guinea. It is that, not only have the living people been deprived of a permanent asset, but their descendants have been as well. Some land sales are essential, but the attempt must be made to replace one permanent asset by another (or at least by a long-term asset).

The New Guineans to whom money is paid for land are merely trustees, not only for today's adults, but also for their children and for those who will come after them. To give the present day adult representatives full and immediate control of this whole resource and the rights to dissipate it immediately is unethical and has no traditional precedent. It should be used by them to acquire substantial long-term interest in industries, commerce, or government securities, or be taken out in part as shares of enterprises which will use the land. In the case of tea estates, for example, it would have been feasible for indigenous people to have supplied the land, by lease or absolutely, and to have been given an equivalent proportion of shares in companies developing them. The same applies to cattle and to many other enterprises. It is encouraging to note that, in 1971, this action was taken in respect of the Bougainville copper industry.

A positive programme is needed to maximise New Guinean ownership of all forms of enterprise. In the allocation of trading licences, not only preference, but an absolute right, should be given to local people. Any form of business which they can manage or could shortly be expected to manage with adequate government or other extension and advice needs to be reserved absolutely for New Guinean businessmen.

### Mining

Here again the principal objectives listed are to attract the maximum amount of foreign investment, to employ the maximum number of indigenes as workers and to 'increase indigenous participation in small scale mining'. It is, in some ways, easier to justify expatriate involvement in plantations because, if properly maintained, they are a continuing asset. If the expatriate plantation owner earned profits before indigenous people were in a position to do so, he has done nobody any harm. The asset continues to be productive, and whether he continues to produce or is bought out by indigenous people, the economy continues to benefit. This is not so in the case of oil, gas, mining and other extractive industries (of which some forms of forestry are an example). To justify their immediate large scale exploitation, very major advantages must accrue to the local people and they must well off-set the probable advantages to the local people of holding on to the resources.

### Manufacturing

Government's first aim is said to be to provide 'employment, training and business opportunities for the indigenous people'. It proposes to do this by providing employment and business opportunities for foreigners. A price must be paid for foreign involvement, but the total cost implied in the plan, in social as well as economic terms, is unnecessarily high.

Industrial undertakings in New Guinea are almost entirely foreign. The Plan notes that indigenous people are being trained for managerial duties, but the current degree of such training is not likely to lead to New Guineans holding the majority of management positions even within the next decade or so.

The proposal to set up a statutory tariff advisory authority is to be welcomed. It is hoped, however, that it has strong New Guinean membership and that all development will be aimed at maximum benefit to New Guinea people—rather than the realities of the plan which give only token support to this principle.[7]

### Air and Sea Transport

There is very important scope for indigenous participation here and steps should be taken immediately to lay a base for their eventual takeover, predominantly by Papuan and New Guinean people. No provisions of this kind were set out in the plan. The granting of air rights gives the airline companies access to a very profitable enterprise. Papua-New Guinea is one of the few places in the Pacific, and in the world, where the ownership of airlines is entirely in foreign hands. The Australian government does not allow foreign airlines to operate within Australia. This lucrative business is understandably reserved for Australians. Likewise, Australia gives landing rights for services from foreign countries only in return for reciprocal rights. These are, in practice, rights to earn substantial money.

Until recently, the Micronesian people of the United States Trust Territory of the Pacific Island had no more experience of running airlines than the people of Papua-New Guinea, yet it was decided that America's trusteeship obligation necessitated substantial immediate Micronesian participation in the ownership and running of internal and overseas air services. When Pan American had a monopoly on internal air services within the Trust Territory, they considered it impossible to provide for local shareholding and the rapid training of local staff, until the government declared that it would seek another airline to do this. Pan American then found it not only possible, but very easy, and planned a new company with Pan American as well as Micronesian shareholders, directors, and management. Pan American saw the light too late, however, and the rights were granted to a newly-formed company, Air Micronesia, in which about 30 per cent of the shares are held by Continental Airlines of the USA, about 20 per cent by Aloha Airlines of Hawaii and about 35 per cent by the United Micronesian Development Corporation, which is a predominantly Micronesian-owned business enterprise. The Micronesian shareholders have privileged access to 51 per cent of the shares after a certain number of years.

Air Micronesia provides jet services within the Trust Territory as well as to the USA and Asia. A similar provision in New Guinea would enable one or more locally based airlines to provide all internal services and have half the landing rights between New Guinea and Australia. This would be substantial business indeed.

In sea transport likewise, American operators are not allowed to compete on equal terms with Micronesians. In Papua-New Guinea, on the other hand, almost all coastal shipping services are in Australian hands. For certain internal routes in the Trust Territory, as well as shipping to the USA, Micronesia Inter-Ocean Line was formed. The basic skills and ships are provided by an American shipping company, half the twelve directors of the local company are Micronesian, and there are specific provisions for rapid training of Micronesians.

All other local shipping (and there is quite a lot of it) in Micronesia is operated by Micronesian individuals, companies and co-operatives. This situation did not arise automatically; it required specific government action to protect and develop the local industry. Such action has been taken to protect and develop the coastal shipping industry in Australia for Australians, and equivalent is needed in New Guinea.

## Tourism

The tourist programme calls for indigenous participation only through 'employment and training and the supply of goods and services'. It was this kind of policy that led the former head of state of Western Samoa, the Hon. Tupua Tamasese, to restrict tourism because his experience in other countries led him to believe that if the role of the Samoan people was to be that of servants, waitresses, taxi drivers, curio sellers and prostitutes, then Samoa preferred to be without it. The proposals for tourism in the five-year plan for New Guinea seem to be of the kind that Tamasese took steps to avoid in Samoa.

It was assumed by foreign investors and foreign governments at that time, that a tourist industry could only be built with foreign people owning the hotels and the major tourist facilities. In recent years, however, both

investors and governments have changed their views on minimum requirements for a viable tourist industry, and most self-governing islands of the
Pacific now insist on substantial local participation. When Intercontinental
Hotels wanted to build an international hotel in American Samoa, the people
opposed the scheme unless they were to derive significant advantages at all
levels and be major owners. The problem was resolved when the Samoan
people formed a company, collected as much money from their people as
they could, and accepted a loan and advice from the United States government to ensure that the hotel was successfully established. The hotel is
owned by the Samoan people who took shares in it (and who have privileged access to buy out the US government's interests) and is leased to
Intercontinental Hotels for them to operate with an almost totally Samoan
staff.

In the kingdom of Tonga, American hotel interests were not permitted
to build until the government had built a major Tongan-owned hotel. The
hotels in the Gilbert and Ellice Islands are owned by local government
councils. In Micronesia, where tremendous impetus is now being given to the
erection of tourist hotels, all of them are required to have very significant
indigenous shareholding.

New Guinea's five-year plan does not prohibit the possibility of locally
owned or joint local-foreign enterprises of this kind. It is protected by their
token existence—perhaps one per cent of the country's hotel beds are owned
by a local government council (in Mt. Hagen), and there has been talk of
minority indigenous shareholding in one small hotel. This is not enough. To
get enterprises of this kind actively functioning requires an express government policy and specific government action.

Consideration might be given to a turnover tax on the travel industry
to provide a fund for the maximum training and participation of indigenous
people at all levels of the tourist industry.

*Man-power*

One of the principal objectives listed is that of attracting and retaining
skilled overseas personnel 'where trained people are not available from
within the Territory'. This is reasonable and necessary provided every effort
is made to train local people to assume these positions. The danger is that
when overseas people are given particularly favourable conditions, there is
not the urgent pressure to pursue the scale of training that is necessary.
The objective of training local people as fast as possible has been stated for
many years but only limited action has been taken to accomplish it. Although
the plan makes provisions for some improvement, they could and should be
expanded considerably.

Another major objective is to 'maintain satisfactory conditions of
employment and stable industrial relations'. This, however, is very difficult
to achieve when the government provides racially discriminatory wages, conditions and privileges. The plan avoids the sharpening conflict between the
races over access to income and other advantages.

Many Asian people who possess skills now being imported from Australia would be happy to work for local rates and local conditions, or much
closer to them than Australians are. Certain other Pacific Islanders, too,
have skills which they could effectually contribute. These people are denied
access to New Guinea because they are not white. The White Australian

policy is Australia's own business, but it is unjustifiable to impose it on New Guinea. The government uses tokenism as a protective screen. Each mission was allowed two non-white teachers, when the need for and availability of well qualified persons was in the hundreds. The Department of External Territories advertised for highly qualified secondary teachers in the United Kingdom several years ago. Dozens of the applicants were qualified in every way, but they were not white. Despite the fact that the department was unable to obtain enough white teachers to fill the vacancies, it rejected all the non-whites. In the early 1960s, New Guinea was unable to import enough expatriate medical assistants, doctors and primary school teachers. The Cook Islands had too many doctors and stopped training more. It also reduced teacher intake and later stopped teacher training for a whole year because it had too many trained teachers (and every child was receiving a minimum of ten years' free and compulsory education). Western Samoa had to dismiss some qualified school teachers because of a financial crisis. The writer pointed out to Mr. Hasluck, the then Minister, that these people were available and that the first schools in Papua-New Guinea had been built and staffed by Cook Islanders and Samoans, before Australia took control of the country and restricted their further contribution. The Minister was not prepared to consider employing them.

If expatriates continue to be paid approximately double what local people are paid to perform the same tasks, there are tremendous long-term savings to be gained by investing in higher education for New Guineans. Yet, at the same time, the government denied the new university adequate finance to train the number of people whom they could and were prepared to train. It thus forced the employment of more expatriates when more local people could have been employed in professional categories by 1973.

The plan makes no study of the possible use of volunteer workers, though a passing reference says that volunteers would not be able to make any significant impact. The unstated reason, however, was that the Australian government would not permit them to enter the country. Significant numbers of volunteers, mostly university graduates, were ready and willing to work in New Guinea for two years at local rates and conditions. In 1967, the then Minister of Territories, Mr. C. E. Barnes, confirmed that he would not allow volunteers, except from Australia and the United Kingdom, into New Guinea. That policy has fortunately been eased, and Canadian and New Zealand volunteers are now being admitted also. The only other Trust Territory in the world used more expatriate volunteers working at local rates of pay and under local conditions than expatriate officers paid at mainland rates. In Western Samoa and the Kingdom of Tonga, there are more expatriates working as volunteers (most of whom are much more highly qualified than the average expatriate working in New Guinea) than at overseas rates.

The plan notes that employers are expected to assist with training their staff. In practice, however, because profits are high and goals short-term, most employers prefer to import many categories of workers who could have been trained in New Guinea. Not until the government provides much stiffer restrictions on the kinds of employment that can be undertaken by foreigners in New Guinea, will the situation improve.

In certain medical and education fields, because more service per dollar spent is available from mission services than from government services, it would seem wise to expand subsidies to missions for this work rather than to expand government activity.

The Department of Public Health is justly credited with substantial advances in training indigenous people for responsible positions. Paradoxically, jobs in that department probably require more training than those in almost any other. The Department of Health is highly indigenised, only because it undertook a very comprehensive programme of training both within New Guinea and overseas. The fact that this department has gone so much further than any other in this field is not only a credit to its Director and other senior staff, but substantiates that a great deal more could and should be done by other departments.

### The Circularity of Elite Communication

One reason why planners have made insufficient provisions for indigenous participation is the circularity of elite communication in and about New Guinea. The Department of Territories economists in Canberra get their ideas largely from a small group of colonial officials, businessmen and academics. And the Port Moresby officials who did the detailed planning, do it again, in association with the same group, and pay regular visits to Canberra to do so.

A simple sociogram showing the frequency, nature and intensity of contacts in these matters would show a very small pool of rather like-minded men, knit together in a typical Establishment, accepting the conventional convictions that New Guineans are 'not ready' for much more economic participation, and that existing caste privileges (which are reinforced by the economic plans and practices) are needed and appropriate. Meeting in a variety of combinations and circumstances at conferences, parties or by mail, and saying much the same things to one another, they hear the same ideas repeated back to them and are reinforced in their conviction as to their validity and reasonableness.

New Guinean communication networks hardly intersect at all with this one, except when occasional New Guineans are selected to attend a cocktail party or sit in on a meeting, but the status relations between them and the terms in which the two parties see any given situation usually reduce communication to platitudinous pleasantries at best.[8] With foreign business interests, on the other hand, the Establishment is in relatively close contact. When foreign businessmen do not get their own way, moreover, the small ones contact the Administrator and the large ones the Minister, and put their case loud and clear. Not only are they of the same culture and 'talk the same language' in both a literal and a metaphorical sense, but they can apply a number of social as well as political pressures.

### The Significance of Race Relations for Certain Enterprises

The probable trend of race relations after self-government is vital to economic planning. In my view, race relations, viewed in total, are likely to continue deteriorating until self-government, partly because New Guinean expectations of what they should be are rising rapidly, partly because people remember how relations were in the past as well as how they are at present, partly because of some unnecessarily discriminatory policies here and now, and partly because New Guineans increasingly doubt the legitimacy of many powers and privileges being held by foreigners. At present, much of this hostility which is directed at institutions, aims at foreign government and foreign business. With the coming of self-government, relation with Europeans in government are likely to improve, as their power roles (which attract the hostility, however essential they may be in some cases) will be gone and they will be seen much more in technical assistance roles which are likely to be increasingly appreciated as New Guineans experience the problems of exercising power.

This will leave the whole weight of racial antagonism (and it may well be an increasing weight) directed against foreign commerce. Whereas many people formerly accepted it as legitimate that foreigners should own these enterprises (though many did not, as many cargo cults demonstrate), this view is increasingly rejected, at a time when New Guineans will soon have the power to do something about it. Such action will not only be taken by the New Guinea government (which will be trying to balance advantages to it from foreign enterprise against pressures for more local participation), but by New Guinean individuals and groups. The Tolai people on the Gazelle Peninsula have begun organised 'walking on' to European plantations and found it politically effective, even though the government sends in teargas and armed police. An independent government would probably not resist so strongly in matters of traditional land rights against foreign claimants. Attacks on foreign commercial and industrial enterprises have begun, but are as yet small. In some areas, New Guinean resentment is greatest against foreign-owned plantations. For the country as a whole, however, the most widespread resentment is that against small-scale foreign owned retail enterprises. These are not the most profitable enterprises in the country, but they are highly visible and they are the ones which New Guineans see themselves as able to run. Most industrial enterprises seem not to be seen in this way, at least not to the same extent, mainly because they are seen as sources of employment.

### The Economic Consequences of Institutionalised Inequality

The government always denied the existence of racially discriminatory laws until it was pointed sharply into focus by Sir Hugh Foot's United Nations Mission. An investigation disclosed racially discriminatory provisions in over 70 laws, and it is a credit to Sir Paul Hasluck, the then Minister, that he had almost all of them amended very quickly. Governmental and commercial institutions, nevertheless, still require and condone many hundreds of unnecessary discriminatory practices. In the same way that many officials and businessmen genuinely did not believe that discriminatory laws existed until Foot pointed them out, many still do not believe that a vast range of discriminatory practices exists. It is the subordinate caste who are conscious of them, and those most painfully conscious are the most educated and most influential.

What constitutes adequate housing? In government, the rental is fixed by race. A New Guinean occupying a two-bedroomed government house paid $15.03 per fortnight for it. A European doing the same work and occupying the same house paid $2.76 per fortnight for it, even though he would be paid about twice the salary for the same work. The Government would deny this on both counts. First they would say it is not a matter of race but of whether, in fact, the person is born locally or overseas. The practice is, however, that white men born locally are issued certificates to the effect that they are to be regarded, officially, as having been born overseas. Secondly, they would say that the rentals are not different, they are identical, but that whites (and a few 'honorary whites') receive a rental subsidy of $12.27 per fortnight. This issue, perhaps more than any other, is creating tensions in the Public Service which are making expatriates, who are needed for economic and other development, prematurely unacceptable.

The Acting Director of Education recently pointed out that the government builds schoolrooms for expatriate children at a cost of about $6,000 each 'because of the need to attract expatriates', but schoolrooms for indigenous children for about $1,500 each 'because there is not enough money'.[9]

This kind of double-think, applying one set of criteria to whites to justify a conclusion advantageous to them, and a quite different set to nonwhites, permeates much practice and policy in New Guinea. To many members of the dominant caste, this kind of thinking is reasonable or inevitable. To members of the subordinate caste it is unjust, exploitative and unnecessarily discriminatory.

There are literally hundreds of instances.

When Mr. Oskar Tammur, M.H.A., lived in Australia and tried to vote in elections there, he was told that, as a New Guinean, he could not. Mr. Tammur now leads the opposition to foreign involvement in the Gazelle Peninsula Council, (for which all resident aliens are entitled to vote), and to foreign commerce and plantations. Some, but not all, of the businesses and plantations concerned provide considerable benefit to the economy, but it is important to recognise the economic as well as social cost of the personal humiliation he has experienced. People who are frequently discriminated against by a dominant caste are unlikely to rate economic criteria very highly when an opportunity appears to change the balance of power. The potential economic advantages of selected foreign skills and capital will not be achieved unless social injustice is removed. A lot has been removed in the last decade. A lot remains.

*Conclusion*

One cannot help but applaud most of the sentiments expressed in the plan. They are expressed so frequently in words that one tends to overlook the fact that they are not implemented in the details of the plan. The major mining industry would 'raise the economy to a new and higher level of activity'. But whose economy? Of up to $100,000,000 that the plan says this might add to the country's annual export income, how much would go to local people? The plan provides for the employment of 1,500 of them in the industry, mostly in low-skilled categories, and notes with approval that the companies will give some scholarships to indigenes. But how many relative to the $100,000,000 worth of minerals exported per year?

'Participation' is the key word in this plan, but when its nature is analysed in terms of the provisions made, it is mainly as labourers for expatriate industry, as savers for expatriate entrepreneurs to invest, as peasant producers for expatriate commerce to buy produce from and supply goods to. The plan is characterized by tokenism—indigenous representation (but usually as a minority) on the statutory authorities; some loans (though proportionately small) to indigenous businessmen; some training (but insufficient to avoid long-term dependence on expatriates) in highly skilled occupa tions. Some significant steps towards overcoming these problems have been taken since the plan was written, but much remains to be done.

## REFERENCES

1 This chapter is adapted from articles in *New Guinea,* Vol. 3, No. 4, and Vol. 4, No. 3.

2 Very limited provisions have been made in recent years to permit some Japanese capital into New Guinea, but it has been forced to take a proportion, usually a majority, of Australian (not New Guinean, it should be noted) share-holding and directors.

3 See SHARP, IAN G. and TATZ, COLIN M. *Aborigines in the Economy,* Jacaranda, 1966 especially at pp. 245-246.

4 GUY HUNTER, 'The Transfer of Institutions from Developed to Developing Countries', *African Affairs,* January, 1968, Vol. 67, No. 266, p. 5.

5 CLIFTON R. WHARTON: 'The Green Revolution: Cornucopia or Pandora's Box', *Foreign Affairs,* April, 1969, Vol. 47, p. 467-8.

6 The Tasman Pulp and Paper project at Tarawera in New Zealand is one example of the successful combination of indigenous landowners and expatriate capital in a huge forest-working enterprise. The Maori landowners are more than proportionately represented on the Board of Directors.

7 The Business Advisory,Committee, for example, represented foreign interests exclusively and had no indigenous membership. The 'business advice' available to government was thus heavily weighed in favour of foreign as opposed to indigenous business interests. The Tourist Board likewise represented almost exclusively the interests of expatriate capital and expatriate government. Only two of the fourteen members of the Board were New Guinean.

   This is a practice reflected in the structure of some of the committees sponsored by Aboriginal welfare organizations on the mainland. It is common for few if any Aborigines to be represented at meetings in which matters of considerable social and political importance to them is being considered (Editor).

8 Subordinate castes, anywhere, learn to accord deference and subservience to dominant castes. In conversation, they must acquiesce, concur, plead ignorance, or withdraw into silence. This has led even many of the officials whose task it is to liaise with indigenous people, to very inaccurate conclusions.

9 *South Pacific Post,* 18 May 1969.

# AUSTRALIA AND AFRICA

# 6

## AUSTRALIAN DIPLOMACY AND SOUTH AFRICA

### W. J. Hudson

South Africa has posed diplomatic problems for Australia on two related fronts since 1945: the colonial question of South-West Africa and the question of racial policies, and especially *apartheid,* in South Africa itself. On both fronts, international opinion has hardened against South Africa as former European dependencies have joined the international community since 1945, and have played a major part in changing international attitudes on race and colour issues. For much of the period, and irrespective of parties in power in Canberra, Australia has been alienated from the anti-South Africa camp. This has not been because of marked Australian official sympathy with South African policies as such, although, for obvious historical and geographical reasons, Australians are perhaps more likely than most to feel at least some sense of *rapport* with white South Africans in their unenviable predicament. Rather, it has sprung principally from a kind of indirect community of interest with South Africa, in that most of the steps taken against South Africa over the period could be seen as precedents for possibly similar steps against Australia on the score of Papua and New Guinea and on the score of Australia's own domestic racial practices. Of course, other factors have been marginally involved: an inherent tendency towards a somewhat inflexible, literal approach to constitutional issues; for long an assumption that, by and large, white government is likely to be more orderly and fruitful than government by under-prepared indigenous elements; a feeling that many of South Africa's loudest critics have been ill-qualified to point the moral finger at Pretoria; a disinclination to allow too expansive a role to international organisation—except when such a role has suited particular Australian policies. It should be stressed at the outset that there has been nothing notably immoral about Australian diplomacy over South Africa. International politics is not conducted in some rarified, potentially more moral sphere than national politics; the entities are governments rather than parties or factions but the nature of the game is the same and, while men and governments doubtless are, on occasions, moved by what they see as moral considerations, morality in politics, if it intrudes explicitly, is more likely to be a weapon, a tactic, than a point of disinterested reference. Whether Australian diplomacy over South Africa has always been wise is another question.

### South-West Africa

German South-West Africa passed to the administrative control of contiguous South Africa in 1919 at the same time, and in the same way, as German New Guinea passed to Australian control and German Samoa to New Zealand control. The administrative mandate was awarded by the senior victors of the 1914-1918 war and was confirmed and supervised by the League of Nations. Although the United Nations charter of 1945 did not dictate it in so many words, it was generally assumed that supervision of mandated territories would be inherited by the United Nations by means of trusteeship agreements negotiated between the administering powers and the United Nations—otherwise, the mandated territories would become 'orphans' without supervision, remembering that the administering powers did not possess sovereignty over them. All the old '*B*' and '*C*' class mandated territories became trust territories under United Nations supervision in this way except South Africa.[1]

When the South African Prime Minister, J. C. Smuts, told the United Nations General Assembly's Fourth (Colonial) Committee, in 1946, that reference to South-West African opinion had shown a desire in the territory for union with South Africa, Australia abstained from voting on a draft resolution carried by a large majority and calling on South Africa to submit the territory to the United Nations trusteeship system. The Australian delegate, K. H. Bailey, argued mainly that submission of mandated territories to trusteeship was not compulsory under the charter. In 1947, South Africa announced that she would not proceed with incorporation, would observe the spirit of the old mandate and would submit information annually to the United Nations on the administration of South-West Africa, but declared that she would not submit a trusteeship agreement for the territory. When many delegations, and especially the Indian, loudly condemned the South African position, arguing that, whatever the legal situation, there was a moral obligation on South Africa to submit the territory to international surveillance under the trusteeship system, Australia's then Minister for External Affairs, Dr. H. V. Evatt, equally loudly defended South Africa. Repeating the view that submission was not compulsory under the charter (the charter said that submission of territories would be a matter for 'subsequent agreement' but did not say between whom), Evatt urged the oddly pragmatic point in the Fourth Committee that 'the system under which South-West Africa was administered mattered less than the way in which the Union Government governed the territory'.[2] He made the same point in plenary session of the General Assembly: 'There is an old saying . . . "For forms of government, let fools contest; what-er is best administered is best". I think South Africa can take its stand on that principle'.[3] In 1948, when South Africa announced that she had returned to a policy of 'close association and integration', with South-West Africa to enjoy representation in the South African parliament, Australia again voted against every attempt to impose pressure by Assembly resolution on South Africa to conform. In 1949, Australia carried on with the same posture, vainly opposing an oral hearing for the Reverend Michael Scott, an informal spokesmen for the territory's indigenes, and even abstaining from voting on a resolution referring the issue to the International Court of Justice. Dr. Evatt once justified his rigorous defence of South Africa as 'an appeal for . . . a spirit of tolerance . . . Delegates were reminded that international morality begins at home'.[4] It remains, though, that his view now, that competent government outweighed the principle of trusteeship, was utterly inconsistent with his publicly expressed view in 1942 that the United Nations must be the agent to effect change in the administration of peoples, with his vain demand for universal accountability for all dependency administrations when the United Nations

Charter was negotiated at San Francisco in 1945—in case of doubt, the Assembly should be the final arbitor, he said then—and with his view that 'each member should faithfully observe the recommendations and decisions of United Nations bodies'.[5]

The opinion of the International Court, given in 1950, was ambivalent but of rather more comfort to her opponents than to South Africa; submission of a trusteeship agreement was not obligatory; on the other hand, South Africa was not free unilaterally to change the status of the territory, to which the mandate terms still applied; the United Nations was qualified to exercise supervision in succession to the League of Nations; the 'normal means' whereby the statutes of the territory could be changed would be by the submission of a trusteeship agreement. The anti-colonial states in the United Nations kept up the pressure throughout the 1950s and Australia continued with abstentions or negative votes on South Africa's side, at times emerging as much more intransigent than, for example, the United States and New Zealand. Besides the now hallowed legal defence, Australian delegations argued that the only hope for a settlement lay in negotiation with South Africa, so that increasingly harsh Assembly resolutions were not merely based on misinterpretation of the charter but were politically counter-productive. By the end of the decade, when the issue was becoming the more sensitive because of the application of *apartheid* policies in South-West Africa, Australia was coming to be in diplomatically expensive company. A lonely line-up of Australia, Britain, Portugal, Spain and South Africa (when she was not boycotting proceedings) was becoming not uncommon.

In the early 1960s, Australia changed her posture markedly, to the point, indeed, of retrospective contradiction. After merely abstaining in United Nations General Assembly voting on a series of resolutions very hostile to South Africa in 1960, the Australian delegation, in 1961, clearly left South Africa's side. Leaving the company, in this case, of Britain, Belgium, France and Spain, Australia moved over to the majority supporting a Fourth Committee draft resolution which referred to South Africa's 'ruthless intensification of the policy of *apartheid*' and 'oppressing the indigenous people' and claimed that South Africa had 'persistently failed in its international obligations in administering the Territory'. In plenary session, Australia retreated to an abstention but it remained that the Australian delegation had approved the draft's denunciation of *apartheid,* its call for self-determination for the territory and the sincerity of its sponsors. And Australia voted for another resolution which accused South Africa of having deliberately deprived South-West Africans of access to satisfactory education levels. By 1962, Australia had turned full circle and it is worth quoting at some length a statement made at the United Nations in that year by an Australian delegate, Laurence McIntyre (emphasis by the author):—

'The Government and people of Australia deplored the practice of racial discrimination, in South Africa as elsewhere, and further considered that *South Africa should have followed the example of other Mandatory Powers and have placed South-West Africa under the Trusteeship System* . . . There was also a clear *moral obligation* on the part of South Africa to promote the Territory's advancement towards self-determination and to put an end to all discriminatory policies . . . The continued failure of South Africa to acknowledge its obligations

or to heed world opinion could not but have explosive consequences.
... the United Nations should seek to avail itself of all possible
channels to bring the pressure of world opinion to bear upon the
South African Government.'[6]

Australia then voted for a resolution of the now customary anti-South African
kind. It was almost equally noteworthy that in the next year, 1963, Australia
abstained (although Britain and even the United States were among those to
vote against) from voting on a draft resolution which, among other things,
called for an arms embargo on South Africa. In 1965, too, Australia went
no further than an abstention on a resolution calling for moral and material
support for an arms embargo on South Africa's indigenes 'in their legitimate
struggle for freedom and independence'. Late in the 1960s, the anti-colonial
majority in the United Nations stepped up their campaign to the point where
even a now sympathetic Australia could not follow, but Australia was not as
diplomatically isolated in this kind of hesitancy as she had formerly been in
her period of intransigence. In 1968, for example, Australia was only one of
eighteen mainly western states to abstain from voting on a resolution which
amounted virtually to a call for sanctions against South Africa.

## Apartheid

Racial policy in South Africa was brought formally to the attention of
the international community in 1946 in respect particularly of Pretoria's
treatment of South Africans of Indian origin. In the early inter-war years,
the old India had raised the issue in British Empire councils but now the
still mainly-white Commonwealth was comprised of autonomous elements
jealous of domestic jurisdiction, and the new India had little option but to
raise the question, if at all, at the United Nations. There it found a
sympathetic audience, especially after the accession to power in South Africa
of the more rigorously racist Nationalist Party in 1948, and with the arrival
in United Nations ranks, in the late 1950s and the 1960s, of a large
number of ex-colonial, race sensitive states. By and large, sufficient majorities
at the United Nations over the years since 1946 have accepted the Indian
view that South African treatment (segregation and political discrimination)
of its inhabitants of Indian origin has impaired friendly relations between the
governments involved and has violated the principles of the United Nations
charter. Assembly resolutions repeatedly have called for negotiations
between South Africa, India and Pakistan. South Africa, of course, has been
uncooperative, claiming that the matter is one of domestic jurisdiction in
which legal competence is enjoyed by none but itself: the people involved
are South Africans subject to the South African government and that is that.

In the late 1940s, Australia was not as enthusiastic a defender of South
Africa in this context as in that of South-West Africa, but neither did she
join South Africa's critics. Evatt's delegations tended to abstain or vote with
South Africa but to say very little. When, in 1946, South Africa submitted a
draft whereby the Assembly would deny its own competence, Australia
quietly abstained. True to his stand at San Francisco in 1945, Evatt did allow
however, that it was appropriate for relevant United Nations bodies to discuss
matters of possible concern. In the 1950s, with Labor in opposition and the
Liberal-Country Party coalition embarked on their long tenure of office,
Australian delgations, in a sense, swung closer to South Africa in that they
sought to prevent even discussion of items which they believed were beyond

United Nations competence. As an Australian delegate argued in 1952, 'discussion in itself is intervention'.[7] Consequently, when, in 1952, the year in which Afro-Asian states began their annual attacks on *apartheid* in general and not just as it affected Indian South Africans, South Africa again tried to have the Assembly recognise its own incompetence, Australia this time joined France and Britain in voting for the South African draft. An almost exclusively legal approach characterised the Australian position throughout the 1950s, although there was associated with it the political argument that hostile annual resolutions were self-defeating, in that they provoked deeper intransigence from Pretoria and thus further alienated the one effective agent of change.

In the early 1960s, Australian delegations largely abandoned their legal approach. In 1961, they supported resolutions critical of South Africa, and delegates' speeches henceforth made explicit Australia's official repugnance for policies of racial discrimination. As in the case of South-West Africa, this did not quite put Australia in line with the majority because, in its frustration, not only with South Africa but with Portugal and Britain (over Rhodesia), the majority, in the 1960s, took to arming their resolutions with the teeth of variously severe sanctions. Typically, for example, the Australian delegation, in 1965, accepted a resolution calling for a United Nations fund to aid victims of South Africa's 'discriminatory and repressive legislation' but abstained from voting on another which called for United Nations members to impose economic sanctions on South Africa and to sever diplomatic relations with her. Non-mandatory sanctions, that is, sanctions recommend in Assembly resolutions, have never been satisfactorily implemented and Australia, anyway, has not much encouraged Assembly aspirations in this direction. Mandatory sanctions, that is, sanctions imposed by the Security Council, have been for Australia another matter and when, for the first time in United Nations experience, they were imposed on Rhodesia in 1966, the Australian government professed its acceptance of them even though manifestly it did not think their imposition appropriate.

*Explanatory Factors*

Several factors should be considered if one is to understand Australian diplomacy with regard to South Africa:—

*Domestic Jurisdiction*   Despite the allowances that must be made for the operations of extra-national ideologies, religions and race loyalties and of variously international institutions, it remains that the nation state has not been displaced as the basic unit in world politics, and that governments of states have not yet been persuaded to see their first responsibility as other than the maintenance of the integrity of their territories and the creation of regional and world conditions suited to the furtherance of what they see as their states' best interests. Their very legitimacy is at stake. At the same time, of course, the wars of 1914-18 and 1939-45 and other lesser, but bloody enough conflicts have persuaded states to cooperate in the development of international institutions, the basic hope for which is that they will encourage peaceful resolution of conflict—whether in containing physical conflict or in removing the political or even socio-economic conditions thought to give rise to physical conflict. But international institutions are dependent first on their charters of constitutions, which represent political compromise by negotiating founder states at a particular time, and on subsequent, almost daily politicking by member states' governments.

When the United Nations charter was written at San Francisco in 1945, Evatt took for Australia a hard line on domestic jurisdiction, but the formula at last agreed on for Article 2, paragraph 7, of the charter was anything but clear, and Evatt's subsequent interpretation of it was typically political. If he thought international peace (and perhaps, at times, domestic electoral advantage) could best be served by taking a permissive view of domestic jurisdiction, he did so—whether the issue was religious persecution in eastern Europe, censure of the government of Spain, or the Soviet Union's disinclination to allow exit rights to citizens married to foreigners. If he thought the Australian interest could be served by taking a permissive view, he did so —as in fervently promoting the cause of Indonesian rebellion against Dutch colonial rule. If he thought that the Australian interest would not be served by taking a permissive view, he did not take it, as in the case of South Africa. His successors in the 1950s rarely, if ever, saw advantage to Australia in softening domestic jurisdiction defences against communist and third world pressures on the western camp in general and on Australia in particular. Reasonably enough, they therefore took up a defensive (and I would argue excessively) legalistic posture.

All this is an inescapable aspect of international politics. Just as Australia saw point in beating the moral drum against the Dutch or the Russians or the Spanish on various issues, so many other states at some time have beaten moral drums on behalf of groups outside their own boundaries and therefore inside other governments' jurisdictions. When they have been on the receiving end, their first thought, as a rule, has been the domestic jurisdiction prerogative. Thus India, for example, free enough in its criticism of policies in South Africa or New Guinea, does not accommodate outside criticism of its handling of its Naga minority—similarly with Ceylon and its Tamil Indians, the Soviet Union and some of its national minorities, Hungary and its Catholics, China and its Tibetan separatists, Canada and its French-speaking minority, and so on. Nation states have recently shown a capacity for allowing areas of activity to international organisation but not yet to the point passively of standing by while politically sensitive issues within their own borders are exploited by other states for a variety of moral and amoral motives. Certainly, it would be farcical to expect an Australian government positively to court external attention towards its own colonial and race problems by leading the hounds against South African foxes, or even to ride with the hounds unless other factors seemed to outweigh the possible consequences of precedents created in respect of South Africa.

*The Cold War*   Little needs to be said about the impact of the Cold War beyond the fact that colonial and race questions have served so well as ammunition in the conflict that they have very often been denied sympathetic, informed and constructive attention. For a variety of reasons, Australia identified in the forties and fifties with the western camp and, while the West might try to stress discrimination and exploitation in the eastern camp, the emerging third world states were interested, for obvious historical reasons, almost exclusively with western iniquities. Inevitably, the result was a tendency towards western solidarity. This solidarity factor should not be exaggerated—often Australia went her own way even during the harshest Cold War years—but it did nevertheless operate to some degree: in defending South Africa, Australia defended part of the West, and so herself, against mischievous attack. When the Cold War thawed in the sixties, Australian defensiveness softened, although it will be suggested that other forces were also at work here.

*The Commonwealth Link*    It is often assumed that Australia almost automatically supported South Africa for just as long as South Africa was a member of the Commonwealth, that Australia at once, and perhaps with relief, deserted South Africa as soon as South Africa left the Commonwealth early in 1961 after opting for republican status and choosing not to court humiliation at Afro-Asian hands by applying for continuing membership. Now it is undeniable that Commonwealth associations have affected Australian diplomacy over the years and that this would have been a factor in Australian relations with South Africa. But two qualifications might be entered.

The first is that Australia has by no means invariably given Commonwealth solidarity top priority, whether under Labor or coalition governments. Over the period from 1946 to 1965, for example, analysis of voting at the United Nations on sensitive colonial issues shows that on about one vote in five Australia did not vote with Britain.[8] Given that Australia's Commonwealth associations have always been principally of a Londocentric, bilateral kind, it can be seen that constant solidarity with South Africa in the period to 1960 is not likely to have sprung simply from Commonwealth sentiment. The second is that at about that time, Australia dramatically switched postures on issues, notably those relating to Portuguese colonies.

It should also be remembered that the Australian government, and certainly Menzies, were shocked by the Sharpeville and Langa killings of 1960. Confessing that he had been horrified by the Sharpeville incident, Menzies subsequently saw *apartheid* as ending 'in the most frightful disaster.'[9] It is the case, too, that in mid-1960 Menzies corresponded with the South African Prime Minister, Dr. Verwoerd, urging some reconsideration of racial policies and especially revision of Pretoria's ban on ordinary diplomatic representation by even Afro-Asian members of the Commonwealth, and that Verwoerd's wordy replies were utterly negative. At about the same time, Menzies wrote to Portugal's Dr. Salazar urging acceptance of United Nations surveillance of her colonies. It may well be that, after trying to talk diplomatic sense to these states at the highest level, and failing, Australia then felt free to leave them to their obloquy.

*Changing Attitudes on Race*    The point here is simply that attitudes on race have changed very markedly and very quickly. In the mid-1940s, for example, Dr. Evatt enjoyed a reputation for radicalism on matters affecting what still politely could be called backward peoples: of the San Francisco conference, it was said at the time that 'no delegation . . . has come out so vigorously and consistently for the interests of the subject peoples of the world as the delegation from Australia'.[10] At the same time, however, Evatt and his kind distinguished between societies held now to be able to govern themselves (the Indians, Filipinos, Burmese, Ceylonese and so on) and those still needing the tutelage of advanced societies. True, he did insist on real tutelage and he did assume ultimate emancipation, but he was a paternalistic, a gradualist, and the view subsequently pushed so hard by India that, whatever the society, self-government always was to be preferred even to good government, would have seemed to him monumentally absurd sentimentality. His successors in the Hasluck mould were equally well-intentioned, equally paternalistic, equally convinced that primitive societies needed long preparation for the jump into modern industrial society. This is not at all to say that they have approved all aspects of *apartheid*, or even the doctrine as such, but it does mean that they have seen the problems for white South Africans urged by the governing elites of Afro-Asia at once to share power with numerically much superior, but in most other respects inferior, non-whites (even if the whites are to blame for that inferiority).

In the 1950s, the Afro-Asians, the communist states (at least to some extent tongue in cheek) and a new generation of radicals in the west made almost absolute racial equality the new orthodoxy. In diplomatic terms, Australian governments can be criticised for slowness to recognise the new faith and pay it appropriate tribute, to realise that, especially at the United Nations, what you say and how you say it matter as well as what you do. To this day, South Africa has persisted with the fallacy that politics is a matter of reason and roman law, so that she just cannot communicate with new states largely indifferent to western notions of reason and law, but explicitly concerned with emotion and feeling. Australia woke to the realities in the early sixties but not until she had created a dubious image for herself as an obscurantist and rather nasty white state.

*Diplomatic Isolation*  Diplomatic politics poses as fine problems as any other: when does consistency become intransigence; when does constitutionalism become barren legalism; when does minority company become isolation? And, anyway, what do these intangibles matter? Different governments take different views at different times. It seems to me that, in the case of South Africa, Australia did take consistency in the 1950s to the point where it became less admirable and more obstinate. In the forties, a western bloc plus cooperative Latin American states could hold their own; in the fifties, new members swelled the radicals' ranks, and increasingly western states took to fence-sitting as they accommodated the new orthodoxy and lost the colonies that gave them a material interest in trying to stem the anti-colonialist and anti-racialist tide. By the end of the decade, the reliable intransigents were reduced to Britain, Portugal, Spain, South Africa and Australia, with France and Belgium nearby. It is my strong impression that this growing isolation, at a time when Australia was becoming increasingly aware of its need to cope with Asia as the British link with the old world wore thin, was one of the two key factors that led to change in the Australian position, not an ideological change of a kind to make Australia a prosecutor of the anti-racist crusade but a tactical change based on a judgment that too bleak an image in this area could jeopardise Australian diplomacy in others. As Menzies is said to have declared when commenting on Australia's departure with Britain from South Africa's side in 1961, 'I won't have Australia isolated'.[11] This, as I say, was one of two key factors; the other was a changing official attitude about Papua and New Guinea.

*Papua and New Guinea*  To put it mildly, Australian governments always have taken a close strategic interest in Papua and New Guinea and the experience of the Pacific war of 1941-5 did nothing to lessen it. Whatever the party in power, Australian governments equated strategic satisfaction with possession. Faced with the anti-colonial onslaught, Australia allowed that self-government or independence were the ultimate ends of administrative policy but stressed repeatedly that 'ultimate' was a matter of generations and not simply of years. In the early 1960s, Australia changed her posture here, too. Independence target dates remained anathema, but Australia now gave every public indication of resignation to self-determination being more or less imminent. One cannot be sure whether this reflected a change in strategic thinking in Canberra, new confidence in the capacity of the territory's indigenes soon to cope, or a realisation that the winds of change were such that verbally to toe the United Nations line would make life more peaceful and probably not in itself shorten the Australian tenure— or a combination of all three. But does seem to be the case that the principal factor in Australian thinking on colonial questions generally, including those posed by South Africa, was concern for control over Papua and New Guinea and that a change in posture on the one seemed to coincide with a change in thinking on the other. There is at least a *prima facie* case for assuming that Canberra, in the early sixties, finally decided that Papua and New Guinea were not worth the diplomatic price that Portugal, South Africa and perhaps Spain were prepared to pay. In such an event, it was, of course, essential also to disassociate from South Africa and Portugal.

*Conclusion*

It is suggested here, that Australia supported South Africa until the early 1960s partly because of the Commonwealth link, Cold War solidarity, assumptions about the nature of international politics in terms of domestic jurisdiction and slowness to accommodate the new racial dogmas, but principally because of a disinclination to support a crusade which was also partly directed against her own status as a colonial power and could be directed against her status as a society with a depressed coloured minority. And it is suggested that Australia abandoned this posture when the diplomatic price of positively supporting an apparently doomed cause seemed to have become too high.

Whether Australia should have gone further in the 1960s, and should now go further in the 1970s, is not as easy a problem as some seem to think. Unfortunately, Australia is still itself vulnerable on the score of its own aboriginal minority and its immigration policy. Although a degree of hypocrisy may be necessary in politics, one can at least understand (even if one should disagree with) an Australian government's unwillingness too emphatically to support an anti-racist cause when her own house is in some disorder. Similarly, one can understand (even if one should disagree with) an Australian government's disinclination to support the virtual outlawing of one state because of widespread distaste for some of its internal practices; there just are not many 'clean skins' in a position to throw the first stone. Until we decide to really do something effective and generous about the aboriginal problem in Australia and until we have much more candidly and successfully put across the reasons for fearing tensions springing from open immigration (or until we have decided to take the chance), Australia should surely take up a modest stance on questions like *apartheid*. When our own house is in fair order, then we can afford the luxury of moral posturing. I suggest this because, while the permissable gap may at times be hard to judge, too wide a gap between external policies and attitudes and internal practices and attitudes (about which Australians have tended to fool themselves) could merely court contempt. We are not a racist state in the sense that South Africa is (if only because we have not faced the same population situation) and it would be unnecessary and costly actively to support Pretoria. But, like many societies, we are racist to a degree and our racism happens to be white racism which is the kind under international fire these days, and it will not be altogether easy for Australian governments to toe the international line without straining credibility.

REFERENCES

1 The 'A' class mandates, all in the Middle East, ultimately achieved independence in one form or another.

2 *General Assembly Official Records,* Second Session, Fourth Committee, 39th Meeting, October 8, 1947, p. 59.

3 *GAOR,* Second Session, 104th Plenary Meeting, November 1, 1947, p. 586.

4 *Report of the Work of the Australian Delegation to the Second Annual Session of the General Assembly of the United Nations, New York, 16th September— 29th November, 1947, by the Rt. Hon. H. V. Evatt, K.C., M.P., Deputy Prime Minister and Minister for External Affairs,* as tabled in the House of Representatives, March 11, 1948 (typescript), p. 85.

5 Herbert V. Evatt, *The Task of Nations,* New York, 1949, p. 39.

6 *GAOR,* Seventeenth Session, Fourth Committee, 1387th Meeting, November 16, 1962, p. 388.

7 See NORMAN HARPER and DAVID SISSONS, *Australia and the United Nations,* New York, 1959, p. 171.

8 See W. J. HUDSON, 'Arithmetic of Diplomacy' in *Politics,* May, 1967, pp. 12-31.

9 *Commonwealth Parliamentary Debates, House of Representatives,* Vol. 30, p. 651 sq. (April 11, 1961).

10 New York *Herald-Tribune,* in *Age,* May 5, 1945.

11 KEVIN PERKINS, *Menzies Last of the Queen's Men,* Adelaide, 1968, p. 234.

# 7

## AUSTRALIA AND RHODESIA: BLACK INTERESTS AND WHITE LIES

### Richard Hall

The Rhodesian question has demonstrated one principle in Australian politics—world public opinion can and always will be able to influence Australian policies. This truth may appear a truism to some but it is worth reaffirming because the domestic rhetoric of conservative Australian politicians can give the false impression that, on issues like Aboriginal land rights or New Guinea's timetable for independence, Australia, or rather their Australia, can go its own way. Any Australian government must be sensitive to world opinion. So, even in the face of manifest uneasiness reaching even into the Cabinet, the Liberal-Country Party Government has felt itself constrained to accept and enforce the United Nations sanctions on economic links and trade with Rhodesia. But the Government's characteristic ambivalence in accepting sanctions formally but stretching the terms of 'humanitarian exemption' to sell wheat has helped to mar the respectable image it set out to achieve.

Rhodesian and South African propagandists like to claim that there is a special relationship between Australia and our cousins across the ocean. Any scrutiny of the political record since the Unilateral Declaration of Independence in November 1965 shows that this kinship line strikes a responsive chord among many Liberal and Country Party politicians. But despite this sentiment, the Government's policy of support for the United Nations has been consistent, even if somewhat bent. If the Pearce Commission had been a peaceful exercise, then an inevitable British-Rhodesian settlement, taken together with the U.S. relaxation of the chrome embargo, would almost certainly have opened the way for Australian recognition of and trade with Rhodesia. But, at the time of writing, it is difficult to see how the pending Pearce Report could provide a basis for settlement.

While it has been the fear of world public opinion that has held us in line, a substantial factor in our initial response to U.D.I. was the firm and vigorous definition by the then Prime Minister, Sir Robert Menzies, of the U.D.I. declaration as illegal. When questioned on 12 November 1965, the day after the declaration, Sir Robert spoke briskly of a 'deplorable error of judgment' on the part of the Rhodesians and promised a considered statement on government policy. Four days later the Prime Minister delivered his promised statement to the House of Representatives:

> 'Recent events in Rhodesia, and the reactions to those events in other countries, have presented to all of us acutely difficult problems.

'It is desirable that I should, on behalf of the Government, set out for the benefit of honorable members what we believe to be the facts and what views we take on the various suggested remedies. First I should point out that as Great Britain is for this purpose the colonial power, only the Parliament of Great Britain could grant independence to Rhodesia. The Unilateral Declaration of Independence by the Rhodesian Government was therefore illegal. The Declaration having been made, and the Governor having dismissed Mr. Smith and his government, a position arose in which the only lawful government in Rhodesia is now the Government of the United Kingdom. ... The Rhodesian problem has twice been discussed at Prime Ministers' Conferences. On each occasion, it was unanimously—I repeat, unanimously—accepted that the authority and responsibility for leading Rhodesia to independence must continue to rest with Britain. It still remains the central truth in the controversy. In the discharge of its responsibilities, the Government of the United Kingdom went to great pains to conduct discussions with the then Prime Minister and Government of Rhodesia. ... It did not take the extreme view, now being advocated by some, that the Constitution of Rhodesia should immediately be altered so as to provide for an immediate African majority. It realised that the people were not yet ready for this, and that to act precipitately might conceivably create what might be called a "Congo situation", of unhappy memory. ...

'The principles, as I took an opportunity of telling Mr. Wilson, were and are completely in line with our own thinking. Having regard to what has happened, I think I should now tell the House that I sent a message to Mr. Smith just as he was entering upon his discussions in London. I said I had a natural understanding of the problems confronting the European settlers in Rhodesia, a country which has enjoyed its own substantially but technically incomplete form of self-government for many years, and in which the contribution of the European settlers to the economic vigour of the country has been most substantial. I repeated my own view, which I have on several occasions expressed, sometimes quite forcibly, I hope, in Prime Ministers' Conferences, that two extreme views that had been put forward were not practicable.

'The first extreme view was that either immediately or within a few months there should be adult suffrage with, in consequence, an African majority. If this view were to prevail then, as I said to my friend, Mr. Smith, I could see all the elements of bad, because inexperienced, government, and possible economic disaster. The other extreme view was that the achievement of an African majority should be indefinitely resisted. This view, as I have repeatedly said, and, as I said to Mr. Smith, was, in the prevailing international political climate, quite impracticable. ...

'It should be clearly understood that a similar line was followed with much patience and reasonableness by the British Government. Mr. Wilson himself, in his speech to the House of Commons, put it in this way—

"Although successive British Governments"

—I emphasise "successive British Governments"; the Home Government and the Wilson Government have followed identical policies in this respect—

"are deeply and irrevocably committed to guaranteed and unimpeded progress to majority rule, the British Government, who alone through the British Parliament have the legal power to grant independence, do not believe that in the present and tragic and divided conditions of Rhodesia, a majority can or should come today, or tomorrow. A period of time is needed, time to remove the fears and suspicions between race and race, time to show that the Constitution of Rhodesia with whatever amendments may later be made can be worked and is going to be worked and that the rule of law equally with the maintenance of essential human rights will be paramount and the time required—"

This, I think, is a very wise statement—

"cannot be measured by clock or calendar but only by achievement."

'In spite of all these efforts this illegal declaration of independence has now been made with the constitutional consequences to which I have referred. . . .

'I have already put and answered the question as to the objective of armed force which, it would appear, would be not only to punish but to create a new Constitution and system of government on a basis which we would not want to see established overnight, or prematurely. *My colleagues and I have had very great reservations about even economic sanctions. . . .*

'Above all things, we hope that none of these measures will be of long duration. It would be a sad commentary on the unwisdom of mankind, if through the obstinate pursuit of an illegal course, this prosperous country should be reduced economically to ruin, to the lasting unhappiness of all of its people, voters or non-voters, white or black.'

This very typical example of Menzies' oratory has provided the foundation of Australian policy ever since. While he expressed doubts about the utility of sanctions and referred to 'my friend, Mr. Smith', there was nothing qualified about his description of the regime as 'illegal' or his affirmation that the Government of the United Kingdom was the ultimate authority for Rhodesia. Unless the Pearce Commission were to succeed in bringing about a settlement adhered to by the United Kingdom, it is impossible to see any Australian conservative government being able to repudiate the logic of Sir Robert's pronouncement on the constitutional status, or rather lack of constitutional status, of the Smith regime. However, in the debate on the statement which followed a few days later, in November 1965, the depth of the unease in the government parties surfaced. After Mr. Calwell led for the Opposition, the first government speaker was Sir Wilfred Kent-Hughes, Liberal member for Chisholm. He did not at that stage explicitly dissociate himself from sanctions, contenting himself with: 'no doubt some of the decisions he announced were as distasteful to him and the Government as they were to members on both sides of the House. Perhaps we should remind ouselves that the essence of statesmanship is to know when to give way on the lesser in order to try, if possible, to gain the greater.' Most of the rest of his speech was an elaborate justification of the Rhodesian Government. The next government speaker, the then Minister for Territories, Mr. C. E. Barnes, told the House that 'those of us who come from rural areas, and who have rural associations particularly, I think, have a great deal of sympathy for those people in Rhodesia.' To an interjection 'which people?' the Minister responded 'the European people'.

The then Minister for External Affairs, Mr. Paul Hasluck, who followed, said of the Rhodesian regime: 'In my view they have acted with very little wisdom. They have acted with great foolishness. They have acted in a way which has not, in my view, paid proper regard to the rights and claims of others. But let us recognise the simple fact that they have acted in fear. . . . The Unilateral Declaration of Independence was, in my view, the result of fear and an attempt to preserve, in conditions of fear, something the Europeans thought precious to themselves.' If Sir Robert's original statement bore the impress of his own personal style, so too did that of the Minister for External Affairs. It was cautious, unemotional and utterly oblivious to the passions aroused by the issue. During a later contribution from Dr. J. Cairns, Mr. Shaw, the Country Party member for Dawson, contributed an interjection which at least honestly and openly expressed the feelings of many members on his side of the House. Dr. Cairns stated: 'Two hundred thousand Europeans govern and rule and completely dominate the four million Africans.' Mr. Shaw interjected: 'Why should they not?'. The last government speaker was Mr. James Killen, Liberal member for Moreton, who was to espouse the cause of Rhodesia in a rather spectacular fashion for the next few years. His speech was in the vintage Tory style with the almost compulsory quote from Edmund Burke and large doses of history. He concluded that the cause of the Rhodesian people, meaning of course, the Europeans, had been greatly misunderstood. An essential part of his argument, often to be repeated, was the prevalence of massacres and undemocratic practices in the black African states.

The terms of debate on the Rhodesian question in Australian federal politics have not changed since that first discussion in the House of Representatives. The Government remains tied to sanctions, uneasy but compelled. A substantial proportion of backbenchers and even some of its ministers make sounds of discontent, but accept the reality of government policy. The Labor Opposition maintains its inflexible opposition to the Smith regime. What the debate did foreshadow was the formation of a group among government members which came to be dubbed 'The Rhodesia Lobby'. This rather over-stated the degree of organisation. It is not that they meet but rather that their world view coincides. White Anglo Saxon Protestant solidarity, a hankering for the lost Empire, a deep suspicion of black regimes who rejected the deserving whites and a feeling that communism lurks behind most critical thinking; all these suspicions contribute to the group's ideology. Its members included the late Sir Wilfred Kent-Hughes and the former Liberal member for Bowman, Dr. W. Gibbs, who lost his seat in 1969. J. McLeay, Liberal member for Boothby, who made a number of dire utterances on the future of the western world during a 1971 visit to Rhodesia, was another. Don Maisey, Country Party member for Moore, is accounted a member and reference has already been made to Mr. Barnes, now a backbencher. The Deputy Speaker, Mr.

P. Lucock, a N.S.W. Country Party member, is a fervent pro-Rhodesian. He was one of the 583 Australians who trained in Rhodesia under the Empire Air Training Scheme in World War II. On 27 April 1971, he linked the British Labour Government's attitude towards Rhodesia with the pernicious influence of the permissive society. Mr. Killen, a Queensland Liberal member has been the most vocal of the lobby, but the basis of his arguments has been a little more sophisticated than the rest. A warmhearted man who enjoys the regard and respect of many of his political opponents, he has a tendency to romantic conservatism reinforced by Chestertonian obstinacy.

In the Senate, those accounted members of the lobby are the Attorney-General, Senator Greenwood, Senators Rae and Young, all three of whom travelled to Rhodesia at government expense in the 1970-71 recess. Senator Nancy Buttfield told the Senate in September 1968 that 'the standard of civilisation in Rhodesia is one of the highest in Africa' and went on: 'I believe it is quite disgraceful that Russia is not censured for her actions, while Rhodesia which has been bringing achievement to its people and minding its own business should have these sanction imposed upon it.' Others on the government side who have expressed favourable sentiments include the President, Senator Sir Magnus Cormack, and, it will hardly surprise many, Senator Sim.

The references from Senator Buttfield came from the only debate where there has been a test vote. On September 10th 1968, a motion from Senator Murphy, Leader of the Opposition, brought forward a motion in the following terms: 'That the Senate approves the United Nations Security Council resolution No. 253 of 29 May 1968 on Southern Rhodesia and takes note of the announcement made by the Minister for External Affairs on 2nd September 1968 of the measures so far being taken by the Australian Government pursuant to the resolution and requests the Government to do all in its power to implement the resolution.' (The motion also included the 23 clauses of the Security Council resolution).

This was a neat tactical move designed to show up divisions in the Government parties. The government had no choice, but to accept the motion, even though calling it 'redundant', but a D.L.P. amendment tacked on a clause attacking the Russian invasion of Czechoslovakia. This gave Senators Buttfield, Cormack and possibly others an opportunty to vote in effect against sanctions by supporting the D.L.P. The amendment lost on the voices, so there is no record of how they did vote. The D.L.P. Senator Byrne, who moved the amendment, had little to say about Rhodesia. There has been no public statement of D.L.P. policy, but it may be appropriate here to cite certain documents which will be referred to again later in more detail. A report of an official of the Rhodesian Information Centre published in part in *The Review* of April 1, 1972, said:

'Mr. Santamaria said we had strong support from the leader of the D.L.P., Senator Gair, who wished on occasions to publicly support us in the Senate, but had been restrained from doing so for party political reasons.'

This ties in with a tendency in the pages of *News Weekly*, the organ of the National Civic Council, to describe critics of *apartheid* as being at least dupes of the Communists. It fits with the strategic plan of Mr. Santamaria for a strategic Indian Ocean alliance between Australia and South Africa.

Members of the Rhodesia Lobby have always been eager to suggest that despite the firmness of Sir Robert's statement in 1965, they really had his support. Certainly in his *Afternoon Light*, which he sub-titles 'Some memories of men and events', published in 1967, he shows some misgivings as to the later course of events; however Sir Robert did reiterate his basic principles of 1965.

'For myself I do not defend Rhodesia's Unilateral Declaration of Independence. I think that it was unlawful, being in breach of constitutional authority. I think it was impetuous and ill-advised. I think that the ruling party in Rhodesia errs grievously if it believes that in this century it can indefinitely maintain white authority in a predominantly coloured population.'

It is true that, in the substantial section of the book dealing with Rhodesia, Sir Robert articulates his profound distaste for the new Commonwealth and the United Nations, and appeals for a compromise on some lines of gradualism, but he sees settlement the fruit of a necessary agreement between the United Kingdom and the existing Rhodesian regime. However much he dislikes the African and Asian critics of Rhodesia, he remains caught in the web of his logic of the November 1965 statement.

The initial U.N. Security Council motion calling for sanctions was passed on 20th November, 1965, but in his 8th December statement in the House of Representatives, Sir Robert contrived to announce the imposition of Sanctions without once referring to the U.N. His announcement included restrictions on transactions between Rhodesia and Australia and the suspension of 90% of exports from Rhodesia. In another development in that month, a special meeting of Commonwealth Prime Ministers was called for Lagos in January by the Prime Minister of Nigeria. The Australian government refused the invitation. This was a great departure for an old Commonwealth man like Menzies. On 28 December he explained:

'My Government has consistently opposed the giving of any Commonwealth orders to Britain as to how she should exercise that authority and discharge that responsibility. To have her in effect attacked and threatened at a special conference would be a grave departure from proper practice in a Commonwealth gathering.'

As it happened, the tone of the Lagos Conference communique was temperate, but to Sir Robert it still deserved reproof because of the use of the word 'rebellion' which 'might have been appropriate at the time of the revolution of the American States, but it is inappropriate today.' Sir Robert consistently failed to understand the unique nature of the South African and Rhodesian regimes in the eyes of those black Africans who saw their cousins oppressed by the whites. From this flowed his offhand dismissal of their protests and communiques. Africans and Asians were sophisticated enough to pick up the nuances of his tone, so what Australia might have gained diplomatically from its adherence to sanctions was, at least partially, lost. Still, the decisions announced to the Parliament by Sir Robert in December 1965 did mean that, when the U.N. Security Council passed further sanctions in December 1966, Australia was already in line. But the ultimate Security Council motion of 29th May 1968 calling for mandatory sanctions demanded further Australian policy decisions. The vigilant Mr. Killen raised the matter in the House of Representatives the next day, to argue that the Security Council's 'assumption of jurisdiction in this matter is illegal.' On 14th June, the Leader of the Opposition,

Mr. Whitlam, asked a probing question on government policy but was brushed aside.

It was more than three months later, on September 2nd, that the then Minister for External Affairs, Mr. Paul Hasluck, released the text of the report forwarded to the United Nations Secretary-General on the steps taken by Australia to comply with the May Security Council resolution. At the time, there was some suspicion that the delay was caused by internal pressures from the Rhodesia lobby; however, the following day, the Minister dealt tartly with Mr. Killen who sought to discover when the decision was made. The Minister concluded his answer with 'At no time in the recent series of considerations of Security Council resolutions—if this is the line on which the honourable member is thinking —did Cabinet face up to the question: Do we obey or disobey our obligations as members of the United Nations?'. That was the line on which Killen had been thinking, but the Minister's answer, given his reputation for integrity, not shared by some of his successors, made it reasonably clear that it was the grinding wheels of interdepartmental discussion that had caused the delay, rather than a policy review.

In the Estimates debates in September, Mr. Killen was supported by Sir Wilfred Kent-Hughes, J. Macleay and Dr. W. Gibbs, a Rhodesia Lobby rally which brought a response from Mr. E. St. John, then still in the parliamentary Liberal Party, and historically the only Liberal parliamentarian to associate himself publicly with criticism of *apartheid* and South African policies. In a question to Hasluck he sought an unequivocal assertion of Government policy on Rhodesia, referring to newspaper reports that 'profound distaste (was) felt by certain ministers for sanctions', and asked: ' Might not these reports, or their inference, cause serious harm to Australia and impair our good relations with the countries of Asia and other nations throughout the world?'

In reply, Hasluck was almost as tart as he had been to Killen, and drew some broad distinctions between emotional sympathy and understanding, but stressed that Australia was fulfilling its obligations as a member of the United Nations.

So, by September 1968, Australia had pledged itself to fulfil its obligations as a United Nations member on Rhodesian trade sanctions. The decision flowed from an assessment that the British government case against Rhodesia's Smith regime was correct, and from the political realities of Australia's relations with the Afro-Asian world. Whatever Mr. Killen might say, the advice of the Minister and the Department of External Affairs had been victorious. But subsequent developments were to show that a pledge was one thing, but the administration of sanctions was another. Until the affair of the Rhodesian Information Centre documents in April 1972, the Australian breaches of sanctions involved two matters: the sale of wheat to Rhodesia, and the issue of Australian passports to Rhodesian officials who had been born in Australia years previously.

Section 3(d) of the U.N. Security Council Resolution of May 1968 reads:

'The sale or supply by their (U.N. members) nationals or from their territories of any commodities or products (whether or not originating in their territories), but not including supplies intended strictly for medical purposes, educational equipment or material for use in schools and other educational institutions, publications, news material and in special humanitarian circumstances, foodstuffs.'

On ... 1970 Mr. Whitlam put on notice a question to the then Prime Minister, Mr. Gorton; 'How is it that despite sanctions, Australia's exports to Southern Rhodesia have risen in each of the last three years and Australia has risen from ninth to second place among exporters to Southern Rhodesia, as appears from Annex 11 of the Second Report of the Committee established in pursuance of the Security Council Resolution of 29th May 1968'. While his question was still unanswered, the Opposition Leader, in an International Affairs debate on April 7th, launched a substantial attack on government policy on Rhodesian wheat sales. Seven days later his question was answered, the facts were admitted, but the answer went on to refer to the May 1968 resolution and the use of the phrase 'special humanitarian circumstances,' but did not define these circumstances.

Next day Mr. Lucock of the Rhodesia Lobby asked Mr. Swartz, the Minister then representing the Minister for External Affairs for 'information' on the subject, a standard 'Dorothy Dix formula'. Swartz responded, but in most misleading terms. The crucial part of his answer was: 'In 1968, that resolution did make some exemptions, for medical supplies, educational facilities and foodstuffs on the basis that the people of Rhodesia should not be deprived of these commodities'. The Minister had conveniently excluded the phrase 'special humanitarian circumstances' which would have posed him with the problem of definition. Subsequently, while wheat exports have continued, the government has never attempted to justify or explain its interpretation. The Country Party needs wheat sales, particularly after the withdrawal of the Chinese orders.

However, if there is some faint argument for the wheat sales, there is no case on passports. It was Whitlam who raised the question on 16th April, stimulated by the visit to Australia of the recently retired Commander of the Rhodesian Air Force, Air Vice Marshall Hawkins, a visit which preceded his taking up a post as Rhodesian Diplomatic representative in South Africa. Mr. Whitlam questioned the Prime Minister, Mr. Gorton, on the fact that Hawkins was travelling on an Australian passport issued on August 13, 1968. Mr. Gorton's response was to speak of a pilot who had 'a most distinguished career fighting for the free world against fascism' and went on to say 'if he is an Australian citizen he has a perfect right to visit Australia.' Later questions, put formally on notice, have revealed that the public servant described as the Secretary for External Affairs in Salisbury, Mr. Stan O'Donnell had been issued with an Australian passport on 23rd June 1967, two and half years after U.D.I. and that the Rhodesian Diplomatic Representative in Portugal, Lt.-Col. William Knox, held a passport issued on 6th December 1967, when he was Chairman of the ruling party, the Rhodesian Front. This means that in recent years the travel of the two most important Rhodesian diplomats stationed abroad has been made possible by the collaboration of the Australian government. The passports could have been cancelled at any time. On 20th April 1972, in the debate arising out of the Rhodesian Information Centre affair, the Minister for Foreign Affairs, Mr. Bowen, answered an interjection on the subject of these passports by promising that the Minister for Immigration, Dr. Forbes, would deal with that matter when he followed. Dr. Forbes made no reference to the passports.

The parliamentary debates and exchanges outlined above did little to influence Australian public opinion, largely because the press has showed little interest in Rhodesia, or for that matter, Africa in general. Apart from the Sydney *Daily Telegraph* which has liked to highlight Killen's various interventions, there has been little comment. Even at the time of U.D.I. the topic passed quickly from the editorial columns. Press comment was, it is true, unanimously against the announcement of U.D.I. although the Brisbane *Courier-Mail* did say that 'Anger and regret ... will be mixed with pity'. The *Daily Telegraph*, at that time, impressed as ever by Sir Robert, echoed his argument on illegality. The occasional press comment in the years up to the Rhodesian Information Centre Affair in April 1972, has been almost universally against the Smith regime. Even in the provincial press, where the sentimental line of fellow-pioneers etc. might have been expected to gain some response, the only consistent supporters have been the *Burnie Advocate* (Tasmania), the *West Coast Sentinel* (South Australia) and the *South Burnett Times* (Queensland). The last two come from areas where there have been strong League of Rights groups. The League of Rights is a kind of Australian John Birch Society, an extreme right wing organisation wedded to a conspiracy theory of history. The League, however, always hotly denies charges of anti semitism and racism. But its associated bookshop sells the *Protocols of Zion,* and the April 1972 issue of its publication *Intelligence Survey* can suggest a conspiratorial link between 'Political Zionism' and the Soviet government behind the issue of emigration permits to Russian Jews. The League has taken the case of Rhodesia to heart. Its founder, Eric Butler, has visited Rhodesia on at least one occasion. The Rhodesia Information Centre documents to be discussed below show that there was considerable co-operation and collaboration with the League of Rights.

The Rhodesian cause in Australia has been mainly propagated through the Rhodesia-Australia Associations in the various states, and the Rhodesia Information Centre which is an undercover diplomatic mission of the Smith government. The centre publishes a periodical *Rhodesian Commentary,* at first fortnightly, but more recently, monthly. Most of the material is supplied from Rhodesia but the last page is an inset dealing with the activities of the Associations in Australia and New Zealand. One issue claimed a mailing list of 5,500, but certainly many of these go to libraries, random lists of politicians etc., and a proportion to New Zealand. The largest attendance reported at a meeting was 250 in Sydney. Projecting from that, it seems fair to speculate that the Associations would not have more than a thousand activists. The picture of the Associations' activities that emerges from the pages of *Commentary* is very much like other small interest group associations, i.e. film nights, annual general meetings, letter writing to newspapers etc. There is a discernible overlap of Liberal Party membership. Two of the most prominent activists in the N.S.W. Association over the years have been J. D. Fell and Dr. Charles Huxtable, both well known in the Liberal Party in N.S.W. The current committee of the N.S.W. Association, apart from Dr. Huxtable as President, also includes E. C. B. MacLaurin, an academic well known in the Liberal Party. But the Committee memberships disclosed in *Commentary* show that the Associations have not been successful in involving any really prominent national political figures in their activities, apart from the Liberal members paying for their trips to Rhodesia by a couple of speeches. Three groups can be discerned among the Associations: the older Australians of the High Tory type with a nostalgia for a long-lost Empire; emigre South Africans and Rhodesians, and finally extreme right wingers of the League of Rights type who see Rhodesia as a bastion against the forces of Communism, etc. One of the latter class is Robert J. Clark, President of the Immigration Control Association, whose publications were recently described by the Prime Minister as 'disgraceful'. Mr. Clark, apart from putting out pamphlets of that kind which set out to rouse racial fears, is also on the current committee of the Rhodesia-Australia Association of N.S.W. and has, in the past, held executive office as Treasurer. To be fair to some members, it must be said that there have been tensions between the first and third groups. Some of the older members have been particularly upset at the intervention of the small cell of Sydney Nazis as a supporter of the cause. It was the Nazis who were mainly responsible for the violence at a meeting of the Association on May 18, 1970, when a number of students who had interjected during a report by John Macleay, M.H.R., were bodily ejected.

Towards the end of last year, the appointment of the Pearce Commission and the African reaction revived news coverage of Rhodesian affairs. The arrest of Judith Todd, well known for a speaking tour in Australia in 1969, also gained wide coverage. (The documents show that the Rhodesian Information Centre was most concerned at the adverse reaction to the arrests.)

However, it was the affair of these documents from the Centre that, for the first time, made Rhodesia and the Smith regime a major issue in Australian domestic politics. On March 31, 1972, the weekly newspaper *The Review* was published a day early, ostensibly because of the Easter Holiday week-end, but actually because it had got wind of the fact that *The Age* had come into possession of photocopies of a number of documents from the Rhodesian Information Centre office at 9 Myrtle Street, Crows Nest, Sydney. *The Review,* which also had these copies, published an extensive analysis by its Canberra correspondent, Mungo MacCallum. The next day *The Age* also published a similar analysis by Ben Hills. The writer of this chapter has also seen the photocopies, and the following comments are based not only on the reports in the two newspapers, but also on a reading of these photocopies.

The documents unequivocally showed that the 'Centre' was not simply an Information office. Letters from Salisbury government departments to its director, K. D. Chalmers, constantly referred to the 'Mission', the same title as that given to the offices run by Hawkins and Knox in Pretoria and Lisbon. The N.S.W. Companies Office had registered the business, after some initial misgivings, after receiving an assurance that it was an office of the Government of Rhodesia. Its cars were registered and insured in the name of that government. It received and dealt with immigration and visa queries. On the information side, the documents give a picture of an extensive but inept campaign to influence media and politicians. Only the free trips to Rhodesia gave any mileage. The 'Centre' had received more than $140,000 since 1968, mostly through a Swiss Bank account. The authenticity of the documents, in whole or part, was not challenged publicly by the Director of the Centre. However, he did state that there had been a burglary on his premises earlier in the year. In one statement he referred to money being stolen but this was not repeated.

From the published reports in the newspapers two groups of questions emerged. They were:

1. Should the Centre, operating as it was as a diplomatic mission, be closed, and could it?

2. Should action be taken against the officers of the Centre for illegal import of films? Should action be taken against John Lotter, Information officer, of the South African Embassy who had collaborated in the import of some films for the Centre?

Resolution 277, adopted by the United Nations Security Council on 18 March, 1970, was the most explicit on the first question. In clause 3 it called 'upon member states to take appropriate measures at the national level to ensure that any act performed by the officers and institutions of the illegal regime in Southern Rhodesia shall not accord any recognition, official or otherwise, including judicial acts through the competent organs of their state.' The N.S.W. government had recognised the office's registration and allowed the Rhodesian government's cars to be insured. Overriding that, the Commonwealth External Affairs power under the constitution could be said to cover such a situation, i.e. Victoria could not have disassociated itself from the declaration of war against Germany in 1939.

On the film importation issue, the Customs (Prohibited Imports) Regulations had been amended on 19th December, 1968 to ban the importation of, among other things, 'cinematograph film, exposed and developed' from Southern Rhodesia, without the consent of the Minister. On the evidence of the documents from the Centre no such permission had been given or even sought; indeed, the Centre complained to its South African counterpart about the stringency of the Australian Customs application of this sanction. *The Review* had published on its front page a photocopy of the letter involving Lotter. While the South African Ambassador has issued a blanket denial of any involvement, he did not make any comment on the actual contents of the letter.

Press briefings from the Department of Foreign Affairs over the weekend of publication conveyed departmental pleasure at the opportunity to act against the mission. On the following Tuesday Customs Department officers raided the Centre. But on return from the Easter break the Foreign Minister acted to quash the enthusiasm or action. By the time the House met on 11th April, supporters of the Rhodesia lobby were boasting openly of a victory. H. Turner, Liberal caught the first call at question time with a question most helpful to Bowen, who rested his case on freedom of information, citing the entry of propaganda from the Peoples Republic of China. The Foreign Minister spoke darkly of how 'people should not think they are able to break into premises, steal property and use it in this fashion.' He concluded that on his own and the Department's advice 'the documents do not constitute grounds for closing the Rhodesia Information Centre.' After that it was really all over. Whitlam pressed the film issue and the Minister for Customs, Mr. Chipp, described the breach of regulations as technical and the 5 films seized as innocuous. (He omitted to say that the 5 were only a fraction of the catalogue.) Whitlam later returned to the role of Mr. Lotter. Bowen was content to rely on the denial by the South African Ambassador. The next week the Government was heavily criticised by the Opposition in an urgency motion on racism, but the cold reality was that the Rhodesia lobby had won.

From the foregoing analysis, it might be clearly deduced that the ruling European dictatorship in Rhodesia has many friends and supporters in Australian governmental circles. In the light of continuing world opposition to the ambitions of the Southern African racists, this has been done at the cost of Australian interests and integrity throughout the world.

As with so many other instances covered by the three volumes in this series, the Rhodesian/Australian alliance demonstrates the continuing influence of racism in the country.

# 8

## AUSTRALIA, RHODESIA AND SOUTH AFRICA: A COMPARISON

### Sekai Holland

*A Black African's Response to Australia*

The most common question asked of me, as a black, by white Australians, is whether Australian society is as racist as either Rhodesian or South African society. I think they expect that, having come to Australia as a student and having been treated well in that regard, I will naturally say that of course it is not. But any honest reply, although it evokes much anger from white Australians must always be the same: Australia, for the Aborigines, (and they are the prime measure of racism here) is worse than either South Africa or Rhodesia for the Africans.

Many white Australians are angered by this appraisal because, as well as ignoring their own individual racism, they also deny the existence of racism throughout Australian society. Some of these people even go on to 'explain' that Aborigines are in their appalling circumstances because, being a Stone Age people, they are unable to grasp the complicated routine of a civilised existence; and that, although everything has been done for the Aborigines, they have failed to help themselves because of inherited characteristics such as laziness, unintelligence and lack of pride in themselves. These attitudes are widely held by many white Australians, although few of them have ever had any personal contact with Aborigines. Those who have met Aborigines perpetuate the myths on which prejudice is based.

Many Australians may dismiss my views as those of an extremist, who does not represent the attitudes of overseas students or of coloured immigrants. Most of them probably do not know about the private criticisms which overseas students make about Australian racism. This criticism must remain private because of the document we are compelled to sign before accepting a scholarship, stating that we will not get involved in Australian politics. As racism is undoubtedly a political topic, overseas students do not publicly criticize it. Likewise, many coloured immigrants feel it impolite and ungrateful to express public criticism of a country which has been 'gracious' enough to admit them as citizens. Yet Australians often use the presence of Asian and African students, and the restricted immigration of coloured people, as evidence for the absence of racism in this country. They ignore or disregard the treatment of Aboriginal people, and this in itself is a kind of racism.

Australian racism cannot be judged by the way Europeans treat visiting students, but rather on observation of the way Aborigines are treated and talked about. The real situation can be gauged more accurately from the statistics available about the numbers of Aborigines in prison; the number of their children dying from malnutrition in what appears such a wealthy country, and in particular the Nancy Young case and the way Dr. Kalokerinos was treated by fellow doctors for saying that it was a vitamin C deficiency rather than neglect by their mothers that caused infant deaths. The only practical accomplishment of the jailing of Nancy Young was to reinforce the widespread Australian view that Aboriginal mothers not only do not love their babies but also bash and starve them to death.

The reason why white Australians can believe that Australia is not a racist country, while at the same time acknowledging that South Africa is one, is that the ideology adopted by South Africa, with its complex set of racist laws and the open practice of segregation as a policy, is more obvious. They are satisfied that South Africa has to have racist laws because it has a colour problem, and believe that separation is the best way to avoid conflict and exploitation. Australia, they believe, would have to do the same thing if Europeans were outnumbered four to one by tribal Aborigines. Yet they insist that this is just hypothetical because Australia does not have a colour problem! People like this are simply not aware of the magnitude of the problem which already exists in Australia.

The following statistics underline Australia's position as one of the most racist countries in the world. On these figures alone, it surpasses the Union of South Africa!

*Infant Mortality Rates, Northern Territory Aboriginals and others*[1]

|                                                          | Infant Mortality Rates per 1,000 Live Births |
| -------------------------------------------------------- | -------------------------------------------- |
| Northern Territory Full blood (1965-67)                  | 131.0                                        |
| Australia (1958-60) excluding Full blood Aborigines      | 20.7                                         |
| NZ Maori (1958-60)                                       | 51.0                                         |
| US Indian (1959)                                         | 47.0                                         |
| South Africa (Asiatic) (1959)                            | 62.2                                         |
| South Africa (Coloured) (1959)                           | 120.6                                        |
| Japan (1959)                                             | 33.7                                         |
| Thailand (1959)                                          | 47.1                                         |
| Philippines (1959)                                       | 93.4                                         |
| India (Rural Sample) (1958-59)                           | 145.9                                        |
| Basutoland (1955-60)                                     | 181.0                                        |

*Racism a Product of Conflict*

Racism is the product of those attitudes of suspicion and distrust which arise from the divisions existing in society where one group has interests in conflict with those of another. Common examples are the division of the Australian community into groups based on wealth, religion, area of residence, type of employment, political belief, or racial standing. Between the different groups based on any one of these categories there can be a certain amount of conflict of interest, the prime example being that found between political parties, because politics is basically the question of seeking and maintaining power and deciding the way in which limited resources are to be distributed. However, behind the differences of all these groups, there lies much that they have in common as a result of being part of the one society. In a developing economy there is relative mobility between groups, not for everyone certainly, but enough so that the boundaries are not rigidly defined. There is also much overlap and neutral ground.

Racism is introduced into political conflict when completely different cultures coincide with political and economic interests. Where one experiences a combination of colour and cultural differences distributed on economic grounds, social and political stratification becomes more patent, and conflict increasingly purposeful. This situation does not inevitably lead to an irresolvable conflict, but seems to be the common pattern of adjustment when white and black societies come into contact.

The circumstances which have led to white racism in Africa are similar to those which have created the gap between black and white societies in Australia.

The fundamental aspect of white racism in both countries is a complete lack of respect for the culture of other racial groups, which are seen and evaluated according to the values which whites regard as fundamental. This means that they are not interested in discovering the real aspirations of these other groups, and leads to the callous destruction of their societies, which are regarded as inferior. White racism is as closely tied up with the beginnings of the slave trade and colonialism in Africa as it is with the development of the White Australia policy, indentured Pacific Island labour and the so-called official policy of assimilation of Aborigines.

When Europeans first started arriving in Africa, they found a

' . . . "cultural gap" between Africa and Europe . . . so wide that many Europeans found it genuinely difficult to believe that Africans were altogether human'.

Yet

' . . . it can be shown without much difficulty that the leading states of Africa and Europe were divided in medieval times, five or six hundred years ago, by no "cultural gap" of any significance'.[2]

In the intervening period rapid changes took place in Europe with the development of science and technology, while Africa seemed to undergo a decline with the collapse of such empires as the Monomotapa, which stretched from the Congo to Zimbabwe (Rhodesia). Yet Africa had produced many societies which were the result of successful adaptation to the difficult environment. In the absence of new challenges to their existence, there was a natural conservative belief that change for its own sake would cause disaster. Nevertheless, the arrival of new situations was the impetus to modify the patterns of behaviour of societies that were to continue to be successful.

As Lévi-Strauss and Malinowski have demonstrated, the question of social and political change in tribal or pre-literate societies raised important environmental questions which, as Europeans are now finding to their chagrin, strike at the very basis of existence. Under colonialism such processes of adjustment were no longer possible, because, by means of superior force, the Europeans divided up the African and Australian continents for their own ends, and in the process, destroyed the traditional societies.

Ignorance of the processes of adjustment was not the sole preserve of the indigenes. The following analysis of the contact situation by a European observer clearly establishes this point:

'One circumstance . . . very detrimental to an increase [in the supply of Aboriginal labour] . . . in the tropical regions of the North . . . is a fact reported to me by the Palatine priests at Beagle Bay Mission. After a tolerably good test of a hundred cases, namely that a black woman, having given birth to a child by a white father, will not again bear to a black father. If this is the case, in order to keep up the splendid supply of labour now available to develop the Northern region, every effort should be made to prevent the intermingling of the races'.[3]

## The Benefits of Colonialism

Too often Europeans emphasise the advantages of colonialism, asserting how much the British did to 'civilise' and modernise Africa and Australia. The truth is that the major effect of colonialism was to destroy African and Australian society and halt its natural progress by excluding the native people from any say in making the decisions that controlled their lives. While they stayed and occupied the land in Africa, the invaders dictated all of the terms by which the native people had to live. This was justified on the grounds that they were primitive and barbaric and incapable of deciding their own needs. As Hartwig has pointed out in Volume Two of this series, many of these arguments were merely rationalisations of the desire to totally dispossess the local people of their land and wealth. In Australia, the same bias has been built into the law, the ultimate source of conventional wisdom, and Aborigines find themselves completely incapable of reclaiming that which is rightfully theirs. In Africa, it was not until the European colonies started to gain independence that they could start on true development. Previously, growth of the economies was merely an accidental by-product of the European haste to exploit the continent.

It might seem a quaint comment on the state of affairs, but that continent colonised and totally devoted to European purposes, North America, is now paying the price for the excesses of the European patterns of material consumption. In Africa, at least, the circumvention of the rape of the continent must stand to the eternal credit of the native people. Australian indigenes are also fully aware of the destructive aspects of 'European progress', hence their wish to gain some control over what remains of their tribal lands.

Racism has developed as a result of the white man's need to justify his cruelty and exploitation by means of myths which he has created about the black races. Basil Davidson has described this aspect of racism by comparing the writings of Stuart Cloete, a widely-read white South African author, with those of Nbabaningi Sithole, an African nationalist at present imprisoned in Rhodesia. Cloete endeavours to prove that Africans are inferior human beings without any right to natural equality with whites.

'There is no word here for "thank you" ', Cloete wrote, 'for the people are without the concept that requires its use'. On the contrary, Sithole replies, and offers a short list of terms for 'thank you' in Ndebele, Shona, Tuganda, Hausa, Tswana and Sotho.

'The African', Cloete explains, 'has been conditioned by centuries of savage competition to seize what he desires wherever he can find it'. Sithole's reply is, 'We do not deny this . . . What concerns us here is the context in which [Cloete] makes this statement. He gives the false impression that it is only the African who has been so conditioned. One could reverse his statement so that it is equally applicable to any race in this world. The European has been conditioned by centuries of savage competitive life to seize what he desires wherever he can find it. The occupation of Asia, Africa, the Americas, Australasia and other non-European lands by Europeans is an historically irrefutable piece of evidence [to this effect] . . .'.[4]

Again, Cloete's desire to distort is illustrated by a statement of his that is widely accepted by whites: 'Let us have no illusions. The Black man hates the white. Above all he hates him for being white, because this is something he can never be.' Sithole's reply is penetrating:

'On a purely human basis the African accepts the white man. In the majority of cases it is the white man who does not accept the African. One of the reasons why the white man fears granting the African full independence is that the African may use against the white man the hateful methods he has seen the white man use against the African.

'What the African hates in the white man is his unfair social, economic, political and educational discriminatory practices which relegate the African to second- or third-rate citizenship in the land of his birth. The African hates the white man's arrogance, his mania for humiliating him in the land of his birth . . . Politically, the white man dominates the African; economically, he exploits him; socially, he degrades his human status . . . It is these things the African hates, and not the white man himself.'[5]

As McQueen, Hall and Brash have treated the question of race prejudice in Australian literature in some detail in the other two volumes of this series, there is little need to give further emphasis to this point. It should be sufficient to connect the development of Australian attitudes with those expressed by Cloete in Africa. The background is, again, supplied by early officials concerned with Aboriginal administration.

'A native living according to his own customs will remain healthy and strong; dress him up and house him and he will soon fade away. The experience of the good bishop Salvado . . . is that we must not forget they are savages, and we must try and make their work worth their food and clothing, and, if they acquire this knowledge, reading and writing might then be taught; but as they can never hope to have the same status as a white man, it is useless to teach them those things that will not be useful to them.'[6]

Prejudice and ignorance were apparently the unfailing companion of the white man on the colonial frontier.

### The Spread of Empire

Without wishing to give a detailed history of Southern Africa, it is necessary to look at some aspects of it which are too often ignored or even, outside the academic world, too often unknown. History as it is taught to whites and blacks in Southern African (and Australian) schools tells very little of the real situation when the two cultures first met. One aspect of the deliberate misrepresentation of the past is the theory that when whites arrived at the Cape, the Africans (called 'Bantu' by the whites) were almost simultaneously coming in from the north, while the area in between was practically unpopulated. The importance of this myth is that it is the justification for the present system of land division in South Africa, with 13 per cent of the land set aside for Africans (14½ million) and 87 per cent for the whites (4 million). It is also significant as an example of a myth which has come to be more widely believed, even outside South Africa, than the truth.

A myth of similar proportions has been maintained about the association between Australian Aborigines and the land. Although it is true that the migratory people of the desert asserted very little control over their extensive domains, in the better watered areas of the continent there was a very clear and detailed appreciation of what rights individuals had over any particular area. In many cases it was possible for the native residents to draw maps of these rights. To dispossess people of their rights it has been of assistance to rationalise their ownership away. The incredible situation has now arisen in Australia where people who have occupied land since time immemorial, have been declared by the courts to have no interest in their domains, finding in fact that their interests have passed to a foreign company whose residence in the country stretches back a mere three years. The courts have been completely unappreciative of the total and inalienable source of inspiration that land plays in the lives of totemic people. Regardless of the decision of the courts, the Aboriginal people cannot forego their land rights without committing cultural and spiritual genocide. While it is doubtful that this is exactly what the court had in mind, it is in keeping with the avowed aims of assimilation of the Australian governments.

In South Africa the oral traditions of the tribes indicate that they crossed the Limpopo River, the northern frontier of the country, in about 900 A.D. Typically, such evidence is ignored by Europeans. The first Europeans were those who were shipwrecked along the coast, such as the survivors of the Portuguese ships *Sao Joao* and *Sao Bento*. The *Sao Joao* was wrecked on the southeast coast near present day Pondoland in 1552, while the *Sao Bento* was shipwrecked along the coast of what is now Zululand. Reports from both the crews mentioned seeing 'Kaffirs, very black in colour', who were herding cattle, which they offered to barter. Similar reports give many instances of survivors of other shipwrecks who stayed to live with the Africans rather than return to Europe. Yet, if the European South African story is to be believed, those areas were at that time uninhabited because the 'almost simultaneous massive migration . . . from the north'[7] was not to begin until 100 years later, when the Dutch arrived at the Cape.

When the whites crossed the Great Fish River they found Africans already well established. This was the southern-most limit of the main Nguni migration which had in fact taken place at least two or three centuries earlier, (in other words one or two centuries before the whites even landed at the Cape). Of more interest however was the existence of other African groups which had settled long before the Nguni migration. Archaeological evidence for this has been provided by the Archaeological Research Unit of the University of Witwatersrand, Johannesburg. The heart of Afrikaner settlement is in the provinces of the Orange Free State and the Transvaal, both of which have archaeological remains of many hundreds of African settlements of pre-White origin. Such old kraals are found near present Johannesburg and in many of the rich mineral areas. In fact, the Africans were mining and smelting copper and gold centuries before the white man came. To quote John Laurence, 'A prime example concerns the rich Phalaborwa (Palabora) copper field in the Northern-eastern Transvaal. The historical evidence here includes the old fifty foot-deep Bantu mine-shafts; the known fact of pre-White Bantu mining there—'The Africans had been smelting odd pockets of copper round Palabora for centuries'.[8] Today, Phalaborwa's riches are for Whites only.'[9] As whites claim that apartheid has simply divided South Africa according to who was living there first, it might be asked when these areas are to be handed over to their rightful owners.

There are also many similar situations in Australia relating to the experience of the Aborigines, although, because of the lack of enthusiasm for recording oral history, much of the evidence has vanished. It is sufficient to recall that black colouring on most Aboriginal bark painting has a manganese base, although Europeans praise themselves for the discovery of the large deposits recently brought into commercial production in North Australia. In similar vein, Donald McCleod, as leader of the Pindan Aboriginal groups in the North West of Western Australia, had been claiming the mineralisation of the area since the early 1930's. The Western Australian government continually harassed him for offering this advice, amongst other things, and refused to assist the Aborigines in the development of their mineral enterprise though the extension of capital aid. Today, Australia stands on the brink of a mineral boom around the areas where Aborigines have survived for years on mining. It is significant that the new towns and mountain ranges bear the names of the more recent discoverers, or should I say owners, of the mineral deposits. The Aboriginal role in the opening up of the country has been all but forgotten.

### Disappearance of the Tribes

The fate of the Hottentots and Bushmen is another neglected aspect of South African history, just as tribal history is in Australia. If prior occupancy is the moral basis for white South Africa's claim to the land, what happened to these two groups of people who were living side by side at the Cape when the Dutch first began to settle after Jan van Riebeeck had set up a revictualling station in 1652? It is now often claimed that on contact with the Europeans the peaceful Bushmen '. . . took refuge from civilisation in the semi-desert of the north-western cape'.[10] To quote John Laurence in *The Seeds of Disaster*:[11]

> 'The facts are rather less idyllic. In 1774, after more than a century of White settlement, a White commander killed 503 Bushmen and took 239 prisoners, and it has been calculated that in the ten years between 1785 and 1795, no fewer than 2504 Bushmen were killed and 669 made captive. An official investigation as late as 1862 confirmed a report that White farmers in the northern Cape Colony were still pursuing a policy of exterminating Bushmen.'

Needless to say, there are very few Bushmen left now, and those remaining are living in the inhospitable Kalahari Desert.

The Hottentots were more numerous than the Bushmen and occasionally fought back against the Europeans were were settling their land and stealing their cattle. Van Riebeeck's Journal of 1660 records his receiving a delegation of Hottentots who

'... dwelt long upon our taking every day for our own use more of
the land which had belonged to them from all ages. They also asked
whether, if they were to come into Holland, they would be permitted
to act in a similar manner.'[12]

There had been a war with the Hottentots in 1657 and another in 1673,
which lasted intermittently for 10 years. Eventually they were defeated
through lack of numbers and were driven into the mountains. All of
their land was thus taken by force, as were most of their cattle.

The basis of the once-stable Hottentot society was thus destroyed and,
by the 18th Century, they were reduced to a poverty-stricken nomadic existence, relying on hunting and collecting wild fruit and vegetables. Many
of them were killed by epidemics of smallpox and measles which the Europeans introduced, or simply died of malnutrition and related illnesses. Three
years after the British finally took control of the Cape from the Dutch, which
had occurred in 1806, they introduced a pass law to control the remains of
the Hottentots. Under the new law any Hottentots not employed by white
masters, as indicated by their pass, were considered vagrants, and after
being arrested were hired out as labourers to white farmers. Any white man,
not just police, had the right to order a Hottentot to show his pass. To
carry a pass, Hottentots had to enter into labour agreements with white
farmers, with no guarantee of even a minimum wage. To prevent the parents
from running away, Hottentot children were 'apprenticed' to do unpaid tasks
on the farm. The absence of restrictions on the farmers meant in effect that
Hottentots still living around the Cape were forced into slavery.

Beyond the Cape, the situation was no better, as Hottentot families
attempting to establish farms were driven out by the encroaching Boers. A
European traveller in 1813 reported:

'We came to a Hottentot kraal ... but their fountain was dry so that
they had no water for man or beast ... From their own account they
had once a better place, but a boor [farmer—later Boer] having
asked permission first to sow a little corn, then to erect a mill,
they allowed it; after which he applied to the government for a grant
of the whole place, which they granted not knowing that it was in
possession of these Hottentots; of course they were driven from it.
An old Hottentot told us that he remembered the time when the
boors were all within five days' journey of Cape Town and the
country was full of Hottentot kraals: but they were all gradually
driven up the country to make room for white people.'[13]

The slaughter of Hottentots continued until around 1860 '... for many white
persons thought and spoke of them as if they were animals, and thousands
were killed'.[14] While some whites were concerned about this genocide, the
attitude of most was that it was wasteful of potential labourers. Thus, those
remaining were made into servants in the new arrivals' households.

Today the Cape Coloured stands as a descendant of this noble race of
maligned men and continues to be maligned to this day. The white South
Africans who talk of their 'prior occupancy' of the Cape have tended to
ignore the historical annexation of land from the Hottentots, and now deny
the Cape Coloureds any land rights whatsoever. Today, like the Africans
also affected by the Group Areas Act, they are still being forcibly moved
from their traditional homes to barren lands which they have never seen

before. By the end of September 1968, 23,587 Coloureds (mainly Cape Coloureds) had been 'resettled', as the government euphemistically calls it.

In Australia, the pattern of suppression of the original inhabitants has been hardly less brutal. Indeed, in the extermination of the Tasmanian Aborigines Australians can lay claim to one of the most goulish accomplishments in the history of man. Both Stevens[15] and Stanner[16] point out that few Aboriginal groups in Australia live in their traditional areas. They have been pushed around and manipulated in the cause of European convenience and national development. At worst, as Berndt noted in his study of industrial relations on the Northern Territory cattle stations in 1945, some eighteen tribes disappeared in the wake of the European cattleman's complete lack of concern for the suffering that his occupation of the tribal lands had brought. Indeed, so convinced were they of the morality of their actions that they set out to engage Berndt as a recruiting agent, in an endeavour to ensure that more Aboriginal labour would be fed into the industrial machine.[17] Fortunately, he saw through their stratagem.

Horner and Hartwig, in Volume Two of this series, deal in some depth with the impact of violence on the Australian Aboriginal community. There is a striking similarity with the African experience, and the rationalisations which have been built into European attitudes towards the suffering. Of all of the historians who have written on the consequences of the European invasion of Australia, only Rowley, in his recent study of Aboriginal society, has shown that the resistance of Aborigines to European encroachment was both widespread and significant.[18] Most writers interpret the alleged submission of Aborigines to European rule as further evidence of the backward nature of Aboriginal society. Nothing is further from the truth. In all, apparently, some 160 of the 380 original Australian tribes have disappeared without trace. This is the graphic accomplishment of European 'civilisation' as far as the native people are concerned.

*Effects of Racism*

The belief of South African regimes in the myth of race has had extreme results for the Africans. Not only the standard of education and the level of employment available, but even residence is completely dictated by the whites. One of the most fundamental aspects of this discrimination is the present distribution of land, by which the Africans have been set aside the use of 13 per cent of the land although comprising 75 per cent of the population.

Back in 1954, the official Tomlinson Commission reported that the African reserves could support only just over 2 million people, unless an additional 1,250,000 jobs were provided at the rate of 50,000 a year, which would raise to 7 million, the number that could be supported. What has in fact happened is that the population in the Reserves as now risen to 7 million (as a result of forced resettlement), but only about 2000 jobs have since been created. Not surprisingly, average income has fallen from $32 per year in 1954 to $27.50 per year in 1969. The reduction, in real terms, is even greater. Similarly, subsistence farming has become less productive because of overcrowding and soil erosion, while programmes for soil reclamation recommended by the Commission were never adopted.

The accomplishments of the Australian Government's so-called assimilation programme are interesting in this respect. The Aboriginal labourer in the cattle industry of the Northern Territory started out on 20 per cent of the European wage rate and by the time the 'assimilation' programme had been developed to its greatest height he ended up with 15 per cent of the European wage rate.[20] Employers complained, however, of inability to pay. None, apparently, stopped to consider that their very fortunes were based on government sponsorship of this fiscal dishonesty—at least until they were called upon to substantiate their claims before the Commonwealth Arbitration Commission, when they allowed their counsel to encourage them to use the argument of racial disparities. Fortunately, the device did not work. However, from most recent reports Aborigines in the Northern Territory cattle industry still continue to be paid a pittance for their labour.

One could multiply the South African experience in Australia many times. However, I shall refer only to residential stratification. Two decades of 'equality' of opportunity in the Northern Territory of Australia, where the Federal Government policies have most influence, has led to a situation where 87 per cent of the European population live in the towns and 92 per cent of the Aboriginal population live in the country. It is not surprising that European employment opportunities in the towns have expanded some 400 per cent over the last decade and a half, whilst in the country the indigenous population, apart from those employed on cattle stations, remain in almost universal unemployment.

Such policies as these in both South Africa and Australia have led to widespread malnutrition and a very high infant mortality rate. In this respect there is little difference between the two countries. 'A survey conducted in 1966 indicated that almost half of the children born in a typical African reserve in South Africa died before reaching the age of five years.'[20] In Australia, 28 per cent of all deaths in the 1-2 year age group are Aborigines, representing 20 times the Australian average.[21]

It is further claimed that apartheid allows all races to develop on their own without the friction that would inevitably result from contact. However, contact does occur for two fundamental reasons. In the first place, the rapid expansion of South Africa's economy is based on the extreme exploitation of black labour, as the Africans are paid very much lower wages than whites in all industries and services. Secondly, because the reserves have almost no industry, and the land is very poor and overpopulated, Africans are forced to immigrate to 'white areas' in search of work. Yet, in the places where we do work in contact with whites there is extreme resentment over the absolute control of wages and conditions exercised by the employers and the Government. The exact processes of discrimination cannot be covered here, but some idea can be gained by comparing average monthly wage rates of whites and Africans in various industries in 1968-9:[22]

| Industry | Whites | Coloured | Asians | Africans | White/Black wage ratio |
|---|---|---|---|---|---|
| Mining | $A 371 | 77 | 95 | 22 | 16.5:1 |
| Building construction | 352 | 122 | 169 | 56 | 6.3:1 |
| Wholesale trade | 306 | 214 | 117 | 60 | 5.1:1 |
| Public service | 264 | 125 | 159 | 45 | 5.9:1 |

Such discrepancies in wage rates are the result of Africans being completely excluded from the wage-fixing process: African trade unions are not legally recognised and have no powers to negotiate industrial agreements.

Militant action such as striking is illegal and carries the risk of fines up to $A1250 or three years in prison.

The question of occupational rewards for Australian Aborigines has been fairly adequately covered in Volume Two of this series, but some figures are worth repeating for the sake of comparison. The similarities between Australia and South Africa in this respect are quite marked. In the example presented, one can be fairly certain that the wages mentioned were actually received by the employees as the institution was government controlled. However, in private industry in Australia there is no certainty of the indigene receiving the wages due to him at all. Indeed, the further one moves away from Government supervision the less likely is the native labourer in Australia to be paid.

*Aboriginal Employees on Queensland Settlements*

|  | Aboriginal weekly wage | European weekly wage |
| --- | --- | --- |
| Truck Driver | $20.00 | $70.00 |
| Tractor Driver | $12.00-$18.00 | $65.00 |
| Labourer | $10.00-$18.00 | $60.00 |
| Mechanic | $24.00 | $75.00 |
| Painter | $16.00 | $65.00 |
| Ganger | $20.00-$25.00 | $80.00 |
| Carpenter (trained on reserve) | $20.00 | $75.00 |
| Police Constable | $12.00-$18.00 | $80.00 |

South Africa is much more proud of its achievements in education, and its whites are very fond of claiming that it has more educated Africans than any other country. Such a claim had some validity in the past, when African education was primarily in the hands of missionaries.

In the first half of this century, a significant number of Africans obtained university degrees at Fort Hare or some of the other universities without a colour-bar, and became doctors, lawyers, scholars or other professionals. Professor D. D. T. Jabavu was a world authority on the classics, as was Professor Z. K. Matthews on education. Writers such as Ezekiel Mphahlele and Lewis Nkosi have achieved international recognition, as have Nelson Mandela and Robert Sobukwe in the legal profession. However, since 1948, South African standards of education have been falling, particularly as a result of the 1953 Bantu Education Act. Dr. Verwoerd himself described the policy: '... Bantu education should stand with both feet in the reserves. What is the use of teaching the Bantu child mathematics when it cannot use it in practice? That is absurd ... There is no place for the Native in the European community above the level of certain forms of labour ... It is of no avail for him to receive a training which has as its aim absorption in the European community.'[23]

Bantu education is thus clearly a system designed to prevent Africans from ever rising above the level of unskilled labour, and to ensure that they are never able to compete on equal terms with whites. 1970 Government expenditure on education confirms this:

White children—$A285 per head per year.
African children—$A25 per head per year.[24]

Although under the policy of 'job reservation', Africans are not allowed to work at skilled jobs retained for whites, the restrictions are sometimes said to apply only in the 'white areas'.

It might be thought that the situation would improve in the reserves, but the standards of Bantu education are so low that, by March 1971, there were no registered African dentists, surveyors, architects, town planners or engineers. Yet there were Africans with all these qualifications before 1948. Only a very small number of doctors graduate each year, so that there is now only one doctor per 100,000 non-whites, one of the lowest ratios in the world. The former Director of Education in Natal underlined the results of Bantu education: '(It) fails not only to prepare African children for life in the general economy of South Africa, but fails even to provide the technicians and artisans required by the Bantustans. There is no need, we are told, for Bantu engineers. Poor Bantustans!'[25]

Possibly one of the most cynical aspects of Bantu education is that Africans, who are supposedly intellectually inferior to the whites, are forced to study in *three* languages. They begin schooling in the tribal language, but are later taught the more academic subjects in Afrikaans and English as well. This extremely burdensome policy is a major reason for the very high proportion of African students who drop out before completing primary school.

In South Africa, the Bantustans are controlled entirely by the white-educated parliament, which has thus determined what kind of education whites want the Africans to receive. There is no question of the Africans being allowed to determine what kind of education they really want for themselves. What we want is an education appropriate to the twentieth century. But we also want to maintain the cultural traditions which have survived mutilation under colonialism.

Australian educational provisions for Aborigines, on the other hand, need little comment. With fewer than one dozen part Aborigines at University and no full-blood Aborigines at the tertiary level of education the situation speaks for itself.

On the Aboriginal reserves it might also be shown that the indigenous Australians are controlled by concepts of paternalism similar to those imposed on their black brothers in South Africa.[26] In both situations, Europeans seem reluctant to allow the development of individual expression of opinion for fear that this will react in a manner unfavourable to their interests. Probably they are right in this respect. But it is an erroneous view of education to believe that it can grow and develop in a situation which is artificially-induced, with no practical meaning for the native people, either in their daily lives as children or for what they might, or might not, do as adults. In South Africa and Australia, education for natives has no purpose. Accordingly, it is rejected by those whom it is supposed to benefit. The Europeans, of course, write this off as the strange workings of the savage mind!!!

## British and Boers

Another aspect of South Africa of comparative interest is the difference between British and Boer racial attitudes. The Nationalist Government, which was formed in 1948, and has since developed the legal framework of apartheid, is predominantly Boer. For this reasons there exists a wide-

| State | Aborigines | Part Aborigines | Totals | Pre-school | Primary | Secondary | University | Technical/Professional | Government Staffed | Mission Staffed | In-Service Training and Adult Education[1] |
|---|---|---|---|---|---|---|---|---|---|---|---|
| NT[2] | 20,120 | 4,000 | 24,120 | 362 | 3,866[3] | 6 | 0 | 13[4] | 37 | 10 | Av. enrolment 640; 130 in special courses: home management, catering, etc. |
| VIC | — | 3,500 | 3,500 | 60 | 500 | 243 | 0 | 4 | 2 | 0 | No classes; adult education officer appointed for 1968 |
| SA | 3,123 | 4,632 | 7,760 | 150 | 1,723 | 195[5] | 5[6] | 12 | 7 | 2 | Literacy classes at Coober Pedy; more classes expected soon |
| WA | 9,905 | 11,985 | 21,890 | 400 | 4,731 | 582 | 0 | 75[7] | 18 | 3 | Full-time officer, 80 adult classes, enrolment 1,200 |
| NSW | 130 | 23,000 | 23,130 | 857 | 5,530[8] | 1,080 | 2 | 2 | 11 | 0 | Sydney and New England University programme; several classes |
| QLD | 12,000 | 29,700 | 49,700 +8,000 TSI[9] | 240 | 2,956 | 490 | 2 | 5 | 21 | 8 | 15 in special courses: kindergarten teaching aides |
| Totals | 44,605 | 77,495 | 130,130 | 2,164 | 19,306 | 2,596 | 9 | 111 | 96 | 23 | |

[1] Number of trainees varies according to nature of courses conducted
[2] Figures apply to full-blood Aborigines only
[3] Includes 316 post-primary pupils
[4] 7 welders at Technical College, Brisbane, and 6 apprentices in New South Wales
[5] Includes 9 post-primary pupils
[6] Two at University and 3 tertiary equivalent
[7] 50 in agriculture courses and 25 in apprenticeship
[8] Includes 192 in super-primary category
[9] Torres Strait Islanders

*Source:* C. M. Tatz, 'Aboriginal Education—present facilities and needs', in T. Roper (ed), *Aboriginal Education: the Teacher's Role*, Melbourne 1969. Published with permission of Abschol.

spread belief that racism in South Africa is the fault of the Boers, and that
the English are much more 'tolerant'. This belief is naturally prevalent in
English-speaking countries such as Britain and Australia. In reality there
is little difference between the two groups. There is no doubt that Boers
are much more direct and outspoken in their attitude towards the Africans than are the English. However, behind the Englishman's expressions
of friendliness lies exactly the same determination to maintain his privileged
position in the racist society. The deep divisions in South Africa between the
Boers and the English are primarily due to conflict between these two culturally dissimilar communities competing for power. In fact, the word 'racialism' in South Africa used to refer to this very conflict.

The English are widely known to have officially abolished slavery after
finally taking over the Cape from the Dutch in 1806, but it is rarely mentioned that they also introduced the system of pass laws for the Hottentots
which amounted to much the same thing. This kind of one-sided approach
is typified by G. H. L. Le May in *Black and White in South Africa*.
While this author is undoubtedly opposed to apartheid, he makes the mistake
of laying the blame for it upon the Boers whose Voortrekker forebears
he describes as 'self chosen by a form of natural selection in reverse. They
represented that part of the community of the Cape which was least able
to come to terms with the new situations posed by the arrival of the
British, and the imposition upon the colonial society of such concepts as legal
equality.' He justifies this view of the British by saying that they had only
property qualifications for the franchise, but fails to mention that the qualifications were simply raised when African voters looked like having any
influence. The same story has been repeated in Zimbabwe (Rhodesia) today.

Any feelings left among the Africans that the British were sympathetic
towards their aspirations were shattered after the Boer War, in which many
had supported the British forces. In 1901, the British governments promised
the Africans that after the war they would be given the same privileges as
whites. But the peace treaty signed at Vereeniging was concerned with
humiliating the defeated Boers, and betrayed the African trust. In fact,
the history of British actions in Southern Africa constitutes a whole series of
betrayals of the Africans. Some of the most significant include the 1910 Act
of Union by which Britain gave South Africa its independence under the
minority control of Boers and English, with a Constitution which restricted
the vote to whites in all provinces except the Cape, which had a limited
non-white franchise; and the 1936 'Hertzog settlement' which deprived the
Cape Africans of their direct franchise and put them on a separate roll.
Against the united opposition of Africans throughout the country, this bill
was passed with unanimous acceptance by white South Africans, including
the 'liberal' English. Characteristically, the area of land which had been
promised by way of 'compensation' to the Africans was never released. Critics
of the Boers should ask themselves if the Anglo-Saxon settlers of Australia
and North American have been any less ruthless in their dealings with
Aborigines, American Indians or black Americans.

### 'Separate Nations'

Under the theory of apartheid it is claimed that South Africa is moving
towards a system of autonomous states for the different racial groups. This
is supposed to allow each group to develop on its own terms without inter-

ference or 'competition' from another group. Following the well-known principle of 'divide and rule', the whites have decided the way the races are to be divided. All whites are thus classified together, whether they came from English or Boer ancestry, or are recent immigrants from southern Europe. Their deep divisions of cultural background, language, and in particular, the marked antagonism which has existed between the English and Boers, are ignored. The Africans, on the other hand, are divided up according to tribes, ignoring the fact that the Swazi, Zulu and Xhosa, who are now forced into separate 'homelands', are all Nguni people speaking dialects of the same language, and having similar social and legal structures. The Pedi, Tswana and Sotho form another group with similar culture and language. Before the whites came these populations were fluid and lived side by side. Far from preventing friction, the whites have separated these tribes in an attempt to develop rivalry and illfeeling between them.

In all the decisions concerning the division of South Africa into racial areas, and the way they are to develop, African opinion has not even been asked for, let alone heard. To date, the Africans, Coloureds and Asians, have all had the right to vote taken away from them. In its place the Africans are told that they can still decide their own affairs through their chiefs. In traditional Nguni society, the chiefs used to wield great power. They had an inner circle of advisers, who were mainly from the nobility, as well as an outer circle of councillors, both of which were consulted on matters of state. In the Sotho and Tswana groups the whole community would be involved in such discussions. Although the chiefs were not obliged to follow such advice, the wise ones would generally do so in order to retain the loyalty of the community. As the Swazis say, 'The king is ruled by his councillors.'

The Bantu Authorities Act of 1951, which controls the formation of the Tribal, Regional and Territorial Authorities within the reserves, took away the traditional powers of the chief. Real power is now vested in the Bantu Affairs Commissioner, a white public servant. He can nominate members of the Tribal Authority, which now takes the place of the traditional councillors, as well as veto appointments made by the chief. The result is a complete distortion of traditional relations between the chief, his councillors and people. The chief is now paid by the government and can even be dismissed by the government. He thus becomes simply a puppet of the Bantu Affairs Commissioner. His duties include reporting any unrest or dissatisfaction in his tribe, and particularly the arrival of strangers without permits.

In the Australian context, it should be pointed out that the system of indentured labour, much favoured by British colonial administrations after the outlawing of slavery, was the basis used by Australian interests in the development of their tropical empire in Queensland and New Guinea. This system still continues in a very open way in New Guinea today. On the mainland, the system of contract labour, and the associated restraint on the legal, civil and social rights of the black worker, is still the basis of European policy and attitudes towards Aborigines.

It is still necessary for Europeans to obtain visas and permits to enter Aboriginal reserves in Australia. These are controlled, not by the people they are supposed to benefit, but by some distant European bureaucrat who is charged with interpreting what he believes are the Aborigines' best interests. Invariably, these amount to what the European government believes is politically expedient.[27]

In South Africa the situation is little different. One of the best-known South African chiefs was Albert Luthuli, who, in 1961, became the first African to be awarded the Nobel Peace Prize. His recognition by the South African Government, however, consisted of a series of banishments and restriction orders, as well as being deprived of his chieftainship when he accepted the presidency of the African National Congress.

In 1959, the characteristically-named 'Promotion of Bantu Self Government Act' removed the remaining white representation of Africans in the Republic's Parliament, and divided the various ethnic groups into national units. This caused great resentment because of the way people who had been living together for generations were arbitrarily divided up and separated into tribal groups which had long lost any distinct separate identities. They were also not fooled by promises that, once they agreed to separation, they would be allowed to vote as national units. Commissioners General were then appointed to continue white control. The source of all decision-making, the Union Parliament, is still an exclusively white body, without even any representation for the African chiefs who are supposed to be able to control their own affairs.

The Australian equivalent of manipulation of the indigenous community for European purposes can be seen in the internal administration of reserves, mentioned briefly above, and the illegal presentation of voting returns.[28] Possibly, a more sophisticated technique has been involved in the election of an Aboriginal senator from Queensland, representing the conservative Liberal-Country Party coalition. Although his claims to represent the Aboriginal people are almost universally decried, he maintains strong support in his own domestic organisation—the One People of Australia League—a state-sponsored political and welfare organisation reminiscent of Fascist Italy. It was W. E. H. Stanner, himself a government nominee to national policy-making bodies on Aboriginal affairs, who drew attention to the numerous Aboriginal leaders who had been illegally removed from their communities to serve the short run convenience of European administrators.[29]

In Australia, all colonies, other than South Australia, were established with letters patent which claimed all land in the name of the Crown. In South Australia the letters patent establishing the colony called on the Governor to protect native property rights and to ensure that these were not interfered with except by due process of law.[30] The instructions to the Governor were soon forgotten, and the pattern of settlement in South Australia proceeded in much the same manner as in all other colonies. Native property rights were all but completely ignored. The disastrous impact of European occupation of the Australian continent, and the large land areas involved, encouraged some remorse for the fate of the indigenes and sizeable tracts of land were put aside for their occupation. The movement to establish native reserves gained pace in the 1920 and 1930s. A background to this generosity was the conviction that the native people were in the process of dying out and all that could be done to assist them was merely putting off the fatal day. Little concern was shown for either the resources or potential of the reserves. Invariably they were situated in isolated or inhospitable environments.

For the past half century, Australian Aboriginal reserves have developed into little more than impoverished holding camps, in which the indigenous community has been restrained from entering the broader framework of Australian society. At first this was rationalised on the basis of miscegenation. However, in more recent times the continuing importance of the reserve system is justified by demonstration of the economic and social impoverishment of the Aborigines—a condition the reserves themselves have been primarily responsible for creating.

*Background of Settlers*

An appreciation of the differences in culture between the black and white people when they first met in South Africa and Australia is crucial to an understanding of later developments in racial attitudes. To the Dutch, and later the English, the Africans were at first regarded as curiosities. Skin colour and physical appearance were the most puzzling to those Europeans, and they invented many theories to explain them. These included the effect of the sun's heat on the skin, excessive sexuality or the curse of God on the descendants of Ham. The latter theory, which is still held by the Dutch Reformed Church in South Africa, seems to rely on the assumption that blackness in itself must have been a curse.

Apart from differences in appearance, Africans were also different in their clothing, housing, farming, warfare, language, government and morals, all of which were classified as 'savage' or 'primitive' when measured against European customs. A great deal of interest was taken in this comparison, but mainly at a very superficial level which did not attempt to understand why Africans found this way of life more appropriate to their environment. When it came to religion, the 'heathenism' of the Africans was regarded as ' . . . a fundamental defect which set them distinctly apart . . . they were not accustomed to dealing face-to-face with people who appeared, so far as many travellers could tell, to have no religion at all. Steeped in the legacy and trappings of their own religion, Englishmen were ill prepared to see any legitimacy in African religious practices. Judged by Christian cosmology, Negroes stood in a separate category of men.'[31]

With the advent of slave-trading and other forms of exploitation a new twist was added to the Europeans' debate about the Africans. Where, before, many commentators had felt that Africans would behave more like them in a better environment, now it became necessary to prove the hereditary nature of the African's supposedly bestial character and to emphasise his inherent inferiority. In justification of their involvement in the slave trade, a group of Liverpool merchants declared in 1792: 'Africans being the most lascivious of human beings, may it not be imagined that the cries they let forth, at being torn from their wives, proceed from the dread that they will never have the opportunity of indulging their passions in the country to which they are embarking.'[32]

In the first contacts between black and white, which occurred mainly with shipwrecked sailors, the whites were treated as guests by the Africans. There are many recorded cases of such Europeans marrying African women and refusing to leave when later offered the chance to return home. In the early days of settlement there were some instances of the social acceptance of mixed marriages. A well-known case is that of the Hottentot woman Eva, who, in 1664, married Van Meerhoff, the explorer. The bridal feast was held in Government House. However, by 1685, such marriages came to be considered a disgrace, and were prohibited by law in that year.

The kind of incident which destroyed the development of friendly relations between black and white can be seen in the treatment of Makoni, chief of a Mashona group in Zimbabwe. Thomson, an English explorer, observed that Makoni had '. . . uniformly treated individual settlers with kindness and consideration. What annoyed him was the pegging-out of the whole of his territory for farms or gold claims.'[33] While he still had faith in the whites as individuals, other Africans could no longer tolerate the encroachments being made upon them. As a result, in 1896, three European traders who came looking for food were killed. Although it was proved that Makoni had not been involved, the British chose to make an example of the very man who was interested in developing friendly relations with them. When they threatened his people with dynamite and a field gun, Makoni gave himself up to be arrested, and was court-martialled and shot on the spot.

Possibly because of the greater isolation of the Australian frontier, many of the examples of European ingratitude to their Aboriginal hosts have either been lost or are now only folklore with little chance of recovery. Mary Durack, in her book *Kings in Grass Castles*, provides ample evidence of the less than favourable terms Europeans meted out to local natives. The hand of gratitude was often a clawed fist. Aborigines who opened up their water-holes to the invaders frequently returned to find them polluted. Many, indeed, by the time European closer settlement had been achieved, found their relatives' bodies staked out in the fields as scare-crows. In other parts of the country Aborigines were frequently shot on sight or even for sport. A more sophisticated version of this pattern of exploitation now exists in the use of Aboriginal wages and trust funds to expand the economic welfare of the European community!

## Christianity

Christianity played a significant role in the long-term destruction of African society as it did in Australia. In the first place, heathenism and savagery were associated together in the minds of the missionaries, who were determined to break down many of the traditional aspects of the African way of life which they disapproved of. The Calvinists found biblical justifications for this subjugation on the grounds of the imputed moral turpitude of the natives, and their belief in being the chosen people of God to whom the heathens were given as an inheritance. Yet such attitudes resulting from religious belief were not limited just to the Calvinists. It is observed that '. . . if the London Missionary Society (arose) out of English Evangelical Protestantism, it still (spoke) with the Reformation language of the Afrikaner.'[34]

Whatever the motives of the missionaries themselves, there is no doubt that whites have been quick to see the advantages to themselves of religious indoctrination in the subduing of the Africans. In 1856, a South African government official, J. C. Warner reported: 'The political and religious governments of the Kaffir tribes are so intimately connected that one cannot be overturned without the other, and they must stand or fall together . . . It seems to me that the sword must first break them up as tribes and destroy their political existence, after which, when thus set free from the shackles by which they are bound, civilisation and Christianity will no doubt make rapid progress among them.'[35] The word 'Kaffir' used above is South Africa's equivalent of the word 'nigger', but its original (Arabic) meaning was simply 'unconverted' or 'heathen'. That this has since come to be used as a term of abuse for all Africans shows the importance of religion in the development of South African racism.

In the Australian situation, it is interesting to note that many of the early anthropological scholars were evangelists. Indeed, the architect of the so-called Australian assimilation programme, A. P. Elkin, was a Christian missionary. A careful reading of some of Elkin's main theoretical writings on the problems of contemporary adjustment of Aborigines will clearly show his belief in Christian, or European ideas, in preference to those of the indigenes.

Christian missionaries in Southern Africa have always had an obsessive preoccupation with the sexual customs of Africans.[36] In Zimbabwe girls began physical preparation for the sexual side of marriage at the age of eight. Anatomical improvements (*not* female circumcision) were made to heighten their later sexual response to their husbands, as well as easing the process of giving birth. At puberty, all girls were isolated and taught what to expect in sexual intercourse. To become acquainted with the sexual movements, they were taught various dances. Boys also were isolated at puberty for initiation and circumcision. Then, according to the tribe they belonged to, they learnt the theory or practice of sexual intercourse themselves. However, such practices, which had succeeded in giving Africans a healthy physical and mental outlook towards sex were declared the work of the devil by the missionaries, and every method was used to stamp them out. Yet, looking around it is obvious that the sexual culture of Europeans is in chaotic confusion. That there should still be conflict in Australia, for example, on the issues of sexual education in schools, availability of contraceptives and abortion, and yet still so much ignorance about sex, is amazing. In Zimbabwe, whites have not yet even reached the stage of public discussion of these issues.

The most powerful influence of Christianity amongst Africans came through the mission schools which were the main educational facilities available. The standard of education was often high, leading up to the English GCE levels, but always at the expense of traditional culture, which it attempted to replace with a peculiar mixture of nineteenth century Christian attitudes.

One custom that survived the Catholic missionaries' control was communal bathing. During childhood, I looked forward to bathing in the creek running by the village every evening after a long day in the fields. The best time was on Saturdays when my sisters and cousins would congregate by the rocks before going in to bathe all afternoon in the nude. The family washing was done whilst teasing each other about the growth of our breasts or pubic hair, but it was all in a spirit of uninhibited playfulness. But when I went to my first mission school, we were given solemn lectures against the evil of girls bathing together, although the reasons were never explained. At one school, two girls who were found taking a shower together were severely caned in front of all the other girls, but not even they were told why what they had done was wrong. Africans learnt to accept such irrational attitudes as the price of obtaining an education.

I was interested to read of the many sexual offences which have been committed on Australian Christian Aboriginal missions. This, taken together with the almost common pattern of brutality and restraint, makes it seem as though the individuals concerned are merely the product of the environment with which they were forced to contend, rather than individuals with their own volition.

It is ironic that European civilisation should owe so much to Christianity in its cultural development and yet be so unprepared to act according to the most fundamental principle of Christ's teachings. In Africa, the same settlers who were stealing land and cattle from us were the ones who judged us according to what they claimed to be civilised Christian standards. Thomson wrote: 'The Zulus are an essentially logical people. "You say it is a wicked thing to drink and lead immoral lives", a Zulu said to one of my friends, "and that if we do shall go to hell. Well hell can't be a very bad place, for you white people don't seem to be afraid of going there. We see that you do all these things." '37

*Zimbabwe (Rhodesia)*

Rhodesia perhaps provides a microcosm of the attitudes that have been prevalent in Africa's recent history of white rule. Whites have been settling in the southern country Africans call Zimbabwe for only the last eighty years, motivated by the desire for riches from reports of extensive gold deposits. Inducements of land (three thousand acres for each person), were promised to each of the two hundred members of the original pioneer column. Since then, the availability of cheap black labour and the use of the country's most fertile land has made Zimbabwe a very desirable country for whites. To justify their total control over its political and economic systems and the extensive privileges they have obtained at the expense of the Africans, the whites have also, in this area, resorted to mythology.

Douglas Reed, an Englishman who has settled in South Africa, epitomises the attitudes of the white population, whether in Zimbabwe South Africa or Australia, to non-whites. Shortly after the Smith regime's unilateral declaration of independence in 1965, he went to Zimbabwe to write about the situation and present what he calls 'the true picture'. His book *Insanity Fair '67*, first published in Cape Town, compares the World's 'conspiracy' against Ian Smith to the situation in Europe in 1936 which led to Hitler's being allowed to invade Austria and Czechoslavakia, and hence to the Second World War. African Nationalism, Mr. Reed claims, is the counterpart to Nazism. Naturally this kind of outlook is enthusiastically received by the whites, and the book was 'the fastest selling in many years' according to the *Rhodesian Herald* which added that Reed was 'A man whose political conclusions—should not be taken lightly'. The South African Broadcasting Company said it had 'remarkable foresight'. With these credentials established it is useful to see the way in which he explains the role of the whites in Zimbabwe. Of the original white invaders he says, ' . . . Their great purpose was to root out slavery, which the warrior tribes and Arab slave traders together practised. They were the banner-bearers of Christian civilization in Central Africa . . . .'

'Prior settlement' is the myth used to justify the white presence in South Africa, but in Zimbabwe reliance is placed on the great understanding the whites have of Africans, and the claim that the Africans support the Smith government because without it Zimbabwe would return to the chaos and confusion which it is believed exists in all the independent African countries to the North. In Reed's words,

> 'I repeat, the white man demonstrably gave the black one in Africa life, and when the white man leaves, the black folk begin again to kill, mutilate, publicly hang and enslave each other; they have not had time to learn otherwise and do not yet wish to change. Against the further spread of this evil process, stands Rhodesia, where law and order and protection in the white man's understanding of the words prevail, and its neighbours in Southern Africa.
>
> 'They stand alone against the menace of a third general war, which in my judgment must inevitably come out of the African shambles if England and America continue their effort to extend the area of chaos Southward from the Zambezi.'[38]

These words are thrown at me everywhere in Australia, in various forms. There is no effort made to see what, in fact, the Africans to the North are doing; neither is there the inclination to find out what the Africans really think and what their situation now is.

Prior to white settlement, Zimbabwe was the home of various communities of the vaShona people, the remnants of the once great Monomotapa Empire which the early Portuguese explorers described with awe. In 1645, following a long period of peace, King Monomotapa IV declared complete disarmament as war had become unnecessary. Instead, they developed special techniques of underground resistance and ways of frustrating enemy plans which ensured their independence for three centuries before the arrival of the British. Many Nguni clans from the South attempted conquest unsuccessfully, and had to proceed north to Malawi and Zambia. The last of these clans were the Amandebele, an offshoot from the Zulus, under Mzilikazi. They raided several Shona clans. In accordance with their tradition, these clans withdrew into the mountains taking their possessions with them. Other clans were conquered by the Amandebele, who married vaShona girls and for some reason adopted the religion of the conquered.

At about the same time, the first whites to come from the South were hunters and missionaries who came only as temporary residents. They lived among the African people who accepted them as guests and gave them permits to travel through their land. Cecil Rhodes, an Englishman whose life-long ambition was to expand the British Empire throughout Africa, looked upon Zimbabwe enviously. In order to gain Queen Victoria's assent to further expansion, he arranged for Charles Rudd to ask the new Ndebele king, Lobengula, for a mining concession. In return, Lobengula was offered a perpetual annuity, one thousand rifles, ammunition and an armed steamboat on the Zambezi river, as well as an understanding that he would be free from the continuing pressures of other foreign agents. The king was suspicious and wary of the British of whom he said:—

> 'Did you ever see a chameleon catch a fly?—The chameleon gets behind the fly and remains motionless for some time, then he advances very slowly and gently, first putting forward one leg and then another. At last, when well within reach, he darts his tongue and the fly disappears. England is the chameleon, and I am that fly.'[39]

However, Lobengula was persuaded by John Moffat, the son of Robert Moffat, a missionary who was a close friend of Lobengula's father Mzilikazi, that nothing more was involved than prospecting for various minerals. Lobengula accordingly granted what is known as the Rudd Concession in October 1888, giving exclusive mining rights in his land to Rhodes. All Lobengula's councillors were opposed to the granting of the concession, which they feared would be used as an excuse to come in and settle on their land, as they had done in South Africa. Within two years their fears were realized as the pioneers hoisted the Union Jack at Fort Salisbury, setting the stage for the problems that have continued to trouble Zimbabwe. The arms and the gunboat were never delivered.

Not only did the whites seize land, and declare the owners squatters, they also decided to force the chiefs to supply the new owners with cheap labour. To force the Africans to work, chiefs were beaten, at times shot or evicted. However, the most effected method was imposing a hut tax payable in cash or labour or in kind in the form of cattle. Each hut cost 10s. per year.

On forced labour, Thomson say:

> 'I have often heard of cases in which wages have been refused when due, and, in some instances, the claimants have been flogged for insisting on payment.'[40]

There was a certain amount of debate amongst the whites, on the morality of forced labour and the hut tax. However, the precedent of not consulting the Africans was quickly established even though we were the ones affected by any decisions taken. The most devastating aspect of this kind of labour in the mines and on white farms was that the men were forced to leave their homes, wives, environment to obtain a mere pittance in return. The serious breakdown of family and communal life in much of Southern Africa can be attributed to conditions imposed on Africans, to make them work for cash rather than live their own lives the way they choose.

The nature of British authority was also strongly resented. Each district was forced to have a white Native Commissioner appointed by the white government without consulting the Africans. Each Native Commissioner had the support of the *status quo,* meaning that no matter what ruthless decisions he took, he had the support of the government. The qualifications of these commissioners were poor. Thomson says of them,

> 'There are many details connected with the treatment of Natives personally known to myself, which prove conclusively that the wrong men were often chosen for handling such raw material both in the mines, on the farms and in government service.'[41]

A typical example occurred, following the killing of a policeman in the Lomagundi district. A sub-inspector immediately sent out a force to punish the suspects. The force rode inside a church where Rev. Eva was in the middle of a service. His congregation was African. Seven chiefs were arrested and taken outside. Five minutes later the minister heard shots and ran out to find 3 chiefs shot dead. The police officer apologised to the minister about the use of guns but was not concerned about the dead chiefs, who had not even heard about the dead policeman. No action was taken when this matter was reported to the government.

The above circumstances, therefore, led to the first two wars of resistance fought by the combined forces of the vaShona and Amandebele. The whites were shocked that the two groups of Africans were fighting together, and explained this by telling themselves that, in fact, the Africans, being so lazy, preferred to unite and overthrow the whites trying to give them jobs. The Protestant ethic of work for its own sake as being part of their belief in righteousness was strong among the settlers. The problem here was the whites' definition of work; which inherently must involve labouring in those industries which were important to the white man's economy. For the Africans, who were used to a subsistence economy, these considerations were subordinate to the important aspects of life, looking after the extended family unit and developing human relationships and involvement in creative cultural activity.

In the Australian case it is not difficult to find many parallels to the Black African experience in Rhodesia. During the early periods of colonial settlement, many Aboriginal tribes were offered the hand of friendship. Once having given up their heritage, they were frequently bludgeoned to death.

Lobengula's tale of the chameleon and the fly is typical of the stealth with which Aboriginal independence and resources have been filched away. In the light of the African experience, it is not surprising that the Christian missions have frequently been the vehicle of dispossession. Using the spread of the Gospel as the reason for their entry on to Aboriginal reserves, missionaries have readily become the agents of European government policy. Not one Christian mission station or Government settlement on Aboriginal reserves in Australia has a fully autonomous and independent local council. Christians have been all too ready to abandon the fundamental concepts of their faith when they come into conflict with the superior claims of indigenous people to the assets they so strongly covet.

But the analogies do not end there. They continue right into present day experience. The Aboriginal reserves, having been established inalienably for indigenous purposes, have now become the pawn in the black/white advantage game—with the Aboriginal community always losing. One only has to look at the structure of the agreements to exploit mineral resources on Aboriginal settlements to appreciate the accuracy of this statement. In these negotiations the common technique of duplicity is to offer the native community the prospects of unlimited employment and economic opportunity, which are never realized in practice.[42]

The African practice of forced labour has its parallel in Australia in the so-called 'contract' system of labour, once used universally, but now limited to the State of Queensland. Despite the passage of laws to regulate the employment of Aboriginal labour for over seventy five years, few employers meet the standards laid down and few have ever been prosecuted for their lapses. Indeed, in the more remote areas of Northern Australia it is still unusual for Aborigines to be paid any kind of wage at all.

Summary execution at the hands of law enforcement officers was also a fairly common method of inter-racial discipline in Australia. Few Australians seem aware of the widespread nature of this form of violence. It will be sufficient to mention two of these cases. In 1928, a police posse rode into an Aboriginal reserve in North Western Australia and executed at least eleven Aborigines, burning their bodies as they went. Their action was in retaliation for the spearing of an isolated settler by some unknown individual. In 1936, a similar posse executed some seventeen unarmed indigenes near Alice Springs, although it was known that they had no connection with the crime involved. The police officer involved in this atrocity was later tried for his misdeeds, found not guilty, and praised for his bravery in the line of duty.

As Jack Horner has shown in Volume Two of this series, the entire pattern of white Australian relationships with Aborigines may be best interpreted in terms of brutality. For it is only here that the figures on infant mortality, arbitrary arrest and the destruction of Aboriginal society have real significance.

In Volume Two of this series, Colin Tatz made certain recommendations in the fields of education and land rights for Aboriginal people. In education, his conclusions involve an emphasis on Aboriginal culture and family relationships, the use of Aboriginal languages and assurance that the education given will be useful and meaningful to Aborigines, rather than being taught in an environmental vacuum as happens so often now. He also strongly criticises assimilation as it has been practised by Australian authorities in the past. There is, no doubt, some point in all of these ideas. However, to arrive at these conclusions, Tatz has taken Bantu education as it is applied in South Africa and somehow managed to extract principles which were never intended by South Africans. There is no similarity whatever between tribalism in South Africa, where it has been distorted and enforced against the wishes of the Africans, and demands by some aboriginal people for voluntary separation on a bi-cultural basis, in a manner which they determine themselves.

Similarly, in South Africa, the use of African languages is enforced at the primary education level. There is then an abrupt switch to English for the Arts subjects, and Afrikaans for mathematics, at secondary level. The whites are not forced to learn any African languages. The effect of Bantu education is traumatic, and so devastating to the African child that there is a 90 per cent dropout at primary school level. Those that do overcome these incredible obstacles form only a very small minority of African students. The instance given of a 90 per cent pass rate at Matriculation level by Colin Tatz ignores the only relevant fact, which is that the absolute number of African students who have passed Matriculation in South Africa has been declining since the introduction of Bantu Education. This is not to say that it is not useful for Aborigines, and whites as well, to be given the opportunity to study their languages in schools, but that the only lessons to be learnt from South Africa seem to be what should be avoided.

Although it is not stated specifically, the underlying assumption behind Tatz's recommendations seems to be that it is a good thing in itself for Aborigines and whites to be segregated at school. The whole chapter illustrates so clearly how even white intellectuals who claim to see the defects of apartheid, can be misled. Also, it illustrates a common failing that afflicts many white South Africans whom we meet in Australia. After their lifetime of positive indoctrination in racism it seems that apartheid places distinct limitations on their ability to reason, perhaps because they are so used to seeing everything in terms of the framework provided by apartheid. More useful lessons could be learnt from studying certain limited aspects of New Zealand, and recent policies adopted towards the American Indians and their land rights. But to take South Africa, whose policies have resulted in extreme mutilation of the original African way of life, seems foolhardy. The whole concept of Tatz's chapter is so divorced from the realities of apartheid, that such an intellectual exercise can only be described as dangerous.

Apartheid means the complete subjugation of Africans by whites, whereas the real interests of the Aborigines can only be articulated by the Aborigines themselves. Africans and Aborigines alike, as they realize the blindness of white people to this basic necessity, will come to see that they cannot depend on liberal philanthropy, and that the answer to their situation lies in a complete overthrow of the existing social system.

*Conclusion*

In South Africa the pattern of racism is complete—a government basing its policy on racial differences and enforcing its will on the majority of people by armed might. To assist in maintaining this situation, four thousand troops are maintained on the country's northern borders. However, South Africa's interest do not stop there. They extend into Rhodesia and Portuguese Mozambique and Angola as well. These latter communities are viewed as buffer states by the South African government, and the maintenance of white superiority in them is vital to the continuation of the South African state.

The real difference between Australia and South Africa rests in the fact that the objectives being sought by South Africa in the dominance of its native people have actually been achieved in Australia. The Aborigines have been completely dispossessed of their land and relegated to an insignificant role in Australian society. Unfortunately, the facts of this accomplishment serve to delude many Australians that there is no problem of racism in Australia. The significance of their position is not that they are unable to recognise the complete triumph of racist ideology—the supplementation and dispossession of one race by another. There can be little doubt that this has been achieved in Australia. South Africa, however, still has a long way to go. It is to be hoped that Australians will not be unduly influenced by the struggles of South Africa to achieve these ends.

## REFERENCES

1   Moodie, P. M., 'Mortality and Morbidity in Australian Aboriginal Children', *Medical Journal of Australia*, 15 January 1969, p. 182.

2   Davidson, B., *Which Way Africa?* Penguin Books. Harmondsworth (U.K. 1971), pp. 35-36.

3   *Report of the Chief Protector*, Western Australia 1906, p. 4.

4   Davidson, *Op. cit.*, pp. 56-57.

5   *Ibid.*, p. 56.

6   *Report of the Chief Protector*, Western Australia, 1899, p. 5.

7   Laurence, J., *The Seeds of Disaster*, Victor Gollancz Ltd., London, 1968, p. 294.

8   *Sunday Times*, London, 9th April, 1967, p. 24.

9   Laurence, *op cit.*, p. 305.

10   *Ibid.*, p. 293.

11   *Ibid.*, p. 293.

12   *Ibid.*, p. 292.

13   *Oxford History of South Africa*, Vol. I, Oxford, Clarendon Press, 1969, p. 68.

14   *Ibid.*, p. 71.

15 "The Role of Aboriginal Labour in North Australia" in SHARP, I. G. and TATZ, C. M., *Aborigines in the Economy,* Jacaranda Press, Brisbane, 1966.

16 STANNER, W. E. H., "Industrial Justice in the Never Never" *Australian Quarterly,* Winter, 1968.

17 BERNDT, R. M., *A Northern Territory Problem: Aboriginal Labour in a Pastoral Area,* University of Sydney, 1948.

18 ROWLEY, C. D., *The Destruction of Aboriginal Society,* A.N.U. Press, 1970-72.

19 STEVENS, FRANK, *Equal Wages for Aborigines, The Background To Discrimination in the Northern Territory of Australia,* FCAATSI, Sydney, 1968, p. 23.

20 'Facts and Figures on South Africa', *U.N. Unit on Apartheid,* New York, 1971, p. 18.

21 MOODIE, *op. cit.,* pp. 180-185.

22 GERVASI, S., "Industrialization, Foreign Capital and Forced Labour in South Africa", *U.N. Unit on Apartheid,* New York 1970, p. 36.

23 BROOKES, E. H., *"Apartheid, a Documentary Study of Modern South Africa",* Routledge and Kegan Paul, London 1969, p. 51.

24 *Financial Mail,* Johannesburg, 9th October, 1970.

25 BROOKES, E. H., *op. cit.,* p. 60.

26 See Frank Stevens, "Aboriginal Policy and the Dual Society in North Australia", *Proceedings of the Cairns Conference on Aboriginal and Island Affairs,* Cairns, Oct. 1968.

27 See, for example, "Palm Island-Hell in Paradise. A Study of Segregation and Prejudice" *Aboriginal Quarterly,* March 25, 1968.

28 HOLMES, CECIL, "The Democratic Way of Life" *The Territorian,* Vol. 2 No. 7, February, 1966. There is probably no element of chance left in Queensland where the Premier of the state has polled 100% of the votes on those missions which are run by Europeans professing the same religion as the chief executive.

29 STANNER, W. E. H., *After the Dreaming,* The Boyer Lectures 1968, A.B.C. Sydney.

30 HASSELL, K., *Relations Between the Settlers and Aborigines in South Australia 1836-1860,* Libraries Board of South Australia, Adelaide, 1966, p. 6.

31 JORDAN, W. D., *White over Black,* Penguin Books, Baltimore (U.S.) 1969, p. 23.

32 DAVIDSON, B., *op. cit.,* p. 18.

33 THOMSON, H. C., *Rhodesia,* Smith Elder, London, 1898.

34 HARTZ, L., *The Founding of New societies,* Harcourt Brace, New York 1964, p. 61.

35 *Oxford History of South Africa,* Vol. I, p. 269.

36 Perhaps this explains the otherwise unexplained numbers of half-caste children born in the vicinity of some of the missions.

37 THOMSON, H. C., *op. cit.,* p. 61.

38 REED, D., *"Insanity Fair '67",* Tandem Books Ltd., London 1967, p. 20.

39 MTSHALI, V., *Rhodesia: Background to Conflict,* Leslie Frewin, London 1967, p. 31.

40 THOMSON, H. C., *op. cit.,* p. 238.

41 *Ibid.,* p. 187.

42 See Address by Dr. H. C. Coombs in *Kunmanggur* No. 5 April, 1970, Canberra and also Frank Stevens 'Weipa: The Politics of Pauperisation', *Australian Quarterly,* Vol. 41 No. 3, September, 1969.

# 9

# AUSTRALIA'S VOTING PATTERNS AT THE UNITED NATIONS

## Jean Skuse

Australia played a significant role in the drawing up of the United Nations Charter in San Francisco in 1945. The Australian delegate, Dr. H. V. Evatt, was sensitive enough to see that world order was not just dependent on the absence of wars but that social justice was equally important. He introduced many amendments to the Charter relating to the cause of colonies and dependent peoples and championed the interests of the small powers.

Critics since then have claimed that Evatt was representing his own point of view rather than Australian foreign policy[1] but it is interesting to note that, in his address to the General Assembly of the United Nations in September 1970, Right Honorable William McMahon saw fit to refer to this early role of Australia,[2] as did Sir Laurence McIntyre in the last session of the Trusteeship Council.[3] Both reaffirmed Australia's interest in the small Powers and in self-determination for dependant Territories.

The record since those early days of the United Nations shows that, in spite of the initial interest in protecting the rights of smaller nations, Australia has allied itself with the major Powers. During the Menzies Government, the tendency was to vote with the Commonwealth. Of recent years, the Australia-United States vote is almost inseparable. In the 1970 General Assembly, there was no recorded vote where Australia and the United States were in opposition to one another. On all resolutions condemning decolonisation, colonisation, non-self governing territories, apartheid and chemical and bacteriological warfare, Australia has recorded a negative vote along with South Africa, Portugal, United Kingdon and United States (and sometimes France).[4]

Australia has never played the kind of independent or mediatory role exhibited by other 'middle power' western countries such as Canada, Belgium, France, Norway, Sweden and New Zealand. Instead, its vote has been so in line with the United States, that one wonders whether it has an independent foreign policy at all.[5] More than once I have heard delegates to the United Nations refer to Australia as a colony of the United States.

In looking at Australia's voting patterns at the United Nations in terms of racism and racial discrimination, it is difficult to determine whether it votes a certain way because of racial attitudes or because it values its alliance with the United States to such an extent it is not free to vote independently. One must draw one's own conclusion on this matter. Although the record clearly shows anti-racist lip service, this is not supported in the voting pattern for implementation of policy. There is little doubt however, as to the interpretation which must be given to this pattern by the non-white colonial and ex-colonial nations.

The United Nations resolutions on racism and racial discrimination which involve Australia can be divided into three broad categories—The Declaration on the Elimination of all Forms of Racial Discrimination, Apartheid and problems of South Africa, Namibia and Rhodesia, and the granting of independence to colonial countries with special reference to Papua-New Guinea. There are many other issues which have racial overtones, especially if we consider the term 'racism' to apply to any conviction that one's own systems or beliefs or way of life is superior to any other, and that domination of power must remain the province of 'superior' nations. We could then include a whole spectrum of issues before the United Nations, such as recognition of mainland China, satellite broadcasting, exploitation of the sea-bed, the development decisions on trade and aid, chemical and biological warfare, disarmament and environment. There are many who would claim with some justification, that the present world system is built on white racism. Taking into account the history of white colonial expansion, the exploitation of the black man and the built-in world trade structures which work to the advantage of the white man, this point of view is understandable. However, for the purposes of this essay, we will confine ourselves to the three areas mentioned.

*The Declaration on the Elimination of all Forms of Racial Discrimination*

The United Nations Declaration on the Elimination of all Forms of Racial Discrimination was adopted by the General Assembly on 20th November, 1963.[6] This Declaration affirms the necessity of speedily eliminating racial discrimination throughout the world in all its forms and manifestations. It provides, as well, that particular efforts shall be made to prevent discrimination based on race, colour or ethnic origin.

The Declaration was followed by the International Convention on the elimination of All Forms of Racial Discrimination in 1965.[7] The Convention defines racial discrimination as 'any distinction, exclusion, restriction or preference based on race, colour, descent or national or ethnic origin which has the purpose or effect of nullifying or impairing the recognition, enjoyment or exercise on an equal footing, of human rights or fundamental freedoms in the political, economic, social, cultural or any other field of public life'. States which are parties to the Convention condemn racial discrimination and undertake to pursue a policy to eliminate it. They also agree to take specific measures to ensure the adequate development and protection of certain racial groups, guaranteeing them the full and equal enjoyment of human rights and fundamental freedoms. A unique feature of the Convention is that it is the first United Nations human rights instrument to provide machinery for its implementation. A Committee has been appointed to receive reports which all Parties must submit regularly on measures that they have taken to carry out their commitments under it; to make general recommendations to the General Assembly; to settle disputes and to receive communications from individuals or groups regarding its violation.

The Convention was opened for signature on 7th March, 1966. 44 States' parties have ratified or acceded to the Convention (October, 1970). 31st December 1971 has been set as a target date for ratification by all eligible states. Australia has not yet ratified the Convention. It did, however, support a resolution in General Assembly condemning racial discrimination and inviting all countries to become parties to the Convention in 1971.[8]

*South Africa and Apartheid*

While the Government of South Africa maintains that its racial policies are outside the jurisdiction of the United Nations, the General Assembly and the Security Council regard the policy of *apartheid* as constituting a violation of the Charter and therefore as coming within their sphere of competence. South Africa's racial policies have been under discussion in the United Nations since 1946. In 1962, the General Assembly went further than the usual condemnations by requesting Member States to take the following action:—

(1) Break off diplomatic relations.
(2) Close their ports to all vessels flying the South African flag.
(3) Prohibit their ships from entering South African ports.
(4) Boycott all South African goods and refrain from exporting goods, including all arms, to South Africa.
(5) Refuse land and passage facilities to all aircraft belonging to the Government of South Africa or companies registered under the South African laws.[9]

The Assembly has also established a special committee to keep South Africa's racial policies under review.

Since this Resolution, the United Nations has followed three main lines of activity in dealing with *apartheid*, urging an arms embargo, economic sanctions and related measures, moral and political and material assistance to the oppressed people of South Africa and dissemination of information to secure full understanding and support for the efforts directed towards the elimination of *apartheid* to avert the grave threat to international peace and security.[10]

Looking at the 1970 General Assembly, one resolution on *apartheid* emphasised the failure of some States to implement previous general Assembly and Security Council resolutions urging States to refrain from selling arms or assisting the manufacture of arms in South Africa.[11] 98 countries voted in favour of the resolution; 2 against (Portugal, South Africa), 9 abstentions (Australia abstained). Australia could support a general resolution condemning *apartheid*[12] but abstained from voting on a subsequent resolution calling for the cooperation of governments in disseminating information on its evils and dangers and encouraging anti-apartheid movements.[13] Australia joined France, Portugal, South Africa, United Kingdom and the United States, the only countries voting against a resolution calling for the termination of diplomatic relations, economic cooperation, tariff and trade preferences and shipping and air services.[14] 91 countries favoured this resolution, but when the main trading partners do not agree to it, it becomes completely ineffective. Australia voted against a resolution calling for economic sanctions against the 'illegal racist minority regime in Southern Rhodesia'[15] and abstained from voting on a similar resolution concerning Namibia.[16]

These examples are typical of the voting patterns of Australia on *apartheid* issues. Couched in general terms, it votes in favour of resolutions, but when these require supportive action, the response is to abstain or to record a negative vote. The usual explanation of the vote is that Australia regards *apartheid* and the policies of the Smith government as domestic issues, quoting clause 2/7 of the U.N. Charter which denounces interference by outsiders in the internal affairs of another State.

In keeping with its desire to support struggles against *apartheid*, the United Nations established a Trust Fund for South Africa in 1965, to provide legal aid to those on trial for opposition to *apartheid* and relief for refugees from South Africa. A Fund for an Education and Training Programme has also been set up. Fifty countries, including the United Kingdom and the United States, have contributed. Australia, whilst supporting an appeal to Governments to assist the oppressed people of South Africa,[17] has not yet made a donation.

The Chairman of the Special Committee on the policies of *apartheid*, Abdulrahim Abby Farah, made the following observation on the *apartheid* issue at the United Nations:—

> 'Too many resolutions and too little action are all that the U.N. can show after having dealt with the problem for twenty-five years. We have had outright condemnations of those racist policies by those major powers which have assumed positions of responsibility for world leadership and which have the means to give a lead in the problem. But their condemnations have not been matched by either performance or precept. Not only has the U.N. failed to halt the progressive erosion of the inalienable rights of the non-white population of the region by white minority regimes, but we have allowed ourselves to become passive witnesses to the development of a situation which now constitutes a real threat to international peace and security.'[18]

Whilst Australia is not a major power, it has allied itself with those who are, turning majority resolutions into no account.

### The Declaration on the Granting of Independence to Colonial Countries and Peoples

On December 14th, 1960, the General Assembly adopted a 'Declaration on the Granting of Independence to Colonial Countries and Peoples'. The resolution was adopted by 89 votes for, none against, with 9 abstentions. (Australia, Belgium, Dominion Republic, France, Portugal, South Africa, Spain, United Kingdom and United States). The paragraphs causing the most difficulty for Australia in the light of its policy in New Guinea were:—

> para. 3. Inadequacy of political, economic, social or educational preparedness should never serve as a pretext for delaying independence.
> para. 5. Immediate steps shall be taken in trust, and non self-Governing territories or all other territories which have not yet attained independence to tranfer all powers to the peoples of those territories without any conditions or reservations, in accordance with their freely expressed will or desire and without any distinction as to race, creed or colour, in order to enable them to enjoy complete independence.[19]

The successful struggles for independence and the de-colonising of over one billion people has been one of the most outstanding achievements of the United Nations. From its inception, it has promoted the self-government and improvement in living standards of dependent peoples. The Trusteeship Council has had the responsibility for territories not yet self-governing and there remain only two under its supervision—New Guinea and the Trust Territory of the Pacific Islands.

Members of the Trusteeship Council have scrutinised Australia's policy in New Guinea and, in its 1970 session, there was some criticism. The questions raised concerned the differences in salary scales for indigenous people and expatriates, the administration of the land tenure system, the reason why only half the number of voters took part in local government elections in 1969, as compared with 1968; and the fact that the amount of loans made by the Development Bank to non-indigenous people was over five times that of loans to indigenous persons. The Special Representative of the Administering Authority, Mr. L. W. Johnson, claimed that there was no discrimination by race in granting credit from the Development Bank and stated there was a single salary scale for indigenous and expatriates except for the public services, which would be remedied soon. He did not have figures available when asked for a comparison of Australian assistance to the territory with the income foreign companies earned.[20]

Nine petitions concerning New Guinea were received by the Trusteeship Council,[21] eight of them concerned with the Bougainville copper scheme, especially with the use of tear gas against men and women to prevent them from rightfully possessing their own land.[22] The petitions were referred to the President of the Trusteeship Council, Sir Laurence McIntyre (Australia) to ascertain which of them raised issues regarding racial discrimination and should therefore be forwarded to the Committee on the Elimination of Racial Discrimination. He announced that there were no such petitions and that consequently no action had to be taken.

A Resolution on Papua and New Guinea before the General Assembly 'calls upon the administering Power to prescribe, in consultation with freely elected representatives of the people, a specific time-table for the free exercise by the people of their right to self-determination and independence and to report to the Trusteeship Council on action taken in that regard', and 'requests the administering Power to intensify and accelerate the education and technical training of the indigenous peoples of the Territories and the localisation of the Public Service'. (98 voted in favour of the resolution; Australia, France, Portugal, United Kingdom and United States abstained).

Some aspects of Australia's policies in New Guinea were criticised in a special report of the United Nations on foreign economic interests.[23] Particular mention was made of the control of major sectors of the economy by Australian interests, excessive profits taken out of the territory, low wages to indigenous workers, special tax privileges to foreign companies and non-indigenous agricultural holdings of more than a million acres, almost two thirds of which are unused.

*Australian Aborigines*

The emphasis on foreign policy by the United Nations means there has been little reference to the Australian Aborigine. Of interest however, is a Special Study of Racial Discrimination in the Political, Economic, Social and Cultural Spheres commissioned by the General Assembly in 1965, and completed in 1970. It is the first comprehensive study on racial discrimination on a world-wide scale prepared by the United Nations. Chapter IX deals with measures taken in connection with the protection of indigenous people.[24] It relies for its information about Australia on a report from the

Government. The Australian report declares that 'in accordance with their declared policies of promoting the advancement of Aborigines to complete social, economic and political equality, the Federal and State Governments are keeping under continuous review all laws and regulations that authorise any differences in treatment between aborigines and other Australians.'[25]

The International Labor Organisation, an agency of the United Nations has sought to safeguard employment rights of indigenous people, but Australia has not yet signed the relevant Conventions.

This chapter has focused on Australia's position on selected issues before the United Nations, leaving the reader to reach his own conclusion as to whether this is a racist stand or not. It is difficult to estimate what importance Australia places on its part in this international organization. Sometimes it seems that regional treaties and alliances with powerful allies are given higher priority. There is very little coverage in Australian press of its role in the United Nations. There is no doubt however, that the image created by voting patterns at the United Nations is important and that the nature of the vote is a declaration of policy.

## REFERENCES

1 e.g. Menzies and McEwan; see WATT, ALAN, *The Evolution of Australian Foreign Policy* 1938-1965, Cambridge University Press, 1967, pp. 72, 97.

2 General Assembly A/P V 1846, 23rd September, 1970.

3 TR/1973, 26th May, 1970.

4 Resolutions of the General Assembly GA/4355, 17th December, 1970.

5 See GEBBER, H. G. *The Australian-American Alliance*, Penguin Books Australia Ltd., 1968.

6 Resolution 1904 (XVIII).

7 Resolution 2106 A (XX).

8 Resolution 2647 (XXV).

9 Resolution 1761 (XVII).

10 'Objective Justice' U.N. Office of Public Information, Vol. 2 No. 1, January 1970, p. 12.

11 Resolution 2624 (XXV).

12 Resolution 2671 (XXV)B.

13 Resolution 2671 (XXV)C.

14 Resolution 2671 (XXV)F.

15 Resolution 2652 (XXV).

16 Resolution 2678 (XXV).

17 Resolution 2671 (XXV)B.

18 Press Release U.N.O.P.I. GA/AP178, 26th February, 1970.

19 Declaration of the Granting of Independence to Colonial Countries and Peoples, U.N. General Assembly, 1960.

20 TR/1976-1980, May-June 1970.

21 T/1702, add. 1.

22 TR/1980, 2nd June, 1970.

23 'Foreign Ecomonic Interests and Decolonization' United Nations, New York 1969.

24 E/C.N.4/Sub.2/307/ add 2, 23rd July, 1970.

25 *Ibid.*, p. 38.

# 10

# THE CAMPAIGN AGAINST RACIALISM IN SPORT

## R. J. Buchhorn

It is ironical that an event as mundane as a routine tour by a South African Rugby Union team should provide the point at which the issue of racism should become most widely raised and debated in Australia in 1971. Sport plays a big part in the life of both nations, and we have been exchanging teams for decades, generally ignoring any attempts to raise the question of racial discrimination.

With the benefit of hind-sight, it is perhaps remarkable that it didn't happen sooner. Again, for decades there has been a core of people in Australia aware of the evil of *apartheid* and its significance for mankind: and sport is obviously an area in which the issue takes on concrete and practical dimensions within the capacity and interest of the 'man in the street', whether in Australia or South Africa.

Not only will the controversy influence relations between the two countries, but also promises to influence the direction of events and attitudes in each. In Australia, demonstrations have already raised the associated issues of authoritarianism, and the maintenance of 'law-and-order' in the face of nonconformity and dissent.[1] To understand how this has come about, it is necessary to know something of the background of *apartheid* in sport, the campaign to exclude South Africa from international competition, and Australia's eventual involvement.

### Sport in South Africa

Of books providing a glimpse of life in South Africa, the one most widely read in Australia would be Alan Paton's *Cry the Beloved Country*. The novel concludes on a high note of hope, with a sturdy flame of new understanding, co-operation and brotherhood dispelling the darkness. Most Australians who have read it are somewhat taken aback when told that this flame has long been extinguished.

The book was first published in 1948. During World War II, South Africa's declaration of war on Germany had divided white opinion, and the resentment of the pro-nazi Afrikaners ran high. Non-whites had had opportunities to strengthen their political organisations, and have their horizons broadened by news from other countries. The presence of a considerable Indian community (about 2.5 per cent of the population) ensured that India's progress towards independence did not go unnoticed. Colonialism and European supremacy seemed to be coming to an end. The portents were full of hope for the non-whites, but struck fear in the hearts of the whites. The stark alternatives—integration and equality or *apartheid* and *baasskap* (mastership)—presented themselves to the white South African voters in the election of 1948; and the Nationalist Party came to power. The die was cast. South Africa turned to tread a new path.

These events had their impact in the field of sport. In South Africa, sport was the preserve of the whites, just as it had initially been for the rich in many western countries.[2] Of course the non-whites—and the poor—did play, their efforts being regarded with an amused tolerance. But the whites were in control. The national championships and records were their preserve. They alone represented their country abroad. Their organisations were the ones internationally recognised. Apart from some individual sports like weight-lifting and table-tennis, they had little or no contact with non-white South African sportsmen. Generally they heard of these only after they had gone abroad and achieved success and recognition—e.g., Ron Eland, a weightlifter who represented England at the 1948 Olympics; Papwa Sewgolum, the golfer; Basil D'Oliveira, the cricketer.

But the war had brought to non-white sportsmen the knowledge of a world beyond South Africa's borders, where sportsmen of all races competed as equals; these green fields beckoned to them. There began, with weight-lifting in 1946, a series of approaches to the international controlling bodies of various sports, seeking recognition, and access to international competition. They were generally able to point out that the all-white national body which enjoyed affiliation debarred them from membership either in practice, or by an explicit clause in their constitution.

The subsequent pattern of events was repeated again and again—initial rebuffs; renewed appeal; suggestions of affiliation with the existing all-white controlling bodies; these in turn either rejecting such suggestions, or making an offer of a most subservient status; increased participation in international meetings by non-white representatives from de-colonised nations; panic deletion of 'whites only' clauses from constitutions of recognised bodies, and renewed attempts to get at least token affiliation of some non-white bodies in South Africa; greater unity in non-white national federations, and adoption of a more militantly non-racial approach, with occasional success in getting white members; acceptance of the non-racial body and expulsion of the all-white body; and sometimes the reversal of this decision, to start the whole process again.

It was not until 1956 that the first victory was won. The International Table Tennis Federation expelled the all-white S.A.T.T. Union from membership, and recognised the non-racial S.A.T.T. Board as the sole controlling body in South Africa. A similar victory was won for Soccer in 1961; the decision was reversed in 1963, and made again in 1964. Weight-lifting had to wait until 1969.

Not only did the Table Tennis victory encourage the efforts of other non-racial sporting bodies, but it provoked a reaction from the Government which made them even more determined.

Until 1956, the Government had said virtually nothing about *apartheid* in sport. Various laws had been in effect, but were not specifically directed against non-racial sport. For example, the Group Areas Act of 1950 provided for the restriction of ownership and *occupation* of land to a specified population group.[3] Occupation was interpreted by the courts as meaning mere physical presence.[4] The Reservation of Separate Amenities Act of 1953 permitted the reservation of public premises or vehicles for the exclusive use of any race.[5] Such measures generally required the granting of a permit for any multi-racial sporting event, or for spectators of more than one race to attend any sporting function. Under this sort of pressure, bodies which had conducted multi-racial events found it easier to segregate into separate bodies. Weight-lifting was one of the first affected.[6]

But the victory of the S.A.T.T. Board provoked angry reactions from government members of parliament. The Minister for the Interior made a statement to the newspaper *Die Burger* on 25th June, 1956, in which he denied Government interference in non-white sport. But he made it clear that sporting bodies must accord with the policies of separate development. They must organise and keep their activities separate. There would be no mixed sport within the Union, and the mixing of races in teams should be avoided. The Government would prefer to see non-white bodies seek international recognition through the aegis of white associations already enjoying recognition. He warned that passports would be withheld from non-whites guilty of 'such subversive intentions' as seeking to have non-racial bodies recognised internationally.[7]

The dismay and consternation manifested by this reaction caught the attention of the opponents of *apartheid*. A chink had appeared in the armour. Their support and encouragement were welcomed by the still comparatively disorganised non-white sporting bodies. In January 1959, the South African Sports Association (SASA), representing some 70,000 sportsmen, held its first meeting. Alan Paton was Patron; Dennis Brutus was Secretary; John Harris a vice-president. It began co-ordinating the efforts of non-white sports bodies to achieve the goal already reached by the Table Tennis Board.

Officials of the 'subversive' non-racial federations and of SASA came increasingly under the eyes of the Special Branch. In the State of Emergency following the Sharpeville massacre in March 1960, a number of their homes were raided and searched, and records confiscated. Dennis Brutus was refused a passport in 1960, and placed under a five-year banning order in October 1961.

Nevertheless, the work went on. SASA made its first representations to the International Olympic Committee (IOC), and were referred back to the controlling body in South Africa, the South African Olympic and National Games Association (SAONGA). This body renewed its offer of subservient status for the non-racial bodies, and inadequate assurances for the inclusion of non-whites in the Olympics. In July 1962, SASA announced a plan to establish a South African Non-Racial Olympic Committee (SANROC), to challenge the membership of SAONGA in the IOC. It was duly formed in October of the same year, and set its sights for the IOC meeting in Baden-Baden in October 1963. SANROC Chairman John Harris had his passport withdrawn as he was about to leave for the meeting: President Dennis Brutus was in prison, after being shot by the police.

The Baden-Baden meeting was a turning point. It laid down conditions under which South Africa could compete in the 1964 Tokyo Olympics. They were:—

(1) firm declaration barring racial discrimination;
(2) SAONGA to be in a position to resist any political pressure;
(3) a change of Government policy regarding racial discrimination in sport within South Africa.

From the outset it was obvious that these conditions would not be met.

In spite of further pleas, South Africa's invitation to the Tokyo Olympics was withdrawn in January 1964. The debate was significant for two reasons.

Firstly, SAONGA did offer to make some concessions. Non-whites of merit would be chosen for the Olympics, but on the basis of separate trials, rather than direct competition with whites. If athletes of different races recorded identical times, tests of 'physiological and psychological capacity' would be conducted to determine selection. It is not clear how members of the boxing team would have been chosen. Even more concessions concerning team unity, common uniforms, travel and accommodation, and selection procedures were to be presented to the IOC in Teheran in 1967. But it was to be a matter of too little too late.

Secondly, the scratch SANROC representative at Baden-Baden, Dr. Robin Farquharson, was assisted by a representative of the British Anti-Apartheid Movement. They were able to show how the selection system now being proposed by SAONGA had functioned when applied to the selection of a team of athletes for a contest in Lourenco Marques, Mozambique, in 1962. There were to be two entrants for each event. In the separate trials, two African athletes recorded times which should have won them selection; but the executive committee of the white S.A.A.A. Union chose whites whom they had beaten. This was their decision, not one imposed by the Government.

They were also able to give details of the ruling given by the full Bench of the Natal Supreme Court in October 1962 on an appeal by the State after it had failed in a prosecution against two whites, five coloureds and two Indians for having played football together. As the body controlling the ground had not laid down conditions restricting its use to one racial group, and as the players did not use dressing-room facilities etc. of other racial groups, the appeal failed. This proved that there was no law against mixed sport in South Africa. It was, of course, opposed to Government policy. But SAONGA could no longer argue that they were merely obeying the laws of their country.

*Pressure from Without*

The presence of the British Anti-Apartheid Movement's representative at Baden-Baden marked a new development. This was the beginning of an active campaign in other countries against the continuation of sporting contacts with white South Africa.

Broadly speaking this activity progressed from the non-white nations, enjoying their new independent status and voice at meetings of international bodies controlling sport, to the allies they won there from among the socialist countries of Europe, thence to America where black power was a significant factor, and finally to New Zealand, England and Australia. It is worth remarking that this order is roughly the inverse both to the extent of sporting links with South Africa, and to the degree of support given to the all-white sporting bodies of South Africa in their struggle to maintain membership of the international bodies.

The initital reaction of the South African Government was to tighten its belt, and also the reins on its own sporting bodies. Provisions of the Group Areas Act were more strictly enforced, and extended by Proclamation R26 of 12th February, 1965, which made it even more difficult for people to be spectators at sporting fixtures of another race. For every 7 permits granted to allow this, 3 were refused.[8] In 1966, the Indian golfer Papwa Sewgolum found it harder to get permits to compete in Open tournaments. For the first time, a permit was refused to allow African Ministers to join in an annual golf-day for the Clergy. A campaign begun in New Zealand in 1960 to ensure that Maoris would not be excluded from the All-Blacks Rugby Union teams to tour South Africa went into top gear during the Springbok tour of that country in 1965. Private assurances were being given that Maoris would be acceptable. But in a speech at Loskop Dam (4th September, 1965) Prime Minister Verwoerd stated:—

> 'When we are guests of another country we have to behave according to their traditions . . . we expect that when other countries visit us, they will respect ours . . . Everybody knows what these are.'[9]

A leading article in *Die Transvaler* three days later commented:—

> '. . . it must be ascribed to one particular factor that the white race has hitherto maintained itself in the southern part of Africa. That is that there has been no miscegenation. The absence of miscegenation was because there was no social mixing between white and non-white. Social mixing leads inexorably to miscegenation . . . It is today the social aim of the communists and supporters of radical liberalism. In South Africa the races do not mix on the sports field. If they mix on the sports field then the road to other forms of social mixing is wide open . . . . With an eye to upholding the white race and its civilization, not one single compromise can be entered into— not even when it comes to a visiting rugby team.'[10]

The All-Black's tour of South Africa for 1967 was cancelled.

This probably had greater impact than exclusion from the 1964 Olympics. It marked the first rejection by one of South Africa's traditional sporting opponents, and in a sport of special significance. Rugby Union is the sport most closely identified with the nationalist identity and aspirations which also find expression in *apartheid*. New Zealand were their traditional rivals for world supremacy.

Mr. Vorster, the new Prime Minister, remained intransigent. He assured Parliament (11th April, 1967) that:—

> '. . . no mixed sports between whites and non-whites will be practised locally . . . If any person, either locally or abroad, adopts the attitude that he will enter into relations with us only if we are prepared to jettison the separate practising of sport prevailing among our own people in South Africa, then I want to make it clear that . . . I am not prepared to pay that price. On that score I want no misunderstanding whatsoever . . . on this principle we are not prepared to compromise, we are not prepared to negotiate and we are not prepared to make any concessions . . . .'[11]

After South Africa's exclusion from the 1968 Mexico Olympics, the movement spread and gathered momentum. In September 1968, the South African Government had refused to accept an M.C.C. team which included Basil D'Oliveira. The tour was cancelled. The campaign in Britain gathered momentum, and the Springbok Rugby Union team which went there in October 1969 met with a sustained series of massive demonstrations which disrupted virtually every match, and set the stage for the widthdrawal of the M.C.C. invitation to the South African cricketers for 1970.

During 1969-70, eleven white South African bodies were either barred from world championships, suspended or expelled from international controlling bodies.

One of the few bright spots for South Africa was the 1970 visit by the All-Blacks. The tour was undertaken in the face of strong protest within New Zealand, and only possible because of the acceptance of three Maoris and a Samoan in the team—as 'honorary whites'. This concession was as traumatic as it was significant. It triggered a split in the Nationalist Party, and precipitated a general election! It does not indicate a change of heart, but rather South Africa's desperation for acceptance in international sport.

*The Campaign in Australia*

In the struggle to maintain official recognition of their all-white sporting bodies on the international level, South Africa has generally found Australia to be one of her staunchest allies. For example, at the IOC meeting in Grenoble, January 1968, it was Australian Hugh Weir who drafted and submitted the resolution which almost got South Africa into the 1968 Mexico Olympics.[12] To compensate for the cancelled M.C.C. tour of South Africa (1968-9), the Australian Cricket Board of Control agreed to send an Australian team for virtually a full tour in January 1970. When the white South African Pentathlon team was excluded from the world championships in Budapest in September 1969, only the Australian team withdrew in protest.[13]

Prior to 1969, there had been occasional, but relatively small, demonstrations against visiting South African sporting teams. The question of cutting sporting ties with South Africa was scarcely even suggested. Two events were to bring a rapid change.

Firstly, in April 1969, Dennis Brutus visited Australia at the invitation of the South Africa Defence and Aid Fund. He was able to open the eyes of some of the people active in their opposition to *apartheid* to the effectiveness of protests against racism in sport. Among these was John Myrtle, a young school teacher, who became convenor of the Campaign Against Racialism In Sport (CARIS). He unearthed two Islanders boarding at G.P.S. Schools who had seen less capable players chosen or sent for trials for the school-boy Rugby Union teams to tour South Africa from August 1969. With another school teacher, Peter McGregor, he staged a lonely two-man demonstration for the team's departure. Thereafter no visiting South African sporting team had a smooth passage: lady bowlers, women's basketball, tennis players, surfers, all encountered demonstrations of increasing dimensions. Peter McGregor became convenor of the Anti-Apartheid Movement, committed to militant non-violent action to disrupt tours by South African teams: CARIS continued the task of education, publicity, petition and representation to sporting bodies maintaining links with South Africa.

Also in the winter of 1969, the Australian Wallaby Rugby Union team toured South Africa. It included Anthony Abrahams, a young Sydney Law graduate who had battled with what, in the Australian context at that time, was a difficult decision—to withdraw from the team as a protest against *apartheid*—or to go, so that he might later be able to speak with greater authority. He went, with eyes open, and introductions to a number of opponents of *apartheid*—Alan Paton, Helen Suzman and others. His movements caught the attention of the Special Branch, and warnings to desist came through the team manager.

This, together with his prior knowledge of South Africa, involved him in the role of a catalyst in relation to his team-mates, enabling them to see *apartheid* in a light very different to the one being presented to them by their hosts. Abrahams went on to Europe after the tour, and in letters to Australian newspapers, called for an end to sporting relations with South Africa. Some time later, four of his team-mates gave an interview on their experiences, showing the political implications of the tour, recommending that there be no more as long as teams in South Africa were selected on a racial basis. They declared that they would not play sport against South Africa under the present arrangements. It received wide publicity, and was published at length in *The Australian* (21st May, 1970). Two Wallabies who had toured South Africa in 1963 later joined their campaign, as did Bryan Palmer, an elder statesman of Australian Rugby Union.

But a survey in March 1971 showed that the percentage of Australians opposed to a visit by a South African Cricket Team had dropped from 16 per cent to 9 per cent in one year. *The Australian* (3rd April, 1971) quoted the comments of some of the Wallabies mentioned above: 'disappointing; very sad; depressing'. But the same paper also carried a news item which was to brings things to life. The South African Government had rejected a request from the country's Cricket Association for two non-white players to tour Australia with the Springbok team in late 1971. That such a request had even been made was itself a significant change. The decision sparked off new controversy in South Africa. It also clarified the issue for many Australians, and galvanised waverers into action.

Two State Labour Governments announced they would boycott the tour. The Prime Minister told the South African Government of his disappointment and regret at the decision, but said the tour could go on. The Australian Council of Trade Unions threatened a boycott on touring teams. The Australian Council of Churches called on Christians to boycott all tours, and take part in peaceful protests. Anthony Abrahams arrived back from Europe to campaign throughout Australia, and anti-tour committees sprang up in all capital cities. South Africa and racism had arrived as one of the big issues of the year.

*Reflections*

One of the perplexing questions confronting mankind in this century is that of effective action: how can we influence society, challenge people to face up to the consequences of their action, or inaction and stir them to take responsibility. Inertia, apathy, nonchalance seem to prevail.

For decades South Africa had been in the news: Treason Trials, the Sharpeville massacre, the break with the Commonwealth, the struggle over South West Africa, support given to Rhodesia, and so on. But the Australian public generally remained unmoved, while the Liberal-Country Party Government actively courted the South African Nationalists. Sir Robert Menzies was Dr. Verwoerd's strongest supporter at Commonwealth Conferences in the fifties; Qantas exchanged rights to passenger flights with South African Airways, in preference to East Africa Airways; Australia has rarely voted against South Africa on United Nations resolutions condemning *apartheid*, and, in fact, has supported South Africa;[14] in June 1969, Mr. J. F. Haak, Minister for Economic Affairs, became the first Nationalist Party Minister to be welcomed on an official visit to Australia; Trade delegations have gone to South Africa, so successfully that our exports trebled in three years, 1968-71;[15] Australia has refrained from contributing to the United Nations Trust Fund for South Africa, used to assist the victims of *apartheid*.[16]

And yet all the while there were anti-*apartheid* groups at work, campaigning in various ways for the reversal of this trend. Their activities caused scarcely a ripple, and had no impact on the Government. There was little awareness of our complicity in the evils of *apartheid*, and little recognition of any obligation to try to influence the course of events in that country.

This paralleled the situation in South Africa itself. Since coming to power, the South African Nationalists have successfully stifled or tamed any opposition to its policies. There has been no lack of opposition. Yet it had no notable success in challenging the course of apartheid, or winning concessions. South Africa's acceptance—as honorary whites—of Maoris in the All Blacks' Team of 1970 divided the Government, was one of the few accommodating steps taken in 22 years of Nationalist rule, and this was in response to campaigns against racialism in sport.

In so far as CARIS has confronted Australians with the question of racism and our relationship with South Africa, it has succeeded. The first reason for this is that the nature of *apartheid* and its intrusion into sport makes it vulnerable at that point.

The myth that *apartheid* means 'separate and equal development' has been sufficiently exploded by the actions of the South African Nationalist Government, and by their own statements:—

> 'We want to keep South Africa White . . . Keeping it White can mean only one thing, namely, White domination, not "leadership", not "guidance", but "control"—"supremacy".' (Dr. Verwoerd as Prime Minister in the House of Assembly, 25th January, 1963.)[17]

In the 1970 election campaign, a Government Minister was reported as having said that white superiority in South Africa would be maintained at all costs, even if it meant civil war:[18] and that in white South Africa only the white man was *baas*, and that the Nationalist Party would maintain this position for ever, with force if necessary.[19]

This explains the stipulation of the Nursing Act of 1957 forbidding the employment of non-whites in posts where they could supervise or control white staff.[20] Similarly non-white policemen are under a standing instruction not to give orders to white policemen even if of lower rank, nor to arrest a white member of the public even if such a person commits an offence in their presence.[21] It led to the ludicrous situation where, having won the Natal Open in 1963, Indian golfer Papwa Sewgolum stood outside the clubhouse in the rain, while the trophy was handed to him through a window, whilst inside his fellow Indians worked as drink stewards.[22] This relationship is a jealously guarded privilege. In 1970, the Government re-affirmed its refusal to allow Indians to employ Africans as domestic servants or nurse-maids.[23]

It is only within this context of *baasskap* that contact between races is to take place. Any other contact would provide an opportunity for the recognition of a common humanity, and thereby jeopardise the concept of racial superiority which provides the underpinning for the policy of *apartheid*.

This explains the efforts to ensure that white school teachers do not teach non-white children. The pupil-teacher relationship is a very human one. Similarly African and Indian children were excluded from a Beethoven music contest, on the grounds that 'different races perform best in their own idiom'.[24] It explains why a Government spokesman should say that contact between white student leaders from Stellenbosch University with their counterparts from the University College of the Western Cape (for coloureds) should be allowed only if it has the 'result of bringing greater separation of the races.[25] It explains, finally, *apartheid* in sport.

Against this background one can understand white South Africa's determination to maintain racial segregation in sport. The *Die Transvaler* leading article quoted earlier shows the dangers envisaged in the inclusion of Maoris in the All-Blacks. Its sentiments were echoed a few days later by a senior Afrikaner Nationalist:—

> 'To-day it is rugby, tomorrow it would be cricket and the next day swimming. Where will it all end? It would be the first step towards social integration. It would be playing right into the hands of our enemies.'[26]

They were taken up again by a recent Government speaker in the House of Assembly. Mr. D. J. L. Mel said that no concession to non-racial sport would satisfy South Africa's enemies; they would make more demands 'until they have the full price, which is the head of South Africa on a platter.'[27] On this point, the South African Nationalists provide the opponents of *apartheid* with ample justification for their campaign against racialism in sport!

The second factor in the success of CARIS has been that in both Australia and white South Africa, sport looms large in the lives of a considerable proportion of the population. Both countries enjoy excellent climatic conditions, as well as a high standard of living, which ensures adequate facilities, abundant leisure time, and scope for professional coaching and playing.

In addition, both groups are, geographically, outposts of western civilisation, and success in international sport provides a boost for national morale. This is particularly true for South Africa. Dr. Danie Craven, President of the South African Rugby Board bears eloquent witness:—

> 'Being a young country we have to prove ourselves, and we try to do that. It's a big world and we are a small country. If you are weak then nobody takes any notice of you. You have to be strong.'[28]

And more recently:—

> 'Isolation will steel us. It will harden us, make us vicious. If you don't want to play with us, we will say "goodbye". We will not crack. We will not change our way of life.
> 'The scenery from Johannesburg to Capetown is as good as any in the world. We have beautiful girls, plenty of drinks, and our sportsmen can enjoy themselves as much in their own country as anywhere else—perhaps these days more so.
> 'We will be the greatest sportsmen in the world but if the world doesn't want to see us then that is up to the world. But I think finally the world will react like a child hankering for an unattainable toy.'[29]

However, the tone of Dr. Craven's remarks indicate that the stronger hankering might be in the opposite direction!

So sport has taken the front line for protest. The complexities of trade, defence and diplomacy between Australia and South Africa place them beyond the understanding and reach of most people. But sport is a field of endeavour in which anyone can be an expert, a field in which the issue of racial discrimination is presented in terms that are within the grasp of the multitude. It is consequently an area in which they can be challenged; an area open to effective means of protest for virtually anyone, and made more attractive by the fact that unlike an economic boycott it does not penalise the non-white majority. It has provided one answer to the question posed at the beginning of these reflections.

There have been inhibiting factors. Australia's tardiness in taking up the issue of sport with South Africa was in keeping with, and reinforced, the image given by our record on racial issues like the White Australia Policy and treatment of aboriginals. We are generally reluctant to face up to controversial questions, and harsh towards those who try to raise them. This conformism and authoritarianism has since been evidenced in reactions to protests against the Springbok Rugby Union tour: extreme Police action against demonstrators and wide public support for same; the cries of law and order; the Government's support for the tour by assurances and the offer of RAAF aircraft; and, as a fitting climax, the Queensland Government's declaration of a State of Emergency to cover the duration of the tour!

That protests have taken place in spite of these factors has made them even more effective as far as South Africa is concerned. Professor Robert Anderson, Principal of Ormond College at Melbourne University, was in South Africa at the time, and described the reaction:—

'It came as a tremendous shock that this little outpost was reacting against *apartheid* . . . In fact, the Australian demonstrations have had a greater impact than those in Britain or any other country, because the South Africans see us as an all-white country with some aspects of their *apartheid* policy.'[30]

Certainly 1971 will be seen as the year in which Australia became aware of *apartheid* in South Africa, and started to question our complicity in the racialism of that country. Hopefully, it will also be a milestone in our confronting racialism in all facets of Australian life.[31]

REFERENCES

1 This association is one of the central themes of '*The Authoritarian Personality*', ADORNO & others, John Wiley & Sons, N.Y., 1964.

2 The Marylebone Cricket Club is a classic example.

3 BRIAN BUNTING, '*The Rise of the South African Reich*', Penguin African Library, 1964, p. 145.

4 *A Survey of Race Relations in South Africa*, 1956-57, published by the South African Institute of Race Relations, p. 27.
These Surveys are produced annually by the Institute, (P.O. Box 97, Johannesburg) and provide an invaluable source of documentation. Hereafter they will be referred to simply as SAIRR Survey, 19. . .

5 BUNTING, *op. cit.*, p. 149.

6 PETER HAIN, '*Don't Play With Apartheid*', George Allen & Unwin, London, 1971, p. 50-1.

7 S. ABDUL MINTY, '*International Boycott of Apartheid Sport*', U.N. Unit on Apartheid Notes and Documents, No. 16/71 (71-06578) p. 6.
CHRIS DE BROGLIO, '*South Africa: Racism in Sport*', International Defence and Aid Fund Pamphlet, London, 1970, p. 6.

8 SAIRR Survey 1965, p. 307.

9 SAIRR Survey 1965, pp. 311-2.

10 Quoted by HAIN, *op. cit.*, pp. 108-9.

11 Quoted by DE BROGLIO, *op. cit.*, p. 10.

12 'You are Condoning Apartheid', an interview with Dennis Brutus in *Outlook*, (Sydney) April 1969. An article by Richard Thompson in the June 1967 issue of the same periodical describes how the Australian representative openly championed the cause of white South Africa at the May 1967 meeting of the IOC in Teheran.

13 Barry McDonald was in South Africa as a member of the Wallaby Team at the time. In an interview he said: 'The Australian action received wide praise and publicity, with the implications that we "understood" South Africa's problems, that we endorsed her policies.' *The Australian*, 21/5/70.

14 e.g., Resolutions 2506B was passed by the General Assembly of the U.N. 22/11/69, by 80 votes to 5, with 23 abstentions. Australia was one of the 5 voting against the resolution. See essay in this Volume by Miss Jean Skuse.

15 Given by Paul Webster in feature article in *The Australian*, 16/4/71.

16 U.N. Unit on Apartheid, Notes and Documents No. 8/70 (70-07503). Over fifty countries have contributed, across the spectrum from Ireland to USSR.

17 JOHN LAURENCE, *'The Seeds of Disaster'*, Gollancz, London 1968, p. 82.

18 U.N. Unit on Apartheid, Notes and Documents, No. 12/70, p. 26. The Minister was Dr. P. Koornhoof, Deputy Minister of Bantu Administration and Development and Immigration, at Stiltfontein, reported in *The Star*, Johannesburg, 21/3/70.

19 *Ibid.*, at Hopetown, reported in *Cape Times*, 17/3/70.

20 ALEX HEPPLE, "Workers Under Apartheid", International Defence and Aid Fund pamphlet, London, 1969, pp. 44.

21 A. SACHS, "The Violence of Apartheid", IDAF pamphlet London, 1969, p. 35.

22 LAURENCE, *op. cit.*, p. 236.

23 *Rand Daily Mail*, Johannesburg, 16/3/70.

24 *Ibid.*, 9/7/70.

25 *Daily News*, Durban, 16/8/69. Initially, there was strong opposition to any contact from the Stellenbosch S.R.C. commission set up to consider the question. Under pressure, they relented to recommend contact by way of correspondence. A youth organization affiliated with the Nationalist Party suggested that white students could gain all the knowledge they needed about coloured people through books, and from the Department of Coloured Affairs. SAIRR Survey, 1969, p. 222.

26 Quoted in LAURENCE, *op. cit.*, p. 248. No name given.

27 *The Australian*, 21/4/71.

28 HAIN, *op. cit.*, p. 44.

29 Interview with Alan Trengove. *Newcastle Morning Herald*, 29/6/71.

30 Professor Anderson, with two other Presbyterian Ministers, returned from a fact-finding mission to South Africa on 16/7/71. cf. *The Australian* 17/7/71.

31 It is significant the many people involved in aboriginal advancement, and a number of Aboriginals themselves, were involved in the campaign to stop the Springbok tours.

# AUSTRALIA AND FUTURE RACE POLICY

# 11

## IN DEFENCE OF AUSTRALIA'S POLICY
## TOWARDS NON-WHITE IMMIGRATION

### John Ray

Among academics there is widespread criticism of Australia's immigration policies. 'White Australia' is definitely a dirty word among much of Australia's intelligentsia. The defences that one normally hears of Australia's policy generally come from politicians rather than from academics in the social sciences (see, for instance 'The evolution of a policy' by the Hon. Phillip Lynch, M.P.—former Minister for Immigration). In this paper I wish, as both a social scientist and as a conservative, to rebut the usual criticisms made by academics and positively to argue for Australia's present policy.

Some of the criticism one reads, even in reputable academic journals, is so incoherent on the rational level as to be very difficult to answer at all. The article by the anthropologist, Ian Bedford, for instance, (in *Politics* of 1970, pp. 224-227) contains the bald assertion that—'If the Australian is not to make war on the Asian in Asia, he must live with him on his own soil'—and a whole series of similar statements whose only support seems to be the moral rectitude of their writer. This writer indeed seems to be characterized by that very 'intolerance of ambiguity' for which the racially prejudiced person has long been slated (e.g. Adorno *et al.*, 1950; Rokeach, 1960). He argues that Australia should allow much more Asian migration *just so* we will have another Rhodesia. For the sake of showing white Australians clearly to belong in the 'Baddie' camp of Bedford's conceptual world, he is prepared to encourage all the suffering among, and injustice toward non-white races that he believes to have arisen in Rhodesia. He *expects* Australia to erupt in bloodshed and riot without the White Australia policy. And it is this that he advocates. It is this that he sees as desirable. For what gain? To show us up as what he believes we really are. This, then, is surely an example of, and a testimony to, the way in which moralism can distort our thinking into working against not only our own self-interest but also against moral ideals themselves.

Among the saner advocates of increased non-white immigration, however, different arguments are generally advanced. As far as I am able to summarize them, they seem to go as follows: 1. Australia is too culturally isolated and inward-looking; 2. Our policy angers other (Asian) nations; 3. We have a moral obligation to help the suffering humanity of Asia in every way we can; 4. Any form of discrimination on racial grounds is, in principle, morally offensive; 5. The gain to Australia would be greater than the loss even in purely material terms. 6. Racism is evil and we should force everybody to become non-racists. I will consider these arguments one by one. The first is certainly the most superficial and easily refutable point. It is abundantly clear that, on the world scene, Australia has more cultural diversity than most. With several million migrants from all parts of Europe in its population, Australia has a wealth of cultural diversity that few societies in the world could equal. Roughly one fifth of Australia's population was not born in Australia. Is this true of India, of China, of the U.S.A. or of most countries Australia might be compared with? The great European cultures that have made the world in their image are all represented here in strength. Asia and Africa are falling over themselves to emulate the Coca-cola culture and successful materialism of the European world. Are we to weep that we are not being exposed to what Asia itself is rejecting? Being electronically open to and in communication with all the world, Australia is right in the main stream of the world's cultural and intellectual developments. The music of a new composer or the new social theories of a great thinker might reach Australia a few months after they have reached the U.S.A. but is this cause for self-castigation or derogatory comparison with someone such as the Asian peasant who is cut off *entirely* from the world's intellectual community? If Australia is indeed culturally isolated and inward-looking, then, on the same criteria, all but a tiny percentage of the world's population must be similarly condemned. Sydney and Melbourne are infinitely closer to the New Yorks and Londons of the world (or whatever other great cultural centres one has in mind) than are the Rangoons or Tim-buctoos. When I go to the theatre in Sydney, I have a choice of plays that would not, in terms of number and variety, invite derogatory comparison with many other cities in the world. I can go to any number of Greek restaurants in Sydney (or for that matter Chinese, Indian, Italian, Lebanese or Yugoslav restaurants) and drink Greek wine while a roomful of Greeks around me drink Australian beer. In terms of cultural variety the comparison we need fear would be hard to draw. Paris? Perhaps. Peking? No. Even Tokyo, for all its commercialized (and Western) variety, hears fewer foreign accents than we. One may, of course, advocate that we be exposed to a *different sort* of variety, but variety *per se* we do have—*par excellence*. I myself feel that I have more to learn from a refugee Romanian Jew than I have to learn from an Asian peasant whose one aspiration in life is to own a bicycle. So then, by any standard of *objective* comparison, I would like to claim that Australia is an intensely cosmopolitan and urban society centred around its two great metropolises—highly advanced, taking the best that the world has to offer and itself contributing at least its fair share to the dominant world culture of which it forms a part. Personally, I might welcome greater immigration to Australia of educated Indians and Africans because of the refreshing skepticism and *joie de vivre* that these groups might respectively contribute to our culture, but so to say is to imply a consciousness that *any* society—even the very best—can be improved. It is not to say that the society we presently have is at all a bad one in the respect under discussion.

The second criticism listed above is that our policy angers Asian nations. This is an assertion about which it is hard for either side to be factual. Most nations of the world do have restrictive immigration policies and ours in fact would rate among the more liberal. Nearly all the Asian nations themselves forbid people other than those of their own race from settling and acquiring citizenship. Indeed, others of their own race might not even be welcome. The one country that has made public protest about our policy in recent times is Japan—a country which itself is almost fanatically ethno-centric and oppressive towards its own small Korean minority. Their protest against our policy is, in fact, the protest of a country which *forbids* perman-ent immigration of foreigners against a country which will accept any number of Japanese applicants of sufficient educational standards. Unlike the U.S.A., there are *no* quota restrictions on Asian settlement in Australia. The only restrictions are educational. Our Immigration Department statistics regularly reveal, in fact, that of those Asians whose application to settle here is approved, not much more than half actually come. From 1966 to 1971 (inclusive), 7,000 applications to immigrate made by Asians were approved but only 3,200 actually arrived. Many Asian countries are in fact themselves most unwilling to allow their people to leave (Taiwan being perhaps the most extreme example), so our policy, in fact, ought to accord well with what they themselves want. In summary then, the only evidence we have for Asian irritation with our policies is the case of Japan. Given Japan's own policy, however, we cannot see this criticism as very deep-seated or defen-sible. A situation that *would*, of course, draw criticism from Asian nations would be if we did have here a substantial minority of their people and ill-treated them. Witness the criticisms of Britain by the Afro-Asian nations or of South Africa by the black African nations. Since it is most implausible to believe that Australians would be more tolerant than Britons, our present policy can be seen as one that ensures that we do *not* anger Asian nations.

The third criticism listed above is that we have a moral obligation to help the suffering humanity of Asia in every way we can. In answer to this I could well make here the usual observations about the relative efficacy of foreign aid versus immigrant intake and I am sure that an impressive case could be made for the claim that the best place to help Asians is in Asia. One could even argue that importing a tiny minority of the Asian popula-tion into our midst (into what is, for them, an alien society) would be *counter*-productive to the welfare of both the individuals concerned and of the countries concerned. What I want to do instead of this however, is to challenge the basic premise that we are under a moral obligation. I would contend that the entire conception of Right and Wrong here involved is faulty. The existence of a *discoverable* right and wrong is implied in the criticism. Against this we must put the commonplace among many educated people today that there is *no such thing* as an absolute Right and Wrong. At least since Nietsche (1906) and Sorel (1915) the existence of moral properties has also been widely questioned among philosophers and social scientists. It is true that the two statements 'X is pink' and 'X is right' have the same grammatical form. While 'pink' does indeed describe a property of the object, 'right' would seem rather to describe *our reaction* to the object or action. The rightness of some action exists in our opinion of it—not in the action itself. 'Rightness' attributed to some action is therefore a fraudu-lent attribution—designed to provoke argument, discussion or consensus in a pseudo-objective form. It is a polite (but misleading) way of saying 'I favour X'—or, at best, 'all men would favour X if they had proper considera-tion for their own long-term self-interest'. If the moralist claims that some-thing other than self-interest is involved, he must at least show where his moral basis emanates from. How does he know whether a thing *is* an instance of the category 'a right action' (or 'an action which we are morally obliged to perform')? If God is the source of our moral information one has to be a metaphysician to be a moralist. Since I am not a metaphysician I am not impressed. Even if I was a metaphysician how could I be sure that I was getting the correct account of what God's will is? Given the divisions among religious people on moral questions, it would seem that moral information is not only metaphysical information but metaphysical information of a particularly uncertain sort. The only possible non-metaphysical answer that a moralist can give for the source of his moral information is to say that what is morally right is what he likes, or what all men would like in some optimum situation. The moral information is not to be gained from the action itself. A moralist will see taking up sword (or whatever example of an action one has in mind) as right on one occasion but wrong on another. The action has not changed—only our response to it (a response that is, of course, dictated by circumstances). Applying this to the question in hand, we must translate the contention here at issue as: 'I would approve of us helping the starving millions of Asia in any way we can'. This, of course, deprives the original assertion of its original imperative force. The utterer wished not only to report his own feelings but also to influence us to act in accordance with those inclinations of his. He could have said, 'Thou shalt help . . . etc.' but this would not have succeeded in influencing us unless he had direct power over us. He therefore resorted to the subterfuge of moralism and endeavoured to convince us that we were under an obligation similar to a contractual obligation. Once this subterfuge is perceived however we must immediately be interested to ask, 'What is the origin of this obligation? Contractual obligations arise when we exchange one service for another but no such exchange has been undertaken on the present occasion'. In answer to this, the moralist can only resort to the Deity or some other mystical or hypothetical source of obligation. Alternatively he can abandon morality altogether and argue that it would be in our best long term self-interest to act in the manner he advocates. If he does this, the burden of proving his new empirical assertion is thrown upon him. He must advance arguments such as the two considered first above in order to show us that it is, in fact, the case that acting as he advocates would further our long-term self-interest. He may, of course, resort to arguments of a more general sort than the ones considered above. He may say something like: 'It is always wise to be benevolent'. This however is a contentious statement and requires proof. If 'benevolent' is defined in some non-circular way, it can surely be shown that some benevolent acts might not lead to the long-term advantage of any party. One has in mind such adages as 'Sometimes you've got to be cruel to be kind'. Surely the European nations were being benevolent in allowing Hitler to remilitarize the Rhineland in the mid-1930s but it would be a brave spirit who would argue that this action was to our long-term self-advantage. Whether benevolence is wise also depends on what our goals are. If we enjoy aggression or the humiliation and suffering of others, then benevolence will obviously be less often wise than if we are otherwise motivated. Obviously then, general rules such as 'It is always wise to be benevolent' just will not work as such. At best they are guides to consider accepting when we have no other information as to the consequences of our actions or when such information as we do have leads to irresolvably conflicting conclusions. In all situations, our first preference must be to argue each case on its individual merits. It is this, then, that the advocate of change in our immigration policies has to do. He has to show that a change is to our advantage *in this particular case*. His primary reason for so arguing may not, of course, be that he believes a change would be to our advantage. While some advocates may be in this category, I believe that the greatest number would be people who have been conditioned in their upbringing to accepting as true, parental assertions that some acts *are* good or bad of themselves. Little Johnny is told that it is *bad* to act in a certain way—not that such an act is disliked by the parent (for whatever reason). Although it will not stand up to rational scrutiny, such children may often accept the inculcated belief that the act itself has this imputed property of 'badness' in some way intrinsic to it. The acceptance that certain acts have a property of 'badness' is also associated with (conditioned) negative affect towards such acts. Therefore, any acts that seem similar to acts that the child has accepted to have this property of 'badness' will suffer from generalization of negative affect. The adult feels (not necessarily consciously) that prohibiting unlimited Asian immigration is similar to acts that he was conditioned to avoid as a child. His advocacy of freer migration may therefore be dictated, not by rational considerations, but by generalized conditioned negative affect. Presumably, however, most of us would want to give more thought to our own long-term advantage in this particular situation than following our immediate emotional impulses. That the moralist's conditioned affect is a poor basis for action can also be appreciated if we reflect that others may not share that affect or even have conditioned affect of opposite effect. Where different people have opposite affective responses to the same actions, we cannot expect argument to alter the affect in any way but we might, if we are optimistic, hope that the policy actually adopted by the parties concerned would be decided on rational considerations of long-term self-interest. If this is to happen, debate on the likely outcomes of the alternative policies is essential before our estimation of the relative advantages to us can be made. Moralistic utterances *cannot* contribute to such a debate. This dismissal of moralistic utterances as nonsensical does then dispose of not only argument 3 above, but also of arguments 4 and 6. Argument 6, however, could be recast as: 'It would be in our interest to force people to become non-racists'. It is in this form that it will be considered below.

Before that, however, we will move on to argument 5—that the gain to Australia of freer Asian migration would be greater than the loss even in purely material terms. Such arguments generally turn on the economic advantages of immigration *per se*—such as the elimination of upbringing expenses and the greater entrepreneurial motivation and rate of capital accumulation among migrants. It is proposed that the latter might be higher among Asian migrants and that we could be more selective of educational level etc. if we gave ourselves Asia to pick and choose from as well as Europe. Also falling under this general rubric, is the argument that we could correct the imbalance of the sexes in Australia by importing large numbers of Asian women.

Since Australia's per capita rate of capital accumulation is second only to Japan's and since the migrants we already get do have an average level of education higher than that of native Australians, it is evident that, even though it might in theory be possible to do better, we are certainly not doing at all badly already. Even if we were to make a concerted effort to get the cream of Asian society here, this would be at great cost to those societies and would certainly not be permitted by them. Because average educational levels are so much higher in Europe than in Asia, anxiety not to offend other nations by attempting to drain off their best talent would alone constitute sufficient reason to concentrate our immigrant-seeking activities on

Europe. The loss of one professional man is an immeasurably greater loss to Asia than it is to Europe. The third proposal to correct the abnormal preponderance of men in Australia by importing Asian women is probably a rather facetious one. It has obvious difficulties associated with the acceptability of women from a vastly different culture to unwed Australian men and is also a policy unlikely to gain acceptance from the Asian nations concerned.

The sixth point listed above is not readily disputable in its revised form—but it also has lost most of its impact in the revision. Obviously if all people were not racists this would solve a lot of problems. The point is, however, that bringing Asian migrants here is certainly not the way to achieve this. Britain's experience suggests in fact that this would lead to the *emergence* of racism. If we want people to become non-racists the only way is the slow sure way of more education.

Having now seen that the reasons why we *should* have more Asian migration do not stand up well to fuller consideration, we may ask: 'Are there any reasons why we *should not* have more Asian migration?' The answers I want to suggest to this are, in general, so well known as to appear passe but the only answer the Left can generally produce to them takes the form of misapplying a psychiatric but clearly pejorative label such as 'paranoid'.

Let us face the fact that large numbers of even educated Australians do not like Jews or 'Wogs'. This is not concentration camp mentality. It is simply the perceptual descrimination of identifiably different characteristics in these people and the personal preference of not liking such characteristics. The concept of national characteristics stands in somewhat of a bad odour today but for all that it remains true that people who travel overseas have no difficulty in naming what those characteristics are (Cf. Madariaga, 1970). To say that Italians are more emotional is not at all to deny that some Italians are not emotional. It is simply to say that emotionality is more common among Italians than it is among us. We all have personal preferences about what we like in other people. If Italians are more emotional and we don't approve of emotionality (for us a cultural value), it makes perfect sense not to like Italians or any other group that is similarly characterized. Disliking Italians in this way is not even inconsistent with liking some individual Italians. I personally don't like marmalade jams but I have occasionally tasted a marmalade jam that I did like. In spite of the exceptions, when I go to the supermarket, I don't buy marmalade. Similarly I once knew even an ardent neo-Nazi who regarded the white race as the only one with a right to exist. One of his best friends and most constant associates was a Pakistani who was nearly as black as the proverbial ace of spades. Some exceptions don't necessarily disturb a rule. Following this line of reasoning through, if Australians like English migrants most and Asian migrants least, it is English migrants we should choose. This may be ethnocentric but it is not racist. The ethnocentric places a high value on those characteristics that are prominent in his own group. The racist actively persecutes members of other groups. Many superbly functioning and well-adjusted Australians I know will justly deny being racists and honestly deplore and condemn Hitlers concentration camps. Yet these same people will, among friends, exchange mocking misnomers for suburbs in which Jews have settled: Bellevue Hill becomes 'BelleJew Hill' and Rose Bay becomes 'Nose Bay'; Dover Heights becomes 'Jehovah Heights'. On the issue of admitting Jews to their exclusive schools and clubs, these WASPs will say: 'We let a few of them in—just to show we're not prejudiced'. If this feeling exists towards a group demonstrably not of inferior educational or cultural standards and which is not easily distinguished by something as salient as skin colour, how much more feeling must be expected against Asians? As happended with Great Britain, ethnocentrism could erupt into racism. Large numbers of Asians are readily accepted in our University communities but outside the sheltered world of academe things are different. We do have in Australia our own long-established Asian communities and we do have a continuing flow of Asian migrants. Pragmatic management has so far kept the proportion of Asians to a level where racism has not evolved. Let not moralists stampede us from this policy into something that can advantage no-one. The misguided compulsions of moralism offer us the prospect of transforming Sydney into another New York. Against this, I advocate enlightened self interest and an Australia not torn by racial tensions. At present I can walk alone at night through the streets of Sydney without fear. I would like to keep it that way.

## REFERENCES

ADORNO, T. W., FRENKEL-BRUNSWIK, ELSE, LEVINSON, D. J., & SANFORD, R. N. *The authoritarian personality*: Harper, N.Y., 1950.

BEDFORD, I. White Australia, the Fear of Others, *Politics*, 1970, 5, 224-227.

DEPARTMENT OF IMMIGRATION *Australia's Immigration policy*: Government Printer, Canberra, 1970.

LYNCH, P. *The evolution of a policy*: Australian Government Publishing Service, Canberra, 1971.

MADARIAGA, S. DE *Englishmen, Frenchmen, Spaniards: An essay in comparative psychology* 2nd. ed.: Pitman, London, 1970.

NIETSCHE, F. *Beyond good and evil* (vol. 12 of *The complete works*. Ed.: O. LEVY) Foulis, Edinburgh, 1911.

ROKEACH, M. *The open and closed mind*: Basic Books, N.Y., 1960.

SOREL, G. *Reflections on violence* (Trans. T. E. Hulme): Allen & Unwin, London, 1915.

# 12

## TOWARDS A MULTI-RACIAL SOCIETY

### A. Barrie Pittock

*Prologue*

This essay is addressed primarily to a group of well-intentioned white Australians. In it I want to present a point of view, and raise questions, which most white Australians have never taken seriously. I want to do this basically because I believe most of us are deluding ourselves about race relations in this country. We see Australia and its racial history, past, present and future as only white men could see her. It is time we took a new look and tried to understand that there are other points of view which may be more realistic than our own; for the reality may require a different response than the myth.

When our British forefathers took this land they termed it 'waste and unoccupied': in reality they conquered the Aboriginal people by force of arms, disease, starvation, and the destruction of Aboriginal social systems.[1] We are heirs to a colonial empire which was built largely on force and a deep and abiding belief in the superiority of the British people and their institutions.

We have tried, partly out of a sense of guilt, to ignore and forget these facts. We even advise Aborigines to 'forget past injustices', ignoring both the sanctimonious overtones and the fact that the injustices continue into the present, and will probably continue into the future, for all we are doing about them.

There have been, and there are, white men who have recognised the truth and stated it clearly. Unfortunately they have been few, and have gone largely unheeded. Notable amongst them is the English Quaker, James Backhouse, after whom this lecture is named.

Backhouse visited the Australian colonies in the years 1832 to 1838, to discharge what he felt to be a 'religious duty'. One of his particular concerns was the state of the Aboriginal inhabitants.

Symptomatic of Backhouse's approach was the following note in the introduction to his 'Narrative':—

> 'In the course of the Narrative, the term Savages is sometimes used in reference to the Aborigines of the countries visited; but it is only intended, by this term, to designate human beings, living on the wild produce of the earth and destitute of any traces of civilisation; and by no means to convey the idea that these people are more cruel than the rest of the human race, or of inferior intellect.'[2]

In 1837 Backhouse put in writing to the Governor of New South Wales his ideas concerning the Aborigines and what might be done to help them:—

'In those parts of the Colony in which the White Population have taken possession of the lands, the Kangaroos and Emus, which were among the chief animals on which the Blacks subsisted, have been generally destroyed, and the grounds on which these animals fed is now depastured by the flocks and herds of the usurpers of the country; who have also introduced profligate habits among the Blacks, that are rapidly wasting their race, some tribes of which have already become extinct, and others are on the verge of extermination.'

'It is scarcely to be supposed that in the present day any persons of reflection will be found who will attempt to justify the measures adopted by the British in taking possession of the territory of this people, who had committed no offence against our Nation; but who, being without strength to repel invaders, had their lands usurped, without any attempt at purchase by treaty or any offer of reasonable compensation, and a class of people introduced into their country, amongst whom were many ... who ... practised appalling cruelties upon this almost helpless race. And when any of the latter have retaliated, they have brought upon themselves the vengeance of British strength, by which beyond a doubt many of the unoffending have been destroyed, along with those who had ventured to return a small measure of these wrongs upon their white oppressors.'

After making a number of practical suggestions, Backhouse continued:—

'... seeing the state to which the Blacks are reduced, and the vast pecuniary advantage derived by the Whites from the possession of their soil, the expense ought not to stand in the way of the amelioration of their condition, especially when it may be amply provided for out of the proceeds of the Government sales of the very lands which were the natural possession of the Blacks, and to which their right has only been questioned by a foe too powerful for them to contend or argue with.'"[3]

About the same time, Backhouse wrote to the chairman of the British House of Commons' Select Committee on Aboriginal Tribes, Sir Thomas Fowell Buxton, in the following terms:—

'The system of colonization that has been pursued by the British Government has been upon principles that cannot be too strongly reprobated and which want radical reformation. Aborigines have had wholesale robbery of territory committed upon them by the Government, and settlers have become the receivers of this stolen property, and have borne the curse of it in the wrath of the aborigines who, sooner or later, have become exasperated at being driven off their rightful possessions.'

'Though the mode of holding property differed among the aborigines of Van Dieman's Land from that used among English people, yet they had their property: each tribe was limited to its own hunting-ground; and into such hunting-grounds the island was divided; and it is said, the tenure on which the aborigines of New Holland hold their country is somewhat more specific than that formerly used by the now almost extinct race of aborigines of Van Dieman's Land.'

He goes on:—

'Perhaps it might be for the best if, in eligible situations, the British Government would become the original purchasers (I do not mean by compelling sale, for that would be next to robbery), and would arrange for the preservation of the rights of the parties making the sale, and take steps to promote their settlement and civilisation, and would encourage missionaries to labour amongst them; and would, also, on as reasonable terms as possible, dispose of the territories so purchased to settlers, maintaining likewise proper civil government at such places.'[4]

The Select Committee to which Backhouse wrote, itself concluded that 'the native inhabitants of any land have an uncontrovertible right to their own soil',[5] and this is recognised in international law and practice outside Australia, which goes back to the Spanish 'Laws of the Indies' of 1594.[6]

The Aborigine, and indeed we ourselves, may well ask how far Australia has progressed in terms of racial justice in the 130-odd years which have passed since the days of Backhouse and the Select Committee of 1837. Regrettably, and to our individual and corporate shame, the answer, as I will show in part, is not very far. There are indeed still many white Australian, some in high places, who believe Aborigines to be of inferior intellect and ability; incapable, for instance, of running their own communities or their own cattle stations. And we still have governments, which we have elected, which deny that Aborigines have any right to land or compensation by virtue of their rightful inheritance.

What have we done individually or corporately, as members of the Society of Friends which Backhouse was so concerned to nurture in this country, to develop and further his insights.

Like most other men of good will we have often done our best to help individuals here and there, providing scholarships or kindergartens, advice and encouragement, and these deeds are not to be dismissed out of hand. However, when it comes to the big issues which question the whole relationship between Aborigines and newcomers (as Backhouse did), and which threaten the whole framework of 'policy' and the 'status quo', how many of us stand committed to morality and justice rather than order and expediency?

## Racism in Australia

Let me review, briefly and inadequately, some of the main areas of concern. First we must start with definitions of some necessary terms such as 'racism' and its two varieties, 'individual and institutional racism'.

(White) 'racism' is 'the conscious or unconscious belief in the inherent superiority of persons of European ancestry, which entitles all white peoples to a position of dominance and privilege'.[7]

Racism in this sense is more than pride in one's own race, or even of preference in personal associations; it is essentially a question of dominance or privilege determined by racial origin.

Such racism can be directed personally from an individual of one race to an individual of another race, for instance by acts of violence or ridicule. This conscious and overt behaviour we may call 'individual racism'.

Contrasted to individual racism is something we may call 'institutional racism'. Institutional racism is not readily attributable to the views or actions of individuals, but to the operation of the established system of laws and institutions of a whole society.[8]

Individual racism still exists in Australia. In recent years I have seen for myself or else can recall newspaper reports of such incidents from every mainland State in the country. Usually it concerns the housing of Aboriginal people in white towns, or discrimination in hotels and other public facilities. Occasionally it involves violence. Such incidents are sometimes, but not always, much publicised and officially condemned.

Regrettably, however, South Australia is the only State to legislate against such acts, and responsible administrations all over Australia tend to minimise and cover up the misdeeds of their employees in this regard. Whatever the truth of particular allegations, the tendency all too often seems to be to avoid the honest and independent inquiries which alone can ensure that justice in these cases not only is done, but is also seen to be done. Real, alleged and rumoured cases of individual racism contribute a great deal to the bitterness and fear felt by many Aborigines.

Institutional racism, although it is widespread and terribly damaging to all concerned, is largely ignored, hidden, or held to be somehow justified in Australia.

Externally, Australia's euphemistically titled 'restrictive immigration policy' is the outstanding example, and one which is symptomatic of widespread racist thinking in this country. Australians, it seems, can get rightly concerned about individual non-Europeans who have somehow got across an image of themselves as persons, but not about the principle and policy which leads to such cases.[9] Australians rightly concern themselves about refugees from Hungary or Czechoslovakia, but largely ignore, for example, the Chinese refugees in Indonesia and Hong Kong.

Aborigines are the victims of many forms of institutional racism in Australia.

Wage discrimination has long been a glaring example.[10] Despite recent favourable changes in some industries, lower wages are still being paid to Aborigines in the Northern Territory under the Wards Employment Ordinance, and in Queensland under the 1966 Regulations of 'The Aborigines and Torres Strait Islanders' Affairs Act of 1965'.[11] The simple principle that there should be only one set of industrial laws for all Australians has yet to be established.

As Backhouse so clearly recognised, the denial of Aboriginal rights to their traditional land is a most basic form of institutional racism—'wholesale robbery'. Land is the only economic asset, apart from their physical strength, with which Aborigines could ward off poverty and degradation in the face of white settlement. It is this continuing loss, more than any other single factor, which has and is making paupers out of most Aborigines. It is not a question of a return to a hunting and food-gathering economy, but of having the economic capital with which to enter the twentieth century on equal terms with the usurpers of their country.

Limitations on the personal freedom and legal rights of Aborigines persist, to a remarkable degree, both in Queensland and the Northern Territory. In these areas Aborigines normally resident on Aboriginal Reserve are subject to the will of often paternalistic or authoritarian administrators armed with the power to arbitrarily direct and interfere in the daily life of the people in a manner which would be regarded as intolerable in white society. Laws ostensibly designed, and no doubt genuinely believed to be protective, have become instruments for the suppression of initiative and the exercise of authoritarianism.[11, 12]

Perhaps most real in terms of the everyday experience of Aborigines is discrimination in the standards of public administration in the case of Aborigines as against non-Aborigines. Unsuitable and unqualified staff, and unfilled but vital staff positions, are common on Aboriginal Reserves to a degree which would cause public outcry and scandal in a white community. Similarly, local authorities commonly tolerate bad housing and sanitation in Aboriginal fringe-dwellings which would never be tolerated if non-Aborigines lived in the same situation.

Effective discrimination in the administration of justice in the courts is also common in such centres as Darwin and Alice Springs. Illiterate Aborigines, often unable to understand and speak ordinary English, let alone legal jargon, are frequently brought before courts in these centres without interpreters or legal representation. The Director of Social Welfare in the Northern Territory, commenting on protests at this state of affairs, has been quoted recently as saying by way of explanation, 'It would result in an intolerable strain on Welfare Officers'.[13]

Frank Stevens, an economist formerly at the Australian National University, has estimated that approximately 8,000 able-bodied Aboriginal men are unemployed or under-employed in northern Australia, and that without major changes in policy this number will not decrease in the foreseeable future.[14] This represents at present approximately 50 per cent of the Aboriginal work force in the area, a figure which would be quite intolerable if it applied to a similar white community.

Similarly, Aboriginal poverty and ill-health is so bad that were it true of a non-Aboriginal community in Australia it would bring immediate and urgent emergency relief measures into action. Dr. F. Lancaster Jones, in a demographic survey of the Northern Territory,[15] found that:—

> 'On any reasonable assumption (as to accuracy) the infant mortality rate amongst Aborigines remains extremely high. In Central Australia, indeed, the registered infant mortality rate was 208 per 1,000 live births, which must be among the highest infant mortality rates in the world.' (p. 96).

He goes on to say,—

> 'the causes of infant mortality among Aborigines in the Northern Territory are not yet under control and that no immediate decline in its incidence can be anticipated. The rapid increase in the number of Aborigines at many Government Settlements and Mission Stations has tended to foster conditions conducive to the rapid spread of diseases such as gastro-enteritis, dysentery and pneumonia, all of which have caused excessive mortality among Aboriginal infants and children' (p. 97).

According to Jones' figures, 1 child in 6 dies in its first four years in the Northern Territory. Although no similar figures are published for other parts of Australia, it is clear from the similar age structure of the part-Aboriginal population[16] and the extreme povery and poor living conditions, that similar death rates must apply to the Aboriginal and part-Aboriginal population as a whole throughout Australia.

From a survey of the part-Aboriginal population of rural New South Wales by Professor C. D. Rowley,[16] it was found that 37 per cent of

Aboriginal dwellings were classified as 'shacks' and that Aborigines averaged 1.6 persons per room. 51 per cent of Aboriginal dwellings did not contain enough beds for the number of people living in them, 49 per cent had no laundry, 46 per cent no separate kitchen, 38 per cent no water in the dwelling, and 41 per cent no garbage disposal service, to mention but a few of the sad statistics.

Whatever rationalisations we can offer in these various instances of institutional racism, certain cold facts remain. One is that, whatever the reason or historical context, Aborigines today suffer many handicaps which truly make them, as a race, under-privileged citizens. A second is that were a comparable number of non-Aborigines suffering in the same way, it would be regarded as a major political issue which would threaten to bring down governments.

Despite long-standing government policies of 'assimilation', we in practice still apply double standards—one for the white folks and one for the black folks.

### Assimilation as Racism

We shall now turn to the most subtle form of institutional racism, and the most all-pervasive: the policy of 'assimilation' itself.

Public attitudes and policies in Australia, right from the time of first settlement, have always demanded conformity to the British-Australian way of life as an unquestioned and at least implicit price which has to be paid for equal opportunity. This has had disastrous psychological and practical consequences, notably in the failure of early and even current attempts by many sincere and devoted people to educate Aborigines.

Education was, and to a large extent still is, based on ignorance and disdain for the Aboriginal way of life. Educational effort has been geared to non-Aboriginal goals, to the objective of turning Aborigines into dark-skinned Europeans, and to the alienation of the individual from his traditions and his 'more backward cousins'.[17]

This same attitude found expression in the Victorian Act of 1887, which sought to 'merge into the general population all half-castes capable of earning their living', by removing them from their full-blood relatives on the reserves. Far from achieving its stated objective, this policy resulted merely in the depopulation and closing of many Aboriginal reserves (for which the land-hungry whites were grateful) and the growth of squalid camps populated by part-Aborigines. It turned potentially productive citizens into alienated paupers.

In practice, although not in name until Professor A. P. Elkin popularised the term in the 1940s, Australia's Aboriginal policies have always been essential assimilationist. Aborigines have been expected to see the self-evident truth that the European way of life is in every respect superior and more desirable than their own. This was stated most explicitly in the following statement, issued in 1961 from a meeting of Federal and State Ministers in charge of Aboriginal affairs:—

> 'The policy of assimilation means in the view of all Australian governments that all aborigines and part-aborigines are expected eventually to attain the same manner of living as other Australians and to live as members of a single Australian community, enjoying the same rights and privileges, accepting the same responsibilities,

observing the same customs and influenced by the same beliefs, hopes and loyalties as other Australians.'

In order to meet criticism of this policy, the wording was changed in 1965 so that now the policy officially *seeks* (rather than *means*) that all persons of Aboriginal descent *will choose* to attain (rather than *are expected eventually to attain*) a *similar* (rather than *the same*) manner and *standard* of living, the words *observing the same customs* are omitted, and so too is reference to their being influenced by the *same beliefs*.[18]

The key element in this change of definition is the insertion of the idea of Aboriginal *choice;* however, it is at the level of practical implementation that we must judge the reality of this theoretical change of policy. One has only to look at the recent case of the Gurindji people at Wattie Creek in the Northern Territory to see the real problem. A 'choice' is only meaningful if positve alternatives are made available. The Gurindji people clearly *chose* to develop their own community on their own land, but the Commonwealth Government just as clearly rejected this choice.

In the words of the Minister for the Interior (9 Aug. 1968):—
'The Government's aim is to ensure that all of the opportunities which the Australian community offers ... are open to every Aboriginal and that all Aboriginals are equipped to take advantage of those opportunities *in the way which most appeals to them.*'
'Singling out the issue of land rights and pressing for areas of land to be granted to *groups of Aboriginals* in remote places *would not serve this purpose.* On the contrary, we could end up with a series of depressed *Aboriginal communities* tied to a form of sub-standard living *with a barrier* between them and the rest of the Australian community. *Separatism and segregation* of Aboriginals would create here problems now being faced in other countries.'
(My emphasis added, A.B.P.).

One might well ask how giving Aborigines ownership of their land would make them poorer than at present, and what new barrier the Minister imagines Aboriginal ownership of economic assets would create between the already largely segregated Aboriginal communities and the rest of Australia. The real threat, it would seem, is not to the Aborigines but to the real policy of the Government, which continues to see Aborigines as individuals who must be brought to conform to the ideas and prejudices of urbanised, individualistic white Australians.

There is, on the other hand, a sense in which the barrier of which the Minister spoke does exist in the minds of many Australians. It is a barrier of *fear*—fear of a state of affairs in which more than one way of life exists side by side. It is fear of the very existence of groups of free men who by choice live according to different customs and traditions.

Australians and their governments seem incapable of distinguishing between such a free but *plural* society and a state of enforced segregation or apartheid. Enforced conformity in a 'homogenous society' is commonly seen as the only alternative to a policy of racism, yet ironically this pressure to conform as the price of equality is itself racist where racial and cultural differences already exist, for it implies that one group should subordinate its values, and even its very existence, to the desires of another.

Two other recent examples may help to illustrate how this attitude of enforced homogenity bears on real questions of administrative policy and racial justice.

The first is a statement to the Legislative Assembly of Victoria on May 4, 1965. The issue under debate was the government's determination at that time to close the Lake Tyers Aboriginal Settlement, instead of developing it as a free and open village community. The speaker was the then Chairman of the Aborigines Welfare Board:—

> 'I do not know how anyone lives in and takes part in society *by being segregated* 30 miles from the nearest habitation and being *permanently segregated* there in such conditions that others *of their kind* are persuaded to go and be *segregated* with them. If that were *allowed* we would finish up with a large scale settlement of people who were not part of *this society of ours* but were, in fact, *an alien race* within it.'

(My emphasis added, A.B.P.).

One might well ask whether the same criteria ought to be applied to people 'segregated' in other country towns '30 miles from the nearest habitation', and to other voluntary communities such as monasteries or old people's villages!

The second example is the statement by the Commonwealth Minister for Immigration, made in the House of Representatives on 24th September 1968. In it he said that was not the wish of the people, and certainly not the policy of the government, to create a multi-racial society in Australia. The purpose of Australia's immigration policy, he said, was—

> 'to *maintain the homogenity of the Australian people*. I feel sure that the people of Australia would not wish the Government to aim at *creating a multi-racial society* and the policy of the Government certainly does not.'

Not only does this attitude beg the question as to whether limited numbers of selected non-Europeans can be admitted without causing racial tensions,[9] but it also completely overlooks the fact that *Australia already is a multi-racial society*.

To come back to the question of the reality of Aboriginal choice in the policy of 'assimilation', one of the great ironies of the policy as it has operated in the past is that, while it provides no *positive* alternative, it cannot avoid a *negative* one. Aborigines, when faced with a given policy, can still choose either to accept and co-operate with it, or else to reject and not co-operate with it. Most Aborigines, again and again, have made the same choice, to reject and oppose the implementation of policies decided for them by white men. More than any other factor, this has been responsible for the historic failure of Australian Aboriginal policies.

When the Meriam Survey of 1928 revealed a similar failure of assimilationist policies in the United States of America, it led to the 'Indian New Deal' under John Collier.

Collier's 'Indian Reorganization Act' of 1934 initiated a policy of cultural revival, with a strengthening of tribal autonomy, and an increase in the Indians' economic base, including land holdings.[19]

The new policy in America was based on Collier's belief that there might be, indefinitely, American citizens with beliefs and affiliations different from the majority, so long as all were equal before the law. Collier recognised that tribal affiliations, rights in tribal lands held in common, adherence to old religions, and the use of old languages might well enrich the total community, and certainly constituted no fundamental threat to other Americans. To Collier it was a simple question of human freedom and diversity: Indians had as much right to stay Indians as Jews to stay Jews, or Catholics to stay Catholics, and an equal right to associate together and run their own communal affairs.

This is not to say that Collier believed that Indians, any more than Jews or Catholics, should retain their traditional way of life unchanged by the impact of the twentieth century. Collier recognised that the Indian had to modernise, but not at the price of ceasing to be Indian:—

'Assimilation, not into our culture but into modern life, and preservation and intensification of heritage are not hostile choices, excluding one another, but are interdependent through and through. It is the continuing social organism, thousands of years old and still consciously and unconsciously imbued with and consecrated to its ancient past, which must be helped to incorporate the new technologies. It is the ancient tribal, village, communal organisation which must conquer the modern world.'[20]

Despite John Collier's fervent and idealistic attitude in defence of Indian rights, his policies were soundly based in economics and the psychological framework necessary for later economic development. This is not the place to discuss cases and details—suffice to say that we Australians, both Aboriginal and non-Aboriginal, have much to learn from the successes and failures of recent American Indian development, not least in terms of the value of ownership of economic assets such as land and mineral rights.[21]

It is perhaps an ironical twist that the very success of the development under the Indian Reorganisation Act has raised the educational and material standards of some Indian groups to the point where individual Indians from those groups are now much more readily assimilated than would have been the case without an initial strengthening of the group. Now that their group identity is no longer under such strong attack, these Indians have lowered their defensive barriers and are more open to the modernising influence of the outside world. Perhaps they also have more chance of influencing it.

### The Impending Crisis

Aborigines are well aware, even if white Australians are not, that individual and institutional racism are wide-spread in this country. Wage discrimination, unemployment, poor health, poverty, and dual standards of justice and administration are everyday experiences to Aboriginal and part-Aboriginal people. Some are bitter, many drown that bitterness in alcohol, or hide it through fear and the well-learned lesson that it is best to tell the white man what he wants to hear.

Far too few Aborigines yet have the education and experience to put into English what they feel and want. Fewer still have the skill to do so in the face of opposition from politicians experienced in the arts of rhetoric and begging the question.

Nevertheless, increasingly articulate spokesmen are appearing. They often lose out on television to the fast and smooth talking representatives of Governments and vested interests. Sometimes their emotions get the better of their logic or their tact, and sometimes they are just too polite to contradict untruths. Sometimes they are accused by politicians of uttering words 'put into their mouths' by sinister and mysterious agitators (how many politicians write all their own speeches?).

Despite all this, leaders are appearing. To the extent that education is succeeding it is producing better informed, more articulate and more radical leaders. It is significant that the new generation, like black people elsewhere, are thinking and talking in terms of economic and political power. In tune with the times, they are impatient for equal rights and freedom from all forms of discrimination *now*.

Modern communications, and the slow but real progress of education (including non-government education through Aboriginal advancement movements) have produced both a revolution of expectations and a revolution of identity and methodology. The Aboriginal residents of shanty dwellings, cattle stations, missions and government settlements are no longer unaware of the possibilities in the outside world. Transistor radios, and to a lesser extent books and television, have brought the whole world into these once isolated and insulated communities.

Now practically all Aborigines are coming to hear of Australia's high standard of living, of the mineral boom, and of Martin Luther King, Stokely Carmichael, and a thing called 'Black Power'. Further, they are finding out about New Guinea, about self-government and land rights there, and about how the United Nations pressure is keeping Australia on its toes.

When the Aborigines on the cattle stations around Port Hedland went on strike, back in the late 1940's, the presence of the lone white man, Donald McLeod, was probably essential.[22] Despite Frank Hardy's somewhat egocentric account,[23] I doubt if any white man was essential to the strike on Wave Hill Station in 1966.

The 89 per cent 'yes' vote on the Aboriginal question in the referendum of 1967 raised the hopes and expectations of many Aborigines, not for the first time. When Mr. Wentworth, as the new Commonwealth Minister for Aboriginal Affairs, virtually offered the Gurindji people at Wave Hill some of the land they had asked for, hopes of a new deal were raised higher still. When these hopes were dashed by Federal Cabinet shortly after, I believe that many Aborigines, and in particular many Aboriginal leaders, began to lose faith in Australian democracy.

There is little talk now amongst Aborigines of trying to change the Government's mind; the talk I hear is of defiance and of going to the United Nations. Far from being 'agitators', most whites in the Aboriginal advancement movement now seem like counsellors of caution. They are among the few remaining leaders with faith in the internal processes of Australian political democracy. Aborigines are tiring of petitions and protest meetings. They want action, even if it means going outside Australia to get it.

The north-western half of Australia contains only some 370,000 people, of whom approximately one quarter are either pure Aboriginal or of Aboriginal or Islander extraction.[10] According to Lancaster Jones[15, 16] the rates of increase of the Aboriginal and part-Aboriginal populations are each about 2 per cent per annum. At this rate these populations will double in about 20 to 25 years. This is appreciably faster than the growth rate of the non-Aboriginal population of Australia, even with our large-scale programme of (European) immigration. If the mortality rates amongst the Aboriginal and Islander populations were lowered by better public health measures and improved diet, the rate of increase of these populations would be even more dramatic. This is best illustrated by considering that about 53 per cent of the Aboriginal population is in the 0-15 year age group, compared to 30 per cent of the total Australian population.

It follows that, despite our racial immigration policy, we already have a multi-racial society in northern Australia, and that Australia *will become increasingly multi-racial* into the foreseeable future. The crucial policy question then is not whether we *ought* to become a multi-racial society, but *what sort* of multi-racial society we want to build—one based on dominance and privilege or one based on real equality and mutual respect.

Consider then the effects of the present widespread institutional racism, and in particular the growing population of coloured Australians who are living in poverty, deprived of their only real economic asset, the land, and largely unemployed or under-employed. The problem should be obvious, for we have the classic ingredients which spell trouble in multi-racial societies elsewhere; the coincidence of economic and racial differences, growing population pressure, under-employment, legitimate grievances, and an increasing awareness of the disparity on the part of the under-privileged group.

*Poverty and Black Power*

Oscar Lewis, the American sociologist, has defined what he calls the 'culture of poverty',[24] which is a style of life adopted by people who have lived for generations in poverty. He bases his definition and description on observations among the poor in Mexico, and among Negroes and Puerto Ricans in the United States of America.

According to Lewis,—

'The culture of poverty is both an adaptation and a reaction of the poor to their marginal position . . . . It represents an effort to cope with feelings of hopelessness and despair which develop from the realisation of the improbability of achieving success in terms of the values and goals of the larger society . . . . Once the culture of poverty comes into existence it tends to perpetuate itself from generation to generation because of its effect on the children. By the time slum children are six or seven they have usually absorbed the basic attitudes and values of their sub-culture. Thereafter they are psychologically unready to take full advantage of changing conditions that may develop in their lifetime.'

He goes on:—

'The lack of effective participation and integration of the poor in the major institutions of the larger society is one of the crucial characteristics of the culture of poverty. This . . . results from a variety of factors which may include lack of economic resources, fear, suspicion or apathy, and the development of local solutions for local problems. However, 'participation' in some of the institutions of the larger society—for example, the jails, the army and the public relief system —does not *per se* eliminate the traits of the culture of poverty. In the case of a relief system which barely keeps people alive, both the basic poverty and the sense of hopelessness are perpetuated rather than eliminated.'

'. . . People in a culture of poverty produce little wealth and receive little in return. Chronic unemployment and under-employment, low wages, lack of property, lack of savings, absence of food reserves in the home and chronic shortage of cash, imprison the family and the individual in a vicious circle . . . . Along with disen-gagement from the larger society, there is a hostility to the basic institutions of what are regarded as the dominant classes. There is hatred of the police, mistrust of government and of those in high positions, and a cynicism that extends to the church. This gives the culture of poverty a high potential for protest and for being used in political movements aimed against the existing social order.'

Such an analysis, based as it is essentially on observation in North America, seems almost prophetic when held up as a mirror to the Aboriginal situation. Doubtless many will think it unduly pessimistic. I do not think so. The proof lies not in northern Australia, where the process is still in its early stages, but in Victoria and New South Wales, where 150 years of effort have produced little but fringe-dwellers whom Professor C. D. Rowley quite clearly regards as fitting into 'a typical culture of poverty'.[16] If you can imagine 25 per cent or more of the population living in such conditions you will begin to see my vision, or nightmare, of northern Australia a generation hence.

There is another parallel we can draw with the ghetto-dwellers of North America besides the 'culture of poverty'. It is the parallel between the old-style civil rights movement in the U.S., with its emphasis on finding the individual Negro a home and a job in an 'integrated' neighbourhood, i.e., out of the Negro ghetto, and the policy of assimilation in Australia.

Both aim at helping the more able and adaptable individuals from the under-privileged community to get out into the 'main-stream' of the domin-ant white society. Both have succeeded in doing so for many individuals. However, both have been defeated essentially by the same basic fact—that the under-privileged community, be it Negro ghetto or aboriginal settle-ment, is growing in population faster than the 'cream' of those societies can be skimmed off into the outside world.

In both cases the continuing process, in which individuals (who through good fortune or exceptional drive and ability 'qualify') are removed from the under-privileged community, deprives that community of its potential leader-ship and ability to raise its own standards and self-esteem. Too often those who move out are completely lost to their former community either by choice or expedient necessity.

It is this, more than anything else, which makes life in a ghetto or Aboriginal settlement such a psychologically self-defeating and self-perpetu-ating existence. If material, educational and psychological standards are to be raised for the bulk of the increasing population in these segregated communi-ties, this must be done *where the people are*, in their own communities. It is only when this has been achieved that 'integration' in the American sense, or 'assimilation' in Australian usage, can be brought about on a large scale.

The American response to this situation, to the *numerical failure* of the old-style, civil rights movement, has been the emergence of the 'Black Power' movement.[8]

In the words of a recent World Council of Churches study document:—
   'Black power ideology tends to reject racial integration as an immedi-

ate goal in favour of building strength within the black ghettos and to de-emphasise inter-racial endeavours. Theorists of the movement see this development as the process of disenchantment of the races on the level of white dominance and paternalism in order to prepare both races for re-engagement at a higher level bottomed (sic) upon full equality and partnership as the fundamental condition precedent to reconciliation and eventual integration. Observers suggest that this is a movement towards abandonment of the traditional goal of cultural assimilation in the United States and an embracing of the goal of cultural pluralism.'

'. . . the Black Power movement, among increasing numbers of Negro youth in the United States (expresses) determination to achieve racial equality through self-determination of the black community and the rapid acquisition of political and economic power. It also seeks to throw off the heritage of a degrading self-concept, imposed by white racism, and to find a distinctive cultural identity consistent with racial pride and with mature, free manhood and womanhood. Hence, the Black Power movement calls for all-black organisations, a black-led struggle for Negro rights, and the acceptance of whites only if they are willing to work under black leadership.'[25]

In their recent book, Stokely Carmichael and Charles Hamilton say:—

'Integration as a goal todays speaks to the problem of blackness not only in an unrealistic way but also in a despicable way. It is based on complete acceptance of the fact that in order to have a decent house or education, people must move into a white neighbourhood or send their children to a white school. This reinforces, among both black and white, the idea that "white" is automatically superior . . . . No person can be healthy, complete and mature if he must deny a part of himself; this is what "integration" has required so far . . . .'[8]

Rather curiously, in view of the sudden prominence of the concept, the idea represented by the Black Power movement is far from new. The American Indian, ever since the coming of the first white men to North America, has been struggling to maintain his own culture and 'power base' in the land and tribal organisation. In this he has been remarkably successful, although until the advent of the Indian Reorganisation Act of 1934 it was a struggle against great odds.[19]

With increasing education and material prosperity on many Indian Reservations, the—

'thrust of young American Indians, especially those who are university-trained, (is) now to reassert their ethno-cultural identity as Indians. In the past, educated Indians sued to be absorbed into white society, thereby depriving the Indian community of forward-looking leadership. They regard this process as anything but a wholesome integration. They resent it as a process of cultural genocide. With this general emphasis, there is also a tendency to revive the spirit of tribal nationalism with renewed pride in the unique culture and language of each tribal nation.'

'The crucial issue for Amerindians is their collective survival in the face of (the) highly individualistic culture of industrial civilisation which has been causing disintegration of their basically communal culture from its foundation up. Today young, intelligent Indians are becoming increasingly militant in this struggle.'[25]

Such an analysis thus leads me to conclude that race relations in Australia are to a large extent wrongly based, with widespread injustice, and the increasing prospect of more organised, vocal and radical Aboriginal protest. With the almost daily example and growing influence of 'Black Power' type movements in the U.S. and elsewhere, this situation puts Australia in a new perspective. We are already a multi-racial society. We now have to face the questions as to where we want to go from here and how we are to get there. These questions raise issues which go right to the core of our traditions and beliefs.

*The Goal of Cultural Pluralism*

If the goal of assimilation of large numbers of individual Aborigines into the Anglo-Australian way of life is not realistic in the short run, not acceptable to the Aborigines, and essentially racist in its assumptions, what then ought to be our goal in race relations.

Clearly a permanent and forced segregation of the races is even less acceptable and less realistic. The races are inextricably bound together by economic inter-dependence, inter-marriage, and by the common recognition of the immorality and stupidity of enforced segregation.

The concept of a tolerant multi-racial society, one in which different races and cultures live freely together in the same country, is a middle way which deserves more attention than it has been given to date. Such a plural society would tolerate and even encourage the preservation of distinct group identities and cultures on a basis of equal opportunity, mutual tolerance, and freedom of the individual to choose his own way of life.

Whether assimilation is the inevitable end product, and the plural society merely a means to that end, is to me an academic question best left to academics and to history. Nevertheless, it is commonly argued that assimilation is the end product of social evolution, and that it should therefore be recognised as such and stated as the goal of racial policy.

Such an argument is questionable primarily because it is undesirable to state *as policy* a goal which is currently unacceptable and psychologically damaging to the minority group. It presumes to impose as policy the wishes or historical judgment of one racial group upon another.

Secondly, it is questionable whether racial and cultural assimilation *is* inevitable in the long run. Even if it were so, one might well ask how long such a process might take, for it hardly seems realistic to state as a goal of social policy a state which might take literally hundreds of years to come about. We might well pause to consider such cultural, national and racial minorities as the Welsh-speaking people of Wales, the French-Canadians, and the various Iroquois tribes of the north-eastern United States and Canada, all of whom have survived centuries of domination.[26]

Discussing the Maori people of New Zealand, Professor W. R. Geddes has stated:—

> '. . . a merging (of the Maoris and Europeans) does not appear likely for a very long time . . . complete merging of the groups (seems) too remote for policy to be based upon the prospect. Policy, one might suggest, had better leave the matter alone . . . . Emphasis on either assimilation or on Maoridom as aims of overall policy would be

unfortunate because it is inconsistent with the more important concept of democracy which supports the rights of all groups within the law and of individual persons to choose their own associations.'[27]

What seems more probable than complete assimilation is a form of plural society in which group differences based on racial origin become less and less important in most daily activities, but which retain importance in certain special areas of activity.[28] Such group differences already exist in white society, for instance different church and political affiliations, different sporting interest, and different professional or spare-time activities. Just as people of Scots ancestry, and even many who have 'adopted' Scots ancestry, can occasionally indulge in Highland dancing and feel a special interest and pride in things Scottish, so perhaps with the Aborigines in years to come.

Another argument commonly used in favour of assimilation as a goal of social policy is that the presence of pluralistic minority groups in a society seems always to harbour the danger of conflict and of the subordination of one group by another.[29] This is largely behind the Australian fear of groups of people who want to be different.

Given that different groups already exist, such an argument loses much of its point if it is conceded that a tolerant plural society is at least an essential pre-requisite for successful assimilation. Assimilation, as opposed to segregation or genocide, is only possible in a racially and culturally tolerant society. A plural society, on the other hand, can arise in an intolerant or racist society as a result of a compromise or balance between opposing forces, and evolve into a more tolerant society. A case in point is the growth of tolerance between the Catholic and Protestant elements in Australian society.

Assimilation *as a policy which is not acceptable* to the minority group in question is more a *cause* of group conflict than a means of avoiding it.

What distinctive elements might Aborigines preserve in a plural society, and of what value are these elements?

Ultimately, this is a question for the Aborigines to answer in their own way and from their own point of view. However, we can catch glimpses of the sort of things which have seemed of value to sympathetic observers. Such elements are not merely the outward signs and symbols of a vanishing past in terms of art, music and dance, however valuable it may be to preserve these as living arts: far more important are the attitudes and ideals which sustained the Aboriginal people in the past, which are still to be found among them, and from which modern technological man may well learn.

T. G. H. Strehlow summed up these ideals as 'the principles of cooperation, nor subordination; of differentiation without inequality; of tolerance for the customs of other peoples in their own country; and of respect for the hunting grounds of other tribes.'[30]

The late John Collier believed fervently that the American Indians, and indeed all tribal people, have a great deal to contribute to twentieth century man. In conversation he put it this way—

> "Any so-called primitive society ... incorporates discoveries and adjustments, spiritual as well as material, (made) across thousands of years. There's the famous view of the anthropologist, Ruth Benedict, of the arc of human potential: no one society embraces the whole arc, it takes a thousand societies to embrace the whole arc of human potential. Each of these primitive societies, almost without exception, has preserved something of universal value—Universal Man.'

'To pass from the general to the particular: if you read Kropotkin's great book on *Mutual Aid* you'll find that mutual aid, intense and profound, existed in nearly all primitive societies—with all that mutual aid entails—feeling for the other person, feeling for the group.'

'Again, generally speaking, the primitive group has integrated itself profoundly with the land—landscape, soil, waters, sacred places; and its feeling towards the earth is essentially religious, mystical, poetical, rhapsodical."

'Again, you'll find that nearly all primitive societies have achieved ways of bringing the child through childhood and adolesence into the full grouphood so that the whole human potential is realised and capitalised by the group. The individual in the primitive society is fulfilled through his group. His group is his fulfilment, but his group is not just a social organism—it is a man in nature, man in the spirit.'

'The feeling among all settled primitives of the sacredness of the earth and man's union with earth certainly is something the world needs—and needs terribly.'

'Another feature which you find in almost all primitive societies is heroism. It expects its people to endure, and to triumph over suffering, triumph over fear. Heroism may be the most important endowment—our own very self-seeking soft age doesn't value heroism very much.'

'Finally I'll mention that among nearly all primitives you encounter the great importance of ritual, that is the social art of sharing deep emotion—that is what ritual is.'[31]

Perhaps Collier's view is a little idealised. Nevertheless, there is sufficient truth in it to give us all pause to reflect on the values which so-called civilised man has lost. In an age of ideological conflict and nuclear deterrence, we need to value co-operation and mutual aid. In an age of growing economic inequalities between peoples and nations, we need different attitudes to the acquisition and sharing of material wealth. In an age threatened by environmental pollution on a world scale, we need a new reverence for nature and the world around us. In an age of hurrying tension, in which we are threatened by the prospect of unemployment due to automation, we need a different sense of time and a different attitude to the supposed moral virtue of labour. In an age of racial conflict, we need a new attitude to the diversity and otherness of our fellow-men.

As Frank Engel, Secretary of the Division of Mission of the Australian Council of Churches, has said:—

' . . . the strength of Aboriginal culture is its stress on spiritual and human values and its discounting of material ones, together with its strong emphasis on human relationships and responsibility to the group. The time has come for a re-evaluation of the two cultures and a facing of the fact that while Christianity has been closely associated with European culture, that culture today is non-Christian, even anti-Christian, and that in certain respects Aboriginal culture is nearer to the spirit of Christ. Obvious examples are the gentleness of Aborigines contrasted with the aggressiveness of the European, and Aboriginal insistence on finding the common mind of the group as against the self-assertion of individualistic European leadership.'³²

Obviously modern technology poses serious problems of adaptation for so-called primitive societies. However, the rapid changes in modern technology also require changes in our society, and we may not be any better equipped to deal with them than are the Aborigines. Some of our values, as has already been suggested, may in fact be less in tune with the times.

A simple example of parallel problems of adaptation may help illustrate the point. Aborigines who settle into village life have serious public health problems due to the change from a semi-nomadic life where sanitation and garbage were not important. Similarly, we have a serious and growing problem of air and water pollution due to the rapid growth of industry and the cities. Are we better able to safeguard our environment with our individualistic materialistic values than are the Aborigines with their traditional reverence for nature. In this, as in many other things, we have little cause to feel superior.

To sum up the discussion of cultural pluralism, our goal ought not to be the unrealistic dangerous and racist one of eliminating group differences, as if they were undesirable in themselves, but rather a fostering of a growing recognition of the values and merits of diverse traditions and cultures. Group differences ought to be removed from the arena of fear, privilege and dominance and placed in the more peaceful and productive realms of creative co-existence.

There is no reason why a multi-racial society, such as the Australia of the present and the future, should not also be a tolerant one in which cultural diversity is a subject of pride, interest and mutual respect. We might even be led eventually to extend this concept to our Asian neighbours! The goal of a tolerant plural society closes no doors: it neither separates people nor extinguishes the insights and values of their diverse human traditions.

*The Role of Violence*

If the goal of a free and tolerant multi-racial society is to be achieved in Australia, it is clear that men of goodwill must become active. However, Australian historical attitudes and the current existence of widespread institutional racism, coupled with the factors of population growth and distribution, pose serious problems as to how one should act. This problem is complicated further by the impact of overseas developments and in particular by the varying influence of events, and fashions in policies and methods, concerned with race relations in the United States.

Consider the question of the role of violence which white people usually associate with the Black Power movement, but which most black people regard as a minor question of tactics, at least in the American ghettos.

The Black Power idea in essence is that black people are more likely to achieve freedom and justice for themselves by working together as a group, pursuing their goals by the same processes of democractic action as any other common-interest pressure group such as returned servicemen or chambers of commerce. Up to this point Black Power is hardly controversial, and the idea, whether known by that name or not, is widely accepted amongst Aborigines who are active in their own cause.

Controversy, and our dilemma, arises over two aspects of the American movement. The first concerns the role of the 'white liberal', or sympathetic non-black, in the movement, and the second concerns the use of violence.

One way of looking at these two questions is to regard them as aspects of a more fundamental question, which is whether in the pursuit of its goals the black advancement movement should be guided more by general principles than by expediency. In a real sense this was Martin Luther King's position, based as it was on a strong Christian faith. Martin Luther King based his campaign on an inclusive Christian love, which not only moved him to work in close and open collaboration with white sympathisers but also moved him to consistently reject violence as an instrument of policy.

This is not to say that King did not go out of his way to find and promote black leadership and self-help. He realised that growing Negro self-respect and a growing sense of Negro achievement were essential to the morale and regeneration of his people, and not in the least inconsistent with love for other men.

It must also be stressed that Martin Luther King was quite ready to sacrifice 'order' for 'justice'. He was quite ready to disobey unjust laws, and indeed regarded this as a Christian duty. He was willing even to go ahead with non-violent protests in the knowledge that these challenges to an unjust *status quo* would 'provoke' a violent reaction.[33]

The difficulty in requiring a *movement*, as contrasted with an individual, to be guided by certain general principles, is that large groups of people seldom have many principles in common. Thus, to ask a given racial interest group to follow a set of principles not common to other racial groups, and which are not clearly in their own interests as expedients, is to be guilty of a form of racial discrimination.

If a movement adopts or accepts violence as a legitimate form of protest or instrument of change, those of us who advocate non-violence on principle have a number of choices. We can sacrifice non-violence in order to preserve our identification with the victims of injustice, opt out of the whole struggle, continue to advocate non-violence on tactical grounds, or attempt to act as a third force advocating non-violence on both sides. This is not a simple or easy choice and we can indeed be thankful, for selfish as well as other reasons, if such a choice is not forced upon us.

Whatever our reaction to this dilemma, American Black Power ideologists have stated their position quite clearly:—

> 'One of the most disturbing things about almost all white supporters has been that they are reluctant to go into their own communities— this is where the racism exists—and work to get rid of it . . . . We are speaking of those whites who see the need for basic change and have hooked up with the black liberation movement because it seemed the most promising agent of such change. Yet they often admonish black people to be non-violent. *They should preach non-violence in the white community.*'[8]

A white community which has no real compunction about using violence as an instrument of national policy, whether in Viet Nam or elsewhere, does not have the moral right to condemn others who resort to violence for the purpose of upsetting an unjust *status quo*.

Preaching non-violence in the white community is not simply a question of advocating it in the physical sense, for example in regard to Viet Nam or police brutality, but of advocating the abolition of institutions and practices which sustain injustice. Those 1 in 6 Aboriginal children who die in their first four years of life in the Northern Territory are just as dead as if they had been killed by bullets or bayonets. Institutional racism in this country is 'doing violence' to Aborigines, and to our professed values, every day.

In a recent report on 'The Role of Violence in Social Change', a working group of the American Council of Churches confessed:—

'The Church is ill-prepared to examine violence as an approach to social change because the tragic urban situation which faces America today can, to some extent, be blamed on the Church. Violence in our land is inherent in value structures and social processes which the Church itself undergirds and participates in as a social institution. The violence which permeates these structures and processes we shall term 'systemic violence'. Rarely does the Church repudiate such violence. On the contrary, the Church frequently sustains systemic violence with its silence, if not its benediction; with preference for order rather than for justice; and with a lack of zeal for the vindication of the victims of injustice.'

'From the genocide practised upon the American Indian in our earliest days to the present disregard for the poor, the Church, which should have exceeded every institution in its righteous indignation and conscientious resistance has, in fact, continued to pronounce its blessing upon the system which produced such inhumanity. Even now the vast majority of Christians support this nation's violence in Vietnam while roundly condemning the violence of embittered black people in the urban ghettos. But how can Christians condemn 'violence in the streets' when the Church itself has not consistently condemned systemic violence in the society but has, too often, actually supported it'.

The report goes on to ask,—

'Can the Church simply condone violence knowing that violence begets violence, that hate multiplies hate, and that unchecked, chain-reaction violence could engulf us all . . . .'

'Christians can insist that violent reactions to systemic violence demand massive understanding and drastic remedial programmes rather than brutal reprisals . . . . One criterion for judging violence is whether or not the violence seeks to preserve privilege based on injustice or to redress wrong. The former is unjustified violence. The latter can be justified.'

'Christians must make every effort to thwart, disrupt and undermine systemic violence by non-violent means . . . . Detailed mobilisation of Church resources must be developed to respond to confrontation between the police-military arm of the State and subjugated, robbed and excluded populations . . . . Christians should use all educational means available to them to teach American racial history, which includes the role of violence in support of racism . . . . In any conflict between the government and the oppressed or between the privileged classes and the oppressed, the Church, for good or ill, must stand with the oppressed, for Jesus did say: "Inasmuch as you did it unto the least of these, you did it unto me".'[34]

How do we relate the above statements, in their American context, to the problem of a multi-racial society in its Australian context.

Firstly, I believe we have to admit that institutional racism and systemic violence are strongly represented in the Australian racial scene. These have already been discussed above; if you still doubt their seriousness then I beg of you, please study them for yourself, for they cannot be lightly dismissed.

Secondly, my personal observations amongst Aborigines (mainly in the more settled areas) is that violence is currently rejected primarily on the grounds of expediency. This is not surprising in areas where Aborigines and part-Aborigines together number less than 1 per cent of the population. I am convinced that bitterness is widespread, if not universal, but that Aborigines and part-Aborigines have learnt well that bitterness should not be shown.

Thirdly, despite all judgments to the contrary and despite arguments as to its futility, violence in the northern areas of Australia cannot be ruled out as impossible. All the ingredients for such a situation already exist—individual and institutional discrimination, the coincidence of colour and poverty, a rapidly increasing substantial, and largely under-employed coloured population, and a growing sense of political and social awareness and frustration.

I do not believe that Aborigines are unique among men in being naturally and one hundred per cent non-violent. It is wishful thinking for either of us or the administrations concerned to believe so. Thus, while we have escaped the dilemma of open racial violence in recent times, I believe the time has come for us to act with the concern and urgency which violence might have prompted in us. If violence does come, it will be because we have failed to eliminate the systemic violence of injustice from Australian society.

It is my hope that in the years to come white Australians of goodwill will not earn the reproach which the late Dr. Martin Luther King once addressed to a similar body of Americans, when he said:—

'... I must confess that over the last few years I have been gravely disappointed with the white moderate. I have almost reached the regrettable conclusion that the Negroes' great stumbling block in the stride toward freedom is not the White Citizens' "Councillor" or the Ku Klux Klanner, but the white moderate who is more devoted to 'order' than to justice; who prefers a negative peace which is the absence of tension to a positive peace which is the presence of justice; who constantly says "I agree with you in the goal you seek but I can't agree with your methods of direct action"; who paternalistically feels that he can set the time-table for another man's freedom; who lives by the myth of time and who constantly advises the Negro to wait until a 'more convenient season'. Shallow understanding from people of goodwill is more frustrating than absolute misunderstanding from people of ill-will. Lukewarm acceptance is much more bewildering than outright rejection.'

'I had hoped that the white moderate would understand that law and order exist for the purpose of establishing justice, and that when they fail to do this they become the dangerously structured dams that block the flow of social progress. I had hoped that the white moderate would understand that the present tension in the South is merely a necessary phase of the transition from an obnoxious, negative peace, where the Negro passively accepted his unjust plight, to a substance-filled positive peace, where all men will respect the dignity and worth of human personality. Actually, we who engage in non-violent direct action are not the creators of tension. We merely bring to the surface the hidden tension that is already alive. We can bring it out in the open where it can be seen and dealt with. Like a boil that can never be cured as long as it is covered up but must be opened with all its pus-flowing ugliness to the natural medicines of air and light, injustice must likewise be exposed, with all of the tension its exposing creates, to the light of human conscience and the air of national opinion before it can be cured.'[33]

*Epilogue*

When the apostle Paul wrote to the Galatians, 'There is no such thing as Jew and Greek, slave and freeman, male and female; for you are all one person in Christ Jesus'[35] he was not stating an anthropological fact, but testifying to the equal worth of all men in the sight of Christ. This is the basis of our belief in the infinite worth of each individual human being, irrespective of race, status or sex. It means, unequivocally, that every man has value and rights, simply by virtue of being a man; human rights do not have to be earned.

There is no denying that men of different racial and cultural background are indeed different. These differences are part of our individuality, part of the spectrum of genetic and environmental differences which make each individual unique. As integral parts of the individual personality, these differences therefore must be respected for what they are, part of the infinite variety of mankind.

Like John Woolman, when explaining his reasons for travelling amongst the Indians of Pennsylvania in 1772, we ought to be able to say:—

> 'Love was the first motion, and then a concern arose to spend some time with the Indians that I might feel and understand their life and the spirit they live in, if haply I might receive some instruction from them, or they be in any degree helped forward by my following the leadings of truth among them . . . .'[36]

I believe we, as Christians, realise something at least of the importance of the individual being part of a group, and that amongst the rights which men have, the right of associating freely with his fellows is important. In some measure the individual finds fulfilment in his group, for man is a social being. So it seems to me that justice towards individuals requires justice towards groups as groups.

Love is a reciprocal relationship between independent personalities, each with rights and spheres of interest. So it is with groups—a proper loving relationship between groups must be based on their rights to co-exist and influence matters in their own spheres of interest. I do not see such group existence and group power as inconsistent with a loving relationship, but rather as the proper basis for such a relationship.

Our task then is not to oppose group differences or *legitimate* group power, i.e. power which does not place one group in a position of dominance or privilege with respect to another, but to welcome such diversity and reciprocity as the basis of creative dialogue in a spirit of love. *Our task is to gain the free, non-violent, and voluntary acceptance by the white power structure of the legitimacy and value of a sharing of power with black people.*

In order to be true to this goal, and to our own values as Quakers and Christians, we need to act in love, truth and responsibility, but also with frankness and radical strength of purpose. We need to speak truth to power on race relations in a way which we have failed to do since the days of James Backhouse.

In conclusion, I would like to quote again from an American context, part of a message to Friends from the Sixth National Conference on Race Relations, held in North Carolina, July 1967.

'We are far from belittling what Friends are already doing to overcome the effects of prejudice on many fronts. We need more Friends personally involved in what is, after all, more a white than a minority problem. We need to develop more sensitivity to the subtler forms of discrimination and injustice, we need to work with church and other groups on many problems of opportunity denied the individual because of his race or colour or culture.'

'But we need to be attacking these too-familiar civil rights problems in the light of a new awareness. It becomes increasingly clear that our existing social-economic-political-legal-military system — the framework within which the white establishment operates—simply cannot be patched up in such a way as to end exploitation and degradation. The changes called for—we are only partly aware of what they must be—will be so great as to constitute a social revolution. Some of the traditional values and concepts we, along with other Americans, hold most firmly—the moral necessity of labour, the nature of property rights—will have to be re-thought. We must be prepared to discover how much we ourselves, sharing in and profiting from the operation of this system, are contributing to the power which maintains the very practices we are fighting against.'

'We do have faith that there is a way for love instead of hate, for inclusiveness rather than exclusiveness, for brotherhood instead of apartheid, to prevail in the end as the spirit of our land. But we shall be able to bring this about only through commitment to a vision of a different social order—a society in which power and responsibility are shared willingly, in which our special privileges are surrendered, in which every man, in all the magnificent variety which God has bestowed, is fully accepted as equal.'

'To such leadings, to such commitment, we ask God to open our minds and hearts.'[37]

*Author's Note*

*Recent developments in Commonwealth policy, some since this essay was written, viz., the payment of full award wages to Aborigines employed by the Commonwealth and the institution of capital loans for "viable Aboriginal enterprises", give cause for increased optimism.*

*It should be clear, however, that these changes do not go far in meeting the serious situation which I have outlined.*

*Further, one must bear in mind that changes in policy and legislation are extremely difficult to implement if they continue to be interpreted and administered by field staff whose whole working life has been devoted to contrary policies.*

*Authoritarian and paternalistic attitudes die hard, and it should not be*

assumed that theoretical changes in policy and attitudes in Canberra necessarily lead to significant changes in practice where the Aborigines are.

## ACKNOWLEDGEMENT

The substance of this chapter was first presented as the sixth in a series
of lectures instituted by Australia Yearly Meeting of the Religious Society of
Friends on the occasion of the establishment of that Yearly Meeting on January 1,
1964. This lecture was delivered in Adelaide, South Australia, on January 5, 1969,
during the sessions of the Yearly Meeting, and is reprinted here with the permission
of The Religious Society of Friends (Quakers) in Australia Incorporated.

## REFERENCES

1 A. Grenfell Price, *White Settlers and Native Peoples* (Georgian House,
Melbourne, 1949), pp. 116-117.

2 James Backhouse, *A Narrative of a Visit to the Australian Colonies* (Hamilton,
Adams and Co., London, 1843), p. xvii.

3 James Backhouse, ibid., p. cxxxiv.

4 Quoted by Clive Turnbull in *Black War: The Extermination of the Tasmanian
Aborigines* (Lansdowne Press, Melbourne, 1965), p. 165.

5 *The Colonist*, 10 October 1838.

6 See the article *The Spanish Origin of Indian Rights in the Law of the United
States* by Felix S. Cohen, in *The Legal Conscience* (Yale University Press, New
Haven, 1960), pp. 230-252.

7 World Council of Churches, *Background Statement on White Racism*, Document No. 12, Fourth Assembly, Uppsala, July 1968.

8 For a fuller discussion see Stokely Carmichael and Charles V. Hamilton, *Black
Power* (Vintage Book V-33, New York, 1967), p. 4 et seq.

9 The Immigration Reform Group, *Immigration: Control or Colour Bar?* (Mel-
bourne University Press, Melbourne, 1962), particularly pp. 35-36; see also
*Hansard,* House of Representatives, 24 September 1968, for a sample of current
Australian parliamentary opinion.

10 Frank Stevens, *Equal Wages for Aborigines* (Aura Press, Sydney, 1968).

11 Colin Tatz, *Aborigines: Equality or Inequality* (*The Australian Quarterly,*
March 1966).

12 Colin Tatz, *Queensland's Aborigines: Natural Justice and the Rule of Law,*
(*The Australian Quarterly,* September 1963). Although this article refers to the
situation in Queensland prior to the new Act of 1965, and the Regulations of
1966, the situation has changed little (see reference No. 11).

13 *Northern Territory News,* 5 June, 1968.

14 Ian G. Sharp and Colin M. Tatz (editors), *Aborigines in the Economy*
(Jacaranda Press, Brisbane, 1966), pp. 279-303.

15 F. Lancaster Jones, *A Demographic Survey of the Aboriginal Population of the
Northern Territory, Occasional Paper No. 1,* Australian Institute of Aboriginal
Studies, Canberra, 1963.

16 C. D. Rowley, *The Aboriginal Householder* (*Quadrant,* November, December,
1967).

17 E. J. B. Foxcroft, *Australian Native Policy* (Melbourne University Press, Melbourne, 1941); see also James Backhouse, op. cit. p. 502.

18 *The Australian Aborigines* (Department of Territories, Canberra, 1967), pp.
39-46 particularly.

19 John Collier, *Indians of the Americas* (*Mentor* MP494, New York, 1963); D'Arcy McNickle, *The Indian Tribes of the United States* (Oxford U.P., London, 1962); Harold E. Fey and D'Arcy McNickle, *Indians and Other Americans* (Harper and Bros., New York, 1959).

20 John Collier, *From Every Zenith* (Swallow Press, Denver, 1963), p. 203.

21 See for instance *Human Organisation*, Vol. 20, No. 3 (Society for Applied Anthropology, New York, Winter 1961-62); A. Barrie Pittock, *Compare Overseas, Crux*, June-July 1965 (Australian Student Christian Movement, Melbourne); A. Barrie Pittock, *Aborigines and the Tourist Industry* (*The Australian Quarterly*, September, 1967); William A Brophy and Sophie D. Aberle, *The Indian: America's Unfinished Business* (U. of Oklahoma Press, Norman, 1966).

22 Donald Stuart, *Yandy* (Georgian House, Melbourne 1959).

23 Frank Hardy, *The Unlucky Australians* (Nelson, Melbourne, 1968).

24 For a popular account see *The Scientific American*, October 1966; for a more extensive account see Oscar Lewis, *La Vida* (Secker and Warburg, London, 1967).

25 World Council of Churches, op. cit. pp. 5 and 10.

26 Edmund Wilson, *Apologies to the Iroquois* (W. H. Allen, London, 1960); Nathan Glazer and Daniel Moynihan, *Beyond the Melting Pot* (M.I.T. Press, Cambridge, Mass., 1963); and Charles Wagley and Marvin Harris, *Minorities in the New World* (Columbia University Press, New York, 1964).

27 W. R. Geddes, *Maori and Aborigine: A Comparison of Attitudes and Policies*, Aboriginal Affairs Information Paper No. 1, 1962.

28 Eugene Hartley and Richard Thompson, *Racial Integration and Role Differentiation*, Journal of the Polynesian Society, Vol. 76, pp. 427-443, 1968.

29 Charles Wagley and Marvin Harris, op. cit. p. 294.

30 T. G. H. Strehlow, *The Sustaining Ideals of Australian Aboriginal Societies* (Aboriginal Advancement League Inc., Adelaide 1962).

31 From a taped interview by the author with John Collier at Ranchos de Taos, New Mexico, December 1963.

32 Frank G. Engel, *Turning Land Into Hope* (Australian Council of Churches, Sydney, 1968).

33 Martin Luther King, Jr., *Letter from Birmingham City Jail* (American Friends' Service Committee, Philadelphia, 1963).

34 U.S. Conference on Church and Society, *The Role of Violence in Social Change, Social Action/Social Progress*, January, February, 1968.

35 The New English Bible, Galatians, 3, 26-28 (Oxford U.P., Oxford, 1961).

36 *The Journal of John Woolman* (Everyman's Library, London, 1952), p. 107.

37 *Black Power, White Power, Shared Power*, Study Guide on Race Relations (Housmans Bookshop, London, 1967).

# POSTSCRIPT

# RELUCTANT FLAME

## John Kasaipwalova

Cold bloodless masks stare me, not for my colour
But for my empty wealth house and passion logic.
I dream to see people, they give me leafless rootless logs
The logs are trimmed, they shine in their trimness
Look how orderedly fat and silent they float this earth
With their guns, their airplanes, their cyclone wheels and their bishops
And all this like a snake's shining eye, they fix straight my looking
So, quickly I say 'this is for me, my food, my soul and my spirits
Masta masta give me more, I will pray, I will obey, yes masta truly!'

I say aa-aa-aa-sah sah sah-aah yessaah
To the logs captive stares believing this for my good
They have no legs, they slithe greasily like snakes
Their thunderous motion blinds my looking face
I do not see the cold seed making roots in my heart
The seed grows, it spreads inside me and I cannot see it
Watered by the mountain fog that covers the deathly silence of the logs
But somewhere in my vein my small blood drop begins to volcano cry
For dawn wind to blow away the fog, to make my vision clear
To see these logs truthfully moving
Have no giving roots to intercourse the humus of humanity
No leaves to quiver the living joy in the timeless wind
For their motion is timed and their wind is time.

Yet why, why, why? Why are the wooden faces so real? Why?
I look back and see my vagueness dreaming in the setting twilight
I look to the right I see fixed grins and armed teeth
I look to the left I see arming teeth fixing its grins
The faces all pale and wooden coaxing and commanding me to laugh
I open my face and laugh like a politician
But this laugh makes night inside me and under its cover
The cold pale seed hatefully grows and spreads

It climbs to my brain I stop feeling and begin to believe
It moulds my face I laugh to the outsider's pricking
It fills my arm veins I drop the bush knife for the pen
It paralyzes my eye-balls to kill their sweeping sight
It captures my soul for the ransom of amen
It clamps my balls and I painfully shout out for a white vagina
It craws over my skin and in shame I moist shirt and trousers
I hate myself and my black lover to forcedly love my hater
The cold seed thrives on my destruction.

YUPELA OL FRENDS NA WANTOKS
YUMI LUKLUK INSAIT NAU LONG YUMI YET !!!

This is the white cradle, this is the white pool
This is the white ocean chasm in which we float steerless and captured
Black destination with villages of joyful living seems impossible
Made unreal and distant by the thick white fog
The fog blankets over, it pierces—no black density withstands the flood
I tremble in fear, the cold westerly chills my flesh and bones
Memory of past warmth swims in my heart like stones
What is this chill, where is that flame to warm and melt me?

The chill is killing the flame, it is everywhere
Chill you're a bastard, I hate you as a panther hates a motherfucker
Every turn of my head sees your tentacles strangling innocent kanakas
You have trampled the whole world over
Here your boot is on our necks, your spear into our intestines
Your history and your size makes me cry violently for air to breathe

Where is that flame !!! Where has it gone !!!
The acid in my heart kicks me with volcanic tremors
My veins, my arteries, they bulge with swelling resentment
I tremble in frenzy to smash open
To let the acid, the fire and the boulder in my throat
Spew outwards into every direction of havoc cyclone and thunder !
Yet the chill wraps me paternally
Till the inner vomit and rotten boilings appear
Like gentle swellings of canvas sail pregnant with caressing breeze
This is the vision that fills my fixed eyes.

I must believe the outward form of this chilling canvas
By this I hide from the distressing truth like the midday sun hiding its day
The pain of castration and splitting-two falsely fade
When I hazily wink my attention on my form from the outside eye
And like a masochistic martyr turning to the grace of christ
I accept pain for pleasure and call my vomit my 'good character'
The white fog and all that it devours
Describes and prescribes me with a three-one criterion
SHIT, VOMIT and PROFIT . . . . . .
            but, but, but in its greedy ignorance
            the fog will not see that . . . . .

Deep in my core that small blood droplet pulses lonely and faint
Each day the weighty cover shrieks arrogantly
Vowing to crush and smother the tiny flame within that pulse
I know the threat, my fear piss is streaming down my legs
I will call my ancestors and all the spirits of my grounds and waters
They will throw their magic over my body
I will stop pissing my leg and cup my palms around my precious flame
My shoulders will stoop under the chilling weight
My back bone will groan and break its suppleness
But my ancestor companions will not loosen my sinews around the flame

Green mountains will boast their size and their foreverness
A passing eye will sing their permanency and solidness
But inside each mountain lies a tiny flame cradled and weighted by above
People will live, people will die
But the tiny flame will grow its arms and legs very slowly
Until one day its volcanic pulse will tear the green mountain apart
To allow pentup blood flow and congested vomit spit freely
Tiny flame of my pulse, you are silent, you are patient
My hands and my aching body will nurse you against the venomous enemy
You will grow, you and I will soon be free to grow our love

Stretch your ear to ground and listen to the distant stirrings
Napalm cannot burn out the flames the guerrillas now open
The green chilly mountain is staggering to burst apart
The tiny flame within its own fence is burning into the icy centres
Look how the flame came from the ghettoes
The flame kept down by chain and hunger
Once reluctant now creeps obviously into the pale coldness
Chubby Checker gave Elvis the twisting flame to throw
Ray Charles gave the Beatles the explosive pulse to shake the total stiffness
That children tempered by this flame will scorch and burn their elders
Listen carefully, this is but one arm of the reluctant flame
Burning and melting the icy bloodless body

My flame take your fuel from these brother flames
Let not the oceans drown your linking pipe
You will grow, you will grow, you will grow like a boil on pale skins
Maybe your vibrant lava will flow to burn anew the world
When Johannesburg and New York is in flames
and the black vomit will fertilize this barren soil
But today your eyes are dimdimed and in your enemy you see your friend
My lover, my me, we will not follow the cold pale reach for the moon
Our ancestors and our spirits sleep on this earth
Let the lunatics meet on the lunacy, we will use the soil to grow our
        brotherly flame
Our reluctant dream flame is burning disconnected like a bush fire
But one day, one day . . . . . one day . . . . .

Is this the dream of an unborn child—a madman imprisoned?
No ! No ! No !
The foetus is already a man; the madman is judgement for his imprisoners
My body has no time for God and the miracles
My poison is your bitter booting and clapping shut my mouth
The voice that will shoot from my stomach
Will be the death axe to smash the ice of my imprisoners
It will not come from heaven nor from the green mountain
It IS the unseen vibrant rhythm from my pulse deep down down inside
Crying violently for me to open my eyes and the time.
For to wait a thousand years it too wait too long.
Reluctant flame you have lifted your skirt to my eyes
I come up truly for your wavy rhythms to burn

But how can you and I make live love
Your flesh and mine shivering to make one soul
To know the burning frenzy of our flesh tremble in unison
As we passionately dig into reality the living shape of love-body-soul?
Yes how! How? How? How can we live the shaping of this love
When the cold seed creeps silently in the cover of the fog
To make our love limbs cold and our souls sensualess?
How? How? How? How can a dying soul make love, yes how?
Where is that flame to thaw out my freezing deadness? Where?
I must open my mouth in search of air !
Cry my soul body, cry violently
For your unseen enemy has the poisoned knife to my throat!

Black faces staring mutely by the dusty bus stops
Our envy hateful hearts crying tears to see them speed past in arrogance
Black shoulder bleeding from the copra bags
Our silent spear strikes inside to see the fortnight scraps
Black angelic voices singing the strange alleluia
Our soul damning itself to feel the memory of sensual dance and song
Black bodies madly showing off white long stockings shirt and trousers
Our laugh spirits cries to wear fully the colours we know
Black feet uniformed blue carry the terror of baton and tear gas
Our eyes hate one another, but somewhere we feel a strand of wantok
Black ears glued to the cheap transistors
Our we yearns to make music instead of feeding senselessly on noise
Black stooges yessarring whitishly to make paper our destiny
Our revolting will be turned against our selves traitors
Black muffled servants clamouring shamelessly for black cars stigma
Our aspirations will forever lie lost in the mess of paper status
      FUCK OFF, WHITE BASTARDRY, FUCK OFF !
        your weighty impotence has
          its needle into
           me !

Please, my black woman, please do not weep your hate against us
You were not satisfied, please my love do not cry
See my tears of shame and anger, please my you, do not cry
Impossible for me to say sorry without seeing my lies
Please, my black flame say for me what you see
Lovers with cold arms, legs, hips, skins and souls
Must weep their tight vaginas and slack penises
My black woman please do not cry helplessly
Look at my tears, I know our grave of rotting flesh
Crawling maggots rippling over one another
To suck the slimy fluid of our colding flesh
Please my lover my me do not cry your fear and hate
The thick fog closes our vision, yes
I cannot in honest clarity show us the way out of our grave
But take my hand and let our fingers make one flesh
Though we sink captured, I know a memory, I feel a small pulse
Inside, inside, where our eyes do not see there is a
      Pulse !

Inside, inside, where our minds do not now recognize there is a living
  Memory!
A flame alives from its ignition and its fuel.

I go past the Palm Tavern
Wantoks dancing one another to the drums
Big beautiful black shouting bursting open
Roofed by rusty scraps, children laughing, crying and fighting
They hit ukeleles, guitars and tins
Music is
People meeting, laughing at Koki
The wind tickling my hair on the back of passenger truck
My smile to you, we say no words, we know
I offer you one betel nut, they talk for us
Wantok we eat our rice and meat together

Firm beautiful black hands stoning police thugs
Proud feet kicking off the liar's cargo on high roads
Determined wills pulling out the devils claims
Voices slapping their faces to tell them 'white bastards'
Smashing the glassy window shows of the thief
To give the warn for flame next time

RELUCTANT FLAME OPEN YOUR VOLCANO
TAKE YOUR PULSE AND YOUR FUEL
BURN BURN BURN BURN BURN
LET YOUR FLAMES VIBRATE THEIR DRUMS
BURN BURN BURN BURN BURN
BURN AWAY MY WEIGHTY ICE
BURN INTO MY HEART A DANCING FLAME

# CONCLUSION TO THE SERIES

# CONCLUSION

## *S. Encel*

A series comprising three volumes and almost fifty authors does not readily lend itself to the drawing of conclusions. There is no simple way of summarizing the diversity of material, of approach, and of theoretical assumptions to be found among the contributors to the series. This concluding chapter is devoted, therefore, not to a summary but to some speculations about the extent to which the series has achieved its purpose, the reactions it has already evoked, and the problems of further research and writing about race relations and racial attitudes in Australia.

Reviewers and correspondents, commenting on the first two volumes in the series, differed widely in their reactions but underlined a few common themes. The picture of race relations and racial attitudes was confusing. The material about the Aborigines was written by white men and women and the Aboriginal viewpoint was insufficiently represented. There was insufficient material about the problems of European immigrant minorities. The existence of a general syndrome of racism had not been demonstrated, except in relation to the Aborigines; apart from that there was only 'prejudice', which also arose from other sources. One correspondent noted the omission of any discussion of anti-German prejudice, as manifested in two world wars, including W. M. Hughes' refusal to allow the Australian-born children of German immigrants to vote in the two conscription referenda of 1916-17. Others criticized our treatment of the churches from various viewpoints; e.g. we should have said more about the failure of the Catholic Church to take a positive stand against racism, instead of publishing a moral homily by the Bishop of Ballarat, and we should have given more credit to the anti-racist activities of the Lutheran missions since the 1930's. And finally—a common observation—the contributions were uneven and our coverage of the subject was patchy.

Many of the criticisms cancel out; others reflect the usual tendency of reviewers to write *de haut en bas* (often with striking lack of justification). However, some of the points made in the reviews are important and will be taken up in the ensuing paragraphs. Before proceeding, a few words of exculpation may not be misplaced. In planning the series, we did not and could not begin with a clear-cut framework for the analysis of the subject. Racism, racialism, prejudice and oppression take many forms and we were concerned to present as many facets as possible. If we did not attract more Aboriginal contributors, it was not for want of effort. Unevenness of treatment reflects enormous variation in depth of interest and appreciation of all these facets, not to mention the remarkable backwardness of the social sciences—especially anthropology, social psychology, and sociology, which are the most relevant in this connection—at Australian universities. It is this backwardness which is one of the prime reasons for the scarcity of research on immigrant minorities. The quality of the series is, with one or two exceptions,[1] an accurate reflection of the state of scholarly inquiry into race relations in Australia.

Until recently, it could also be said to reflect the lack of public concern with race relations. The fact that public concern, dormant for a long time, did exist was verified by the South African football tour in 1971, which led to violent demonstrations not seen in Australia since the depression years of the 1930's. Since then, the question of race relations has continued to simmer, and the pot has occasionally boiled over. At the beginning of 1972, it was freely predicted that the White Australian Policy would be a major issue at the 1972 federal election because of the adoption by the Australian Labor Party of a policy of non-discriminatory immigration. Political leaflets declaring 'If you want an Asian for a neighbour, vote Labor' made their appearance. The dispute within the A.L.P. over immigration policy which occurred in the early months of 1971 was revived when its former leader, Mr. Arthur Calwell, declared in April, 1972 that he did not want to see a 'chocolate-coloured Australia'. The racism indicated in this comment was consistent with the historical development of attitudes as indicated in these volumes, in which opposition to non-European immigration is matched by 'colour blindness' about the Aborigines, the original chocolate-coloured inhabitants who were dispossessed, slaughtered and repressed by white settlers. The reaction to Mr Calwell's statements also underlined another point made in these volumes, that racism and racialism have roots which are independent of class and party allegiances.

The existence of public concern with these issues can no longer be doubted, and it may be assumed that scholarly concern will soon reflect the rising level of public awareness.

On one major issue, many reviewers concurred with the editor's general assessment. In his foreword to Volume 1, Frank Stevens argued that the existence of racism was amply established by the evidence of Volume 2, on black-white relations within Australia. In the other two volumes, evidence of prejudice, intolerance, and discrimination was presented but not proof of racism, i.e. the existence of a deterministic belief system which ascribes social differences to fixed physical and cultural criteria.[2] Or, in other words, the enormous differences between black men and white men can be shown, without difficulty, to engender the whole gamut of ideologies, prejudices, discriminatory laws, economic exploitation, repressive administration and sexual hypocrisy which make up racism in other parts of the world. When the differences are more subtle and more complicated, the analysis becomes correspondingly more difficult and more controversial.

The problem is not confined to Australia. The study of race relations and related phenomena—racism, racialism, ethnocentrism, colonialism, prejudice, paternalism, apartheid—is in a highly confused state. According to van den Berghe, it has contributed little to an understanding of social relations in general because it focuses on the 'problems' of prejudice, discrimination, conflict etc., and abstracts the racial issue from its wider social context.[3] Attempts to construct models for the explanation of racial situations are usually based on one or two specific situations whose characteristics are not found elsewhere.[4] In particular, conclusions drawn from situations where skin colour is an important factor do not carry over into other situations where physical differences are insignificant. Anti-semitism is not the same phenomenon as colour prejudice, although prejudiced persons commonly show a high correlation between the two. Again, colour consciousness can be highly selective, as was the case in Queensland two generations ago in relation to the Kanakas, the Aborigines and the Chinese. The political character of racism is another major complication. Social scientists generally take a liberal or radical view of politics, and the association of racist ideologies with right-wing political movements makes detached analysis particularly difficult. Moreover, views of politics are closely related to views of human nature, and the views which are most influential in the social sciences are those derived from philosophers like Locke and Marx, which readily lead to the proposition that racism is an 'epiphenomenon' or, more simply, a cloak for other motives of an economic and political character. This viewpoint is manifested in Professor Stanner's introduction to Volume 1, which argues that we are usually prejudiced about race because of other things. As against this, all three volumes provide evidence of the way in which racist and racialist attitudes enter into private social relations and into government policy, both foreign and domestic. It is difficult to believe that these attitudes are, in every case, a cover for something else, especially when the range of situations is so varied.

The common factor is, perhaps, that Australia is a product of the colonial era, and like all colonial territories there is a basic element of racism in its social fabric. We are leaving our colonial past behind us, and this involves the re-examination of many assumptions about the past, the present, and the future, including the meaning of words like 'assimilation' and 'integration' which denote an essentially racialist perspective. Further investigation of the areas opened up for discussion by the present series will enable us to link the undoubted racism that pervades our treatment of the Aborigines with its penetration into other aspects of social relations where its influence is, as yet, only dimly understood. In this way our three volumes may help to make a long-term contribution towards the understanding which must precede action to combat racism and racial discrimination.

## REFERENCES

1 One exception relates to the history of Kanaka labour on the Queensland sugar plantations. In seeking contributors, the editors were unaware of the scholarly work done on this subject by Mrs. Kay Evans of the University of Queensland, and there was insufficient time to incorporate a contribution by her in the third volume.

2 JOHN REX, 'The Concept of Race in Sociological Theory' in SAMI ZUBAIDA (ed.), *Race and Racialism*, London, Tavistock, 1970 p. 39.

3 PIERRE VAN DEN BERGHE, *Race and Racism*, N.Y., Wiley, 1967, ch. 1.

4 JOHN REX, *Race Relations in Sociological Theory*, London, Weidenfeld and Nicolson, 1970, ch. 1.

# INDEX TO VOLUMES 1-3

References indicate volume (in **bold** type) and page numbers

References indicate volume (in **bold** type) and page numbers

References indicate volume (in **bold** type) and page numbers